MW00773570

BAPTISM AND THE REMISSION OF SINS

BAPTISM AND THE REMISSION OF SINS

David W. Fletcher, Editor

College Press Publishing Company, Joplin, Missouri

Copyright © 1990
College Press Publishing Company
Second Printing, 1992

Printed and Bound in the
United States of America
All Rights Reserved

Library of Congress Catalog Card Number: 89-81420
International Standard Book Number: 0-89900-422-9

Table of Contents

DEDICATION

To the pioneers of the American Restoration Movement who had both the courage to search the Scriptures anew and the courage to declare the results of their search with boldness. We who stand on their shoulders are grateful for the courage God gave them. May we have the same courageous spirit that moved them as we too search the Scriptures anew and proclaim it with boldness.

INTRODUCTION

The American Restoration Movement is one of the largest religious movements indigenous to North America. Although its beginning is variously dated,[1] it is certain that by the beginning of the *Millennial Harbinger* in 1830 the theology and practice of the American Restoration Movement was fundamentally intact. The formative period of this development was the 1820s. This movement is now represented by three major religious groups — Christian Church (Disciples of Christ), Christian Churches and Churches of Christ (Instrumental), and Churches of Christ (Non-instrumental) — with a total membership of over five million.

The most distinctive aspect of the American Restoration Movement was its baptismal theology. In contrast with the theological setting of the day, the Restoration Movement's teaching on the subject of baptism was unique. It certainly contrasted with the Presbyterians, Methodists and Lutherans who practiced infant baptism. The Restoration Movement was baptistic. It advocated the immersion of believers only as baptism. However, the Restoration Movement also stood in contrast with the Baptists — something which the Reformers themselves were quick to point out. The difference with the Baptists focused on the movement's peculiar understanding of the phrase "baptism for the remission of sins" which was announced by the Reformers across the American frontier. As a consequence, the baptismal theology of the Restoration Movement was unique and novel in the eyes of the mainline Christian communities.

This distinctive view of baptism focuses on the issue of baptismal efficacy. In the aftermath of the Protestant Reformation, the debate concerning baptismal efficacy centered around two positions.[2] First, there was the position of the "Sacramentalists." This is basically the position of Roman Catholics, Eastern Orthodox, Anglicans (Episcopalians) and Lutherans. Jewett defines this view as one that "regards the sacraments as inherently efficacious to mediate the inward grace (blessing) of which they are the outward sign."[3] The sacraments, particularly baptism in this case, have a "causative significance for the salvation of the one receiving the rite."[4] Second, there is the position of the "Evangelicalists." This is basically the position of the Reformed theology exhibited in Presbyterian, Baptist and Wesleyan traditions. Jewett defines this view as one that regards baptism as that which " 'signifies and seals,' but does not effect, the blessing of cleansing and renewal in Christ."[5] Baptism is the sign and seal of righteousness and salvation. It is the outward sign of the inward grace previously received.

The baptismal theology of the American Restoration Movement does not fall into either one of these two categories. It is neither "sacramental" nor "evangelical."[6] It rejects any kind of magical efficacy to the waters of baptism, and it requires faith on the part of the one who receives the grace mediated by baptism.[7] It does not view baptism as a mere ordinance, nor does it view it as an empty symbol of a grace already bestowed. Rather, the American Restoration Movement has argued that baptism is a true means of grace for those who receive it in faith. The thing signified by baptism, i.e., washing away of sins in the blood of Christ, is actually bestowed at the point of baptism. It is not only a sign, but a true means.[8]

Unlike the sacramentalist view of baptism, it does not see a strict "causative" connection between baptism and salvation. The baptismal water does not effect anything in and of itself. Instead it is the faith in Christ's blood that is effectual. However, the Restoration Movement argues for a chronological connection between baptism and salvation — a connection in which there is both symbol and true mediation. The obedience of faith in the submission to the command to be baptized is the chronological point at which one is saved. It is this chronological connection which distinguishes it from the baptismal theology of evangelicalism. Here the debate should not be about the efficacy of baptism or the efficacy of faith, but rather about the chronological point of salvation. In other words, the question is not, "Does faith save?" Rather, the question is: "When does faith save?"

This is a distinctive position in the history of Post-Reformation theology. However, it is not unique in the history of theology viewed from the beginning. In the first chapter, Dr. Cottrell demonstrates that the consensus of theology prior to the rise of Reformed theology was essentially the viewpoint of the American Restoration Movement. Consequently, while Alexander Campbell's exposition of "baptism for the remission of sins" was unique and novel to the American frontier, it was also a return to the biblical and historical roots of Christian theology.

In the second chapter, Dr. Cottrell stresses the uniqueness of Reformed theology in contrast with the earlier consensus of Christian theology. Concentrating on Zwingli, Dr. Cottrell gives a clear exposition of the view of baptismal efficacy which would later dominate Baptist thought. In Zwingli and Reformed theology as it developed, "we have," as Jewett comments, "the beginning of a new constellation of ideas in the theological heavens."[9] It was in the climate of Reformed theology that the

11

early American Reformers lived and moved. The American frontier was dominated by Calvinism, and this had a tremendous impact on the beginning of the American Restoration Movement.[10] The theology of Stone, Scott and Campbell began in and was influenced by Reformed theology.[11] Indeed, the Restoration Movement was largely a reaction to what they perceived as hyper-Calvinism. Consequently, as their distinctive view of baptismal efficacy developed, they were careful to distinguish themselves from not only the sacramentarians (they wanted to avoid the *ex opere operato* of Roman Catholicism), but also the "evangelicalism" of Reformed theology. They perceived themselves as proposing a *via media* (a middle way) by returning to a solid biblical foundation.

Although the American frontier shaped the American Restoration Movement, its European heritage also played a significant role. Both Campbell and Scott were born in Europe, and came to America with clear understandings of their own respective Presbyterian traditions. Dr. McMillon, in chapter three, outlines the various backgrounds which influenced Campbell and set the stage for the introduction of restorationism in America.

Chapters four and five, written by Dr. John Mark Hicks, detail the development and mature views of Alexander Campbell on the design of baptism. Beginning in Presbyterianism, Campbell moved through the Baptist adaptation of Reformed theology to embrace a "novel" view of the design of baptism which became the distinctive mark of the new movement in the late 1820s. Chapter five, in particular, deals with the issue of Campbell's attitude toward the sects around him who did not agree with his "novel" views on baptism for the remission of sins. In this chapter Campbell's views on both "right-wing" and "left-wing" issues are examined.

In chapters 6 and 8, Mr. Chestnut and Mr. Gross deal with some "right-wing" issues that arose within the Restoration Movement. The issues boiled down to this question: should those immersed without respect to the remission of sins be reimmersed for

12

the remission of sins? Campbell battled Dr. John Thomas on this issue in the 1830s. The battle continued in the 1880s between David Lipscomb and Austin McGary. The issue even now causes debate within moderate and conservative quarters of the American Restoration Movement.

In chapters 7 and 9, Mr. Greene and Dr. North deal with some "left-wing" issues that arose within the Restoration Movement. The issues boiled down to this question: should the American Restoration Movement accept the unimmersed into the fellowship of the visible church? Mr. Greene approaches the question by following the career and baptismal theology of Barton W. Stone. Stone advocated fellowship with the unimmersed. As such he prefigured those who advocated "open membership" in the 1920s. Dr. North details the "open membership" debate which triggered the division between the Christian Church (Disciples of Christ) and the Christian Church/Churches of Christ (Instrumental).[12] This remains a major point of division between the Christian Church (Disciples of Christ) and the Churches of Christ (both Instrumental and Non-instrumental).

In the final chapter of the book Mr. Fletcher, a member of the American Restoration Movement, gives a contemporary overview of the biblical data. Mr. Fletcher underscores an aspect of baptism often neglected in the movement. He emphasizes the role of the Spirit of God in mediating the salvation bestowed at baptism.

It is the purpose of this book to give a comprehensive overview of the development of baptismal theology in the American Restoration Movement. The rise of the distinctive view of baptismal efficacy must be placed against the backdrop of Reformed theology. The tensions which developed within the Restoration Movement over Campbell's view of baptismal efficacy, both from the left and the right, must be seen as part of the struggle to come to terms with a baptismal theology radically different from that in Reformed thelogy. It is the history of this

13

development and controversy which is the subject of this book.

David W. Fletcher
Chaplain, US Air Force
Sembach, Germany

John Mark Hicks
Associate Professor of Christian Doctrine
Harding University Graduate School of Religion

Endnotes

1. Some date the beginning of the movement from the dissolution of the Springfield Presbytery under Barton W. Stone in 1804. Others date it from the publication of the *Declaration and Address* by Thomas Campbell in 1809. Others date the beginning of the movement with the introduction of the *Christian Baptist* in 1823. While the events of 1804 and 1809 were necessary to the development of the Restoration Movement, these events signaled nothing unique in the total environment of religious history at the time. Britain had seen similar principles and movements initiated prior to these dates. However, with the publication of the *Christian Baptist* the American Restoration Movement began to have a defined essence and a unique program: the Ancient Order and the Ancient Gospel. This becomes most apparent in the development of Campbell's baptismal theology.

2. This terminology with its definitions is adopted from Paul K. Jewett, *Infant Baptism & the Covenant of Grace* (Grand Rapids: Eerdmans, 1978), pp. 3-4; 75-82.

3. Jewett, p. 3, footnote 2.

4. Jewett, p. 3.

5. Jewett, p. 3, footnote 2.

6. The definition of the Reformed view of baptismal efficacy as "evangelical" is rather prejudicial. This implies that all other views are non-evangelical, i.e., they are not consistent with the gospel of Jesus Christ. This is not a good use of the term "evangelical." However, the term is used here in a strictly historical sense, according to Jewett's categories.

7. It is important to note that all sacramentalists are also advocates of infant baptism. Sacramentalism does not require faith on the part of the recipient in order to enjoy the benefits of the grace given in baptism. Lutherans are a possible exception since they argue for the reality of "infant faith" (that is, the faith which the infant possesses).

8. This is supported biblically by the instrumental use of *dia* (through) in Romans 6:4 and Titus 3:5. See chapters 1 and 10 for a look at the Biblical data.

9. Jewett, p. 78.

10. See Arthur Schlessinger, Jr., "The Age of Alexander Campbell," in *The Sage of Bethany: A Pioneer in Broadcloth*, edited by Perry E. Gresham (reprint; Joplin, Missouri: College Press Publishing Co., 1988), pp. 25-44.

11. These three men all began their religious life in the context of Presbyterianism, and consequently in the context of Reformed theology.

12. The issue of baptism had nothing to do with the division between the Christian Churches/Churches of Christ (Instrumental) and Churches of Christ (Non-instrumental). That division centered around the application of certain hermeneutical principles with regard to church order and worship.

1

THE BIBLICAL CONSENSUS: HISTORICAL BACKGROUNDS TO REFORMED THEOLOGY

Jack W. Cottrell

In religious and theological circles the word *Reformed* refers to one of the two main streams of Protestantism flowing from the Reformation of the sixteenth century, the other being the Lutheran. The Reformed branch originated in Switzerland principally in the minds of Huldreich Zwingli and John Calvin.

Zwingli is actually the fountainhead of Reformed theology. He launched the Swiss Reformation in Zurich around 1520, or about the time Martin Luther was doing the same thing in Germany. Zwingli's work was cut short by his untimely death in 1531; but the basic elements of his thought were adopted by John Calvin, who, operating out of Geneva, took over the reigns of the reforming movement in Switzerland. The general system of theology and church practice thus begun by Zwingli and worked out by Calvin goes by the name *Reformed*.

The term *Reformed* should thus be distinguished from the Reformation in general, since it is but one specific branch of the Reformation. It should also be distinguished from *Calvinism* per se. The latter is a narrower concept, being specifically that aspect of Reformed theology which comprises the doctrines of sin and salvation (i.e., the "five points" of Calvinism, or TULIP). This is a part of Reformed theology; but also included is a particular view of the church, its ministry, and its sacraments. This last point is what is at stake here.

In formulating its doctrine of the sacraments, Reformed theology introduced a fundamentally new understanding of the meaning of baptism, one which has had profoundly unhappy consequences for Protestantism in general. We are referring here only to the meaning and purpose of baptism, since the issues of its mode and subjects had been compromised long before the Reformation. With regard to meaning, however, there existed a remarkably consistent agreement within Christendom for fifteen hundred years, up to and including Martin Luther himself. This agreement consisted in two main points: (1) baptism is a work of God, i.e., the main action in baptism is something being done by God and not by man; and (2) the divine work accomplished during baptism is the initial bestowal of saving grace upon the waiting sinner, i.e., it is the point of transition from wrath to grace for the individual.[1]

The Reformed theologians, however, created an entirely new approach to baptism. Some of them denied that baptism is a work of God in any significant sense, making it primarily a work of man. Others did not go quite this far, but nevertheless they denied that baptism is the time of the initial bestowal of saving grace. God may be working in baptism, but He is doing something other than this. Needless to say, such denials constitute a complete reversal of biblical doctrine.

My purpose in the first two chapters of this book is to describe the nature of this change in understanding of the meaning of baptism.[2] The plan of the present chapter is first to survey the principal passages in the New Testament itself. Second, a few representative authors from both the early church and the medieval church will be surveyed. Finally, this chapter will conclude with a look at the baptismal theology of Martin Luther.

A. The Bible*

The Bible's own teaching concerning the meaning of baptism can be seen by examining the biblical passages which say anything at all about what exactly is accomplished in this event. In every case the work associated with baptism is not primarily a human work, but is a saving work which only God can perform.

1. Matthew 28:19

Our brief survey of the Bible's teaching will omit references to John's baptism, since this was an Old-Covenant ceremony not equivalent in meaning to Christian baptism.[3] We begin with Christ's institution of baptism in Matthew 28:19, "Go therefore and make disciples of all the nations, baptizing them in the name of the Father and the Son and the Holy Spirit."[4] The outward action is of course that of the baptizer, but the purpose and result of this action is the establishment of a saving relationship with God the Father, God the Son, and God the Spirit. Sinners were baptized "into the name of" the Trinity. The word for "in" or "into" is *eis*, which indicates the actual entrance into the relationship. The total expression, "into the name of," is *eis to onoma*, which was an expression used in the Greek business world to indicate the entry of a sum of money or an item of property into the account of its owner.[5] This seems to be saying that baptism unites us with

---

*A detailed and in-depth study of these Biblical passages appears in Jack Cottrell, *Baptism: A Biblical Study* (Joplin, MO: College Press, 1989).

God in an ownership relation; we become His property in a special, intimate way.

Such a union is one which can be accomplished by God alone. He paid the price to acquire us as His property, namely, the blood of Christ (I Cor. 6:19-20; I Pet. 1:18-19); and He applies the seal which marks us as His own, namely, the Holy Spirit (Eph. 1:13). All of this comes into sharp focus in baptism, where the blood of Christ is applied (Romans 6:3-4) and the Holy Spirit is given (Acts 2:38). No wonder, then, that baptism is baptism into the name of (into an ownership relationship with) the Father, the Son, and the Spirit.

2. Mark 16:16

Mark 16:16 reports that the Great Commission included these words: "He who has believed and has been baptized shall be saved; but he who has disbelieved shall be condemned."[6] This passage likewise indicates that baptism is not man's work but God's. The fact that the passive voice is used ("has been baptized") shows that baptism is not something the sinner himself does; it is something done to him. (This is the consistent witness of the New Testament.) Also it should be noted that the statement is not in the form of a command, which might suggest that baptism is but one among many acts of Christian obedience. Rather, it is in the form of a *promise*, wherein God Himself promises that *He* will do something. In baptism *He* is the one who acts. And what specifically does God promise to do for the one who is baptized? He promises to *save* him.

3. John 3:5

In John 3:5 Jesus says, "Truly, truly, I say to you, unless one is born of water and the Spirit, he cannot enter into the kingdom of God." Not everyone agrees that Jesus is referring here to Christian baptism. But if He is, as I believe, then once again baptism is seen as God's saving work. The very idea that in baptism the sinner is experiencing a kind of birth eliminates the idea that it is his own work: birth is an eminently passive experience. That it is a work of God is seen from the Greek construction. The phrase "of water and the Spirit" is a single preposition (ek) with two simple objects (water and Spirit) joined by "and" (kai). Such a construction points to a single event including both of the objects, namely, a birth of both water and Spirit. The birth is of water, i.e., baptism; but the essential power causing the birth is from God the Holy Spirit.

Is this Spirit-caused birth taking place in baptism a saving event? It seems to be nothing less than regeneration or the new birth (John 3:3), a necessary condition for entering the Kingdom of God (John 3:3,5).

4. Acts 2:38

On the day of Pentecost, when the guilt-laden Jews asked what to do to be free from this burden, Peter replied, "Repent, and let each of you be baptized in the name of Jesus Christ for the forgiveness of your sins; and you shall receive the gift of the Holy Spirit" (Acts 2:38). The result of baptism is described as two-fold: forgiveness of sins and the gift of the Holy Spirit. These are indeed saving works, removing the sinner's guilt and giving him new life (new birth). And who except God can perform such works?

The fact that an imperative or command is used here (and in Acts 22:16) should not lead us to think that the main point in baptism is our own work, i.e., our obedience to God's command. The imperative is used not simply to add another command to the long list of laws and duties incumbent upon us. It is used rather to tell us how to escape our predicament of sin and guilt, or how to be healed from our soul's fatal disease. It is as if a person with a serious heart ailment asked his doctor how he might be cured; and the doctor says, "Have open-heart surgery." Such a response would be taken more as a promise than a command, and the ensuing operation would be the surgeon's work, not the patient's. Even so, in Acts 2:38 Peter's words are a promise of the efficacy of God's work upon the sinner's heart. See verse 39: "For the promise is for you."

5. Acts 22:16

The assumption that Saul of Tarsus was saved on the Damascus Road prior to his baptism is an inference without foundation. It is inconsistent with Ananias' instruction to the repentant Saul in Acts 22:16, "And now why do you delay? Arise, and be baptized, and wash away your sins, calling on His name." The action linked here with baptism is the washing away of sins (equivalent to the forgiveness of sins), which is obviously a saving work which only God can perform. So again we see God as the principal agent in baptism.

The passage is significant because it does mention something that the sinner himself is doing in relation to his baptism, namely, calling on the name of the Lord. This is a reference to the prophecy in Joel 2:32, "And it will come about that whoever calls on the name of the Lord will be delivered." See also Acts 2:21 and Romans 10:13.

But this human act only serves to establish further the fact that the divine action is the main content of baptism. The recipient of baptism is merely calling upon God (in petitionary prayer) to work His promised work in the baptismal moment. And this promised work is no less than salvation. This is seen in the very reference to "calling on His name." This can be understood only against the background of the promise in Joel 2:32, where the petitioner is granted salvation. Thus Saul is instructed to be baptized, calling on God to save him therein. The "calling on His name" would lose its significance if Saul were already saved.

6. Romans 6:3-4

Another passage which speaks of what is accomplished in baptism is Romans 6:3-4, "Or do you not know that all of us who have been baptized into Christ Jesus have been baptized into His death? Therefore we have been buried with Him through baptism into death, in order that as Christ was raised from the dead through the glory of the Father, so we too might walk in newness of life." Here we should note first that baptism is the act that brings us into union with Christ or into a relationship with Christ: we are "baptized into Christ Jesus." More specifically, we are baptized into a union with those deeds of Jesus which are the very fountain of salvation, namely, His death and resurrection. The result is our own death and resurrection: the slaying of the old sinful self and resurrection to spiritual life. These experiences, accomplished in baptism, are deeds which only God can perform. Only God can crucify us with Christ (verse 6). Being buried and raised again are obviously works done to us, not works which we can do for ourselves.

That such language describes the initial bestowal of salvation should be clear. In view is the beginning of our union with Christ, signified by the word "into" (*eis*) in "baptized into Christ." Also in view is the initial washing with Christ's atoning blood (i.e., forgiveness of sins), since we are "baptized into His death." Likewise indicated is regeneration or the new birth, described in terms of being resurrected from the dead (verse 5).

7. I Corinthians 6:11

Paul's statement in I Corinthians 6:11 almost certainly refers to baptism, though the word itself does not occur. Used instead is a form of *apolouo*, translated "washed": "And such were some of you; but you were washed, but you were sanctified, but you were justified in the name of the Lord Jesus Christ, and in the Spirit of our God." Connected with the washing are justification and sanctification, which again are divine works. They are accomplished by (*en*) the Spirit of God.

Justification is the forgiveness of sins, and sanctification is the initial setting apart or transition from the kingdom of Satan to the Kingdom of God. (All three verbs — *washed, sanctified,* and *justified* — are in the aorist tense, indicating a completed action in the past.) That the washing or baptism is named first might suggest that it occurs prior to or at least no later than the justifying and the sanctifying. The word order alone may not be decisive on this point, however.

8. I Corinthians 12:13

In I Corinthians 12:13 Paul again affirms that the baptismal operation is performed by God, i.e., "by one Spirit": "For by one Spirit we were all baptized into one body, whether Jews or Greeks, whether slaves or free, and we were all made to drink of one Spirit." What is accomplished in baptism is the uniting of the seeking sinner with the one body of Christ, the church. This reminds us of Acts 2:47, which says that the Lord is the one who adds to the church the one who is being saved.

9. Galatians 3:27

The next passage which speaks of what is accomplished in baptism is Galatians 3:27, "For all of you who were baptized into Christ have clothed yourselves with Christ." This repeats a theme already encountered: we are "baptized into Christ," thus being united with Him there. It adds the idea that in baptism we "put on Christ," as the King James Version says, like a garment or a cloak. This brings to mind Isaiah 61:10, "I will rejoice greatly in the Lord, my soul will exult in my God; for He has clothed me with garments of salvation, He has wrapped me with a robe of righteousness." This robe of righteousness is no less than the blood of Christ which covers our sins. Thus the most blessed of God's saving works — forgiveness of sins — is here said to result from baptism.

10. Colossians 2:12

One of the clearest testimonies to baptism as a saving work of God is Colossians 2:12, "Having been buried with Him in baptism, in which you were also raised up with Him through faith in the working of God, who raised Him from the dead." This is similar to Romans 6:3-5 in that it mentions baptism as the time of

24

burial into a union with Christ's atoning blood and of resurrection from our own spiritual death. So that there will be no mistake, Paul says specifically that these initial gifts of salvation are received *en to baptismati*, "in baptism."

This verse also mentions our own main contribution to the baptismal event, i.e., faith. We are buried and raised through faith. Nothing could make it plainer that baptism is a divine work and not a human one, for the verse goes on to say that the object of our faith is "the working (*energeias*) of God." God is the one doing the work (burying us with Christ; raising us from the dead); we merely yield ourselves to Him in faith, trusting that He will do for us what He has promised.

11. Titus 3:5

Titus 3:5 is similar to I Corinthians 6:11 in that the word "washing" (*loutron*) is used instead of baptism, but it still most probably refers to the act of baptism: "He saved us, not on the basis of deeds which we have done in righteousness, but according to His mercy, by the washing of regeneration and renewing by the Holy Spirit." Here the work specified as occurring in baptism is called "regeneration and renewing," which is the same as the new birth and resurrection from spiritual death — one of the prime saving acts of God which mark the beginning of the Christian life.

It is specifically said that God saves us through (*dia*) this washing; the work accomplished therein is attributed directly to the Holy Spirit. That is, the regeneration and renewing are "by the Holy Spirit."[7]

12. I Peter 3:21

By now the reader must be struck by the monotony of the pattern, but there is still one verse to consider, namely, I Peter 3:21, "And corresponding to that, baptism now saves you — not the removal of dirt from the flesh, but an appeal to God for a good conscience — through the resurrection of Jesus Christ." Without referring to any specific aspect of salvation, this verse makes the unequivocal assertion that baptism saves.

Some see the reference to a "figure" (*antitypon*) in the first part of the verse (translated "corresponding to" in the NASB), and think that this is referring to the manner in which baptism saves, i.e., only figuratively. But that is not the point. This word is referring back to verse 20, which says that Noah and the others on the ark were in a sense saved by the water of the flood (presumably as it kept the ark afloat). This is a figure or type of baptism, in that each has a saving power or function. This reference to baptism's saving power magnifies the divine side of the event.

Exactly how does baptism save? Peter very clearly shows that it is not through some physical property in the water itself; it is not just a matter of using water to wash dirt off the body. Nor does the water function as a cleanser for the soul in some metaphysical sense. So how does baptism save? As the *eperotema* ("an appeal," NASB) of a good conscience toward God.

The meaning of *eperotema* is very important here. Some have translated it in such a way that the main significance of baptism seems to be a human accomplishment. This is seen in Luther's use of the German word *bund* as a translation, which means a covenant or pledge. The New International Version uses the word *pledge*. If this is the meaning, then baptism's saving significance lies in man's own efforts, i.e., it is the baptized person's symbolic pledge both to God and to his fellow Christians that he will live a pure life.

This does not seem to be the proper translation of *eperotema*, however. The verb form of this noun means "to ask, to question, to request," and the noun itself (as used here) is best understood as an appeal or a request or a prayer.[8] It is an appeal made unto God (*eis theon*) for a good conscience, for a conscience freed from the guilt of sin. As Greeven says, it "is to be construed as a prayer for the remission of sins."[9] This expression, then, is identical in meaning with Acts 22:16: in baptism the sinner is calling upon God to wash away his sins. (See also Hebrews 10:22).

Thus I Peter 3:21 epitomizes the essence of baptism as taught throughout the New Testament. It is a work of God, with man's only role that of calling upon God to do what He has promised. And it is a work of salvation, wherein a person who comes burdened with the guilt of his sins appeals to God for the remission of that burden and receives it by His grace.

13. Conclusion

We have surveyed the New Testament passages which specifically mention the results of baptism. It is clear that the works associated with baptism are works of salvation; they are works which only God can perform, not man. These are union with Christ; union with Christ in His death and resurrection; union with the Father, the Son, and the Spirit; the remission of sins; the washing away of sin; justification; the gift of the garment of Christ's righteousness; a clear conscience; death to sin; burial of the old nature and resurrection of the new; the gift of the Holy Spirit; regeneration and renewing; the new birth; sanctification; union with the body of Christ; and, in short, *salvation*.[10]

On the other hand, the only human acts associated with baptism are the passive and dependent acts of prayer — calling upon God to do what He has promised, and faith — fully trusting that he will do it. We never once read that in baptism man is making a response, making a commitment, expressing his faith, testifying to his faith, announcing his faith, confirming his salvation, demonstrating his discipleship, or pledging to live a Christian life. Such words as these — response, commitment, expression, testimony, announcement, confirmation, demonstration, pledge — all refer to something man is doing; and they are totally absent from the New Testament descriptions of baptism.[11]

Why is it, then, that the latter terminology has all but replaced the former in so much of Christendom, including an increasing number of pulpits in the Restoration Movement? This chapter and the next will provide the background for answering that question.

B. The Historical Witness

The above understanding of the New Testament teaching on baptism may sound strange in most Protestant circles today, but this would not have been so during Christendom's first fifteen hundred years. For this entire period the accepted baptismal doctrine was built around the core of ideas presented above, namely, that baptism is primarily a work of God and that it is the point of time when salvation is initially received. In this section a brief survey of representative theologians will show that this is the case.

1. The Early Church

a. *Justin Martyr (A.D. 110-165).* Writing in the mid-second century A.D., Justin Martyr gives the clearest and most detailed explanation of the baptismal practice of that period. New converts, he says, are first instructed to fast and pray. "Then they are brought by us where there is water, and are regenerated. . . . For . . . they then receive the washing with water." Justin then quotes John 3:5. He specifically says that "we have learned from the apostles this reason" for baptism, i.e., "in order that we . . . may obtain in the water the remission of sins."[12] Thus the essential elements of the New Testament doctrine are presented.

b. *Tertullian (A.D. 145-220).* The earliest extant treatise specifically on baptism comes from Tertullian in the early third century. It is in the form of a discourse to baptismal candidates, who are being instructed as to the nature and purpose of the rite which they are about to receive. The opening words set the tone for the whole piece: "Happy is our sacrament of water, in that, by washing away the sins of our early blindness, we are set free and admitted into eternal life."[13] Tertullian continues to speak of the saving acts of God in baptism. The baptismal waters, he says, wash away death[14] and give life.[15] "The act of baptism . . . is carnal, in that we are plunged in water, but the effect is spiritual, in that we are freed from sins."[16]

c. *Cyril of Jerusalem (c. A.D. 315-386).* The fourth century theologians continue to teach the Biblical significance of baptism. Cyril of Jerusalem is a good example of this. For him baptism gives salvation by the power of God, as he succinctly states: "When going down . . . into the water, think not of the bare element, but look for salvation by the power of the Holy Ghost."[17] Cyril placed before the candidates for baptism this marvelous promise:

> Great is the Baptism that lies before you: a ransom to captives; a remission of offences; a death of sin; a new-birth of the soul; a garment of light; a holy indissoluble seal; a chariot to heaven; the delight of Paradise; a welcome into the kingdom; the gift of adoption! . . .[18]

d. *Gregory of Nyssa (A.D. 334-394).* Gregory of Nyssa shared the same high view of baptism found in the other early theologians. Its effect is to save, but only by the divine power working therein: "Despise not . . . the Divine laver, nor think lightly of it, as a common thing, on account of the use of water. For the power that operates is mighty, and wonderful are the things that are wrought thereby."[19]

What are the "wonderful things" wrought by God in the baptismal waters? They include "remission of what is to be accounted for, release from bondage, close relation to God, free boldness of speech, and in place of servile subjection equality with the angels. For these things, and all that follow from them, the grace of Baptism secures and conveys to us."[20] "Baptism, then, is a purification from sins, a remission of trespasses, a cause of renovation and regeneration."[21] The baptismal water "renews the man to spiritual regeneration, when the grace from above hallows it."[22]

2. The Catholic Church

The main elements of the Biblical consensus on the meaning of baptism were accepted and taught by the developing Catholic

Church, and they have continued to be a part of Catholic theology throughout the Middle Ages, the Reformation era, and the modern age. Here only two representatives will be discussed, Augustine and Thomas Aquinas.

  a. *Augustine (A.D. 354-430).* Augustine's doctrine of baptism can be summed up in three words: efficacy, power, and necessity. First, with regard to the *efficacy* of baptism, Augustine does not deviate from those who went before him. He sees it as the point of time wherein God works the works which apply redemption to the soul. It is indeed "the sacrament of . . . redemption."[23] Baptism is nothing else than salvation itself;[24] it "brings salvation."[25] We are "saved by baptism"; "the salvation of man is effected in baptism."[26] We are "joined to Christ by baptism";[27] indeed, a person "is baptized for the express purpose of being with Christ."[28]

  The second element of baptismal doctrine stressed by Augustine is the *power of baptism.* Certainly whatever can accomplish the saving work described above is filled with power. But whence comes this power? From the act itself? No! It is from God alone, who Himself is acting on the heart of the person being baptized. The human agent baptizes with water, but at the same time Christ Himself is baptizing "by a hidden grace, by a hidden power in the Holy Spirit," and "by the invisible working of His majesty. For in that we say, He Himself baptizes, we do not mean, He Himself holds and dips in the water the bodies of the believers; but He Himself invisibly cleanses, and that He does to the whole Church without exception."[29] John 3:5 shows that the new birth is by water in its outward form, but "by the Spirit who bestows the benefit of grace in its inward power, cancelling the bond of guilt, and restoring natural goodness."[30]

  A final point is the *necessity of baptism.* On this point Augustine is quite emphatic and almost absolute: baptism is necessary for salvation. He refers to the "apostolic tradition, by which the Churches of Christ maintain it to be an inherent principle, that without baptism . . . it is impossible for any man to attain to salvation and everlasting life."[31]

b. *Thomas Aquinas (c. A.D. 1225-1274)*. Thomas Aquinas is considered by many to be the foremost theologian of Catholicism. His systematic work, the *Summa Theologica*, contains his view of baptism.[32] Here he states unequivocally that baptism is necessary for salvation:

> . . . Men are bound to that without which they cannot obtain salvation. Now it is manifest that no one can obtain salvation but through Christ. . . . But for this end is baptism conferred on a man, that being regenerated thereby, he may be incorporated in Christ. . . . Consequently it is manifest that all are bound to be baptized: and that without Baptism there is no salvation for men (68:1, p. 2398).

This includes all infants, even those born to Christian parents. They all have original sin, "wherefore they need to be baptized" (68:1, p. 2399). "It became necessary to baptize children, that, as in birth they incurred damnation through Adam, so in a second birth they might obtain salvation through Christ" (68:9, p. 2405).

Baptism saves because it is the time when grace is received (69:3, p. 2410); "the grace of the Holy Ghost and the fulness of virtues are given in Baptism" (69:4, p. 2411). This is true basically because baptism is what unites one with Christ, whose suffering is the sole source of salvation. "By Baptism a man is incorporated in the Passion and death of Christ. . . . Hence it is clear that the Passion of Christ is communicated to every baptized person, so that he is healed just as if he himself had suffered and died" (69:2, p. 2409). "Baptism opens the gates of the heavenly kingdom to the baptized in so far as it incorporates them in the Passion of Christ, by applying its power to man" (69:7, pp. 2413-14).

3. Martin Luther

Many have assumed that because Martin Luther championed the Protestant doctrine of justification by faith, he must have taken a "faith-only" approach to baptism. Nothing could be further from the truth. Luther's view of the meaning of baptism stands in direct continuity with the New Testament, the early church fathers, and the Catholic scholars who preceded him. Although he rejected certain excesses of the Catholic view, he still regarded baptism as a mighty work of God in which the Father, Son, and Holy Spirit pour out the full blessings of salvation upon the penitent believer.

a. *The blessings of grace are bestowed in baptism.* "Baptism is a thing of great force and efficacy," says Luther.[33] "In it we obtain such an inexpressible treasure."[34] This treasure includes practically the whole scope of the contents of God's redeeming grace.

Specifically, Luther asserts that forgiveness of sins is initially bestowed in baptism. In his "Small Catechism" in answer to the question, "What gifts or benefits does Baptism bestow?", he says first of all, "It effects forgiveness of sins."[35] This is part of the work of baptism; in it "the forgiveness takes place through God's covenant."[36] "As we have once obtained forgiveness of sins in Baptism, so forgiveness remains day by day as long as we live."[37] Forgiveness takes place in baptism because that is where the blood of Christ is applied to the sinner: "Through Baptism he is bathed in the blood of Christ and is cleansed from sins."[38] An even more forceful statement is as follows:

Holy Baptism has been purchased for us by the same blood which Christ shed for us and with which He paid for our sin. This blood, with its merit and power, He has deposited in Baptism so that men attain it there. For the person who is receiving Baptism in faith is in effect actually being visibly washed with the blood of Christ and cleansed from sins.[39]

According to Luther baptism brings not only forgiveness of sins but also a new birth, a change in the inner man that actually eradicates sin. For "it is one thing to forgive sins, and another thing to put them away or drive them out. . . . But both the forgiveness and the driving out of sins are the work of baptism."[40] Thus it is appropriate to speak of baptism as the time when "a person is born again and made new."[41] This "new birth . . . is wrought in Baptism."[42]

In summary, "What Baptism promises and brings" is this: "victory over death and the devil, forgiveness of sin, God's grace, the entire Christ, and the Holy Spirit with his gifts. In short, the blessings of Baptism are so boundless that if timid nature considers them, it may well doubt whether they could all be true."[43] "No greater jewel, therefore, can adorn our body and soul than Baptism."[44] It is indeed a "flood of grace."[45]

b. *Baptism is God's Work.* One may well ask, How can baptism accomplish all this? Or as the "Small Catechism" asks, "How can water produce such great effects?" Luther answers very plainly, "It is not the water that produces these effects."[46] There is no magical power in the water nor in the act itself;[47] the only power at work is *God's* power. The truly efficacious element in baptism is God's word of promise (e.g., Mark 16:16), and even this power is dormant unless and until it is activated by faith. Thus the two elements that produce the effects of baptism are these: "The Word of God connected with the water, and our faith which relies on the Word of God connected with the water."[48]

The conclusion of the whole matter is this: man is not saved by his own works, which baptism is not, but by faith in God's work, which baptism is. In response to his critics who thought that his view of baptism was a kind of works-salvation, Luther said, "Yes, it is true that our works are of no use for salvation. Baptism, however, is not our work but God's."[49] "Although it is performed by men's hands, it is nevertheless truly God's own act,"[50] as if the Lord Himself were thrusting us under the water with His own hands.[51] "Hence we ought to receive baptism at human hands just as if Christ himself, indeed, God himself were baptizing us with his own hands. For it is not man's baptism, but Christ's and God's baptism, which we receive at the hand of a man."[52]

"Baptism is the work of the entire Holy Trinity," says Luther.[53]

The Father removes our death and sin and misery, and gives us eternal righteousness and life and joy, all through the blood of His dear Son. The Holy Spirit enlightens us and warms us with His fire.

> . . . Now, since all this takes place in the holy sacrament of Baptism, we should, in justice, not like a cow, consider it mere water but the very blood of the Son of God and the very fire of the Holy Spirit, in which the Son sanctifies us through His blood, the Holy Spirit bathes us with His fire, and the Father quickens us through His light and splendor. Thus all three Persons are present, jointly produce the one divine result, and pour all their power into Baptism.[54]

"This is why Baptism is a water that takes away sin, death, and every evil and helps us to enter heaven and eternal life," namely, because "God the Father, Son, and Holy Spirit are indeed in and with this water."[55]

c. *Baptism is for salvation.* In all his writings Luther stresses the fact that baptism is for salvation. "Through baptism man is saved," he says;[56] God "saves us by baptism."[57] In answer to the question of the purpose of baptism, i.e., "what benefits, gifts and effects it brings," he gives this answer: "To put it most simply, the power, effect, benefit, fruit, and purpose of Baptism is to save."[58] Baptism is God's work, and "God's works . . . are salutary and necessary for salvation."[59] One is baptized so that he "may receive in the water the promised salvation."[60]

No wonder Luther speaks of baptism as "excellent, glorious, and exalted," as "a most precious thing," as "an infinite, divine treasure."[61]

C. Conclusion

I have called the view described in this chapter the "Biblical consensus." It is the view that baptism is principally the time when

34

God Himself is working to bestow upon the penitent, believing sinner the benefits of the redeeming work of Christ. This is the New Testament's own doctrine of baptism, and it was recognized as such by fifteen centuries of Biblical scholarship.

If this view sounds strange to the majority of modern Protestants, it is because the Biblical consensus has been replaced in most Protestant groups with an interpretation of baptism which originated in the sixteenth century in the mind of Huldreich Zwingli. It is known as the Reformed view of baptism, and it differs from the Biblical consensus in several crucial respects. This is the topic of this book's second chapter.

Endnotes

1. When infant baptism was first introduced (toward the end of the second century A.D.), its purpose was not to bring the infant from wrath to grace, since the doctrine of inherited guilt and liability to wrath was not developed until the time of Augustine in the early fifth century A.D. At first there was only the idea of inherited spiritual sickness or depravity; infant baptism was adopted as the time when God bestowed on the infant His cleansing and healing grace.

2. We shall not deal here with infant baptism as such, because this was not a new practice with the Reformed churches. We must include a discussion of their new *rationale* for infant baptism, however, since this is the source of their new understanding of the meaning of baptism in general. The question of mode will not be discussed at all.

3. It was in fact Zwingli who introduced the notion that John's baptism and Christian baptism have the same meaning. In asserting this point Zwingli said he was going against all the theologians he had ever read or could call to mind. It was "the common error of the older theologians that the baptism of John was different from that of Christ." (Zwingli, "Of Baptism," *Zwingli and Bullinger*, "Library of Christian Classics," vol. 24, tr. G.W. Bromiley [Philadelphia: Westminster Press, 1953], pp. 143, 161).

4. This and other quotations from Scripture are from the New American Standard Bible (NASB) unless noted otherwise.

5. Hans Bietenhard, *"onoma,"* in *Theological Dictionary of the New Testament*, ed. Gerhard Friedrich, tr. G.W. Bromiley (Grand Rapids: Eerdmans, 1967), V:245. Bietenhard himself does not think this is the meaning in Matthew 28:19 (ibid., p. 275), but Oepke disagrees (Albrecht Oepke, "bapto," *Theological Dictionary of the New Testament*, ed. Gerhard Kittel, tr. G.W. Bromiley [Grand Rapids: Eerdmans, 1964], I:539).

6. For our purposes here we may assume that the textual difficulties with regard to this verse may be resolved in favor of canonicity. Even if not, there is nothing stated here that is not stated many times and even more specifically in other passages.

7. The cadence of this verse is not

"The washing of regeneration

and

the renewing of the Holy Spirit,"

but rather

"The washing

of the regeneration and the renewing

of the Holy Spirit."

8. Heinrich Greeven, ."*eperotao*," in *Theological Dictionary of the New Testament*, ed. Gerhard Kittel, tr. G.W. Bromiley (Grand Rapids: Eerdmans, 1964), II:687-688.

9. Ibid., p. 688.

10. Each of these terms does not necessarily refer to a separate and distinct divine work; some are synonymous. The full range of expression is listed here so that the full impact of this point will be felt.

11. Except for the NIV translation of I Peter 3:21, which I believe is erroneous.

12. Justin Martyr, "The First Apology of Justin," 61, tr. Dods and Reith, in *The Ante-Nicene Fathers*, ed. Alexander Roberts and James Donaldson (Grand Rapids: Eerdmans reprint, 1979), I:183.

13. Tertullian, "On Baptism," tr. S. Thelwell, in *The Ante-Nicene Fathers*, ed. Alexander Roberts and James Donaldson (Grand Rapids: Eerdmans reprint, 1978), III:669.

14. Ibid., II, p. 669.

15. Ibid., III, p. 670.

16. Ibid., VII, p. 672.

17. Cyril of Jerusalem, "Catechetical Lectures," III:4, tr. Edward H. Gifford, *Nicene and Post-Nicene Fathers*, ed. Philip Schaff and Henry Wace (Grand Rapids: Eerdmans reprint, 1978), VII:15.

18. Ibid., Procatechesis [Prologue], 16, p. 5.

19. Gregory of Nyssa, "On the Baptism of Christ," tr. H.A. Wilson, *Nicene and Post-Nicene Fathers*, ed. Philip Schaff and Henry Wace (Grand Rapids: Eerdmans reprint, 1979), V:519.

20. Ibid., p. 518.

21. Ibid.

22. Ibid., p. 520.

23. Augustine, "On the Soul and Its Origin," II:13, *The Works of Aurelius Augustine, Vol. XII: The Anti-Pelagian Works, vol. ii.*, ed. Marcus Dods, tr. Peter Holmes (Edinburgh: T. & T. Clark, 1874), p. 257.

24. Augustine, "A Treatise on the Merits and Forgiveness of Sins," I:34, *The Works of Aurelius Augustine, Vol. IV: The Anti-Pelagian Works, vol. i.*, ed

Marcus Dods, tr. Peter Holmes (Edinburgh: T. & T. Clark, 1872), p. 35.

25. Augustine, Letter #98, "To Boniface," 1, *The Works of Aurelius Augustine, Vol. XIII: Letters, vol. ii,* ed. Marcus Dods, tr. J.G. Cunningham (Edinburgh: T. & T. Clark, 1875), p. 14.

26. Augustine, "Against Two Letters of the Pelagians," III:5, *The Works of Aurelius Augustine, Vol. XV: The Anti-Pelagian Works, vol. iii,* ed. Marcus Dods, tr. Peter Holmes and R.E. Wallis (Edinburgh: T. & T. Clark, 1876), p. 301.

27. Augustine, "A Treatise on the Merits and Forgiveness of Sins," I:55, p. 53.

28. Ibid., p. 54.

29. Augustine, "Answer to Petilian the Donatist," III:xlix, *The Works of Aurelius Augustine, Vol. III,* ed. Marcus Dods, tr. J.R. King (Edinburgh: T. & T. Clark, 1872), p. 462.

30. Augustine, Letter #98, "To Boniface," 2, p. 15.

31. Augustine, "A Treatise on the Merits and Forgiveness of Sins," I:34, p. 35. The only exception to this rule is in the case of a martyr.

32. Thomas Aquinas, *Summa Theologica,* 3 vols., tr. Fathers of the English Dominican Province (New York: Benziger Brothers, 1947-1948). All citations here are from vol. 2 of this edition, and from Part III of the *Summa.* The numbers given in the text refer to the specific question and article, e.g., 68:6 means question 68, article 6 of Part III. Page numbers are also given.

33. Martin Luther, *A Commentary on St. Paul's Epistle to the Galatians,* ed. Philip Watson (Westwood, N.J.: Revell, n.d.), p. 341.

34. Luther, "The Large Catechism," IV:26, in *The Book of Concord,* tr. and ed. Theodore Tappert et al. (Philadelphia: Fortress Press, 1959), p. 439.

35. Luther, "The Small Catechism," IV:6, in *The Book of Concord,* p. 340.

36. Luther, "The Holy and Blessed Sacrament of Baptism," 15, tr. Charles Jacobs and E.T. Bachmann, *Luther's Works,* American Edition, Vol. 35, *Word and Sacrament, I,* ed. E.T. Bachmann (Philadelphia: Muhlenberg Press, 1960), pp. 38-39.

37. Luther, "The Large Catechism," IV:86, p. 446.

38. Luther, "Kleine Antwort auf Herzog Georgen," *Werke,* Weimar Edition, Vol. 38, p. 147, cited in *What Luther Says: An Anthology,* ed. Ewald M. Plass (St. Louis: Concordia, 1959), I:46.

39. Luther, "Zwo Predigten auf der Kindtaufe des Jungen Herrleins Bernhards," *Werke,* Weimar Edition, Vol. 49, pp. 131f., cited in Plass, I:46. Also in "Sermon at the Baptism of Bernhard von Anhalt, 1540," *Luther's Works,* American Edition, Vol. 51, *Sermons, I,* ed. and tr. John W. Doberstein (Philadelphia: Fortress Press, 1959), p. 325.

40. Luther, "The Holy and Blessed Sacrament of Baptism," 15; p. 38.

41. Ibid., 3; p. 30.

42. Luther, *A Commentary on . . . Galatians,* p. 341.

43. Luther, "The Large Catechism," IV:41-42; pp. 441-442.

44. Ibid., IV:46; p. 442.
45. Luther, "The Holy and Blessed Sacrament of Baptism," 6, p. 32.
46. Luther, "The Small Catechism," IV:9-10, p. 349.
47. Luther, "The Babylonian Captivity of the Church," tr. A.T.W. Steinhauser et al., *Three Treatises* (Philadelphia: Fortress Press, 1960), pp. 188-189.
48. Luther, "The Small Catechism," IV:10; p. 349.
49. Luther, "The Large Catechism," IV:35; p. 441.
50. Ibid., IV:10; p. 437.
51. Luther, "The Babylonian Captivity of the Church," p. 184.
52. Ibid.
53. Luther, *Werke*, Weimar Edition, Vol. 45, p. 181; cited in Plass, I:48.
54. Luther, "Von der heiligen Taufe Predigten," *Werke*, Weimar Edition, Vol. 37, p. 650; cited in Plass, I:48.
55. Luther, *Werke*, Vol. 52, p. 102; cited in Plass, I:48.
56. Luther, The Holy and Blessed Sacrament of Baptism," 6, p. 32.
57. Luther, "The Babylonian Captivity of the Church," p. 187.
58. Luther, "The Large Catechism," IV:23-24; p. 439.
59. Ibid., IV:35; p. 441.
60. Ibid., IV:36; p. 441.
61. Ibid., IV:7, 8, 34; pp. 437, 440.

2

BAPTISM ACCORDING TO THE REFORMED TRADITION

Jack W. Cottrell

Protestants tend to think that all the changes brought about by the Reformation were for the better. Luther, Calvin, and company are regarded as having rescued important doctrines and practices from a kind of Roman Catholic "Babylonian captivity." This is especially true with reference to the so-called sacraments.

Without question important changes were made regarding the sacraments, and many of them were definitely needed. However, not all the changes were good. This is true especially of the Reformed revision of the meaning and purpose of baptism. This chapter will describe that revision as it was inaugurated by the first Reformed theologian, Huldreich Zwingli (1484-1531).

Zwingli wrote a great deal about the sacraments, since they were the subject of two of the main controversies in which he was involved. He fought bitter verbal battles with Luther over Christ's presence in the Lord's supper and with the Anabaptists over infant baptism. His general summaries of the Christian faith also addressed the question of the nature of the sacraments as such. Like most people Zwingli assumed that "sacrament" is a general category and that whatever particular rites belong to that category share a common meaning. Thus his conclusions regarding sacraments as such will apply to his view of baptism just as much as his statements about this sacrament in particular.

A. Zwingli's Rejection of the Biblical Consensus

Zwingli began his theological career exactly where Luther and other Reformers did — as a true son of the Roman Catholic Church. As such he first believed that the water of baptism washes away sins, including the inherited sin present in infants.[1] However, by 1523 he had repudiated this understanding of baptism. Although he acknowledged that all teachers before him had held to this view, he rejected it. "In this matter of baptism," he said, "all the doctors have been in error from the time of the apostles. . . . For all the doctors have ascribed to the water a power which it does not have and the holy apostles did not teach."[2] "The Fathers were in error . . . because they thought that the water itself effects cleansing and salvation."[3]

1. Baptism and Salvation Are Not Connected

The last statement quoted above is an exaggeration and is really not fair to "the Fathers," since few if any would have said that the water itself is what cleanses and saves. They generally agreed that God alone does this via the blood of Christ and the Holy Spirit, with baptism being either the means or occasion of God's working. Acknowledging this distinction would not have affected Zwingli's sweeping dismissal of all prior baptismal doctrine, though, since he rejected the latter idea also. There is simply no connection between baptism and salvation as far as Zwingli is concerned. "Christ himself did not connect salvation with baptism."[4] "The two are not to be connected and used together."[5] Since Christ did not rest salvation on external baptism, then salvation does not depend upon it.[6]

Over and over from as early as 1523[7] up to his death in 1531, Zwingli emphasized his view that baptism does not wash away sins. At one point in 1524 he declared that this is the only baptismal issue worth fighting over, namely, that we must not attribute to baptism what belongs to the grace of God alone, i.e., we must not think that the water of baptism cleanses the soul.[8] If anyone says, "External things are nothing! They avail nothing for salvation!" — he speaks correctly.[9] "No external thing can make us pure or righteous."[10] "Water-baptism cannot contribute in any way to the washing away of sin."[11] It "does not justify the one who is baptized,"[12] nor is one born again by baptism.[13] "Everlasting life has nowhere been promised on the terms that unless one has been . . . baptized he shall in no wise attain it."[14] "A sacrament . . . cannot have any power to free the conscience. . . . They are wrong, therefore, by the whole width of heaven who think that sacraments have any cleansing power."[15] In his last major work (1531) Zwingli said that "it is clearly frivolous to teach that . . . the sacraments can remit sins or confer blessings."[16]

In these statements Zwingli is denying that baptism or the water of baptism has any inherent power to remove the effects of sin from the soul. This entire polemic is in a sense misguided and wasted, however, since few if any of Zwingli's opponents would have affirmed such a thing anyway. Tertullian at times comes close to doing so, as may some of the more unguarded expressions of the Roman Catholic *ex opere operato* concept. But this is not the point of the Biblical consensus as held by the majority of the church fathers, Martin Luther, or even the Catholic Church as a whole. Their main concern was to affirm that God works His saving works upon the repentant sinner's soul in or through baptism, i.e. simultaneous with the action of water baptism.

Zwingli recognizes that this is the case, at least with reference to Luther and his followers. He himself distinguishes between the idea that a sacrament can by its own power free the conscience, and the idea that an inward purification is surely performed at the time the sacrament is outwardly administered. But he specifically denies not just the former view, but the latter as well, calling it a "vain invention."[17] "Therefore this second view has no value, which supposes that the sacraments are signs of such a kind that, when they are applied to a man, the thing signified by the sacraments at once takes place within him."[18] God is free to work salvation before, during, or after baptism, as He chooses. The inner, saving baptism "need not be concurrent" with external baptism.[19] The general rule is that salvation precedes the baptism which symbolizes it. As Zwingli says, it "is incontrovertible in baptism and the eucharist" that "that which is symbolized by the sacraments is at hand before we use the sacraments."[20]

The main point, as stated at the beginning of this section, is that baptism and salvation are not to be connected in any way. In fact, Zwingli came to the conclusion that baptism is not intended to have any effect at all upon its recipient; it is given only for the sake of the audience. "For baptism is given and received for the sake of fellow-believers, not for a supposed effect in those who receive it."[21]

2. The Rationale for Separating Baptism and Salvation

It was a rather bold thing for Zwingli to declare that every teacher since the apostles had been wrong about the meaning of baptism. He must have felt that he had good reasons for rejecting the Biblical consensus and introducing a new view. What are these reasons?

Zwingli's fundamental theological rationale for denying that baptism saves is that salvation can be accomplished only through the blood of Christ. He declares that we are justified solely by God's grace, not by the sacrament.[22] No one comes to the

Father except through Jesus (John 14:6) — and therefore not through any sacrament.[23] The blood of Christ, not the sacraments, washes away sins; therefore whoever boldly believes on the blood of Christ receives remission of sins.[24] Washing away the filth of the soul "is the function of the blood of Christ alone."[25] Speaking of original sin in particular, Zwingli says it is "removed only by the blood of Christ and cannot be removed by the washing of baptism."[26] If baptism is necessary for washing away sins, then Christ died in vain, and it is false that God alone forgives sins.[27] Christ's death is superfluous if water can purify the soul.[28]

Underlying this theological reasoning is a basic metaphysical assumption, namely, the absolute dissimilarity and disjunction of matter and spirit. It is essentially impossible for baptism to effect salvation because water is a material element and the soul is a spiritual entity, and never the twain shall meet. Baptism does not purify the soul, says Zwingli, for how could it possibly be that an incorporeal substance could be cleansed by a corporeal element?[29] "Absolutely no sin is taken away by the washing of baptism," for "external things cannot cleanse the conscience."[30] "Material water cannot contribute in any way to the cleansing of the soul."[31] "It is clear that the external baptism of water cannot effect spiritual cleansing. . . . No external element or action can purify the soul."[32]

> . . . How . . . could water, fire, oil, milk, salt, and such crude things make their way to the mind? Not having that power, how will they be able to cleanse it? In fact, what is the cleansing of the mind? Is it a sort of contact with some clean thing? But what can the mind touch, or what touch the mind? Since, therefore, no creature can know a man within to the core, but only God, it remains that no one can purge the conscience save God alone. . . . [33]

This very principle, which Zwingli found in John 6:63 — "It is the Spirit who gives life; the flesh profits nothing," is what he used to exclude the bodily presence of Christ from the Lord's supper.

His statements in that context apply equally to baptism: the application of carnal body to the soul does nothing toward justification, because the soul cannot be fed by the flesh of the body.[34]

The essence of this argument — that the water of baptism cannot wash away sins (1) because only the blood of Christ can do that and (2) because material elements cannot cleanse the spirit — would hardly be disputed by anyone whom Zwingli was opposing, for (as we have noted) most of his opponents did not really attribute the power of washing away sins to the water of baptism in the first place. Hence Zwingli must have had some other reason for separating baptism from salvation, not only as its cause but also as its occasion. That is to say, granted that the agent which cleanses the soul is God alone (on the basis of the blood of Christ) and not baptism, why could God not arrange it so that He would effect this cleansing *during* baptism, as the Biblical consensus had taught for fifteen hundred years?

Zwingli gives two basic reasons why this could not be the case. The first is that this would violate the sovereign freedom of God to act when and where He chooses. Like the wind, which blows where it wishes and is not under our control, the Holy Spirit must be free to work regeneration according to His will and not ours (John 3:8). "Therefore, the Spirit of grace is conveyed not by this immersion . . . . For if it were thus, it would be known how, where, whence and whither the Spirit is borne."[35] If salvation were necessarily linked to baptism in any way, "the liberty of the divine Spirit which distributes itself to individuals as it will, that is, to whom it will, when it will, where it will, would be bound. For if it were compelled to act within when we employ the signs externally, it would be absolutely bound by the signs." We simply cannot have "the divine Spirit be such a slave to the sacraments that, when they are performed, it is compelled at the same time to operate within."[36]

The second reason why salvation cannot be connected with baptism is that the question of an individual's salvation has already been decided by God's gracious, unconditional election before the foundation of the world. Thus since election itself is the ultimate source and guarantee of salvation, the actual time when the salvation is bestowed is irrelevent — whether as an infant or an adult, and whether before, during or after baptism. Even faith itself is not the deciding factor, since whether one becomes a believer or not is dependent solely on election. A person believes only because he has been elected and predestined to eternal salvation. A person might even be saved without faith, if he should die before coming to faith (as in infancy), as long as he is among the elect. "For the elect are ever elect, even before they believe." If a person does believe, he will doubtless be saved; but the salvation is the result of his election, not his faith. The faith itself is the fruit of election. Thus election stands "above baptism and circumcision; nay, above faith and preaching" as the only true cause of salvation.[37] "Election, therefore, precedes faith. . . . Faith is the sign of the election by which we obtain real blessedness. If election as a blossom had not preceded, faith would never have followed."[38] It is election, therefore, which saves.[39] When salvation is attributed even to faith, this is only a figure of speech in which that which belongs to the earlier and to the source is attributed to the later.[40]

The conclusion is that baptism is not necessary for salvation, neither as its cause nor as its occasion. Time after time Zwingli declares that faith alone is necessary for salvation: "Christ himself did not connect salvation with baptism: it is always by faith alone."[41] "The one necessary thing which saves those of us who hear the Gospel is faith."[42] "Faith is the only thing through which we are blessed."[43] "We are saved by faith only."[44] "And since faith is a gift of the Holy Spirit, it is clear that the Spirit operated before the external symbols were introduced."[45] If we say baptism takes away sins, that is just a figure of speech; for it is not baptism which takes them away, but faith.[46] But as we have seen, Zwingli says the same is true even when we say faith saves us. This too is a figure of speech, for in the final analysis election alone is the source of salvation.

45

3. Key Biblical References to Baptism Are Re-interpreted

In the first chapter of this book we saw that numerous Bible passages directly link salvation with baptism. How does Zwingli handle these? Obviously his new view of baptism will not allow him to interpret them as they had been interpreted for centuries. So how does he reconcile them with his denial of any connection between baptism and salvation?

First of all he suggests that they may be explained symbolically; they are figures of speech which do not really mean what they say. We have already noted how he explained to Thomas Wyttenbach in a letter written in 1523 that when it is said that baptism takes away sins, this is a figure of speech. He specifically identifies the figure as *katachresis*, which the dictionary defines as a misuse or strained use of words, or a forced figure of speech which seems to involve a paradox. This is the same kind of symbolic language used when we refer to the bread of the Lord's supper as Christ's body, and the wine as His blood, says Zwingli.[47]

Another figure of speech used in the Bible, according to Zwingli, is *metonymy*, which is defined as the use of the name of one object or concept for that of another to which it is related or of which it is a part. Zwingli defines it as "the name of the sign being transferred to the thing signified, for metonymy is a transposition of names." In this way "baptism is sometimes used for the blood or passion of Christ," as in I Peter 3:20-21, where "we are not to understand . . . the washing of baptism, but Christ Himself or His blood and death, for by these we have been redeemed . . . . How foolish, therefore, would any one seem, who because of these words should maintain that we are washed clean of our sins by the baptismal waters!" The same applies to Ephesians 5:26 and Romans 6:3-4, which are not to be taken literally. We must judge them to be "figurative expressions . . . by faith and our knowledge of heavenly things."[48] This applies to Galatians 3:27 also,[49] as well as to Titus 3:5. Regarding the latter Zwingli says, "Who does not see that there is attributed here to the washing of regeneration that which really and truly belongs only to the divine Spirit?"[50]

Knowing Zwingli's penchant for appealing to figures of speech helps us to understand how he could make an occasional strong statement about baptism, e.g., "We are baptized in order to be new creatures,"[51] and "We are made free in baptism,"[52] and "We who were outside of Jesus Christ have entered into him by baptism."[53] He is speaking figuratively.

The second device used by Zwingli to reconcile his new view of baptism with specific Biblical passages is his distinction between water baptism on the one hand and non-water baptisms on the other. In his treatise on baptism he identifies three kinds of baptisms besides water baptism. The most important is Holy Spirit baptism — "the inward enlightenment and calling when we know God and cleave to him" — which is administered by God how and when and to whom he chooses.[54] "God moves inwardly according to his own sovereign choice."[55] This inner baptism of the Spirit is the only one necessary for salvation, for this is the time when the Spirit bestows the gift of faith.[56] Readers will recognize that Zwingli is speaking of what has come to be called "irresistible grace" in the Calvinistic system. He sums it up thus:

> . . . The inward baptism of the Spirit is the work of teaching which God does in our hearts and the calling with which he comforts and assures our hearts in Christ. And this baptism none can give save God alone. Without it, none can be saved — though it is quite possible to be saved without the baptism of external teaching and immersion. . . .[57]

One must not confuse the two baptisms, says Zwingli, for although outer baptism is good and proper, only inner baptism is sure salvation to the one who has it.[58]

Another kind of non-water baptism is external teaching, especially teaching about water baptism but not about this alone. For example, "the baptism of John" refers not only to his baptizing people in the water of the Jordan River, but also to his activity

47

of teaching. Thus John could "baptize" someone without that person's actually being water-baptized.[59] This is how Zwingli explains the incident in Acts 19:1-7 without admitting that it was a re-baptism — an important point in his polemic against the Anabaptists.[60] This is also an alternative explanation of I Peter 3:21, where *baptism* may actually be a name for "Christ" or for "the gospel," i.e., for the whole teaching of the Christian faith.[61]

At times Zwingli identified yet a third way in which the word *baptism* may be used, i.e., to mean "the inward faith that saves us." This is used as still another possible way of explaining I Peter 3:21, "for neither as water nor as external teaching does baptism save us, but faith."[62] (Here he is using *faith* in the sense of the *fides quae* or the subjective faith by which one believes. In the previous meaning the term *faith* is also used, but in the sense of the *fides qua*, the objective faith or body of doctrine which is believed.)

Having thus isolated several possible non-water meanings for the word *baptism*, Zwingli found it relatively easy to interpret key New Testament passages regarding baptism in a way that was entirely different from the Biblical consensus which preceded him. The fact is that after Zwingli's view of baptism was fully developed, very little if any of the Biblical consensus remained. None of God's great works of salvation — uniting us with Christ, forgiving our sins, regenerating us through the Holy Spirit — is accomplished in water baptism. In fact, there is almost no sense at all in which baptism can be called God's work. For Zwingli it has become almost entirely a work of man. This will now be explained in the next section.

B. *Zwingli's New Doctrine of Baptism*

It was one thing for Zwingli to reject the old doctrine of baptism; it was quite another to come up with a new meaning for it. We have seen that as early as 1523 he had set aside the Biblical consensus. This put him under considerable pressure to find a substitute. Other factors contributing to this pressure were his need to redefine the meaning of the Lord's supper and his need to defend infant baptism.

Regarding the former, it will be remembered that there was agreement that *sacrament* is a legitimate general category and that all the rites belonging to that category to some extent share a common meaning. In Roman Catholic doctrine a sacrament was a ceremony by means of which God bestows grace upon the recipient. Both baptism and the Lord's supper bestow the grace of remission of sins. We have seen that Martin Luther, retaining the Biblical consensus regarding baptism, gave it a very strong meaning. He did the same for the Supper, seeing Christ's body as actually present in it and relating it to the forgiveness of sins. From 1523 Zwingli vigorously opposed the Catholic view and later the Lutheran idea of the Supper, and sought to establish a more moderate view. This was a very high priority for him. But we must emphasize that whatever conclusions he reached regarding the Supper would have to apply to baptism as well, since he took it for granted that both are *sacraments* and sacraments must have the same meaning.[63]

Regarding the defense of infant baptism, two factors made this a pressing need. One was the loss of the traditional rationale, i.e., to remit original sin. Zwingli could not use this rationale, since he rejected the idea that baptism has anything to do with remission of sins as such. Besides, he was revising his understanding of original sin itself, eliminating the idea of original guilt and limiting it to a kind of inherited sickness or depravity.[64] The other factor was the problem of the Anabaptists, who since 1523 were loudly opposing infant baptism in the Zurich area. At first Zwingli was sympathetic with them and even agreed that it was better not to baptize infants,[65] but he soon changed his mind on this. He mercilessly attacked the Anabaptists for disrupting the unity of the church,[66] and began to champion the cause of infant baptism. The only problem was that he had given up the traditional theological reason for it, so now he had to come up with a new one. His search for this new rationale for infant baptism ultimately played a determining role in the formulation of his new doctrine of the meaning of baptism as such.

1. Covenant Unity as the Key to the Problem

In the end Zwingli's new doctrine of baptism was built around a completely new hermeneutical approach to Scripture as a whole, i.e., the idea of the unity of the covenant of grace. This was a doctrine forged in the heat of the Anabaptist controversy in the summer of 1525. It was first used to bolster the argument for infant baptism in Zwingli's "Reply to Hubmaier" in November of that year.[67]

The traditional approach to the covenant idea was that there are basically two main testaments or covenants, the old and the new. The former was essentially the Mosaic covenant, which in a sense absorbed the main elements of the Abrahamic covenant which preceded it. The latter is the "new covenant" established by the blood of Christ (Luke 22:20); it replaces the old one, which was deliberately temporary and preparatory according to the book of Hebrews.

But Zwingli reinterpreted the whole Biblical structure of the covenants. In his view the Mosaic covenant (a covenant of law) is still the old covenant and has been set aside by the work of Christ. But the "new" covenant — that's another story. The new covenant or covenant of grace actually began as far back as Adam, was renewed with Noah, and was formally renewed and clarified at the time of Abraham. In the "Abrahamic covenant" God makes clear His purposes of grace, pledging to bless Abraham and in turn to bless the world through him.[68] This covenant did not cease when the Mosaic covenant was introduced, nor did it end when the latter was set aside. The fact is that the covenant which God made with Abraham and which included the Israelites in Old Testament times still continues today. It is the same and only covenant under which Christians live. Though it is called the "new" covenant, it is really older than the "old" one.

Zwingli stresses this point in his reply to the Anabaptist Balthasar Hubmaier. It is evident, he says, that the Christian covenant or new testament is the old covenant of Abraham, except that we have Christ in reality whereas they had Him only in promise.[69] Jesus' parable in Matthew 22:1ff. shows that we are not called to some other wedding feast, that is, not to a new faith or covenant, but rather to the faith and covenant of Abraham which is the eternal covenant.[70] Christian people stand in the same gracious covenant with God as Abraham did.[71]

Zwingli continued to explain this point in later writings. In his "Refutation of the Tricks of the Baptists" he declares, "Therefore the same covenant which he entered into with Israel he has in these latter days entered into with us, that we may be one people with them, one church, and may have also one covenant."[72] "It is one and the same testament which God had with the human race from the foundation of the world to its dissolution. . . . One and the same testament has always been in force."[73]

Having concluded that there is but *one covenant* which spans the whole of history, Zwingli's next step is to show that there has been but *one covenant people* throughout the ages. If there is but a single covenant with the same promise of grace and the same Savior, then it naturally follows that there is but one people, one church. The Israelites of old and the Christians of today are part of the same body; "there is one church of them and us."[74] "As they had one and the same Saviour with us they were one people with us, and we one people and one church with them."[75] "All the apostles believed this, that there is one testament, one people of God, . . . one church of God."[76]

The final link in this chain is that there is also *one covenant sign*. When God entered the covenant with Abraham, he instituted circumcision as the covenant sign, i.e., the sign to be applied to those (males) who belong to the people of God to mark them as members of the covenant people. Since the same covenant still exists and embraces all of God's people today, an equivalent covenant sign also exists, i.e., baptism.

The idea that baptism in some sense takes the place of circumcision was not a new idea in Zwingli's time; it had been used in one way or another at least since Gregory Nazianzen in the fourth century.[77] Zwingli himself was already using it as an argument for infant baptism even before 1525. In his letter to Lambert (December 1524) he asserted that baptism took the place of circumcision altogether; baptism is the circumcision of Christians.[78] In his book on baptism (May 1525) he declared that the idea that baptism has taken the place of circumcision is so clear that even if we have no clear proof-text, we would still clearly see it as the mark of God's people and would thus conclude that it is one thing to be circumcised and to be baptized.[79] The outward form of the sign changes with the shedding of Christ's blood on the cross, which made the bloody sign of the Old Testament inappropriate and obsolete. Thus circumcision was replaced by the unbloody sign of baptism, but they are otherwise the same.[80] Thus the development of the idea of a single covenant is not the source of the equation of circumcision and baptism, but it does provide it with a stronger foundation. Hence from the time he began emphasizing the unity of the covenant, Zwingli continued to emphasize the oneness of circumcision and baptism.[81]

Here, then, is Zwingli's trilogy: one covenant, one covenant people, and one covenant sign. This is the set of ideas that ultimately determines the doctrine of baptism. This is true with regard to both its subjects and its meaning.

2. Infant Baptism Established

The application of this line of thinking to infant baptism is clear enough, but this will explain how Zwingli spells it out. First, if Christians are the people of God today in the same way as the Israelites were in ancient times, then the covenant should apply to us in the same way as to them, at least in its main points. And what are these main points? Briefly, these: that God is our God, and we are His people. There is no difference between Old Testa-

ment Israel and the New Testament church as far as these promises are concerned.[82] "Since therefore there is one immutable
God and one testament only, we who trust in Christ are under the
same testament, consequently God is as much our God as he was
Abraham's, and we are as much his people as was Israel."[83]
Whatever it meant for Israel to be the people of God applies to us,
too.

Now here is where the specific application begins. Zwingli's
point is this: in Old Testament times, ever since Abraham, the
"people of God" has included both adults and infants. The babies
were considered to belong to God no less than their parents.
Therefore, in the Christian era infants must be regarded as
belonging to God and to the people of God no less than adults.
This is how Zwingli put it in his reply to Hubmaier: "The children
of Christians are no less God's children than their parents, just the
same as in the Old Testament." The last part of this statement
means this: "Just as in the Old Testament the children were just
as much God's, just as much the people of God, and just as much
the children of God as their elders, thus also in the New Testament the children of Christians are members of the people and
church of God."[84] Even if the New Testament does not specifically state this, it must be the case because of the unity of the covenant and the unity of the covenant people. "For how is the testament and covenant the same if our children are not equally with
those," i.e., the Israelite children, a part "of the church and people of God? Is Christ less kind to us than to the Hebrews? God
forbid!"[85]

Therefore, if the covenant sign (circumcision) was applied to
infants as well as to adults in the Old Testament, then it (baptism)
must be applied to infants today also. The logic is unassailable:
circumcision in the Old Testament was given to infants; baptism
has come in the place of circumcision; therefore infants should be
baptized.[86]

It results then, after all this that just as the Hebrews' children, because they with their parents were under the covenant, merited the sign of the covenant, so also Christians' infants, because they are counted within the church and people of Christ, ought in no way to be deprived of baptism, the sign of the covenant . . . .[87]

3. The New Meaning of Baptism

Though the doctrine of covenant unity was formulated mainly to undergird the case for baptizing infants, it had an even more significant consequence in another direction. It is not too much to say that this doctrine ultimately decided the *meaning* of baptism not only for Zwingli but for Reformed theology as such and for the large segment of Protestantism that has embraced the Reformed view of the sacraments.

We have seen that Zwingli emphatically rejected the Biblical consensus regarding the meaning of baptism. He denied that baptism is the occasion when God works His marvelous works of grace and salvation for the repentant believer. But once he had given up this idea, exactly how did he explain the meaning of baptism?

a. *A means of assurance.* Zwingli's earliest attempt to redefine baptism was worked out closely in connection with his changing views on the Lord's supper, i.e., on the nature of the sacraments in general. From approximately 1523 to late 1524 his main emphasis was that baptism (or a sacrament as such) is a seal of faith, that is, a means by which the believer has his faith strengthened. It is a means by which one's own assurance of his personal salvation is bolstered. From God's perspective it is His pledge or oath to continue to be gracious.

Zwingli's first significant explanation of the sacraments is in his "Exposition and Defense of the Sixty-seven Articles," completed in July 1523. It is very important, he says here, to distinguish between those ordinances instituted by God and those instituted by man. How one uses terms is not the important thing, but it is better to reserve the term *sacrament* for those things ordained by the infallible word of God, namely baptism and the Lord's supper.[88]

Now, why did God ordain these ceremonies? One thing is clear: they are not essential to salvation in any way. As soon as one believes, he is assured of God's grace and certain of salvation.[89] However, because of the frailty and weakness of men, God gives these signs in order to strengthen faith. This is why Zwingli does not object to calling the sacraments "signs or seals."[90] They are signs and pledges which God has given in his own word.[91]

The fact is that if faith were strong enough in itself, nothing more would be needed, not even for assurance. But because human nature is weak and frail, God gives the sacraments as outward signs to strengthen weak faith. Regarding baptism specifically Zwingli says,

> . . . Therefore it is faith which is required there, which if it is so great, that it has need of no certain point of time or (no certain) place or person or any other thing, by which, through the circumstance itself, it would desire to be made assured and secure, it has no need of baptism. But if he is still a little too simple-minded and unsophisticated, and needs a demonstration, let the believer be washed, so that now he knows that he is cleansed by faith within just as he is by water without.[92]

Concerning Mark 16:16 Zwingli says, "Whoever has confessed with the mouth that he believes that Christ is his Saviour, him have the disciples comforted with the assurance that God has forgiven his sins, and to this end (i.e., assurance) they have baptized him."[93]

Such external assurance is needed more by the outer man than the inner man. For just as the latter is not able to learn or to become a believer through visible signs, so is the former not able to grasp anything which is not experienced through the senses. Therefore so that God may give adequate proof for the whole man — both inner and outer — he commands that the person who already believes should be baptized with water. This is not for the soul's purification, but so that the outer man by the visible sign may become certain of his salvation.[94]

This last statement was written in late 1524 and was the last time Zwingli explained baptism in exactly this way. In fact, in 1525 he specifically repudiates this whole approach to the sacraments. The idea that sacraments are given to confirm an existing faith, he says, is a mistake that once deceived him. But now he sees that baptism does not confirm faith, for it is impossible for an external thing to confirm faith.[95] This is one of the views of the sacraments that he specifically rejects in the "Commentary on True and False Religion," namely, that "a sacrament is a sign which is given . . . for the purpose of rendering the recipient sure that what is signified by the sacrament has now been accomplished."[96] Such a view is false, "for if the heart already trusts, it cannot be unaware of its trust. . . . For if your faith is not so perfect as not to need a ceremonial sign to confirm it, it is not faith."[97] True faith originates from the Holy Spirit, not from external things; so how can it be strengthened by externals?[98] Christ alone is God's sure pledge of salvation to us.[99]

Why did Zwingli abandon this view of the sacraments and of baptism in particular? One probable reason is that it did not fit in very well with the practice of infant baptism, which he was struggling to justify at this particular time. If baptism is meant to confirm faith, then it would seem to follow that it should be given only to those who already have faith. Such an idea could be seen as strengthening the Anabaptists' position, so Zwingli dissociated himself from it.[100]

In any case, Zwingli continued to exclude this idea from his explanation of the sacraments after 1524. About a year before he died he did resurrect the notion that the sacraments are an aid to faith, but not as a confirmation of it in the sense of increasing one's assurance. The basic idea, as he explains in his letter concerning Eck (1530), is that the sacraments as visible signs simply help us to bring our faith to the forefront of our consciousness and concentrate upon it. They act "as a sort of a stimulant" and "call into action the faith . . . which is already there."[101] They "turn the senses toward faith and call it into use."[102]

In his last published work, "An Exposition of the Faith," Zwingli repeats this idea in slightly stronger terms, but still not in the same sense as his earlier view of the sacraments as seals of faith. One of the virtues of the sacraments, he says, is that they "augment faith and are an aid to it." They "support and strengthen faith," and "assist the contemplation of faith." This is especially true of the Lord's supper, but it also applies to baptism. "In baptism sight and hearing and touch are all claimed for the work of faith," which "perceives that Christ endured death for the sake of his Church and that he rose again victorious. And that is what we hear and see and feel in baptism." In this way "the sacraments are like bridles which serve to check the senses when they are on the point of dashing off in pursuit of their own desires, and to recall them to the obedience of the heart and of faith."[103]

Though these ideas are quite consistent with Zwingli's view of baptism and the Supper from 1525 on, some may think that he was beginning to return to the earlier view of the sacraments as a confirmation of faith and assurance. Unfortunately Zwingli was killed shortly after the "Exposition" was written. We will never know whether he was planning a programmatic revision of his doctrine, or whether the slightly stronger statements in the "Exposition" were just a concession to the political pressures which were the occasion for its writing.[104]

b. *A pledge of allegiance.* The second main aspect of Zwingli's doctrine of baptism is that it is the recipient's pledge of allegiance, an outward sign of his commitment to live the Christian life. From late 1524 and following, this basically replaced the previous idea. Instead of viewing it as God's faith-strengthening pledge to the believer, Zwingli described baptism as the Christian's pledge to his fellow-believers that he is indeed one of them.

Here Zwingli seems to be drawing the meaning of baptism mostly from the meaning of the Latin word *sacramentum*, which was earlier used for the initiatory oath of allegiance sworn by an inductee into the Roman army. This is how Zwingli describes

John's baptism, i.e., as an oath of allegiance (*sacramentum*) by which John was enrolling penitents into the service of the coming leader. But John's baptism is exactly the same as Christian baptism. Therefore Christian baptism is a *sacramentum* also.[105] It is "an initiatory sign or pledge initiating us to a lifelong mortification of the flesh and engaging or pledging us like a soldier at his enlistment."[106] It is "the first pledge and bond of membership in the Christian army," says Zwingli.[107] He explains how, in addition to the military oath, the term was also used to describe the pledge or guarantee which litigants deposited at some altar prior to a civil trial, with the winner getting his pledge back. Both of these meanings are then transferred to baptism and the Lord's supper:

> So I am brought to see that a sacrament is nothing else than an initiatory ceremony or a pledging. For just as those who were about to enter upon litigation deposited a certain amount of money, which could not be taken away except by the winner, so those who are initiated by sacraments bind and pledge themselves, and, as it were, seal a contract not to draw back. . . .[108]

Thus the sacraments "act as an oath of allegiance. For in Latin the word *sacramentum* is used of an oath."[109]

Baptism, then, represents the pledge which the Christian makes to God that he will live for Him and not draw back. Thus it is a *covenant sign* in that it represents the *Christian's* covenant to God. "Baptism is a covenant sign which indicates that all those who receive it are willing to amend their lives and to follow Christ. In short, it is an initiation to new life. Baptism is therefore an initiatory sign."[110] In terms of a covenant sign or pledge, "the man who receives the mark of baptism is the one who is resolved to hear what God says to him, to learn the divine precepts and to live his life in accordance with them."[111] In the case of infants it is the sign of the parents' pledge to teach the child and lead him in the way of the Lord.[112]

But now comes the key question in this aspect of the meaning of baptism, namely *for whose sake* does the believer submit to

58

baptism and thus receive the sign of his covenant with God? It is not for his own sake nor for God's but rather for the sake of the Christian congregation that he does it. "For baptism is given and received for the sake of fellow-believers, not for a supposed effect in those who receive it." It is "not given as a sign to those who receive it, but for the benefit of other believers."[113] This is the whole purpose of sacraments, that by them believers "may give evidence to the rest as to whom they have given their allegiance."[114] "The sacraments are, then, signs or ceremonials . . . by which a man proves to the Church that he either aims to be, or is, a soldier of Christ, and which inform the whole Church rather than yourself of your faith."[115] This applies to the Lord's supper as well as to baptism.[116] This point is made because by 1525 Zwingli had concluded that true faith needs no confirmation from externals; therefore the external signs must be for someone else's sake.[117]

Herein arises the whole idea of baptism as a *public testimony* or *witness*. Everything that baptism signifies has *already happened*; baptism is the way in which one makes this known to other Christians. "Not that baptism bestows the thing, but that it bears witness to the multitude of the previous bestowal of the thing."[118] It is "a public testimony of that grace which is previously present to every individual. Thus baptism is administered in the presence of the Church."[119] "Immersion in water is simply a ceremony by which they testify that they are of the number of those who repent."[120] "Baptism is an initiatory sign or pledge with which we bind ourselves to God, testifying the same to our neighbor by means of the external sign."[121] Zwingli paraphrases Acts 22:16 to read, "Be baptized, that you may testify or bear witness that you believe the remission of sins is of the grace of God alone."[122] Anyone who enrolls in Christ's army ought to receive its public badge or public sign, "that all men may see that he has promised allegiance to that leader whom he has agreed to serve."[123] Baptism is a "public witness" and a "public testimony."[124] "The recipient of baptism testifies . . . that he belongs to the Church of God."[125]

In summary, this second aspect of the Zwinglian doctrine of baptism says that baptism is the individual's pledge or testimony to his fellow believers that he is a member of the Lord's army and that he intends to live like it.

c. *A Sign of Belonging.* We come now to the third and final aspect of Zwingli's teaching concerning the meaning of baptism, i.e., that it is a covenant sign or sign of belonging. This concept was the direct result of Zwingli's new doctrine of covenant unity, which was discussed above. After determining that the "new covenant" to which Christians belong is the same as the Abrahamic covenant, Zwingli declared that Christian baptism is simply the new version of the Old Testament circumcision and therefore has the same meaning. And what was the meaning of circumcision? It was the sign given to those who belonged to the covenant. Therefore this is the meaning of baptism, too.

The key idea here is that whoever is under God's gracious covenant (i.e., whoever belongs to the covenant people) should receive the mark which signifies membership in the covenant. That is the way it was in Old Testament times; those who were in the covenant received circumcision as the covenant sign.[126] Likewise in the New Testament age, baptism is simply the external covenant sign which should be received by everyone who is in the covenant.[127] With regard to meaning, they are exactly the same; "for as circumcision was the signature of the covenant, so is baptism."[128] A sacrament is an external sign of some thing. "Baptism is a sacrament, indicating this thing, namely that the recipient belongs to the Church."[129]

It should be noted that Zwingli came to this conclusion while developing his rationale for infant baptism. In his book on baptism (1525), he stresses over and over that the main reason why infants should be baptized is that they belong to God, just the same as their parents do. Parents and children alike are part of the one flock, the one church of God. How can it be right, then, that not all of his sheep are marked with the one sign?[130]

In this connection we should note how this aspect of the meaning of baptism differs from the second one discussed above. In both cases baptism is a kind of covenant sign, but the nature of the covenant is not the same for both. In the second view above the covenant is the individual's own covenant or pledge to live as a Christian; in baptism he expresses that pledge before the congregation. In this latter case the covenant is God's own covenant, i.e., the whole sum and content of God's covenant or testament with His people, the whole of the Christian faith. In baptism a person is marked as being within the sphere of this glorious covenant. This is why baptism can be called a covenant sign for infants, for in their case the covenant is not their own personal pledge of faith but God's covenant toward them.[131]

We emphasize again that for Zwingli, baptism as a sign of belonging presupposes that one already is saved, that he already is in the covenant, that he already belongs to the elect people of God and to the invisible church before he receives the sign. Receiving the sign merely acknowledges the fact and initiates one into the visible church. It is "not that this sign unites one to the Church, but that he who is already united to it receives the public badge."[132] "The grace of the spirit by which we are admitted into union with the church precedes the sign of union. For no one is sealed unless he has first been enrolled into the army or service."[133] Baptism associates visibly with the church those who have previously been received into it invisibly.[134] By baptism we receive into the church sacramentally those who have already been received in fact.[135] "By baptism, therefore, the Church publicly receives one who has previously been received through grace. Hence baptism does not convey grace but the Church certifies that grace has been given to him to whom it is administered."[136]

One thing should be very clear by this time, namely, that the only biblical source for Zwingli's whole concept of the meaning of baptism is the Old Testament. This he freely admits, arguing that we look to the Old Testament for teaching about other externals, too (e.g., marriage among relatives). So why should anyone object to looking to the Old Testament for teaching about baptism? Certainly we can find such teaching there, for in the Old Testament we can find that which had the same value and meaning for that time as baptism has for this time, i.e., circumcision.[137] And this is precisely how we prove that baptism is nothing more than a covenant sign, namely, by this syllogism: baptism is the Christian circumcision (Colossians 2); circumcision is a covenant sign (Genesis 17); therefore it follows that baptism also is a covenant sign.[138]

C. Zwingli's View of Baptism Analyzed

Without a doubt Zwingli's doctrine of baptism was a radical revision of fifteen hundred years of Christian thinking. It was practically a complete substitution of one view for another. The Biblical consensus had described baptism as a work of God, the time during which God applies the benefits of Christ's work to the believing, submitting sinner. Zwingli, however, abandoned this view for the idea that God's saving work as applied to the individual occurs as a rule prior to baptism. The result was that baptism itself came to be regarded not as a work of God but as almost exclusively a work of man.

This is true in two ways, corresponding to the two main elements in Zwingli's mature view of the meaning of baptism. First, as noted above, Zwingli taught that baptism is one's symbolic pledge to his fellow-believers that he is indeed a follower of Christ. But we should note very carefully that if and insofar as this is the case, baptism ceases to be a work of God and becomes a work of man. The *baptized person himself* is the one performing the essential action (as distinct from the outward or external action) of baptism. It is his pledge, his testimony, his public witness toward others.

Second, as also already noted, Zwingli held that baptism is

the sign of belonging to the people of God. This is not significantly different from the other aspect, except with regard to the person responsible for accomplishing the essential work of baptism. In this case the work is applying baptism as the sign of membership in God's covenant people; it is an acknowledgement of such membership and a reception of the individual into the ranks of the visible church. But again, if and insofar as this is the case, baptism is not a work of God but a work of man. This time it is the *baptizer*, acting for the whole church, who performs the essential action of baptism. By applying baptism the church *admits* and *receives* and *acknowledges*.

In neither case is the idea simply that a human agent is performing the outer physical rite while God is working spiritually. Rather, in both cases even the spiritual meaning or essence of baptism is something done by man. The divine working is already completed before baptism is applied.

All of this leads us to a very important question, namely, what caused Zwingli to depart so radically from the prevailing Biblical consensus on baptism? At least two main factors may be identified. One is his own peculiar understanding of and application of Augustinian theology, especially the concept of sovereignty. A sovereign God, according to Zwingli, cannot be bound with regard to His actions. He cannot be put into the position of waiting for some human act or decision as a precondition for His own work, nor can He be required to act just because somebody somewhere decides to submit to baptism. To maintain His sovereignty, God must remain free from such bondage. (Apparently Zwingli did not understand that divine sovereignty includes the freedom for God to bind Himself, if He so chooses, to act in certain ways in connection with human choices. Such a self-limitation is not a violation of sovereignty but an expression of it.)

But in addition to this concept of divine freedom, and probably even more fundamental, is the doctrine of election which Zwingli's concept of divine sovereignty entails. In the final analysis a person's eternal salvation is completely decided by God's un-conditional, foreordaining election. This is the sole condition upon which salvation depends. The elect person is saved from eternity, saved from the moment he is conceived and the mo-ment he is born. He is saved before he believes; indeed, the very reason he believes is because God has elected to save him and give him faith. If all this is the case, then certainly a mere physical action such as baptism cannot stand above God's sovereign elec-tion. (Being a thorough-going and consistent determinist,[139] Zwingli had no use for an election conditioned upon divine fore-knowledge of free human choices to believe and be baptized.)

I said above that Zwingli's rejection of the Biblical consensus regarding baptism can be traced to his own peculiar understand-ing and application of divine sovereignty. Basically, his concept of sovereignty was in the Augustinian tradition, which I take to be a form of determinism which is at variance with the Biblical view of sovereignty.[140] But the pre-Zwinglian Augustinians such as Augustine himself and Martin Luther,[141] though thoroughly com-mitted to the same kind of sovereign freedom and sovereign elec-tion as was Zwingli, did not see this as somehow contradicting the Biblical view of baptism. Whether Zwingli or those who preceded him were more consistent is a matter which might be debated; the fact remains that it was Zwingli who first decided that this view of sovereignty must be applied in a way that precludes the Biblical consensus on baptism.

This leads us to ask whether there may have been another factor influencing Zwingli even more deeply than his view of sovereignty and causing him to make this peculiar application of sovereignty itself. This seems to be the case, and I would identify this second factor as an incipient philosophical dualism. Though he was not a complete dualist in the Manichaean sense, never-theless Zwingli held to a strong antithesis between body and soul, between matter and spirit. As already noted above, this caused him to deny any link between the physical act of water baptism and God's spiritual acts of salvation. Our purpose at this point is to probe more deeply into Zwingli's dualism in order to show that this was indeed a foundational and influential principle affecting his theology in significant ways.

With passages such as John 6:3 and Galatians 5:17 in the background, one of Zwingli's most basic assumptions was the duality of spirit and matter. On one side is "divinity, spirit, the superior nature."[142] Opposed to spirit is matter, especially the earth, which by nature is dull, dark, inactive and rebellious.[143] This carries over into the nature of man, who is composed of body and soul, "two most widely different things."[144] It was necessary for man to be both spirit and body, in order to contemplate the divine and heavenly with his soul while living with the brutes with his body.[145]

The soul itself is described by Zwingli in only the best of terms. It is godly, selfless, and self-sacrificing.[146] It loves truth and worships God; there is nothing base, disturbing or defiling in it.[147] It "yearns for light, purity and goodness, inasmuch as its nature is light, its substance pure and devoted to the right."[148] It is the part of man that is akin to God, created in His image.[149] Thus the soul is equipped to follow after God; it desires to live according to the law and will of God, in which it delights.[150] It is receptive of holy things.[151] It receives God[152] and is taught by the Spirit.[153]

Zwingli could speak so highly of the soul because he apparently accepted the pagan idea that its essence is derived from the very essence of God. The contrast between the two parts of man, he says, is the result of their respective origins. The body is dull and dark because it consists of earth, but "the mind yearns for light, purity and goodness, inasmuch as its nature is light, its substance pure and devoted to the right, seeing that it derives its origin from the Godhead."[154] The soul "is inspired, fostered, ruled, and fed by God, consisting of the Spirit of God,"[155] and "flowing forth from the Godhead itself."[156] "The mind loves the truth and, therefore, worships the Deity, from whose substance it derives its kinship."[157]

By contrast the earth-derived body is spoken of in the most

negative of terms. At times Zwingli seems at first to be speaking of the body only as it has been affected and infected by sin, but closer examination shows that this is not the case. The earthly body in and of itself is devoid of good. Commenting on Paul's statement in Romans 7:18 ("in my flesh dwells no good thing"), Zwingli grants that Paul is not talking about the bodily flesh we have in common with cattle, "for who does not know that there is no good thing in that?" This fact is so self-evident that it would be a waste of time for an apostle to proclaim it.[158] That "there is nothing good in our perishable flesh" is "a fact that even a blind man can see."[159]

The body has this nature because of the substance from which it is made. "The body inclines to idleness, laziness, darkness and dullness, as it is lazy and indolent by nature, and without reason and intelligence, seeing it consists of earth."[160] Being nothing but a "dull mass,"[161] or "mire,"[162] or "a lump of muddy earth,"[163] "it yearns for the things of earth and lets those of heaven go."[164] It "decays and perishes"[165] and will be forever dead,[166] contrary to the spirit, which is "ordained to possess eternity"[167] and will be raised up to God.[168]

The flesh is "ever rebellious,"[169] "ungovernable,"[170] obstinate,[171] and impetuous.[172] It is self-seeking and does all things only for its own sake.[173] It is defiled by "shameful weaknesses,"[174] especially "the weakness which gives rise to sin" or "proneness to sin."[175] The body "by nature is always prone to violence and lust."[176] The flesh itself is not sin, but that which the flesh does is sin.[177] It is blind and in darkness;[178] it "has nothing to do with wisdom, nay rather is a poison and an impediment to knowledge and intelligence."[179] In its wickedness and wantonness it resists holy things and rejects God's law.[180]

In light of these descriptions, it is not surprising that Zwingli understood the body and the soul to be in a state of constant conflict. These two aspects of man are not just diverse in nature,[181] but are actually opposed to each other to the extent that there is a "duality or contradiction" within us.[182] Man is "half beast and half angel."[183] The result is that man is "never at peace with himself"; for whichever part is dominant, the other is always in rebellion.[184] There is a "constant battle between the flesh and the spirit,"[185] with the flesh attacking and assaulting the spirit.[186] Though the inward man desires to live according to God's law, it is opposed by the outward man.[187] The desire of the flesh (which we call our will) strives against the will of the mind and spirit,[188] and desires things contrary to the spirit.[189] "Hence that sort of internal war in which the mind and the body are engaged against each other," with the flesh always trying to draw the soul from its pursuit of God.[190] "The body resists, because by its nature it scorns whatever the soul greatly values."[191]

In this battle the soul cannot help but be affected. It is weighed down by the body,[192] "held bound by the weight of that clay as by fetters," so that it cannot live according to its perfection.[193] Obscured and darkened by the flesh,[194] man by nature is errant. "It is impossible to live with this flesh without defilement. . . . The flesh is mire; hence whatever comes from man is stained."[195] Man is likened to "a lump of muddy earth plunged into a very clear, pure brook." The stream is now clouded, and "we cannot even hope for the former clearness as long as the lump of earth stays immersed in it."[196]

This duality and inner conflict exist within man even where there is no sin as such, but the principal effect of original sin is that the spirit becomes inclined toward the beastly nature. As created, the godly nature is not selfish but gives itself to be useful to all creatures. The earthly or beastly nature, however, is self-seeking and does all things only for its own sake.[197] But fallen man is *wholly* flesh — "flesh altogether," since the soul itself has taken on the character of flesh with its disease of self-love.[198]

With such a dualistic view of matter and the spirit (body and soul), it is no wonder that Zwingli felt constrained to separate the physical act of baptism from God's saving work in the heart of the sinner. The two are simply not compatible. "For the flesh receiveth not what is opposed to it; and whatever the heavenly

Spirit does is opposed to the flesh."[199] Thus the sacrament is unable either to remit sins or to strengthen faith, for such things belong to divinity (spirit, the superior nature) alone. We must be careful not to fuse the qualities of the two natures.[200]

Thus we conclude that Zwingli rejected the Biblical consensus regarding the meaning of baptism primarily because of his Augustinian theology and his dualistic philosophy. On the other hand, both elements of his new doctrine of baptism were derived from non-New Testament sources. The idea of baptism as the recipient's witness or confession before men seems to come primarily from the meaning of the Latin word *sacramentum* — a non-Biblical word applied somewhat arbitrarily to baptism in the first place. The idea of baptism as a sign of belonging to the people of God is taken wholly from the Old Testament, i.e., from the meaning of circumcision. *In formulating his new doctrine of baptism, Zwingli completely ignored everything the New Testament itself has to say about the subject.*

D. Conclusion

Zwingli's new sacramental theology is undoubtedly one of the most successful new doctrines in the whole history of the church. His basic approach was adopted by John Calvin and made a part of what is called Reformed theology. The Reformed concept of the sacraments was then in turn taken over by most of the newly-developing denominational groups. The bulk of modern Protestantism thus holds to the Zwinglian doctrine of the meaning of baptism.

John Calvin (1509-1564) owes much more to Zwingli than is usually recognized. This is especially true with regard to his understanding of the sacraments, including baptism. Calvin followed Zwingli's lead in rejecting the Biblical consensus regarding the meaning of baptism, and he accepted the Zwinglian idea of covenant unity as the basic framework for his own explanation of the purpose and result of baptism.

Some isolated statements in Calvin's writings seem to be in full agreement with the Bible's teaching. For example, the Geneva catechism affirms that "both pardon of sins and newness of life are offered to us in baptism, and received by us."[201] In another place Calvin says, "In baptism, God washes us by the blood of his Son, and regenerates us by his Spirit."[202] Also,

> . . . We assert that the whole guilt of sin is taken away in baptism, so that the remains of sin still existing are not imputed. That this may be more clear, let my readers call to mind that there is a twofold grace in baptism, for therein both remission of sins and regeneration are offered to us. We teach that full remission is made, but that regeneration is only begun and goes on making progress during the whole of life.[203]

Commenting on the effects of Christ's death and resurrection, Calvin affirms that "by baptism we are admitted into a participation of this grace."[204] He also says "that we put on Christ in baptism, and that we are baptized for this end — that we may be one with him."[205] Commenting on Colossians 2:12, Calvin says we are buried with Christ and crucified with him "through means of baptism"; thus there is an efficacy to the sacrament. "By baptism, therefore, we are *buried with Christ*, because Christ does at the same time accomplish efficaciously that mortification, which he there represents, that the reality may be conjoined with the sign."[206] Regarding the sacraments, Calvin even says that "the use of them is necessary, and that all those who make no account of them declare themselves despisers of the grace of God."[207] Regarding "the necessary observance of Baptism," he declares, "We are agreed that Infants ought to be baptized, and that the omission of the sign is not optional."[208]

Though these statements appear to be quite consistent with the Biblical consensus, Calvin himself did not intend them to be understood in this way. It would be a serious mistake to think that Calvin viewed baptism as the point where the believing, repentant sinner first receives pardon and regeneration. He did not regard baptism in this way, nor as being necessary for salvation. When he says that baptism is "necessary," he is speaking of the necessity of precept and not the necessity of means.[209] He specifically says, "Few realize how much injury the dogma that baptism is necessary for salvation, badly expounded, has entailed."[210] Regarding this statement, John T. McNeill asserts, "There is a popular belief, wholly unfounded, that Calvin taught the doctrine he here condemns"; however, "Calvin does not teach . . . that 'baptism is necessary to salvation.' "[211] Speaking specifically of infant baptism, Calvin says that infants need it, "not as a necessary help to salvation, but as a seal divinely appointed to seal upon them the gift of adoption."[212]

When is salvation received? Adults receive it when they believe, and the children of the godly are born saved.[213] The "faith-only" concept is clearly stated: "After we have embraced Christ by faith, that alone is sufficient to salvation."[214] This is the proper order of things: first salvation, then baptism. Concerning Acts 2:38 Calvin says, "Although in the text and order of the words, baptism doth here go before remission of sins, yet doth it follow it in order."[215] On Acts 10:47 he says, "He which hath received the Spirit is also apt [fit] to receive baptism; and this is the (most) lawful order."[216] The same is asserted in the following statement: "Baptism must, therefore, be preceded by the gift of adoption, which is not the cause merely of a partial salvation, but bestows salvation entire, and is afterwards ratified by baptism."[217]

The apparent contradiction between these two groups of statements from Calvin seems to be explained in the following way. The same salvation which is received in its fullness prior to baptism is offered anew in baptism itself so that it might be apprehended with greater faith and assurance. As Calvin says, the sacraments strengthen and enlarge faith in hearts that have already been taught by the Holy Spirit.[218] "Hence, any man is deceived who thinks anything more is conferred upon him through the sacraments than what is offered by God's Word and received by him in true faith."[219] Whatever is received in the sacraments is not received as if for the first time; it was already there and is only enlarged upon. As applied to baptism, "it makes those who are already ingrafted into the body of Christ to be united to him more and more."[220] "Thus the sins of Paul were washed away by baptism, though they had previously been washed away. So likewise baptism was the laver of regeneration to Cornelius, though he had already received the Holy Spirit." Furthermore, "inasmuch as faith is confirmed and increased by the sacraments, the gifts of God are confirmed in us, and thus Christ in a manner grows in us and we in him."[221] The Biblical consensus, that baptism is the point of one's initial reception of saving grace, is thus denied.

This leads to a brief word about Calvin's main emphases concerning the meaning of baptism as learned from Zwingli. The key terms are *sign* and *seal*, neither of which in the New Testament is used of baptism but rather of circumcision (Romans 4:11). This, of course, is fully consistent with Calvin's acceptance of the doctrine of covenant unity with its equation of circumcision and baptism.[222]

The point most often emphasized by Calvin is that baptism is a seal that confirms God's promises and our faith in those promises and thus strengthens our assurance of salvation. Though this aspect of baptism was abandoned by Zwingli in his later years, Calvin adopted it and made it central. It is the very point already noted above as the explanation of the statements that make a strong connection between baptism and salvation. It is the idea that baptism is "a token and proof of our cleansing" whose purpose is "to confirm to us that all our sins are so abolished, remitted, and effaced that they can never come to his sight, be recalled, or charged against us."[223] It is erroneous to think that the sacraments confer grace; "the only function divinely imparted to them is to attest and ratify for us God's good will toward us. . . . They do not bestow any grace of themselves, but announce and tell us, and (as they are guarantees and tokens) ratify

71

among us, those things given us by divine bounty."[224]

This is Calvin's basic explanation of such passages as Ephesians 5:26 and Titus 3:5. Paul does not mean that baptism or water causes salvation, "but only that in this sacrament are received the knowledge and certainty of such gifts."[225] Baptism "seals to us the salvation obtained by Christ" and "is intended to confirm our faith"; this is the extent of its efficacy as a "washing of regeneration."[226] Also, the point of Acts 2:38 is that baptism is "the seal whereby the promise of grace is confirmed."[227] Thus, "because baptism is the seal whereby he doth confirm unto us this benefit, and so, consequently, the earnest and pledge of our adoption, it is worthily said to be given us for the remission of sins."[228] The same is true of Acts 22:16. "For seeing Paul had the testimony of the grace of God, his sins were already forgiven him. Therefore, he was not washed only by baptism, but he received a new confirmation of the grace which he had gotten."[229]

The idea of baptism as the believer's own sign or pledge to his fellow-believers is secondary for Calvin, but nevertheless it is an important part of his baptismal doctrine. He says,

> But baptism serves as our confession before men. Indeed, it is the mark by which we publicly profess that we wish to be reckoned God's people; by which we testify that we agree in worshiping the same God, in one religion with all Christians; by which finally we openly affirm our faith. . . . Paul had this in mind when he asked the Corinthians whether they had not been baptized in Christ's name [I Cor. 1:13]. He thus implied that, in being baptized in his name, they had devoted themselves to him, sworn allegiance to his name, and pledged their faith to him before men. . . .[230]

These two ideas — baptism as sign and seal — are often affirmed in summary statements about the sacraments and about baptism in particular. For example, the sacraments should first of all "serve our faith before God; after this, . . . they should attest our confession before men."[231] Calvin gives the following definition of a sacrament:

. . . It is an outward sign by which the Lord seals on our consciences the promises of his good will toward us in order to sustain the weakness of our faith; and we in turn attest our piety toward him in the presence of the Lord and of his angels and before men. Here is another briefer definition: one may call it a testimony of divine grace toward us, confirmed by an outward sign, with mutual attestation of our piety toward him. . . .[232]

Now God gave baptism for the same ends common to all sacraments, "first, to serve our faith before him; secondly, to serve our confession before men."[233]

This, then, is the essence of baptism according to the Reformed tradition. It is the view commonly found today in Presbyterian and Reformed denominations, in Baptist and Mennonite groups, in the Wesleyan tradition (e.g., Methodists, Nazarenes), and indeed in most of Protestantism. It was the view which prevailed in the early part of the nineteenth century when the Restoration Movement was taking shape. One of the distinctives of this movement was the rejection of the Reformed revision and a return to the Biblical consensus regarding the meaning of baptism. During the 1820s the doctrine of baptism for the remission of sins was beginning to be taught by such men as Wentworth Roberts, Barton Stone, John Secrest, Alexander Campbell, and Walter Scott.[234] It has continued to be taught down through the decades by those who have caught the vision of these early Restoration pioneers and who desire to be true to the Bible itself. The tragedy is that many in this very movement have begun to doubt its validity and are espousing and proclaiming the Zwinglian heresy instead. If there are others who are being tempted to do the same, perhaps this brief study of Scripture and history will show them the folly of such a choice.

Endnotes

1. Huldreich Zwingli, "Of Baptism," in *Zwingli and Bullinger*, "Library of Christian Classics," Vol. 24, ed. and tr. G.W. Bromiley (Philadelphia: Westminster Press, 1953), p. 153. (Hereafter, "Baptism.")

2. Ibid., p. 130.

3. Ibid., p. 156.

4. Ibid., p. 134.

5. Ibid., p. 136.

6. Zwingli, "Von der Taufe," *Huldreich Zwinglis Samtliche Werke*, Corpus Reformatorum edition (CR), ed. Emil Egli et al. (Leipzig: M. Heinsius Nachfolger), IV:302. This is the same document as "Of Baptism," but this portion has not been translated into English. (Hereafter, "Taufe.")

7. In July 1523 he said, "In dem touff das tuncken nit abwascht die sund," or "Sins are not washed away in baptism." This statement is in "Auslegung und Grunde der Schlussreden," in *Werke* (CR), II:143. (Hereafter, "Auslegung.")

8. Zwingli, Letter to Francis Lambert, Dec. 16, 1524, *Werke* (CR), VIII:269. The idea that sins are taken away by the sacrament is an abuse of grace, he says in a letter to Fridolin Lindauer, Oct. 20, 1524, *Werke* (CR), VIII:237. (Hereafter, "Lambert" and "Lindauer.")

9. Zwingli, "Taufe," p. 206. See ibid., pp. 302-303.

10. Zwingli, "Baptism," p. 130; see also "Taufe," p. 333.

11. Zwingli, "Baptism," p. 153; see also "Taufe," p. 333.

12. Zwingli, "Baptism," p. 138.

13. Zwingli, "Quaestiones de sacramento baptismi," *Huldreich Zwinglis Werke*, ed. M. Schuler and J. Schulthess (SS), III:579. (Hereafter, "Quaestiones.")

14. Zwingli, "On Original Sin," tr. Henry Preble and William J. Hinke, *The Latin Works and the Correspondence of Hulderich Zwingli*, Vol. 2, ed. William J. Hinke (Philadelphia: Heidelberg Press, 1922), p. 12. (Hereafter, "Original Sin.")

15. Zwingli, "Commentary on True and False Religion," tr. Henry Preble, *The Latin Works of Huldreich Zwingli*, Vol. 2, ed. C.N. Heller (Philadelphia: Heidelberg Press, 1929), pp. 181-182. (Hereafter, "Commentary.")

16. Zwingli, "An Exposition of the Faith," *Zwingli and Bullinger*, p. 248. (Hereafter, "Exposition.")

17. Zwingli, "Commentary," pp. 179-180.

18. Ibid., p. 183.

19. Zwingli, "Baptism," p. 135.

20. Zwingli, "Letter to the Princes of Germany Regarding the Insults of Eck," tr. Henry Preble and W.J. Hinke, *The Latin Works of Huldreich Zwingli*, Vol. 2, ed. William John Hinke (Philadelphia: Heidelberg Press, 1922), p. 117. Hereafter, "Eck.")

21. Zwingli, "Baptism," p. 136.

22. Zwingli, "Lindauer," p. 235. See also "Quaestiones," p. 581.

23. Zwingli, "Lindauer," p. 233.

24. Ibid., p. 236.

25. Zwingli, "Commentary," p. 121.

26. Zwingli, "Original Sin," pp. 25-26.

27. Zwingli, "Antwort uber Balthasar Hubmaiers Taufbuchlein," *Werke* (CR), IV:617. (Hereafter, "Antwort.")

28. Zwingli, "Original Sin," p. 27.

29. Zwingli, "Lindauer," p. 236: "Nam qui fieri posset, ut incorporea substantia elemento corporeo ablueretur?"

30. Zwingli, "Original Sin," p. 27.

31. Zwingli, "Baptism," p. 154.

32. Ibid., p. 156.

33. Zwingli, "Commentary," p. 181.

34. Zwingli, "Amica Exegesis," *Werke* (CR), V:626.

35. Zwingli, "An Account of the Faith," tr. H.E. Jacobs and W.J. Hinke, *The Latin Works of Huldreich Zwingli*, Vol. 2, ed. William John Hinke (Philadelphia: Heidelberg Press, 1922), p. 46.

36. Zwingli, "Commentary," p. 183.

37. Zwingli, "Refutation of the Tricks of the Baptists," tr. Henry Preble and George Gilmore, *Selected Works of Huldreich Zwingli*, ed. Samuel M. Jackson (Philadelphia: University of Pennsylvania Press, 1901), pp. 237-243. His point is to defend infant baptism by showing why faith does not have to precede baptism.

38. Zwingli, "On the Providence of God," tr. Henry Preble and W.J. Hinke, *The Latin Works of Huldreich Zwingli*, Vol. 2, ed. William John Hinke (Philadelphia: Heidelberg Press, 1922), pp. 199, 201. (Hereafter, "Providence.")

39. Zwingli, "Quaestiones," p. 570: "Electio est, qua salvi reddimur." See ibid., p. 572: "Electio igitur est quae salvum facit."

40. Ibid., p. 572.

41. Zwingli, "Baptism," p. 134.

42. Ibid., p. 137.

43. Zwingli, "Original Sin," p. 29.

44. Zwingli, "Exposition," p. 272.

45. Zwingli, "Providence," p. 190.

46. Zwingli, Letter to Thomas Wyttenbach, June 15, 1523, *Werke* (CR), VIII:86. (Hereafter, "Wyttenbach.")

47. Ibid.

48. Zwingli, "Original Sin," p. 28. See also "Baptism," pp. 150-151, for a longer discussion of Romans 6:3-4. In this passage Paul simply "introduces water-baptism as a figure or illustration." See also "Subsidium sive coronis de eucharistia," *Werke* (CR), IV:500, where Zwingli says that in I Peter 3:21 "baptism" is used for "Christ."

49. Zwingli, "Quaestiones," pp. 575-576.

50. Zwingli, "Eck," pp. 109-110.

51. Zwingli, "Commentary," p. 134.

52. Zwingli, "De canone missae epichiresis," (CR), II:579.

53. Zwingli, "Baptism," p. 150.

54. Ibid., pp. 132-133.

55. Ibid., p. 163.

56. Zwingli, "Commentary," p.187.

57. Zwingli, "Baptism," p. 137.

58. Zwingli, "Antwort," pp. 620-621.

59. Zwingli, "Baptism," pp. 132-135.

60. Ibid., pp. 169-175.

61. Zwingli, "Antwort," pp. 621-622.

62. Zwingli, "Baptism," pp. 132-134. See also "Lindauer," p. 236, for the same idea.

63. Zwingli, Letter to Matthew Alber, Nov. 16, 1524, *Werke* (CR), III:342. (Hereafter, "Alber.")

64. Zwingli, "Taufe," pp. 307-309.

65. Zwingli, "Baptism," p. 139. Later, in 1530, Zwingli denied ever being in sympathy with the Anabaptists: "That I was ever averse to infant baptism or was tinged with Catabaptism, no lover of the truth and right ever said of me." (Zwingli, "Eck," p. 126).

66. Zwingli, "Taufe," p. 206. See the discussion of this point in Jack Cottrell, "Covenant and Baptism in the Theology of Huldreich Zwingli," an unpublished doctoral dissertation (Princeton, N.J.: Princeton Theological Seminary, 1971), pp. 166-172.

67. Zwingli, "Antwort," pp. 634-635.

68. Zwingli, "Refutation of the Tricks of the Baptists," pp. 220-221. (Hereafter, "Refutation.")

69. Zwingli, "Antwort," pp. 634-635.

70. Ibid., p. 636.

71. Ibid., p. 637.

72. Zwingli, "Refutation," p. 227.

73. Ibid., pp. 233, 234.

74. Ibid., p. 229.

75. Ibid., p. 230.

76. Ibid., p. 232.

77. See G.H.W. Lampe, *The Seal of the Spirit*, 2nd edition (London: S.P.C.K., 1967), pp. 245-246.

78. Zwingli, "Lambert," p. 271.

79. Zwingli, "Taufe," p. 327.

80. Zwingli, "Baptism," p. 132. See "Antwort," p. 638.

81. Zwingli, "Antwort," p. 638; "Refutation," p. 237.

82. Zwingli, "Refutation," p. 234.

83. Ibid., p. 235.

84. Zwingli, "Antwort," p. 629.

85. Zwingli, "Refutation," p. 236. Zwingli had been making this point (i.e. that Christians' children are God's people no less than their parents, just as in the Old Testament) even before he began speaking about covenant unity (e.g., "Taufe," p. 333). The new idea of covenant unity provides him with the needed basis for affirming this.

86. Zwingli, "Wer Ursache gebe zu Aufruhr," *Werke* (CR), III:410. This was written in late 1524, even before the covenant unity argument was developed.

87. Zwingli, "Refutation," p. 236.

88. Zwingli, "Auslegung," pp. 124-125.

89. Ibid., p. 89.

90. Ibid., p. 122.

91. Ibid., p. 122.

92. Zwingli, "Wyttenbach," pp. 85-86. This important discussion of the sacraments was published about a month earlier than the "Exposition and Defense," but was probably written after the section on the sacraments in the latter work.

93. Zwingli, "Auslegung," p. 388.

94. Zwingli, "Lindauer," p. 236.

95. Zwingli, "Baptism," p. 138. He still calls the sacraments "a concession to our frailty" (ibid., p. 131), but for a different reason. Since all people have special signs, God gives them to His people so that they will not be tempted to follow after some false god for whom there are such signs. ("Taufe,") p. 292.

96. Zwingli, "Commentary," p. 179.

97. Ibid., pp. 183, 184.

98. Ibid., p. 213.

99. Zwingli, "Baptism," p. 166. This is an idea that appears throughout the "Commentary"; see pp. 99, 100, 123, 124, 211, 253.

100. See his statement in the 'Commentary," p. 183, that those who hold such a view "refuse baptism to all who have not previously so well learned and confessed the faith that they can respond to all its articles."

101. Zwingli, "Eck," p.113.

102. Ibid., p. 117.

103. Zwingli, "Exposition," pp. 263-264.

104. See G.W. Bromiley's introduction to this work in *Zwingli and Bullinger*, p. 240.

105. Zwingli, "Lambert," p.270.

106. Zwingli, "Baptism," p. 147.

107. Zwingli, "Providence," p. 189.

108. Zwingli, "Commentary," pp. 180-181.

109. Zwingli, "Exposition," pp. 264-265.

110. Zwingli, "Baptism," p. 141; see also pp. 145, 150, 151.

111. Ibid., p. 131.

112. Zwingli, "Taufe," pp. 292-293.

113. Zwingli, "Baptism," pp. 136, 137.

114. Zwingli, "Original Sin," p. 25.

115. Zwingli, "Commentary," p. 184.

116. Zwingli, "Alber," pp. 345, 349; "Amica Exegesis," pp. 646, 645.

117. Zwingli, "Commentary," p. 184.

118. Zwingli, "Eck," p. 109.

119. Zwingli, "An Account of the Faith," p. 47.

120. Zwingli, "Baptism," p. 147.

121. Ibid., p. 148. Zwingli draws some of this meaning from his equation of John's baptism and Christian baptism (see ibid., p. 143).

122. Zwingli, "Quaestiones," p. 577.

123. Zwingli, "Original Sin," p. 28.

124. Zwingli, "Antwort," p. 621: "offne verzugnus," "offne kundtschaft."

125. Zwingli, "An Account of the Faith," p.48.

126. Zwingli, "Antwort," p. 631.

127. Ibid., p. 618.

128. Zwingli, "Refutation," p. 237.

129. Zwingli, "Eck," pp. 108-109. "In baptism the thing is belonging to the Church." (Ibid., p. 107).

130. Zwingli, "Taufe," p. 318; see also pp. 313, 325.

131. Zwingli, "Antwort," pp. 621-622.

132. Zwingli, "Original Sin," p. 28.

133. Zwingli, "Refutation," p. 223.

134. Zwingli, "An Account of the Faith," p. 48.

135. Zwingli, "Quaestiones," p. 577.

136. Zwingli, "An Account of the Faith," pp. 47-48.

137. Zwingli, "Taufe," p. 326.

138. Zwingli, "Antwort," p. 628.

139. See Jack Cottrell, *What the Bible Says About God the Ruler* (Joplin, Mo.: College Press, 1984), pp. 75-77.

140. See ibid., chapter five, "Special Providence and Free Will," especially pp. 168-228.

141. Luther was just as strong a determinist as Zwingli. See ibid., pp. 73-75.

142. Zwingli, "Amica Exegesis," p. 627.

143. Zwingli, "Providence," pp. 160, 162.

144. Ibid., p. 160; "Commentary," p. 81.

145. Zwingli, "Providence," p. 181.

146. Zwingli, "Taufe," p. 308.

147. Zwingli, "Providence," p. 161.

148. Ibid., p. 162.

149. Zwingli, "Of the Clarity and Certainty or Power of the Word of God," *Zwingli and Bullinger*, p. 65. (Hereafter, "Clarity.")

150. Ibid., pp. 66-67; "Providence," p. 171.

151. Zwingli, "Providence," p. 171.

152. Zwingli, "Commentary," p. 339.

153. Zwingli, "Wyttenbach," p. 85.
154. Zwingli, "Providence," p. 162.
155. Ibid., p. 154.
156. Ibid., p. 161.
157. Ibid.
158. Zwingli, "Commentary," pp. 144-145.
159. Ibid., p. 81.
160. Zwingli, "Providence," p. 162.
161. Ibid., p. 161.
162. Zwingli, "Providence," p. 173.
163. Ibid., p. 161.
164. Zwingli, "Commentary," p. 340.
165. Zwingli, "Clarity," p. 65.
166. Zwingli, "Commentary," p. 152.
167. Zwingli, "Clarity," p. 65.
168. Zwingli, "Commentary," p. 152. "For what need would there have been of knowledge of God, and of laws, if the end of the soul were the same as the body?" (Ibid., p. 340).
169. Zwingli, "Providence," p. 171.
170. Zwingli, "Commentary," p. 341.
171. Zwingli, "Providence," p. 172.
172. Ibid., p. 165.
173. Zwingli, "Taufe," p. 308. See "Original Sin," p. 10.
174. Zwingli, "Clarity," p. 65.
175. Ibid., p. 66.
176. Zwingli, "Of the Upbringing and Education of Youth," *Zwingli and Bullinger*, p. 111. (Hereafter, "Upbringing.")
177. Zwingli, "Original Sin," p. 10.
178. Zwingli, "Wyttenbach," p. 85.
179. Zwingli, "An Account of the Faith," p. 37.
180. Zwingli, "Providence," p. 171.
181. Ibid., p. 160: they are "two most widely different things." See also "Commentary," p. 81.
182. Zwingli, "Clarity," p. 61.
183. Zwingli, "Upbringing," p. 106.
184. Zwingli, "Providence," pp. 162-163.
185. Zwingli, "Commentary," pp. 340-341.
186. Zwingli, "Providence," p. 172; "Clarity," p. 65.
187. Ibid., p. 66.
188. Ibid., p. 61.
189. Zwingli, "Original Sin," p. 10.
190. Zwingli, "Providence," p. 162.
191. Zwingli, "Commentary," p. 340.
192. Zwingli, "Wyttenbach," p. 85.
193. Zwingli, "Providence," p. 162.

194. Zwingli, "Clarity," p. 65.

195. Zwingli, "Providence," p. 173.

196. Ibid., p. 161. Changing the metaphor slightly Zwingli says, "The body is clay, taken from the earth, and when you attach this to the soul it is like letting a wild boar into a liquid spring."

197. Zwingli, "Taufe," p. 308.

198. Zwingli, "Commentary," pp. 78-81.

199. Zwingli, "Providence," p. 339.

200. Zwingli, "Amica Exegesis," p. 627.

201. John Calvin, "Catechism of the Church of Geneva," *Tracts and Treatises*, tr. Henry Beveridge (Grand Rapids: Eerdmans, 1958), II:87.

202. John Calvin, "Acts of the Council of Trent with the Antidote," *Tracts and Treatises*, III:176.

203. Ibid., p. 86.

204. John Calvin, *Commentaries on the Epistle of Paul the Apostle to the Romans*, tr. John Owen (Grand Rapids: Eerdmans, 1955), p. 221.

205. Ibid., p. 220.

206. John Calvin, *Commentaries on the Epistles of Paul the Apostle to the Philippians, Colossians, and Thessalonians*, tr. John Pringle (Grand Rapids: Eerdmans, 1948), p. 185.

207. John Calvin, "Confession of Faith in the Name of the Reformed Churches of France," *Tracts and Treatises*, II:152.

208. John Calvin, "Appendix to the Tract on the True Method of Reforming the Church," *Tracts and Treatises*, III:354.

209. This is a very important but often-overlooked distinction. From the Biblical perspective baptism is necessary as a means of receiving salvation, but the Zwinglian-Reformed revision rejects this kind of necessity. In the new view it is necessary to be baptized in the same sense that it is necessary for us to obey any of God's commands, i.e., since God has commanded it, we ought to do it. It is simply one of the many precepts or commands God has prescribed for us. To ignore it would be a sin, but it would not directly affect our salvation. For a contemporary Reformed statement on this view, see Louis Berkhof, *Systematic Theology* (London: Banner of Truth Trust, 1939), pp. 618-619.

210. John Calvin, *Institutes of the Christian Religion*, IV.xv.20, "Library of Christian Classics," Vols. 20-21, ed. John T. McNeill, tr. Ford Lewis Battles (Philadelphia: Westminster Press, 1960), II:1321. (Hereafter, *Institutes*.)

211. John T. McNeill, footnote 39, Calvin's *Institutes*, II:1321.

212. Calvin, "Articles Agreed Upon by the Faculty of Sacred Theology of Paris," *Tracts and Treatises*, I:74.

213. Calvin, *Commentary upon the Acts of the Apostles*, tr. Henry Beveridge (Grand Rapids: Eerdmans, 1949), I:363.

214. Ibid., II:122.

215. Ibid., I:118.

216. Ibid., I:453.

217. Calvin, "The True Method of Giving Peace to Christendom and

Reforming the Church," *Tracts and Treatises*, III:275.

218. Calvin, *Institutes*, IV.xiv.9; Vol. II. p. 1285.

219. Ibid., IV.xiv.14; Vol. II. p. 1290.

220. Calvin, "Second Defense D of the Faith Concerning the Sacraments in Answer to Joachim Westphal," *Tracts and Treatises*, II:336.

221. Calvin, "Mutual Consent in Regard to the Sacraments," *Tracts and Treatises*, II:218. See also the "Second Defense," p. 337: "Thus the sins of Paul were washed away in baptism, though he had previously obtained pardon of them by faith."

222. See Calvin's treatment of this in the *Institutes*, IV.xvi; Vol. II, pp. 1324ff.

223. Calvin, *Institutes*, IV.xv.1; Vol. II. p. 1304.

224. Ibid., IV.xiv.17; Vol. II. pp. 1292-1293.

225. Ibid., IV.xv.2; Vol. II. p. 1304.

226. Calvin, *Commentaries on the Epistles to Timothy, Titus, and Philemon*, tr. William Pringle (Grand Rapids: Eerdmans, 1948), pp. 332-333.

227. Calvin, *Commentary upon the Acts of the Apostles*, I:117.

228. Ibid., p. 119.

229. Ibid., II:303.

230. Calvin, *Institutes*, IV.xv.13; Vol. II. pp. 1313-1314.

231. Ibid., IV.xiv.13; Vol. II. p. 1289. Again, the sacraments are given "first, to foster, arouse, and confirm faith within; then, to attest religion before men." (Ibid., IV.xiv.19; Vol. II, p. 1296.

232. Ibid., IV.xiv.1; Vol. II. p. 1277. Another definition is that sacraments are "at once an attestation to the grace of God to ratify it in us, and external signs, by which we declare our Christianity before men." ("Confession of Faith in Name of the Reformed Churches of France," p. 152).

233. Calvin, *Institutes*, IV.xv.1; Vol. II. pp. 1303-1304.

234. Dean Mills, "The Development of a Doctrine," *Christian Standard* (June 8, 1986), CXXI:11-12.

3

THE RESTORATION OF BAPTISM BY EIGHTEENTH AND NINETEENTH CENTURY RESTORERS IN BRITAIN

Lynn A. McMillon

The ideal of restoring the faith and practice of first century New Testament Christianity distinguishes the Restoration Movement from other theological stances. Not only have restorationists sought to recover the organizational design of the New Testament church, but also all of the beliefs and practices of the New Testament as well.

This chapter focuses on one of these beliefs, baptism. The doctrine of baptism is an essential doctrine because it marks the point at which a person becomes a Christian. Restoration churches see in the New Testament three crucial issues related to the doctrine of baptism. Since the New Testament gives God's inspired pattern for His church, each of these three baptismal issues is essential to a complete and accurate understanding of baptism.

Restoration churches, such as the Church of Christ, emphasize that the mode of scriptural baptism is always immersion because the New Testament Greek word *baptizein* means "to immerse." Furthermore, the examples of baptism in the New Testament support the conclusion that baptism was always by immersion. Baptism by immersion also is essential because immersion represents burial with Christ (Romans 6:3-4).

The second crucial baptismal issue stressed by Restoration churches is the necessity of faith on the part of the baptismal candidate. This limits baptism to adults who are capable of faith in Jesus Christ. Therefore the Churches of Christ today stress that infants cannot be candidates for baptism since they bear no sin, are already spiritually safe, and are not capable of faith.

The third baptismal issue emphasized by Restoration churches, is the belief that baptism marks the fulfillment of a person's faith in Jesus Christ into salvation. At baptism the blood of Jesus washes away a person's sins (Acts 22:16), and the person becomes a Christian. Therefore, the New Testament teaches that baptism is essential to salvation, and is the primary line of fellowship among Restoration churches.

A. The Historical Background
Eighteenth and Nineteenth Century Britain

1. Catholic and Protestant Practice of Baptism

No subject in the history of the Restoration Movement has attracted more study than the meaning of baptism. More than two hundred years ago, the debate began in the Restoration Movement on the mode, subjects, and purpose of New Testament baptism. Sixteenth century reformers and eighteenth century restorers alike struggled to comprehend the scriptural teachings on each of these three crucial areas of baptism.

The scriptural organization of the church, rather than baptism, was the major concern of the eighteenth century Scottish restorers. Because of this they devoted little attention to the meaning and practice of baptism. The same was true of Alexander Campbell (1788-1866), who did not develop an understanding of baptism until his debate with W.L. McCalla in 1823. This chapter shows the studies and conclusions of several of the earliest Scottish restorers in their search to understand New Testament baptism, a search which set the backdrop for the next generation of Restoration study by such men as Alexander Campbell, Walter Scott, Barton W. Stone and others in America.

But first, notice the deeper historical rootage of baptismal study. For hundreds of years prior to Calvin, the Catholic Church baptized infants to remove what they called "original sin," the belief that infants inherit a nature tainted by sin. The mode of baptism practiced by the Catholic Church for hundreds of years was sprinkling or pouring small amounts of water on the forehead of infants. Thus Catholic tradition also held that the mode of baptism was sprinkling or pouring.

Since Europe was predominantly Catholic during the Middle Ages, the practice of infant baptism was universally established throughout Europe. This accounts for the difficulty of both the reformers and restorers in seeing through the theological fog of their day to recover the truth of New Testament baptismal teaching.

Major sixteenth century reformers such as Martin Luther and John Calvin made little progress toward a Biblical understanding of baptism, since they devoted their attention mostly to the subjects of religious authority, the Lord's Supper, and the meaning of faith. When Calvin's theology was imported to Scotland by John Knox in 1555, it impacted the religious thinking not only of Scotland, but of all of the British Isles. Specifically, Calvinism eventually permeated official British and Scottish theological thought through the theology of the Westminster Confession of Faith formulated in 1643.

Much of the difficulty encountered by eighteenth century Scottish restorers (such as John Glas, Robert Sandeman, James and Robert Haldane, Alexander Carson and Archibald McLean) in understanding New Testament baptism lay in the theological meanings given to baptism by the Roman Catholic Church during the Middle Ages. For instance, when the IV Lateran Council of 1215 defined the Seven Sacraments of the Catholic Church, it not only identified baptism as a sacrament, but codified the sprinkling of infants for the removal of "original sin."

2. Westminster Confession of Faith

a.*Background to the Westminster Confession of Faith.* Catholic baptismal belief carried over to the English and Scottish Protestants in 1643, when the Solemn League and Covenant was enacted between the Scots and the English Parliament. The agreement supported the Presbyterian form of church government (regional presbyteries, synods, etc.) in the Church of Scotland, uniformity among the churches in Britain, the extirpation of popery and prelacy, and the mutual defense of the two countries. Thus, when the Westminster Assembly began revising the "Thirty-Nine Articles" of the Church of England, the delegates progressed as far as Article XV before they discovered that the Solemn League and Covenant required uniformity of doctrine between England and Scotland. Therefore, under Scottish influence, Parliament ordered the framing of a confession of faith that would unite Scotland and England theologically in accordance with the provisions of the Solemn League and Covenant. The Westminster Confession of 1643, the creedal statement that resulted, consisted of thirty-three chapters which defined and interpreted major doctrines of Christianity.

b. *Baptism in the Westminster Confession of Faith.* The Westminster Confession baptismal statement "Of Baptism" in chapter XXVIII states: "Dipping of the person into the water is not necessary; but baptism is rightly administered by pouring or sprinkling water upon the person"[1] (Marginal notes in the confession cross-reference Hebrews 9:10,19-22; Acts 2:41; 16:33; Mark 7:4).[2]

The Westminster Confession also addresses the subject of infant baptism: "Not only those that do actually profess faith in and obedience unto Christ, but also the infants of one or both believing parents are to be baptized."[3] (Marginal notes in the confession cross-reference Mark 16:15-16; Acts 8:37-38; Genesis 17:7,9; Galatians 3:9,14; Colossians 2:11-12; Acts 2:38-39; Romans 4:11-12; I Corinthians 7:14; Matthew 28:19; Mark 10:13-16; Luke 18:15).[4]

Next, the Westminster Confession requires infant baptism by sprinkling or pouring. This practice already was well established in the Roman Catholic Church. The Westminster framers further explained that baptism is merely a symbol and does not represent the beginning of one's relationship to God: "The efficacy of baptism is not tied to that moment of time wherein it is administered. . . ."[5] (Marginal notes in the confession cross-reference John 3:5,8).[6] From this creedal statement one sees the teaching that soon was spread by the Westminster Confession throughout Britain.

Thus, when retracing the steps of the early Scottish restorers through the theological obstacles of the seventeenth and eighteenth centuries, one recognizes the ingrained theological barriers they faced. The theological challenge for the restorers was enormous since they struggled to understand the New Testament and shed the centuries of traditional Catholic and Calvinistic belief.

B. Thomas Grantham's Pioneering Theology.

Church historians have divided British Baptists into two major doctrinal fellowships: the General Baptists, who believed that the election of salvation was conditional and potentially effectual for all men, and the Particular Baptists who believed that only a select few were unconditionally elected to salvation. Both groups were Calvinistic, but "independent" in their view of church organization. The term "independent" is used to describe a wide range of English and Scottish churches that were not affiliated with any of the established churches. Both groups of Baptists disagreed with the Calvinists and Independents on their interpretation of the mode and subjects of baptism, however. Baptists believed that baptism was by immersion (hence the name) and that only believers could be baptized. They rejected infant baptism as unscriptural.

Whereas the sixteenth century Protestant Reformers labored to return the Bible and the Lord's Supper to the people, not until the seventeenth and eighteenth century would the restorationists restore the scriptural meaning of baptism.

Of the contribution made by the British Baptists to the understanding of baptism, Sam Hester observes: "The baptized churches have restored baptism just as the Protestants have restored the Lord's Supper."[7] Throughout the sixteenth century Reformation, Protestant leaders were mostly concerned with returning the bread and wine of the Lord's Supper to the laity; whereas previously the priest had withheld the cup of wine from lay members.

The Reformation emphasis on the Lord's Supper is easily observed in the writings of Luther and Zwingli particularly, whereas baptism was given much less attention. Luther, Calvin and Zwingli gave most of their attention to papal authority, the doctrine of faith and theology. Not until the appearance of the Baptists was a greater emphasis placed on adult believer's baptism by immersion.

Thomas Grantham (1634-1692) was an English Baptist minister who broke with Baptist theological tradition to examine the Biblical doctrine of baptism. His work is of significance because he taught that restoring New Testament baptism is an integral part of restoring Christianity to its first century form. In his monumental work published in 1678, "Christianismus Primitivus," Grantham stated the purpose of his book: "The Restauration [sic] of Christianity wherein it is either neglected or

abused to its pristine integrity, both in the form and power of it."[8]
For that reason his pioneering work is here noted as a beginning
point in the recovery of New Testament baptism.

When Grantham was nineteen, he joined a local Independent
church in Lincolnshire, he described as

> congregated upon the foundation principles of Christ's doctrine,
> Hebrews 6:1,2. . . . to keep close to the scriptural rule, respecting
> baptism by immersion, upon the profession of faith.[9]

Grantham taught his readers that they were to "devote themselves to the impartial search after primitive Christianity."[10] It is
clear from this and other passages in Grantham's works that in
his concern for the recovery of New Testament Christianity, baptism was the principal doctrine upon which he focused. When addressing the meaning of baptism Grantham spoke of the "restoration" of baptism as opposed to the "reformation" of it. Grantham
wrote that the revival of Christianity and the restoration of baptism would help to weaken the Catholic Church.

Grantham insisted that the Greek word *baptizein* could not be
translated as sprinkling. He further reasoned that the New Testament mode of baptism was immersion since it was practiced in
rivers and places that had much water. Grantham taught that immersion was the only scriptural mode of baptism.

Of Grantham's understanding of the purpose of baptism,
Hester concludes:

> From Grantham's thorough coverage of baptism, in the 'power,'
> 'extent,' and 'end' of it, one can detect in his thought baptism's
> purpose, namely: (1) the means for remission of sin, (2) a condi-
> tion whereupon one shall receive the gift of the Holy Spirit, and
> (3) the way of incorporating persons into the church of Christ.[11]

When Grantham explained the purpose of baptism, he took a
unique approach to his understanding of the scriptures. Though
he believed baptism was for the remission of sins, he did not

believe that baptism was necessary for salvation. His position was that the only persons required to be baptized for salvation were those who knew that such was required of them.

In summary, in discussing the proper candidates for baptism, Grantham explained that only persons who were old enough to believe were proper subjects for baptism, the usual approach of the Baptists. He saw that it was only for adults, that it was by immersion and that it was for the remission of sins. Yet, in misperceiving that baptism was not essential for salvation, Grantham fell short of the full Biblical understanding of the meaning and import of baptism. Fuller understanding of baptism would have to wait on the studies of later restorers.

C. John Glas' Understanding of Baptism

John Glas (1695-1773), a former minister in the Church of Scotland (Presbyterian) and known as the "father of Scottish Independency," was the fountainhead of the Scottish restoration movement which itself emerged as the forerunner of the nineteenth century American Restoration Movement. Because his initial Biblical concern was over the scriptural relationship of the church to the state, the majority of Glas' theological writing was devoted to the New Testament teaching on the organization of the local church. Glas did, however, write two short treatises on baptism.

More clearly than any other religious thinker up to his time, Glas defined the scriptural composition of a local church, including its leadership by elders, its weekly worship by observing the Lord's Supper, a capella singing, scripture reading, prayer, and contribution.[12] Though Glas was the first restorationist in modern times, he devoted very little attention to baptism.

John Glas' understanding of baptism, however, bears a striking similarity to later thought among American restorationists such as Alexander and Thomas Campbell and Walter Scott.

However, Glas understood baptism as nothing more than the sign of forgiveness in the blood of Christ and not the point of forgiveness. Glas held a Calvinistic view of the meaning of baptism. In one of his writings on baptism, Glas observed:

> . . . to place our salvation in anything beside Christ's blood purifying us, is evidently contrary to the very design of the institution of baptism, and is, in effect, denying the faith of that great truth signified in baptism. To place salvation thus in the sign, is to set it so far instead of, and in opposition to the thing signified, and to make the dispensers of the sign our saviours.[13]

Glas further believed that salvation occurred when the mind responded to the truth of Christ rather than when the body was baptized.

1. Glas on the Mode of Baptism

Though Glas acknowledged that the Greek word *baptizein* meant "to dip, to immerse or to plunge,"[14] he insisted that the primary usage of the word meant "to wash" rather than "to immerse" as seen in the following statement: "But it appears from its use in the New Testament that it signifies *washing*, in whatever way that be done, — and so it is sometimes translated, as in Matthew 15, the washing of tables."[15] From his conclusion that baptism was a washing, Glas reasoned, "Now, if the scripture calls the pouring forth of the Holy Ghost on men, baptizing them with the Holy Ghost; then pouring forth water on men, is baptizing them with the water and the scripture use of the word baptism."[16] Thus, Glas affirmed as "washing" the mode of baptism and believed that any use of water that showed washing was a scriptural mode.

> If it can be inferred from the thing signified in baptism, (as expressed Romans VI.3, 4, 5 and Colossians II.11, 12, 13), that the washing must be by bearing under water, and raising up again; then it can also, by the same rule, be inferred from the

thing signified in baptism, (as expressed Hebrews X.22), that the washing must be by sprinkling; because the thing signified, as expressed there, together with the sign of washing with water, is sprinkling our hearts from an evil conscience.[17]

A final example of Glas' understanding of the mode of baptism as washing, will reinforce his position:

Shall we say upon it, that the scripture confines us so to any manner of washing, that another way of it cannot at all be called baptism? And when our communion with Christ in his death and resurrection, whereby we are saved, is only by pouring out on us the renewing of the Holy Ghost; shall we say, that this cannot be signified in baptism by pouring water on us?"[18]

2. Glas on the Candidates for Baptism

Attention is now turned to Glas' understanding of the proper candidates for baptism. He saw the circumcision of infants in the Old Testament as a parallel to the baptism of infants of believing parents in the New Testament:

Though the children could not in themselves know anything of repentance or remission at the time of their baptism, as did their parents; yet they were, even then, as capable as they of the renewing of the Holy Ghost, and saving change from which repentance flows, and as capable as they of justification, by remission, and by the imputation of righteousness without works.[19]

In this statement Glas insists that adults are not capable of doing anything meritorious. He, therefore, justified infant baptism by claiming that infants no more contribute to their own salvation than adults do. "We contribute as little to our salvation by baptism, as do our infants. They enter the kingdom of God by the same title as we do; and we contribute no more to our entrance than they."[20]

Glas reasoned from Colossians 2:11-13 that baptism for infants was comparable in the New Testament to circumcision for infants in the Old Testament. He concluded that the "circumcision made without hands" is the baptism of the New Testament:

> Now, if the apostle gives us baptism with the thing signified in it, in place of circumcision of the flesh, and calls it the circumcision of Christ; then baptism must be to the true Israel, who were born of the spirit, as circumcision was to the typical Israel, who were born of the flesh . . . baptism belongs to the children of the spiritual Israel unto whom the promise is; even as circumcision belonged to the children of the fleshly Israel. . . .[21]

Following Calvinistic form, Glas believed that infant baptism was limited to the infants of believers:

> Baptism being the sign or seal of our union with Christ, and his body the church, cannot be administered to any infants as members, but the infants of believers; because there can be no baptism without teaching, or making of disciples by teaching, and without a profession of the faith; and we cannot know a child to be holy but by the profession of the parents' belief of the word.[22]

3. Glas on the Meaning of Baptism

While Glas did not associate baptism with remission of sins, he emphasized the ceremonial importance of baptism:

> A great Christian truth, concerning salvation by the death and resurrection of Jesus Christ the Son of God, in whom the Father is well pleased, and the purification of sinners by his blood shed, for the remission of sins, is so expressed in the institution of baptism, and so signified in it.[23]

Glas clearly wanted to distinguish between the symbolism of baptism and the action signified by baptism. This is specifically seen in his interpretation of I Peter 3:20,21: "Peter's words, set forth the putting away of the filth of the flesh, as the sign in baptism, in distinction from the thing signified, wherein he says our salvation only lies."[24] Glas cites the following New Testament passages in support of his understanding of baptism:

> The New Testament speaks of washing as the outward sign of the Ordinance: Hebrews X, "your bodies washed with pure water;" Titus III, "the washing of regeneration;" Acts 22:16, "arise, be baptized, and wash away thy sins;" 1 Peter 3:21, "the putting away of the filth of the flesh," — signifying the washing away of sin, — the purging of the conscience or sprinkling of the heart from an evil conscience.[25]

Glas believed that baptism declares a person a member of the invisible church which is the body of Christ worldwide, but he did not believe that baptism ever made a person a member of a local or visible congregation. He explained this when he said:

> There is no ground in the scripture for thinking, that any one is acknowledged in baptism as a member of any visible church. It only declares the baptized to be members of the body of Christ, the true church, into which all Christians are baptized, though it be invisible; even as they are baptized into Christ.[26]

In conclusion it is recalled that Glas believed that baptism meant to plunge, immerse, or dip but that its principal action was washing. Therefore, to Glas, any mode of baptism that signified washing was to Glas scriptural. He further saw infants of believing parents as proper subjects for baptism, reasoning that baptism in the New Testament was comparable to circumcision in the Old Testament. Glas insisted that the remission of sins was not to be associated with the act of baptism, but with the sacrifice of Jesus signified by the act of baptism.

D. Robert Sandeman on Baptism

Robert Sandeman (1718-1771), Scotsman and son-in-law to John Glas, was responsible for spreading John Glas' teachings throughout England and later to New England. The most concise yet comprehensive statement by Robert Sandeman on the meaning of baptism comes from a recently discovered letter dated March 10, 1736. In this letter to Jean Smellom, Sandeman wrote:

Concerning the ordinances of the Gospel, and first baptism. Many things were said which you have most partly heard, and which I cannot now write; as concerning its belonging to infants, who are the objects of it; its being done with water; of its being an ordinance to continue in the church after the death of the apostles; of the manner — to wit, washing, — whether it be by plunging, sprinkling, or any way else; of its being shadowed forth by circumcision, from Colossians II and 12, of its being no further the ordinance of the visible church than that it must be administered by the elders or bishops of a visible church; lastly, concerning the spiritual grace signified therein, according to the several scriptures that allude to it, as its being the antitype of Noah's ark, and the Israelites being baptized unto Moses in the cloud and in the sea; as it points out putting off the body of sins, the washing of regeneration, and renewings of the Holy Ghost, the answer of a good conscience through the resurrection of Jesus Christ, the having our hearts purged from an evil conscience and our bodies washed with pure water.[27]

E. Description of An Eighteenth Century Baptistry

The only description of a baptistry among the Independent churches in England or Scotland is found in Wilson's *History of Dissenting Churches* which describes the baptistry in the Paul's-Alley meeting place in Barbican, London around 1778.

This Baptisterion, or cistern, is fixed just before the pulpit, the sides and bottom of which are made with good polished stone, and round the top is put a kirb of marble about a foot wide; and round it at about a foot or two distance, is set up an iron rail, of handsome cypher work. Under the pulpit are the stairs that lead down into it, and at the top of these are two folding doors, which open into the three rooms behind the meeting house, which are large, and handsomely wainscotted. Under one of these rooms there is a well, sunk down to the spring of water; at the top of this there is a leader-pump fixed, from which a pipe goes down into the basin, near the top of it, by which it is filled with water; at the bottom of the basin there is a brass plug, from whence there goes another pipe into the said well, to empty it again.[28]

F. The Haldane Brothers on Baptism

James Haldane (1768-1851) and Robert Haldane (1764-?) were Scottish aristocrats reared in the Church of Scotland. Early in their lives they became deeply interested in evangelism. At one time they proposed to go to India, but when permission was denied, they focused their attention on evangelizing Scotland. From 1795 to 1808 these brothers preached by whatever means they could. They seemed to be less concerned with doctrine than with preaching.

G.C. Moore, a contemporary of James Haldane, relates an incident that was crucial in Haldane's rejection of infant baptism and acceptance of believer's baptism by immersion. According to Moore, the incident occurred after Haldane had sprinkled an infant, when his own six year old son asked him, "Father, did that child believe?" "No," said the surprised Haldane. "Why do you ask me such a question?" "Because, Father, I have read the entire New Testament, and I find that all who were baptized believed. Did the child believe?"[29]

Haldane, shocked and astonished, decided to search the New Testament for its teaching on baptism. In the spring of 1808, Haldane informed his Edinburgh congregation that his year-long study of the New Testament had taught him that he could no longer baptize infants. Haldane was himself baptized by immersion shortly afterwards, an event which divided the Edinburgh church he had served for many years.

Prior to 1808, both Haldane brothers had held firmly to the paedo-baptist (infant baptizing) views, but in that year both were baptized by immersion. Even before his own baptism, James Haldane wrote to John Campbell, an associate in Edinburgh, that he had frequently questioned the practice of baptizing children, but each time previously, his doubts were satisfied. After much study, James Haldane was baptized as he wrote to John Campbell in April 1808: "If I had not been compelled to baptize, I should never have mentioned my doubts till they were fully satisfied. At the same time, I informed the church that, although I were baptized I should be of the sole mind as formerly. . . ."[30] By the end of the year Robert Haldane was also baptized along with two hundred members of his congregation, and within a few months, adult baptism was accepted in most of the congregations in the Haldane connection throughout Scotland.

G. The Scotch Baptists

1. Archibald McLean (1733-1812)

a. *McLean becomes a Scotch Baptist.* The Scotch Baptists, who practiced adult baptism by immersion for remission of sins, owe their origin primarily to Archibald McLean (1733-1812), a Scottish highlander, who was brought up in the Church of Scotland (Presbyterian Church). McLean first questioned the scriptural authority for a national church when he read John Glas' *The Testimony of the King of Martyrs.* This work eventually led McLean to withdraw from the Scottish national church and join the Glasites in Glasgow.

McLean withdrew from the Church of Scotland in 1762 and joined the Glasite fellowship in Glasgow where his printing business was located. He continued with that fellowship until 1765, when he was deeply disappointed over the handling of a local case of church discipline. McLean felt so strongly about the incident that he wrote a letter to the elders of the church and to

John Glas. When he did not receive a reply from the elders, McLean felt that there was nothing he could do but resign his membership.

About this same time Robert Carmichael, a former Anti-burgher minister from Coupar-Angus, also resigned from the Glasites.[31] Shortly after both men had severed ties with the Glasites, Carmichael asked McLean what he thought about baptism. Since McLean had given little thought to the subject, he promised to do so, which he did by reading the entire New Testament and noting every reference to baptism. At the end of his study, McLean wrote to Carmichael that he found no scriptural authority for practicing infant baptism.[32] Carmichael first rejected McLean's findings, but soon he determined to make his own study.

A year later, Carmichael wrote to McLean, indicating that he had also come to the conclusion that the New Testament does not authorize infant baptism. Focusing their attention next on adult baptism, the two men decided that Carmichael would travel to London to be baptized by immersion by Dr. Gill, the famous London Baptist minister. Thus, Carmichael was baptized at Barbican, in London, October 9, 1765. Shortly after Carmichael's return to Scotland, McLean traveled to Edinburgh and was baptized by him. In 1768, McLean was chosen as co-minister to serve with Carmichael at the Edinburgh Scotch Baptist church where the two men served together for many years.

The preceding events mark the beginning of the Baptist movement in Scotland. Though these Scotch Baptists later allied themselves with the English Baptists, they were, nevertheless, founded on a much different basis.[33] The Scotch Baptists followed the Glasite form of doctrine and church order on every point with the exception of the doctrine of baptism. It was at this time, ca. 1765, that McLean and Carmichael began teaching that New Testament baptism was by immersion for adult believers and for the remission of sins. Theologically, the American Restoration Movement bears more similarity to the Scotch Baptists than to any other group.

In England, these people were often called Sandemanian Baptists.[34] In New England they were also called Sandemanian Baptists.

b. *McLean on baptism for the remission of sins.* Archibald McLean must be regarded as the first restorationist who not only understood the nature, organization, and work of the New Testament church but who also recovered the New Testament teaching on adult baptism by immersion for the remission of sins.

In McLean's monumental work, *The Commission Given By Jesus Christ To His Apostles*, which analyzed Jesus' Great Commission in Matthew 28, McLean began by asking what the action of baptism is — washing, pouring, sprinkling, or dipping? "Many will tell us that it is any of them we please; which indicates no great reverence for Christ's authority."[35] About the word *baptizein*, McLean observed: "It signifies properly to *dip, plunge,* or *immerse*; and that in distinction from every other form of washing, as well as from sprinkling or pouring, which are expressed in the original by other words."[36] This statement clearly represents the beliefs of the Restoration Movement both then and today.

Furthermore, McLean's study probed the meaning and usage of the Greek prepositions *en* and *eis* with reference to baptism. Of these important Greek prepositions, McLean wrote:

> For instance, *en* or *eis, in* or *into* Jordan (Matthew 3:6; Mark 1:9); *en, in* water, *in* the Holy Ghost (Matthew 3:11); *eis, into* the name (Matthew 28:19), *into* Moses (1 Corinthians 10:2), *into* Christ (Galatians 3:27), *into* his death (Romans 6:3). *Eis* cannot be translated *unto* or *towards* in the case of baptism; because it would be nonsense to say that John baptized *unto* or *towards* Jordan.[37]

McLean stressed the meaning of these Greek prepositions in order to establish the New Testament teaching on immersion. If sprinkling or pouring were the mode of baptism taught in the New

Testament, then the wording would be "baptized with water."

McLean expanded his analysis to consider the name into which believers are to be baptized. He concluded:

> The phrase *in the name*, sometimes signifies *for the sake of, in the strength of, by the authority of, invoking the name of* . . . but here, I apprehend, the expression *into the name* chiefly signifies *into the faith of the gospel*. . . . Here his *name* signifies the same thing with his *faith* or *word*.[38]

Summarizing his study on baptism, McLean wrote: "The faith of the Father and Son must therefore be professed in baptism, for it is a baptism into that faith; and so the apostle connects with the one baptism, the one faith which respects one Lord, and one God and Father of all."[39]

McLean believed Jesus taught that baptism was for adult believers only. In his study of Jesus' Great Commission, McLean observed that the phrase "baptizing them" signifies the subjects that are to be baptized.

> Not every individual in the nations; but only such as they should previously teach with effect, or make disciples by teaching. . . . It is plain, therefore, that none are commanded to be baptized, but such as are first taught or made disciples, and profess to believe the gospel.[40]

In affirming that baptism was for adult believers only, McLean answered the "household" baptism argument traditionally used by paedo-baptists[41] by showing that in the New Testament the only ones who were baptized were those who believed and that they were not baptized until they did believe, citing Acts 2:32, 33 and 34, as well as the example of Cornelius, Lydia and the jailer. McLean further noted that paedo-baptists admitted that there was no scriptural authority for the baptism of infants other than the analogy between circumcision in the Old Testament and baptism in the New Testament. He went on to show several differences that existed between the circumcision of the Old Testament and baptism in the New Testament.

McLean also refuted the argument for infant baptism based on paralleling circumcision with baptism, by citing the differences between them. First, he observed that circumcision belonged to Abraham's natural seed, whereas baptism belongs to Abraham's spiritual seed. Second, circumcision was restricted to males, but baptism is extended to male and female alike. Third, circumcision was not a seal of Abraham's righteousness of faith; therefore no argument can be drawn from it for the baptism of natural infant seed of believers.[42]

Archibald McLean concluded from the New Testament that baptism was for the remission of sins. He observed that so much attention had been given to the proper candidates for baptism that inadequate attention had been given to the purpose of baptism: "The universal practice of sprinkling infants, with the principles adopted and arguments used in support of that human invention, have not only set aside the *subjects* and *form* of Christ's institution, but in a great measure obscured and perverted its *signification*."[43]

McLean next focused on the purpose of baptism as a sign of regeneration, as a figure of remission of sins, and as conformity to the death and resurrection of Jesus. Speaking again of baptism for the remission of sins, McLean writes in his commentary on Hebrews 6: "As to remission of sins, new converts are exhorted to be baptized in the name of Jesus Christ for the remission of sins, Acts 2:38, and to be baptized and wash away their sins, chapter 22:16."[44]

John Glas worked for the restoration of the organization and worship of the church, whereas Archibald McLean restored a clear understanding of New Testament baptism. McLean's work, however, did not directly affect the American Restoration Movement as Alexander Campbell and others did not seem to be aware of his study.

McLean arrived at his conclusions by reading the New Testament rather than studying theology. Contemporary theology would not have yielded this understanding of the Biblical practice.

McLean's understanding of baptism, combined with the Glasite understanding of the organization of the church makes the Scotch Baptists decidedly different from English Baptists and made the Scotch Baptists in America feel affinity with the Campbell-Stone Restoration Movement[45] on the American frontier in the early 1800's. For example, a few of the members of the church that Robert Sandeman began in Danbury, Connecticut, around 1771, allied themselves with the Restoration Movement of Alexander Campbell in the mid 1800's, because of their insistence that adults had to be baptized to receive remission of sins. Furthermore, Walter Scott, one of Campbell's co-workers in the frontier Restoration Movement, was influenced greatly by the writings of Glas, Sandeman, and the Scotch Baptists of New York.

2. Alexander Carson (1776-1844)

Alexander Carson was an Irish minister-scholar who adopted and later advanced the cause of the restoration. As a young man, he attended the University of Glasgow, where he became a recognized Greek scholar whom Robert Haldane called the "first scholar of his time." At age twenty-two he became a minister for the Presbyterian Church in Tubermore, northern Ireland, and served there until ca. 1801.

a. *Carson becomes a Baptist.* In 1801, Carson resigned from the local Presbyterian Synod because he believed that it restricted his religious freedom, so he wrote "Reasons for Separating From the Synod of Ulster," a document similar in content and message to Barton W. Stone's "Last Will and Testament of the Springfield Presbytery" which was written in America about the same time (1804).

Early in his ministry, Carson, influenced by the religious independents of his day, insisted on accepting the authority of the New Testament only. Comparing the Independents to their Presbyterian counterparts, Carson wrote:

> The Bible is their code of laws; they have no other confession or book of discipline. They can do nothing without it; it must be continually in their hands; the rulers rule only by the word of God. But a man may be a Presbyterian all his life, either pastor or private member, with a very slender acquaintance with the Bible. A knowledge of forms and of ancient usages, of ecclesiastical canons and books of discipline, is the chief qualification necessary for Presbyterian judicatory.[46]

Indeed, what distinguished the Scottish independents was their loyalty to and insistence on Biblical authority and their willingness to change when they discovered truth in the New Testament.

Carson first separated from the Presbyterian Church over the place and importance of the Bible in religion and over the form of church government. In 1808, his understanding of baptism was transformed when a Scotch Baptist missionary, sent to Ireland by the Haldanes, taught the doctrine of adult baptism by immersion only. Carson later recalled the incident, "I thought that I could demolish the arguments of that Baptist as easily as you could crush a fly."[47] Carson was never the same after that experience. From that time he began his study of baptism that eventually resulted in his *Baptism: Its Mode and Subjects* in 1831.[48]

Though Carson was a minister in a small Irish village, his eminence as a Greek scholar is seen in his later writings, including a written debate with Samuel Lee, a professor at Cambridge. Friends later observed that nothing ever stirred Carson's intellectual curiosity and spiritual devotion as much as his original encounter with that humble Scotch Baptist who first invaded the secure tranquility of Carson's Presbyterian beliefs.

Though Carson's Greek analysis of baptism in the New Testament was often maligned by the established churches in Ireland and Scotland, his work eventually was recognized in 1840, when he was awarded the LL.D. degree by Bacon College in Kentucky, the first institution of higher education of the American Restoration Movement.

b. *Carson's baptismal theology.* Carson based his understanding of the mode of baptism on the meaning of the Greek word *bapto* from which is derived *baptizo.* Carson insisted that *bapto* has the primary meaning of *to dip* and has a secondary meaning *to dye.* He insisted that every occurrence of the word has one of these two meanings, as he wrote: "*Baptizo* not only signifies to dip or to immerse, but it never has any other meaning."[49]

Some of Carson's contemporary Independent ministers, however, insisted that *baptizo* also meant *to wash,* thus allowing any mode of baptism as long as washing was signified. This is the position that John Glas took on the meaning of the word when he wrote: "The New Testament speaks of washing as the outward sign of the Ordinance; Heb. X. . . . Acts XXVII.16. . . . 1 Peter III.21 . . . signifying the washing away of sin. . . ."[50] In regards to baptism as a washing, Carson observed in his book: "Dipping is the thing expressed, washing is a consequence."[51] Carson produced examples from classical Greek to illustrate the two meanings which he gives to the word baptism. He further systematically covered the passages on baptism in the New Testament to show that their meaning could only be *to dip* or *to dye.*

Much of Carson's attention was devoted to Greville Ewing's interpretation (c. 1795) that *bapto* could be reduced to its radical letters, and by interposing labials and vowels one could form the word *pop.* From this Ewing concluded that a small amount of water could be "popped" or sprinkled on the face of a child and that was baptism. This type of argument Carson dismissed as linguistically unsound and absurd.[52]

In his writings, Alexander Carson constructed a solid case for immersion as the only mode of baptism. He explained that as a result of the immersion into Christ, a person is colored or dyed by the character of Christ: "When a person is dipped in pure water, he is washed; still dipping and washing are two different things. Baptism is a washing, not from the meaning of the word itself, for as far as that is concerned, it might be a defilement; but because it is an immersion in pure water."[53]

Carson also wanted to know who were the proper candidates for baptism in the New Testament. The traditional line of reasoning for infant baptism was to argue from Acts where whole "households" such as those of Lydia, Cornelius and the Jailer were baptized. This represented the primary argument of the paedo-baptists and thus was the principal point attacked by Carson in his study of the scriptural subjects of baptism:

> We are indeed warranted to assume, that it was the usual practice to baptize every family that believed. But from the baptism of a thousand families, we are not warranted to conclude the baptism of every family when the head of it believed. The baptism of one family will prove that, all families in the same circumstances ought to be baptized.[54]

Carson concluded that "None can be saved by the gospel, but such as believe the gospel; none can be baptized with the baptism of the gospel, but such as believe the gospel. There is no exception to either."[55] He further reasoned from the Great Commission:

> That believers only are included in the baptism of this commission, is clear also from the command to teach the baptized: "teaching them to observe all things whatsoever I have commanded you." Here the persons baptized are supposed to be capable of being taught the other ordinances enjoined by Christ.[56]

Of infant baptism Carson remarked, "Ahh, my brethren! It is an awful thing to do in the Lord's name, that which the Lord has not appointed."[57] Finally, Carson summarized one of his own canons for Biblical authority.

Carson saw remission of sins as the primary purpose for baptism. Concerning Acts 2:38 he wrote: "Here baptism is connected with repentance and remission of sins. This baptism, then, cannot extend to infants."[58] In further reference to Acts 2:38 Carson wrote: "Can language be more clear? Does not this show, that in baptism, repentance and remission of sins are supposed with respect to the baptized . . . and this passage proves that none ought to be baptized but such as repent, and have their sins forgiven."[59]

Though earlier in his book Carson made the point that the word *baptizo* does not mean wash, he nevertheless insisted that washing was an effect of baptism:

> The death, burial, and resurrection, which are ascribed to baptism, take place in baptism, and by means of baptism. The washing away of sins, ascribed to baptism, is effected by baptism. This washing, this death, this burial, and this resurrection, then, cannot be the washing, death, burial, and resurrection, which are effected by faith, and which take place before baptism.[60]

H. Conclusion

The eight men surveyed in this chapter span 130 years of careful and devoted study of God's Word to discover its teaching on baptism. What an example they give of the restoration ideal in action. These early restoration pioneers were men of fierce independence and diligent study. The very thought that they were able to overcome the religious prejudices of their day and discover the New Testament teaching on anything is both astonishing and inspiring. They have shown us that restoration is not just a historical movement, but an ideal to follow in applying God's Word to their lives.

Students of restoration history have often asked who was the first person since the New Testament period to come to a full understanding of New Testament Christianity. The first was not John Glas, Robert Sandeman, Alexander Carson, or even Alexander Campbell. The first man was Archibald McLean who understood both the organization and worship of the church as well as all three aspects of New Testament baptism.

Endnotes

1. Philip Schaff, ed., "The Westminster Confession of Faith, 1647," *The Creeds of Christendom, With a History and Critical Notes*, III (New York: Harper and Brothers, 1919), p. 662.

2. Ibid., p. 662, footnote.

3. Ibid., pp. 662-663.

4. Ibid., p. 662, footnote.

5. Ibid., p. 663.

6. Ibid., p. 663, footnote.

7. Samuel Edward Hester, "Advancing Christianity to Its Primitive Excellency: The Quest of Thomas Grantham, Early English General Baptist (1634-1692)" (unpublished Th.D. dissertation, New Orleans Baptist Theological Seminary, New Orleans, 1977), p. 151. The author is indebted to Hester for making him aware of Grantham's work. Hester's work gives an excellent treatment of this early English Baptist who struggled with the meaning of baptism and was a seeker of New Testament Christianity.

8. Thomas Crosby, *The History of the English Baptists from the Reformation to the Beginning of the Reign of King George I*, Vol. 4 (London: n.p., 1738-1740), p. 77 cited in Hester, "Advancing Christianity to Its Primitive Excellency," p. 12.

9. Thomas Grantham, *Christianismus Primitivus; Or, the Ancient Christian Religion* (London: Francis Smith, 1678), "The Epistle Dedicatory."

10. Grantham, Ibid.

11. Hester, "Advancing Christianity to Its Primitive Excellency," p. 60.

12. See Lynn A. McMillon, *Restoration Roots* (Dallas: Gospel Teachers, 1983), for more information on the teachings and practices of John Glas and Robert Sandeman.

13. John Glas, *The Works of John Glas*, IV (Edinburgh: Alexander Donaldson, 1761), p. 194.

14. Glas, *Works*, IV, p. 207.

15. James Morison, ed., *Supplementary Volume of Letters and Other Documents. By John Glas, Robert Sandeman, and their Contemporaries* (Perth: Morison and Duncan, 1865), p. 8; and Glas, *Works*, IV, p. 207.

16. Glas, *Works*, IV, p. 208.

17. Glas, *Works*, IV, p. 209.

18. Ibid.

19. Glas, *Works*, IV, p. 198.

20. Ibid.

21. Glas, *Works*, IV, p. 201.

22. Morison, *Supplementary Volume*, p. xi.

23. Glas, *Works*, IV, p. 192.

24. Ibid.

25. Morison, *Supplementary Volume*, p. 38.

26. Glas, *Works*, IV, p. 202.

---

27. Daniel MacIntosh, ed., *Letters in Correspondence by Robert Sandeman, John Glas and Their Contemporaries* (Dundee: Hill and Alexander, 1851), p. 13.

28. Walter Wilson, *The History and Antiquities of Dissenting Churches and Meeting Houses in London, Westminster, and Southwark*, II (London: R. Edwards, 1810), pp. 228-229.

29. Alexander Carson, *Baptism: Its Mode and Subjects* (Reprint: Grand Rapids: Kregel Publications, 1981), p. xxxii.

30. Letter, James Haldane to John Campbell, February 19, 1808, cited in Alexander Haldane, *Memoirs of the Lives of Robert Haldane of Airthrey, and of His Brother, James Alexander Haldane* (New York: Robert Carter and Brothers, 1853), p. 325.

31. John T. Hornsby, "John Glas: A Study of the Origins, Development and Influence of the Glasite Movement" (unpublished Ph.D. dissertation, University of Edinburgh, 1936), p. 251.

32. Ibid.

33. Information on the meeting places of this and other groups is found in Wilson, *The History and Antiquities of Dissenting Churches and Meeting Houses in London, Westminster, and Southwark*, 3 vols. (London: R. Edwards, 1810).

34. Wilson, *History of Dissenting Churches*, explains that since in London there were several types of Baptists, the Scotch Baptists were called Sandemanian Baptists to describe the type of church government they practiced.

35. Archibald McLean, *The Commission Given By Jesus Christ to His Apostles* (10th ed.; Elgin: Peter MacDonald, 1847), p. 84. This work was originally published in 1786. Additional information on the Scotch Baptists can be found in D.W. Bebbington, ed., *The Baptists in Scotland* (Glasgow: The Baptist Union of Scotland, 1988).

36. Ibid.

37. Ibid., p. 85.

38. Ibid., p. 87.

39. Ibid., pp. 88-89.

40. Ibid., pp. 88-90.

41. Ibid., p. 90.

42. Ibid., p. 98.

43. Ibid., p. 100.

44. Ibid., p. 209.

45. Development of this point is found in Chapter VI of Lynn A. McMillon, "The Quest for the Apostolic Church: A Study of Scottish Origins of American Restorationism" (unpublished Ph.D. dissertation, Baylor University, 1972).

46. In attempting to refute Haldane's *New Views of Baptism*, he converted himself and published Alexander Carson, *Baptism: Its Mode and Subjects* (Grand Rapids: Kregel Publishing, 1981), p. 29. This work was originally published in 1831.

47. McMillon, "The Quest for the Apostolic Church," p. 157.

48. The 1981 edition of Carson, *Baptism: Its Mode and Subjects*, is a reprint of the 5th American edition of 1853 by Philadelphia: American Baptist Publishing Society, which was a reprint of the 1844 enlarged edition of the original.

49. Carson, *Baptism: Its Mode and Subjects*, p. 19.

50. James Morison, ed., *Supplementary Volume of Letters and Other Documents, by John Glas, Robert Sandeman, and their Contemporaries* (Perth: Morison and Duncan, 1865), p. xxxviii.

51. Carson, *Baptism: Its Mode and Subjects*, p. 77.

52. Ibid., p. 87.

53. Ibid., p. 34.

54. Ibid., p. 184.

55. Ibid., p. 173.

56. Ibid., p. 174.

57. Ibid.

58. Ibid., p. 180.

59. Ibid., p. 203.

60. Ibid., p. 161.

4

THE RECOVERY OF THE ANCIENT GOSPEL: ALEXANDER CAMPBELL AND THE DESIGN OF BAPTISM

John Mark Hicks

Alexander Campbell (1788-1866) was the acknowledged leader of the American Restoration Movement during its first years of expansion across the American frontier. It was his leadership and writing that gave the Restoration Movement its impetus in the 1820s and 1830s. Indeed, it was his call for a restoration of the "Ancient Order" and the "Ancient Gospel" which became the battle-cry of the American Restoration Movement.[1] Campbell's theology, then, through the pages of the *Christian Baptist* (1823-1830) and the *Millennial Harbinger* (1830-1870)[2] dominated the movement, but never more so than its initial stages.

In the beginning of the movement, his theology was not only

111

influential, but programmatic. He set the agenda for the movement. This is particularly true with respect to the issue of baptism. It was his debates, writing and influence which pushed the subject of baptism to the forefront of discussion. In fact, Campbell believed that baptism was an issue upon which his program of reform and unity depended. In 1851, reflecting on almost 30 years of controversial discussion about the subject, he states:

> I say, then, that in order to the *union of Christians*, we must have a definite and unmistakable term indicating one and the same conception to every mind. If, then, the Christian Church ever become really and visibly one, she must have one immersion, or one baptism.[3]

Baptism, then, in Campbell's mind became the one institution which could signal the union of all Christians in the visible church. Consequently, the discussion of the subject became a top priority for Campbell in the first years of implementing his unity movement. After all, if everyone believed that believer's immersion was right and proper, why could not everyone unite on that form of institution alone instead of offering conflicting opinions about it? Thus, Campbell spent most of the first 10 years (1823-1832) of his reformation calling upon the sects to give up their opinions and unite on what all believed was a scriptural baptism: the immersion of believers.

However, in the course of discussing the scripturality of believer's immersion, Campbell "discovered" what he believed was the true design and meaning of baptism. This discovery would have a significant impact on the progress of his unity movement. In fact, this discovery would ultimately be the reason the "Reforming Baptists" (as Campbell's followers were known) and the "Regular Baptists" (the Baptist group Campbell was associated with at the time) would separate. The Regular Baptists could not accept the legalism of "water salvation." As a result they drew a line between themselves and Campbell's followers.[4] It is the purpose of this chapter to detail this "discovery," its formulation and implementation within the context of Alexander Campbell's thought.

A. Historical Background

1. Campbell's Theological Background

Thomas Campbell (1761-1854), the father of Alexander Campbell, was an ordained minister in the Seceder, Anti-Burgher Church of Scotland.[5] The Seceder church was Presbyterian in form and Reformed in theology. Alexander Campbell, born in Ireland, was trained by his father in conjunction with a number of schools. In fact, Alexander taught with his father at the Rich Hill Academy beginning in 1805. In 1807, due to health problems, Thomas preceded his family to America where he was appointed to the Chartiers Presbytery of the Associate Synod of North America within the Seceder Church.

Alexander, while waiting for a ship to America, studied at the University of Glasgow for one year (1808-1809). In addition to his time at Glasgow, he also attended the Seminary of George Ewing, the Independent leader who had recently separated from the Haldanes due to their acceptance of immersion as the only scriptural form of baptism. Consequently, Campbell's theology at this point was thoroughly imbibed with Reformed and Paedobaptist concepts.

However, by the time that A. Campbell had reached American shores in 1809, he had become dissatisfied with the Presbyterian form of church order and was moving in the direction of Independency (e.g., Ewing and the Haldanes). In the spring of 1809 Campbell had even refused to participate in communion with the Seceder church due to the state of the church at that time. When Alexander arrived in America, he found that his father had been disciplined and suspended from the Seceder ministry on a variety of charges. One charge was that Thomas believed that there was no divine warrant for holding confessions and creeds as terms of communion. Eventually, on May 18, 1810, Thomas was deposed by the presbytery of Chartiers.

In the meanwhile, Thomas along with some other Independent Presbyterians had started the "Christian Association of Washington" in Washington, PA (August 17, 1809). Thomas wrote the basic document for this Association which is entitled *The Declaration and Address*. Its major emphases included an appeal for unity among Christians, the authority of the Scriptures alone, the right of private judgment and the evil of sectarianism. When Alexander arrived from Scotland in October of 1809, father and son found themselves in fundamental agreement. They had both rejected sectarian Presbyterianism (i.e., the Seceder Church), and both were now advocating Independency.

After attempting to unite with other Presbyterian bodies without success, the Campbells began an independent church on May 4, 1811. It was called the "Brush Run Church" located near Bethany, Virginia (now Bethany, West Virginia). What is interesting for our purposes is the attitude of the Brush Run Church toward baptism. The church determined that only one thing was required for admission into the visible church, and that is the correct answer to this single question: "What is the meritorious cause of a sinner's acceptance with God?" Of course, the answer is the blood of Jesus Christ. But it is important to note that baptism played no role in the acceptance or non-acceptance into the fellowship of the visible church at Brush Run. In fact, one of the reasons that the Campbells were not accepted into the Synod of Pittsburg (a Presbyterian synod of Unionists [as opposed to the Seceders]) was that the Campbells did not make baptism an indispensible term of communion, and they had raised doubts about the authority behind infant baptism.[6] In fact one member of the Brush Run church had never been baptized at all until his immersion on July 4, 1811.

Alexander Campbell, then, as the son of a Presbyterian minister, had been baptized as an infant. He was raised within a Presbyterian church whose theology was thoroughly Reformed or Calvinistic. As he turned toward Independency, he rejected baptism as a term of communion and began to doubt the propriety of

114

infant baptism.

2. Campbell's Immersion

Almost immediately after the beginning of the Brush Run church, two of the members refused to participate in the communion of the church[7] because they had not been immersed. Thomas Campbell reportedly admitted that only immersion was baptism, and he consented somewhat hesitantly to immerse them. They were immersed along with one other person on July 4, 1811. Interestingly, James Foster raised the question whether one unscripturally baptized (as Thomas Campbell was since he had been sprinkled as an infant) could immerse others. The question was apparently side-stepped for some time. At this point the Brush Run church totalled about 30 members.

The Brush Run church gave little attention to baptism. The Campbells had only publicly preached on the matter three times (Feb. 3, 1810; May 19, 1811; and June 5, 1811). It was becoming clear that the Campbells had rejected infant baptism as a human invention. This was obvious when, after the birth of Alexander's first child, Jane, on March 13, 1812, he did not baptize her. Instead, he devoted himself to a thorough study of the subject. The conclusion of that study would change the life of the Campbells.

The question had changed. No longer was the question: "May we omit believer's baptism which all admit to be divinely commanded?" Alexander came to the determination that he was an unbaptized person, and therefore was in violation of the command of God to be baptized. Consequently, he decided to be immersed upon a confession of his faith.

Alexander immediately informed his father of his decision. While the father was not immediately enthused, he accepted his son's decision. They finally obtained the services of Mathias Luce, an ordained Baptist minister of the Redstone Baptist Association, to baptize Alexander on a simple confession of faith. On June 12, 1812, Alexander Campbell and his wife, Thomas Campbell and his wife, Thomas' daughter Dorothea, and Mr. and Mrs. James Hanen were immersed. The next day 13 other members of the Brush Run church requested immersion at the hands of Thomas Campbell.

Alexander often recalled that he was not baptized in Regular Baptist fashion.[8] He had neither testified about some saving experience of the Holy Spirit nor had some Baptist church voted upon his immersion. Rather, he was immersed by Luce upon a simple confession of his faith in Jesus as the Messiah. As Campbell understood the Scripture that was all that was required of him. Campbell would never waver from that position. Anyone who was immersed upon that simple confession would be accepted by Campbell as a brother and a fellow-member of the visible church.

3. Campbell as a Baptist

In the fall of 1812 Alexander Campbell visited the annual meeting of the Redstone Baptist Association. Although he was relatively unhappy with the proceedings, Alexander began to accept preaching appointments in local Baptist churches. Through his acquaintance with them he gained a greater appreciation for their viewpoints. In the fall of 1813 the Brush Run church petitioned to unite with the Redstone Association as long as "no terms of union or communion, other than the Holy Scriptures, should be required." Their application was approved in 1815.

What had begun as an Independent Association in Washington, PA, had now become part of a Baptist Association. The Brush Run church, though still quite independent in thought, had associated itself with the Regular Baptist communion in Pennsylvania and Virginia. Alexander would spend most of his time doing itinerant preaching among the Baptist churches of Ohio, Pennsylvania and Virginia. He even travelled to the eastern seaboard (Trenton, New York, Washington) to raise money to build a church building in Wellsburg, Virginia.

However, the Redstone Association was not always

hospitable to the Campbells. When Thomas Campbell and his independent immersionist group in Pittsburg applied for membership in the Redstone Association in 1816, they were denied because they would not adhere strictly to the Philadelphia Confession of 1747. In 1816 Campbell delivered his soon-to-be infamous "Sermon on the Law" which was nòt well received by the Association. Campbell had too sharply divided the Old Testament and the New Testament for most of the Association's members. From that time on, only about 10 of the Association's 33 churches used Campbell's itinerant services.

The Campbells, however, did not limit themselves to the Redstone Association. In 1818, Campbell established the Buffalo Seminary which he conducted out of his own home. His father, beginning in 1819, assisted him in the training of young men. While the school was not long-lived (it closed in 1822), Campbell saw it as an opportunity to disseminate his reformation ideas. When the school closed, he immediately began his first journal, *The Christian Baptist*. The Campbell movement was not strong, but there were six independent churches associated with it by 1819 with a total of 200 members. Only one of these churches, the Brush Run church, was a member of the Redstone Baptist Association.

B. The Debates of 1820 and 1823

During his years as a member of Baptist Associations (1815-1830),[9] Campbell was working through his concept of unity and reformation. He attempted to work from within the Baptist fellowship as a whole. Indicative of this is the name of his first journal, *The Christian Baptist*. His ultimate separation from the Baptists is directly attributable to his developing views on the design of immersion. In this section we turn to the early years of that development.

1. The Campbell-Walker Debate[10]

117

In the fall of 1819 Mr. John Birch, a Baptist minister, became rather successful in baptizing a number of people near the town of Mt. Pleasant, Ohio. To counteract his influence, the local Seceder minister, Mr. John Walker, delivered a series of sermons in defense of infant baptism. Birch heard one of these lessons, and a lengthy correspondence began between the two. Walker issued a challenge to debate the issue with any Baptist minister. Birch sought the services of Alexander Campbell (who lived about 23 miles from Mt. Pleasant, Ohio). After three attempts, Birch finally persuaded Campbell to debate Walker.

The debate began on June 19, 1820 and ended the next day. The immediate result of the debate was the promotion of Campbell's reputation. All hands acknowledged that Walker had done poorly in the debate, and that Campbell was masterful. Campbell's fame spread across the Western Reserve (western Pennsylvania and eastern Ohio). The debate was published and immediately sold 4,000 copies.

The debate affords us an important reference point in the development of Campbell's baptismal theology. It gives us an extended discussion from which to glean Campbell's view of the purpose or design of immersion. It is important, then, to give close attention to what Campbell has to say at this early stage of his developing career as a reformer.

a. *The Basic Issue of the Debate.* Walker attempted to defend infant baptism along traditional lines. In particular, he rooted his argument in the covenant of grace. In good Presbyterian fashion, he argued that both baptism and circumcision are covenantal seals or signs of the same covenant of grace. Just as circumcision confirmed, or sealed, the blessings of the covenant of grace to Abraham and his descendants, so baptism confirms, or seals, the blessings of the covenant of grace to the Christian and his descendants. As Walker succinctly states in his opening address (p. 9):

I maintain that Baptism came in the room of Circumcision — That

118

the covenant on which the Jewish Church was built, and to which
Circumcision is the seal, is the same with the covenant on which
the Christian Church is built, and to which Baptism is the
seal . . . consequently the infants of believers have a right to Baptism.

Campbell responded that baptism could not have come in the
room of circumcision because they both represent two different
covenants. He denies that one single covenant lies behind both
ordinances. Circumcision "conveyed only temporal blessings to
the Jews" (p. 17). Circumcision was a sign and seal of the temporal promises of God to Abraham. Baptism, on the other hand,
"promises the remission of sins, and the gift of the Holy Spirit"
which circumcision did not (p. 18). Baptism is emblematic of the
spiritual blessings which derive from the new covenant, but circumcision belongs strictly to the old covenant. Since the new
covenant says nothing about baptizing infants, there is no authority for it (p. 25).

   b. *The Design of Baptism in the Debate.* It is important to
note that while, according to Campbell, baptism promises
spiritual blessings to its recipients, it does so only "figuratively" or
as a symbol (pp. 136-137). For instance, the phrase from Titus
3:5 ("the renewing of the Holy Ghost") is used "figuratively" with
respect to baptism and not in reality (p. 137). The "doctrinal import" of baptism is that it is "emblematic" of the gospel just like the
Lord's Supper is a "representation" of the Lord's body and blood
(pp. 136-137). Campbell summarizes his viewpoint in this
lengthy quotation (p. 138):

Hence *"the renewing of the Holy Spirit,"* is a phrase that denotes
the influence of the Holy Spirit, exerted on the whole soul of man;
and implies a death unto sin, a new life unto righteousness. But
the apostle illustrates this subject in the most clear and convincing
manner, in those passages I have read from him [i.e., Romans
6:4-6; Colossians 2:12; I Peter 3:21, JMH]. He shews it to be a
spiritual discovery of the import of the death and resurrection of
Christ, that produces this change upon the mind; and which leads

the subject of his gracious work to submit to "be buried with Christ in baptism" — "to be planted in the likeness of his death, that he may be in the likeness of his resurrection." The outward rite, then, must bear an analogy to the doctrine exhibited in and by it. Hence immersion in water, is a beautiful and striking representation of our faith in the death and burial of Christ; and our emerging out of it, a suitable emblem of his resurrection from the grave, and of our obligations to a new life: so that the sprinkling of a few drops of water has no analogy to the thing signified in Baptism.

It is important to note that Campbell explicitly argues that baptism is an emblem or sign of something that has already happened. The "renewing of the Holy Spirit" has already taken place and has led the subject of it to be baptized in order to signify or represent this work of the Spirit. The outward rite is a "representation" of the thing itself which has already been accomplished by the work of the Spirit. The blessing of justification is given to the sinner before his baptism, and can be obtained without baptism. As Campbell said earlier in the debate (p. 56):

> The called, cannot mean those whom every preacher invites to Baptism, but those whom the Lord calls by his grace or spirit. In this sense it is used, when calling is esteemed a blessing — "whom he called, them he also justified."

c. *The Design of Baptism in the Appendix.* When Campbell published the debate, he also published an extended appendix in which he deals with various subjects connected with infant baptism. The appendix was written during the summer of 1820 immediately following the debate. His main concern is to critique the concept of the "covenant of grace" and describes the various "covenants" of the Bible. He argues that there are multiple covenants in the Old Testament. He lists them as (pp. 154-165):[11]

1. The Covenant with Adam
2. The Covenant with Noah
3. The Covenant confirmed of God in Christ

4. The Covenant of Circumcision
5. The Covenant with all Israel at Sinai
6. The Covenant of Peace, or concerning the Sacerdotal Office
7. The Covenant of Royalty with David

Of these seven covenants, Campbell argues that only three of them had a "seal," or, as Campbell prefers "*confirmative mark*": Adam had the tree of life, Noah had the rainbow, and Circumcision had the mark of the flesh (p. 168). "These tokens attached to these covenants were truly seals, or *marks of confirmation*; visible and evincive of the thing" (p. 168). They are God's acts of guarantee to those who receive them.

In the New Testament, the only seal or confirmative mark which God gives is the Holy Spirit. Campbell writes (pp. 169-170):

> Under the New Testament, the only seal is the *mark* or *impression* which the spirit of God makes upon the heart or soul of the believer. . . . The only *seal* spoken of in the New Testament as the guarantee and property of all Christians, is *"this seal of the holy spirit."* Neither Baptism nor the Lord's supper are ever so called, nor can they be so called, in conformity to the meaning of words. . . .

Baptism and the Lord's Supper can only serve to confirm the faith of the individual, but they cannot serve to "seal" the salvation of God to the person. Only God can "seal" or "guarantee" His gift. "Baptism is an ordinance by which we formally profess Christianity" (p. 170), but it is not a seal. The seal of the Holy Spirit is all that is necessary for the assurance of the believer. It "is a sufficient guarantee and earnest, and *requires not any external ordinance to perfect it*" (p. 171; emphasis mine, JMH).

Baptism, therefore, is not necessary for the seal of the Spirit. Any believer may enjoy the "full blessings" of the new covenant without baptism or the Lord's Supper. Campbell makes this clear in the following paragraph (pp. 170-171):

121

The whole blessings of this covenant, have been as fully enjoyed by many who are now in Heaven, who could not, who did not, receive those ordinances, as by other saints in Heaven or in earth. The thief upon the cross, had as full enjoyment of them, as any other in ancient or modern times. And many, both under the Patriarchal and Christian age, have had all the blessings of redemption as fully bestowed upon them, as any who have been baptized, and have participated of the Lord's supper. Now if Baptism and the Lord's supper, were *the seals* of this covenant, it would follow that they who never had received them, were deprived of the security, for the enjoyment of this covenant, and of course, had no confirmation of it to them.

Campbell's point is simple. Believers of all ages whether in the Patriarchal, Mosaic or Christian ages are sealed by the Holy Spirit as a pledge or guarantee of heaven. They receive this by faith alone without the use or aid of any external ordinance or act. Campbell, it is clear, is simply explaining his own brand of Reformed baptismal theology. In Campbell's view, those whom he baptizes have already received the Spirit as a pledge and guarantee.[12] They are baptized to symbolize the spiritual blessings and to confirm their own faith.

    d. *The Design of Baptism in the Strictures.* In the second edition of the published Debate, Campbell added some 60 pages of response to a series of three letters written by Samuel Ralston which appeared in the *Presbyterian Magazine* of 1821. Campbell's response was written late in the fall of 1821 and appeared in the 1822 edition of the debate. As a result it gives a look at Campbell's thinking about baptism one year after the debate with Walker.

    In his *Strictures on Three Letters*, Campbell evidences the same view of the design of baptism as was apparent in his *Appendix* to the Debate. Campbell spends most of his time answering misrepresentations of his own position and key assertions by Ralston. The issue still centers around whether or not the Covenant of Circumcision and the New Covenant (to use Campbell's

122

terminology) are actually one and the same covenant of grace. Ralston takes, of course, the Presbyterian side of the argument. Campbell follows his premises through in disputing with Ralston.

In the course of his letters, Ralston made this statement to which Campbell strenuously objected: "I do not consider circumcision and Baptism as primarily designed for the purpose of building up believers in holiness; but as ordinances *designed for the conversion of sinners of a certain character*" (p. 241; emphasis mine, JMH). Campbell replied (pp. 241, 243):

> I fearlessly assert that Mr. R[alston] cannot produce one instance from the whole volume of Inspiration, of one person being converted by either circumcision or Baptism. . . . It is predicated on at least four gross errors. . . . The second, that the unregenerate are commanded by God, to make use of certain means to become regenerated, or those destitute of the spirit are to make use of means without the spirit, to obtain the spirit.

Campbell denies any relationship between baptism and the saving of the sinner other than an emblematic one. When Ralston argues that infants are regenerated "through Baptism as the appointed mean" (p. 244), Campbell responds (p. 244):

> Well spoken, Baptism the appointed mean of regeneration for those in the church!! Baptism the mean too of infant regeneration!!! Romanists, shake hands with the Rev. Samuel Ralston. . . .

By late 1821, then, Campbell's position had remained fundamentally the same. His view of the purpose and design of immersion is basically Reformed. It differs little, if any, from the views of his Baptist brethren of the day. Campbell makes no claim to be saying anything different nor do his Baptist readers understand him to be saying anything different. Instead, he is praised by them for the debate and its outcome.

2. The Reading of Errett's Pamphlet

When Thomas Campbell had been in Pittsburg in 1816, he had established a small church founded upon Independent principles in addition to teaching in an Academy. This was the church that had been rejected by the Redstone Association. One of the members of that church was Robert Richardson who was not only a one-time student of Thomas Campbell but who was also Alexander's future son-in-law. The Campbells would make frequent visits to Pittsburg due to their friendly relations with this church.

In Pittsburg, however, there was another congregation founded upon Independent principles. This church was founded by George Forrester who was also the principal of an Academy there. Robert Richardson attended this Academy as well. Forrester was a follower of the Haldane brothers. On occasions he lectured at the Buffalo Seminary until a drowning accident took his life in the summer of 1820. The man who replaced Forrester as both the leader of that congregation and the teacher in the academy was Walter Scott. Under Scott, this congregation would ultimately unite with the other Independent church in 1823 with the assistance of the Campbells.

Scott had moved to Pittsburg in 1819 as a Scottish Presbyterian (Unionist variety). Soon after meeting Forrester he was immersed and began to read the works of Haldane, Glas, Sandeman and Carson. Scott became so imbibed by the reading of these authors that by the time that he and Campbell met in the winter of 1821-22, they were fully of the same spirit and mind. Although the two had met previously in 1820 while Forrester was still alive and Scott was still a Presbyterian,[13] the first *significant* meeting between the two men took place in the Winter of 1821-22 when Alexander paid a visit to the city of Pittsburg. At this meeting they discussed for the first time the meaning of baptism in connection with the remission of sins.[14] In 1838, Campbell remembered that he had given some attention to the topic when he was preparing to publish the debate with Walker. He states he had not yet

124

turned his thoughts to the special *meaning* of Christian baptism. Either during that discussion or in transcribing it for the press, an impression was made on his mind that baptism had a very important meaning and was some way connected with remission of sins; but engaged so much in other inquiries, it was put on file for further consideration.[15]

Certainly Campbell's musing on the subject did not show up in his debate with Walker. On the contrary the sentiments expressed there were the opposite of what he would eventually conclude is the scriptural meaning of baptism.

The single item which seems to have turned the attention of both Alexander Campbell and Walter Scott to the topic of baptism's design is a pamphlet by Henry Errett, a Scotch Baptist in New York City. It was written in 1820, but came into Scott's hands first early in 1821. Scott was so excited by the pamphlet that he spent three months in New York City that year studying the practices of this Scotch Baptist Church. Though disappointed with the church, the impression that tract made upon his mind would excite him to study the matter of the design of baptism further. Also in the early fall of 1821, Mrs. Robert Forrester sent a copy of the tract to Campbell by way of John Tate. Just like Scott, Campbell obtained his first impressions of the design of baptism from this tract by Errett.[16]

The tract is straight-forward and simple in its approach. The first several pages are simply quotations from various New Testament passages (including Mark 1:4-5; Matthew 3:7; John 3:5; Mark 16:16; Acts 2:38; Acts 22:16; Romans 6:2-11; Galatians 3:26-28; Ephesians 5:25,27; Ephesians 4:4-6; Colossians 2:12,13; Titus 3:5-6; I Peter 3:21). In quoting these passages, Errett occasionally remarks that baptism is "connected" with "salvation," "forgiveness of sins," etc.[17] He summarizes his overview of these texts in this way:

From these several passages we may learn how baptism was viewed in the beginning by those who were qualified to understand its meaning best. No one who has been in the habit of considering it merely as an *ordinance*, can read these passages with attention, without being surprised at the wonderful powers, and qualities, and effects, and uses, which are there apparently ascribed to it. If the language employed respecting it, in many of the passages were to be taken literally, it would import, that *remission of sins* is to be obtained by baptism; that an *escape from the wrath to come* is effected in baptism; that *men are born the children of God* by baptism; that *salvation* is connected with baptism; that men *wash away their sins* by baptism; that men become *dead to sin and alive to God* by baptism; that the Church of God is *sanctified and cleansed* by baptism; that men are *regenerated* by baptism; and that *answer of a good conscience* is obtained by baptism. All these things, if all the passages before us were construed literally, would be ascribed to baptism. And it was a literal consideration of these passages which led professed Christians, in the early ages, to believe that baptism was necessary to salvation.[18]

It would be a mistake to stop here, however. Errett does not believe the passages should be taken in a "literal" sense. He compares a "literal" understanding of the words of Jesus at the Last Supper which gave rise to the "awful notion of transubstantiation." He decries the fact that a "literal" understanding implies the necessity of baptism for salvation. Such a notion gave rise to the "unauthorized" custom of infant baptism.[19]

Errett simply wants to argue that baptism should not be thought of *"only as an ordinance"*[20] or, as quoted above, "merely as an *ordinance*." Somewhere between the "literal" understanding of these passages (which yields the necessity of baptism) and the neglect of baptism as a mere ordinance of the church lies a middle ground, a *via media* for understanding the meaning and import of baptism. Errett saw this in the idea of "profession" whereby one "professes" his faith by act as well as by word. Just as men are to confess by word that they "have the remission of sins through the death of Jesus Christ," so also "by deed" they should "in baptism" confess that they have had their sins remitted. Believers, then, in baptism, have "professed to have their sins washed away . . . professed to be purified and cleansed. . . ."[21] Errett sees this profession of faith in the act of baptism as the act by which disciples recognize each other. It is to be regarded as "a prominent part of the Christian profession, or, in other words, that by which, in part, the Christian profession was made."[22] Errett concludes the extract provided by Baxter by noting the necessity of this immersion for fellowship among disciples:

> And if, on reflection, it should appear that these uses and pur-
> poses appertain to the one baptism, then it should be considered
> how far any can now be known, or recognized, or acknowledged
> as Disciples, as having made the Christian profession, as having
> put on Christ, as having passed from death to life, who have not
> been baptized as the Disciples were.[23]

Errett's tract, if put in the historical context of the Scotch Baptist movement, is easily understandable. It is an argument for the exclusion of the unimmersed from the fellowship of the visible church. It does not argue that baptism is necessary for salvation. In fact, it denies that very conclusion. Further, it does not argue that the remission of sins is obtained in immersion. Indeed, Errett understands that to be the "literal" interpretation to which he dissents. Rather, Errett's point is simply this: Christian profession involves immersion. Those who have not been immersed, then, cannot be recognized or acknowledged as Christians in the full sense of that term. Immersion, then, is to be regarded as a term of communion in the sense that the immersed cannot recognize the unimmersed since they have not professed their Christianity in deed as well as word.

This understanding of Errett's tract fits well against the background of the Scotch Baptist groups who were divided over the question of the unimmersed. Should the unimmersed be invited to commune with the immersed? Errett's tract, without making baptism essential to salvation or marking it as the point at which one receives the remission of sins, answers the question in the negative. Errett stresses the "connection" of baptism with the remission of sins only to show that baptism was more than a mere ordinance or command of God, but that this command had a special connotation. That connotation is not salvation itself, but the profession of salvation.. Therefore, baptism is not like other ordinances (such as to pray, sing, etc.), but is to be regarded as that ordinance by which one is "recognized" (not "becomes") as a disciple of Christ.

The effect of Errett's tract upon Campbell and Scott was to raise this very question with them, and to impress upon them the "professional" nature of immersion itself. Further, they seem not to have been altogether satisfied with Errett's dismissal of the "literal" understanding. However, it will be some time yet before either Campbell or Scott will come to a "literal" understanding. But in Campbell's next debate, the effect of the tract and subsequent discussions with Scott are quite evident.

3. The Campbell-Maccalla Debate

a. *Background to the Debate*. At end of the Walker Debate, Campbell had issued a general challenge to debate any Paedobaptist minister of good standing on the issue of infant sprinkling.[24] General dissatisfaction with Walker on the part of the Presbyterians made certain that someone would seek to answer Campbell's challenge. Rev. William L. Maccalla decided to accept the challenge. Campbell agreed to meet Maccalla in Washington, Kentucky in October, 1823. The debate began on October 15 and lasted till the 22nd.

After Campbell received the first letter from Maccalla, dated May 17, 1823, he "resolved to settle the true meaning of baptism before" he debated the subject again. Over several months Thomas and Alexander Campbell discussed the subject in some detail. In July or August of that summer Scott visited Bethany (the home of Alexander) for the first time, and they pursued the discussion further. The three agreed that Campbell should present arguments in the debate based upon the design of baptism and give full airing to them. In 1838, reflecting on the debate, Campbell wrote that the arguments based upon the design of baptism were the "cardinal aim and purpose of the whole discussion." Yet, Campbell admits, the views were, at the time, "perfectly *novel*" to them all.[25]

In the months just prior to the debate Campbell began his first journal, *The Christian Baptist*.[26] The prospectus for the journal was published in the spring of 1823, and the first issue rolled off the press on July 4, 1823. Campbell's purpose in issuing the journal was to "see sectarianism abolished and all Christians of every name united upon the one foundation upon which the apostolic Church was founded. To bring Baptists and Paedo-Baptists to this is my supreme end."[27] It was in the second issue of the *Christian Baptist*, September 1, 1823, that the connection between baptism and the remission of sins was first noted in print by a member of the fledgling American Restoration Movement. In an article entitled "Essay on the Proper and Primary Intention of the Gospel, and its Proper and Immediate Effects," Thomas Campbell made this statement:

Such being the gospel testimony concerning the love of God, the atonement of Christ, and the import of baptism for the remission of sins: all, therefore, that believed it, and were baptized for the remission of their sins, were as fully persuaded of their pardon and acceptance with God, through the atonement of Christ, and for his sake, as they were of any other article of the gospel testimony. . . .Or why could he have received baptism, the import of which to the believer was the remission of sins, had he not believed the divine attestation to him in that ordinance, concerning the pardoning of his sins upon his believing and being baptized? Every one, then, from the very commencement of christianity, who felt convinced of the truth of the gospel testimony, and was baptized, was as fully persuaded of the remission of sins, as he was of the truth of the testimony itself.[28]

Campbell's article did not seem to raise a stir in the pages of the *Christian Baptist*. Perhaps it went largely unnoticed since the

129

paper was so new. But clearly Thomas Campbell had also learned something from Errett's tract and from subsequent discussions with his son and Walter Scott. However, it is unclear to what extent this article represents a mature view. It seems, in fact, to rehearse Errett's tract more than advance upon its views. Campbell stresses full persuasion and assurance rather than the point at which remission of sins is received. While this article is significant as the first printed statement of the connection between baptism and the remission of sins, it does not appear to say anything more than Errett's tract nor is it identical to the position that will be preached across the Western Reserve in a few years.

One month prior to the debate, Alexander Campbell was in Pittsburg for the annual meeting of the Redstone Baptist Association. While no longer a member of the Association, he was present as a spectator.[29] During this time Campbell met with Scott and his father for the final time before the debate. The new understanding of the design of baptism was to be used as a major argument in the debate. This decision had tremendous significance.

b. *Campbell's Argument Based upon Design.* It was not until the second day and at the end of his first speech that Campbell raised an argument from the design of baptism against infant baptism. He did not even have time to fully make his argument, but only to slightly introduce it (p. 100).[30] He did, however, have opportunity to lay the bare groundwork for his presentation of the full argument. He emphasized that baptism is not like other ordinances such as praying, singing, praising, etc. Baptism is only "but *once* administered" and its unusual significance is indicated by various scriptures. Campbell then began to quote some of the same passages that Errett had quoted. From the quotations Campbell concludes, "I have thus, in the naked import of these testimonies, shown that it is of vast *import*, of glorious design" (p. 100). This is nothing more than what Errett had said in his tract, and clearly he is dependent upon it at this point.

While Maccalla understandingly ignored Campbell's argument at this point, Campbell returned to it in his third speech to give it a full definition (pp. 114-119). This is the fullest presentation that Campbell makes in the debate concerning the design of baptism. Campbell actually had two points to raise against infant baptism based upon the design of baptism. The first point is rooted in the necessity of faith for the forgiveness of sins. If faith is necessary for forgiveness, and baptism is connected with the remission of sins, then "baptism without faith is an unmeaning ceremony" since how can it be administered to those as a sign to whom the thing signified has not been given (p. 117)? In sum, "the nature and design of baptism is suited to believers only" (p. 126). The second is this: since baptism has some connection with the "remission of sins" (note the plural), why baptize infants who have never sinned or who are only guilty of one "sin" (note the singular, referring to "original guilt" or "original sin")? Campbell summarized his point in this way (p. 117):

> Our argument from this topic is, that baptism, being ordained to be for a believer a formal and personal remission of all his sins, cannot be administered unto an infant without the greatest perversion and abuse of the nature and import of this ordinance. Indeed, why should an infant that never sinned, that, as Calvinists say, is guilty only of *"original sin,"* which is an unit, be baptized for the remission of *sins!*

The premise of these arguments, of course, is that the design of baptism has some connection with the remission of sins. This was Campbell's major burden of proof. Campbell argues that he is not to be faulted for connecting baptism with the washing away of sins if Ananias did the same in Acts 22:16. Just as Paul believed him, Campbell believed him. Here, however, is what Campbell understands Ananias to mean (p. 116):

> When he was baptized he must have believed that his sins were *now* washed away in some sense that they were not before. For if his sins had been already in every sense washed away, Ananias'

address would have led him into a mistaken view of himself; both before and after baptism. Now we confess that the blood of Jesus Christ alone *cleanses* us from all sins. Even this, however, is a metaphorical expression. The efficacy of his blood springs from his own *dignity*, and from the *appointment* of his Father. The blood of Christ, then, *really* cleanses us who believe from all sin. Behold the goodness of God in giving us a *formal* proof and token of it, by ordaining a baptism expressly *"for the remission of sins!"* The water of baptism, then, *formally* washes away our sins. Paul's sins were *really pardoned* when he believed, yet he had no solemn *pledge* of that fact, no *formal* acquital, no *formal* purgation of his sins, until he washed them away in the water of baptism. To every believer, therefore, baptism is a *formal* and *personal remission*, or purgation of sins. The believer never has his sins formally washed away or remitted until he is baptized. The water has no efficacy but what God's appointment gives it, and he has made it sufficient for this purpose. The value and importance of baptism appears from this view of it.

This extended quotation is significant. It is the fullest statement available in the Maccalla Debate, and consequently must be used to interpret other statements by Campbell in the debate which appear isolated or unconnected with the argument based upon design. Indeed, this section should also serve as an hermeneutical tool for interpreting Thomas Campbell's article in the *Christian Baptist*. It is certainly the clearest statement on the design of baptism available in the writings of Campbell up to this point.

The vital question of our inquiry is this: When does a person receive or obtain the remission of his sins? Campbell answers that there are two senses in which a person receives the remission of his sins. There is a "real" or actual sense, and there is a "formal" or "personal" sense. The "real" sense corresponds to the actual point at which one receives the forgiveness of his sins. Campbell explicitly stated that "Paul's sins were *really pardoned* when he believed" and therefore he was immersed. The blood of Christ accomplished this without the waters of baptism. However, baptism was the point at which this *real* remission was personally assured to Paul when God gave his *"formal pledge"* (p. 118) to Paul that his sins had actually, even though previously, been remitted. No one is baptized, according to Campbell in the Maccalla Debate, to receive the *actual* or *real* remission of his sins, but everyone is baptized to receive or "obtain the *formal remission* of his sins" (p. 118).

Sometimes Campbell may refer to this "formal remission" without the term "formal." For instance, in his second speech, Campbell explicitly states "that remission of sins is bestowed through his name to all who believe and are baptized" (p. 110). However, it is clear from his later statements that he does not mean that baptism is the point at which one receives the *real* or *actual* remission of his sins. One receives this when he believes. Rather, baptism only bestows the *formal* remission of sins. Consequently, faith and baptism both bestow the remission of sins, but faith in the *real* sense and baptism in the *formal* sense.

c. *Campbell and the Baptists on Design.* Since Campbell believes that one is *"really pardoned"* when one believes, how does his view differ from that of the Baptists of his day? Campbell, in his own mind, saw a distinction between his view and that of his Baptist brothers. Indeed, he perceived within himself a movement from an old position to a new position.[31] Campbell did not lose the opportunity of the Maccalla Debate, with so many Baptists present, to distinguish his position from that of the Baptists in general. In the fourth speech of the second day, Campbell specifically addresses his Baptist friends (p. 125):

> My Baptist brethren, as well as the Paedobaptist brotherhood, I humbly conceive, require to be admonished on this point. You have been, some of you no doubt, too diffident in asserting this grand import of baptism, in urging an immediate submission to this sacred and gracious ordinance, lest your brethren should say that you make every thing of baptism; that you make it essential to salvation. Tell them you make nothing essential to salvation but the blood of Christ, but that God has made baptism essential to their *formal* forgiveness in this life, to their admission into his king-

dom on earth. Tell them that God has made it essential to their happiness that they should have a pledge on his part in this life, an *assurance* in the name of the Father and of the Son, and of the Holy Spirit, of their actual pardon, of the remission of all their sins, and that this assurance is baptism. Tell the disciples to rise in haste and be baptized and *wash* away their sins, calling on the name of the Lord.

In distinction from the Baptists, Campbell attaches a special importance to the formal significance of baptism. The concept of baptism as God's pledge to the believer that his sins have already been remitted Campbell perceives as not commonly accepted by his Baptist brothers. He urges them to begin to practice it. Baptism's special significance and importance derives from its connection with the "formal" remission of sins. Any "believer unbaptized has not his sins washed away in a very important sense" (pp. 124-125). Ministers of the gospel ought to use baptism as a means of formally assuring the believer that his sins have been forgiven. The event is God's pledge of the act.

The context for Campbell's statement is two-fold. First, baptism was often regarded by Baptists as simply another moral duty which ought to be rendered to God. It had no special significance other than it was a command to be obeyed. Campbell complained of this earlier in his second speech (p. 117-118):

> We have heard some Baptists reduce this significant ordinance to the level of a moral example, or a moral precept. . . . You place honesty and baptism on the same footing, as alike moral duties. "But," says another, "I was baptized in *obedience* to a divine command." I presume you *"don't steal"* for the same reason. You then make baptism and honesty alike moral duties. The intelligent and well-instructed christian, however, is baptized to obtain the *formal remission* of his sins.

Second, Campbell speaks to a Calvinistic audience which grew up on revivalistic evangelism and the mourning bench. It was the practice to ask the sinner to seek God at the altar of

134

prayer, and wait for His answer. The answer expected was some experience of the Holy Spirit which would assure the believer of his salvation. Campbell is implicitly arguing that instead of asking the believer to wait for an experience of the Spirit, he ought to be commanded to obey God in baptism and there receive the assurance that his sins have been forgiven. Baptism, not an experience of the Holy Spirit at the mourning bench, is God's "*formal pledge on his part* of that believer's personal acquittal or pardon" (p. 118).

d. *Campbell and Errett: Is There A Difference?* Campbell, like Errett, saw himself occupying some middle ground. On the one hand, both Errett and Campbell are clear that baptism is not the point at which one receives the *actual* remission of his sins. Campbell stated this explicitly with regard to Paul, and Errett dismissed the understanding as too "literal." Further, Errett and Campbell both regard baptism as more than a mere ordinance, or simply one of God's many commands. In particular, they both see baptism as the institution through which one is admitted to the visible church, or the kingdom of God on earth. Baptism is designed for entrance into the visible church. Errett stated that no one can be "known, or recognized, or acknowleged as Disciples" if he has "not been baptized as the Disciples were."[32] Campbell, using some of the same terminology, makes the same point in the Maccalla Debate (pp. 170-171):

> . . . that baptism was never designed for, nor commanded to be administered to a member of the church. Except a man be born of water he could not constitutionally enter it. But no one, recognized as a member of the christian church was baptized from the beginning of the New Testament to the end of it. —We read of them being added to the church when baptized, but not once of any being baptized as members of the church.[33]

On the other hand, while they both attached a special import or significance to baptism, Errett referred to baptism's "professional" nature. It is the believer's profession of faith in deed in ad-

135

dition to the formal profession by the mouth. Errett, therefore, attached the special significance of baptism to the *believer's action*.

Campbell, however, attached the special significance of baptism to the *action of God*. Baptism, according to Campbell, is God's pledge, not man's. It is God's profession, not the believer's. In the ordinance of baptism, God gives the believer a full assurance and a formal pledge of forgiveness. Baptism is God's gift which assures the believer of his salvation.

Consequently, while Campbell clearly draws on Errett in several places, the final result is that Campbell emphasizes the divine work of baptism and Errett emphasized the human work of baptism. This distinction is profound, and will, in the final analysis, motivate Campbell's development of his baptismal thought.

4. Analysis of Baptismal Development

In this section we have surveyed Campbell's baptismal theology from the Walker debate of 1820 to the Maccalla Debate of 1823. There can be little doubt that Campbell's view of the design of baptism has changed within these years. In 1820 Campbell held a strong Zwinglian view of baptism where no external thing can have any relationship with salvation. This is particularly exhibited in his *Appendix* to the Walker Debate.

However, by the fall of 1821 his views began to moderate somewhat. There is not a strong emphasis on the design of baptism in the *Strictures* against Ralston written during the Fall of 1821. Perhaps he had already read Errett's pamphlet before or during the writing of the *Strictures*. Yet, it is clear that Campbell did not devote a great deal of time to thinking through the issue of the design of baptism.

It was only in his meetings with Scott and his father Thomas Campbell that the issue was raised. Apparently, after all the parties had read Errett's tract, there was considerable discussion about the issue when they met during the winter of 1821-1822. However, these occasional meetings were not enough to

136

motivate a renewed study of the subject in earnest.

After his challenge was accepted by Maccalla in May, 1823, Campbell began to devote himself to the study of the design of baptism. He says that he determined "to examine this matter . . . with the zeal of a freshman."[34] After discussions with his father, and then discussions between himself, Thomas Campbell and Walter Scott, Campbell came to a firm conclusion about the design of baptism. Determined to teach the Baptists as much as the Paedo-baptists, he presented an argument against infant baptism based upon the idea that baptism is the formal pledge of God that the sins of the believer have been remitted. This position, both in his own mind and in fact, was a reversal of his attitude during and in the aftermath of the Walker Debate. This change in position is directly attributable to three things: (1) Errett's tract; (2) discussions with his father and Scott who were coming to similar conclusions; and (3) his own renewed study of the New Testament from this perspective.

However, Campbell's position did not remain static after the Maccalla Debate. And although Campbell often protested that he began to preach baptism for the remission of sins in the Maccalla Debate, he did not preach it in the Maccalla Debate the same way and in the same sense as he would later. In particular, Campbell moved from his position that Paul's sins were *"really pardoned"* when he believed, and only "formally" remitted when he was baptized. In 1828, Campbell had amended his position to argue that baptism is not only the point of "formal remission," but is also the point of the actual or real remission of sins. This is clearly evidenced by two statements in the *Christian Baptist*:

Nor do we lose sight of the forgiveness of our sins in immersion, because Papists have made a saviour of a mere ceremony. We connect faith with immersion as essential to forgiveness — and therefore, as was said of old, *"According to thy faith, so be it unto thee,"* so say we of immersion. He that goeth down into the water to put on Christ, in the faith that the blood of Jesus cleanses from all sin, and that he has appointed immersion as the medium, and the act of ours, *through* and *in* which he *actually* and *formally* remits our sins, has, when immersed, the actual remission of his sins.[35]

This, then, becomes ours when we become Christ's; and if we formally and actually become Christ's the moment we are immersed into his name, it is as clear as day that the moment a believer is immersed into the name of Christ, he obtains the forgiveness of his sins as actually and as formally as he puts him on in immersion.[36]

These statements cannot stand in any stronger contrast with Campbell's extended remarks in the Maccalla Debate. In the Maccalla Debate Campbell argues that baptism is only a "formal" washing away of sin, and that the actual washing took place prior to baptism at the point of faith. In the *Christian Baptist* of 1828 Campbell argues that the "actual" and the "formal" washings occur simultaneously. The blood of Christ still actually washes away the sin and the baptismal waters still formally washes away the sin, but the two actions are tied together. When one is formally washed, he is at the same time actually washed, and no believer has any assurance of the actual washing without the formal one. There can be no doubt that between 1823 and 1828 there has been a shift in Campbell's baptismal theology.

Within the five years between 1823 and 1828, Campbell underwent a deepening of his understanding of the design of baptism. It is no coincidence that his mature view of 1828 coincides with the explosive revival that began within the Restoration Movement in late 1827. We now turn our attention to Campbell's mature understanding of the design of immersion.

C. The Formulation of the Ancient Gospel

1. The *Christian Baptist* from 1823-1827.

a. *Christian Union*. In the April 5, 1824 issue of the *Christian Baptist* Alexander Campbell penned an article entitled "The

Foundation of Hope and of Christian Union."[37] Here, for the first time in the *Christian Baptist*, he addresses the issue of baptism. He raises the issue in connection with unity and the assurance of hope. His point is summarized in one sentence: *"The belief of this ONE FACT, and submission to ONE INSTITUTION expressive of it, is all that is required of Heaven to admission into the church"* (p. 177). The one fact is that Jesus of Nazareth is the Messiah and the one institution is immersion. "Every such person is a christian in the fullest sense of the word, the moment he has believed this one fact, upon the above evidence, and has submitted to the above mentioned institution" (p. 177). This is sufficient for admittance into the visible church, or the church on earth. This, therefore, ought to be the foundation for unity among the sects. Campbell's point here is not an exposition of the design of baptism. Instead, he is setting forth the essentials of unity among Christians in the visible church. Two things are required: belief of one fact and submission to one institution. Campbell has not, in this article, advanced beyond the understanding of baptism set forth in the Maccalla Debate. In fact, Campbell states that the belief of the one fact "can suffice to the salvation of the soul," but the "overt act of baptism" is "sufficient" for entrance into the church if accompanied with faith (p. 177).

b. *Christian Religion.* In the October and November 1824 issues of the *Christian Baptist* Thomas Campbell, under the byline "T.W.", wrote a two-part article entitled "Essay on the Religion of Christianity."[38] Campbell divides the Christian Religion into two aspects: internal and external. The internal principle is faith. The external principle is "certain acts and exercises of divine appointment" (i.e., "what is commonly called worship"; p. 62). "The first instituted act of christian worship is baptism into the name of the Father, and of the Son, and of the Holy Ghost" (p. 62). Here Campbell focuses on the Greek term *eis* which is translated "into" in the phrase "into the name of the Father," etc. The *eis* expresses relationship. "Thus a new and blissful relation to the Father, and to the Son, and to the Holy Spirit, is publicly recognized towards the believer, by an ordinance divinely and graciously instituted for this purpose" (p. 63). Baptism, then, is the "very first instituted act of obedience, in and by which the believing worshipper is openly declared to be of the household of faith and of the family of God . . ." (pp. 62-63).

Campbell is again repeating what has been previously said in the Maccalla Debate and reiterating the sentiments of the Errett tract. However, Campbell now sees an "indispensible necessity" of order between faith, baptism and all other acts of worship, including prayer (p. 73). While prayer is certainly the next immediate act of worship after baptism, baptism is a prerequisite for acceptable prayer (or worship in general). Campbell sees this order in Acts 22:16: first, be baptized and wash away sins, and second, call on the name of the Lord. He summarizes his point in this manner (p. 63):

> The heart first sprinkled from an evil conscience by faith in the blood of the atonement; and next, the body washed with pure water, declarative of the universal sanctification of the whole man, body, soul and spirit. Then, and not till then, can the believing subject draw near with a true heart, in full assurance of faith, and worship the Lord in the beauty of holiness, first having believed and obeyed the gospel.

Several matters of interest are raised here. First, it is important to note that Campbell still argues that the internal exercise of faith is the point at which the heart is sprinkled with blood. Consequently, one has a purified conscience previous to baptism. Second, baptism is a prerequisite for true and acceptable worship of God. "Now, and not till now, can the believing sinner, first sprinkled at the altar, and then washed in the laver, enter into the holy place without fear, as a qualified and acceptable worshipper" (p. 63). This statement must, again, be set in the context of the visible church, and the Campbells' quest for the unity of the church. The visible church, according to Thomas, can only ac-

140

cept immersed believers as "qualified and acceptable" worship-pers.

The importance of this position is seen when it is contrasted with the "mourning bench" scenario so common in the early nineteenth century. Campbell decries the fact that many are "in-discriminately urged to pray, as a means of salvation, that they may escape hell, without any immediate respect either to the altar or the laver" (p. 73). The apostolic order was: believe the gospel, be baptized, and then pray. With this order the one who seeks salvation can be assured that he has received it when he is im-mersed. Instead, the sects seek at the mourner's bench "inward impressions, exercises, and feelings; predicated upon some peculiar inward work of the Spirit, in order to ascertain the regeneration of the subject" (p. 72). Once the sectarian is satisfied with the "feelings" of the subject, then he baptizes him "merely, as an act of obedience to a positive command, and in imitation of Jesus Christ" (p. 72). Thus, baptism is "sunk to the dead level of a mere moral duty" rather than the formal pledge of God to the believer that his sins have been remitted (p. 72).

The Campbells, therefore, in the context of the *Christian Bap-tist* are calling for a reevaluation of the role of baptism in the con-version process, namely, to substitute baptism for the mourning bench. If one has enough faith to come to the mourning bench, he has enough faith to be immersed. If he is immersed upon faith, then he has God's solemn pledge that his sins have been remit-ted. This is the essence of their distinct plea to the Baptists. As yet, their position has not placed the point of salvation at the mo-ment of immersion. Rather, the saved believer, already cleansed at the altar, comes to the laver for the formal declaration of his salvation in order that he might be recognized as a true worship-per of God.

c. *The Unimmersed.* 1825 passed without anything but pass-ing references to baptism.[39] However in 1826 the issue of the unimmersed was raised in the *Christian Baptist*. "R.B.S." of Virginia wrote Campbell a letter, dated December 6, 1825, in which he decried the lack of "forbearance" among Haldane communities among whom he placed the adherents to the *Christian Baptist*.[40] Further, he opines that if any congregation would implement all that the *Christian Baptist* teaches, then he would say that "a new sect had sprung up, radically different from the Baptists, as they now are."[41] After responding to the charge that he was a Haldane, Alexander Campbell addresses the issue of "forbearance." He points out the Haldanes are more forbearing than the Virginia Baptists. He writes:

> . . . but one thing I do know, that several congregations in this connexion are far more "forebearing" than the Baptists in Virginia; for several of them receive unbaptized persons to the Lord's table, on the ground of forebearance. The congregation in Edinburgh in connexion with James Haldane, and that in Tubermore in connexion with Alexander Carson, two of the most prominent congregations in the connexion, do actually dispense with baptism on the ground of *"forebearance"*. . . . They say that when a Paido-Baptist gives evidence that he is a christian, and cannot be convinced that infant baptism is a human tradition, he ought to be received into a christian congregation as a brother, if he desires it, irrespective of this weakness.[42]

Interestingly, Campbell apparently agrees and disagrees with the Haldanes on this point. In his response to "R.B.S.," Campbell is willing to "allow a brother to exercise his own judgment" in matters of opinion, and Campbell himself is "willing to carry this principle to its greatest possible extent." This includes acknowledging, where possible, unimmersed persons as Christians. He states:

> So long as any man, woman, or child, declares his confidence in Jesus of Nazareth as God's own Son, that he was delivered for our offenses, and raised again for our justification; or, in other words, that Jesus is the Messiah, the Saviour of men; and so long as he exhibits a willingness to obey him in all things according to his knowledge, so long will I receive him as a christian brother and treat him as such.[43]

Thus, Campbell will accept the unimmersed as Christians under certain circumstances. However, this does not imply that he will admit them to the Lord's table or recognize them as members of the visible church. In fact, in the next issue of the *Christian Baptist* (May 1, 1826) Campbell admits that he is rather uncertain about some particulars in this connection. "An Independent Baptist" wrote, letter dated February 11, 1826, that Campbell was inconsistent in being united with the Mahoning Baptist Association (and consequently with the whole Baptist society) when the Baptist Society is founded upon the Philadelphia Confession of Faith.[44] Campbell responded that he was not a Separatist (though he once was one[45]), and admitted that he was struggling with the concept of communion among the sects. While Baptists generally sing and pray with Paedo-baptists, neither one would sit at the Lord's table with each other. In this context Campbell renders his own verdict:

> There is something like inconsistency here. It must be confessed, too, that the New Testament presents baptism as prior to social prayer and praise, as indispensably preceding these, as the Lord's supper. I have thought, and thought, and vacillated very much, on the question, Whether Baptists and Paido-Baptists ought, could, would, or should, irrespective of their peculiarities, sit down at the same Lord's table. And one thing I do know, that either they should cease to have communion in prayer, praise, and other religious observances, or they should go the whole length. Of this point I am certain. And I do know that as much can be said and with as much reason and scripture on its side, to prove that immersion is as necessary prior to social prayer, praise, &c., as it is to eating the Lord's Supper.[46]

It appears that, at this point, Campbell is uncertain what his attitude toward communing with the unimmersed is. He clearly believes that if an unimmersed person is obeying God according to his knowledge, then he is to be regarded as a Christian brother. Yet, he is also certain that immersion is a prerequisite to social worship and the Lord's table. Apparently, Campbell has yet to

143

draw a line, but he is moving ever closer to the exclusion of the unimmersed from the social worship of the church, particularly the Lord's table. As his perception of the design of baptism becomes clearer, he will draw that line, but yet retain a "forebearing" view of the unimmersed who are obeying God to the best of their knowledge.[47]

2. The Historical Background of the "Ancient Gospel" Series.

The rest of 1826 and the first half of 1827 passed without any significant reference to baptism in the *Christian Baptist*. In the fall of 1827 both theology and practice began to develop quickly. In the beginning of 1828 Campbell initiated his monumental series on the "Ancient Gospel." It was the events of the last six months of 1827 that enabled and encouraged Campbell to publish the views which he had only recently come to believe. There seems to have been two events that prompted Campbell to air his views: (1) his relationship with John Secrest; and (2) the success of Walter Scott's preaching and the related success of the Kentucky brethren.

a. *Relationship with John Secrest.* Elder John Secrest, a minister for churches in Belmont and Monroe Counties in Ohio, was a member of the "Christian Connection" associated with Barton W. Stone.[48] In the early summer of 1827, John Secrest had paid Alexander Campbell a visit at Bethany, Virginia along with William Mitchell. They discussed the issue of baptism, and particularly the design of baptism. After ascertaining that Secrest immersed believers, Campbell asked: "Into what do you baptize them?" When Secrest was dumbfounded, Campbell then explained to them the greater significance of the institution.[49]

Over the next three months Secrest baptized *"three hundred"* persons. The total number of baptized individuals exceeded one thousand when Secrest's co-laborers are also taken into account. When Campbell and Secrest saw each other on August 27th, Secrest reported the fruits of his labor and told Campbell that he "immersed them into the name of Christ for the remission of their

144

sins." Campbell went on to explain the fuller story in the *Christian Baptist*:

> Many of them were the descendants of Quakers, and those who had formerly waited for "the baptism of the Holy Spirit," in the Quaker sense of those words. But Brother Secrest had succeeded in convincing them that the *one baptism* was not that of Pentecost, nor that repeated in Caesarea, but an immersion into the faith of Jesus for the remission of sins. . . . Immense have been the crowds attending, and great the excitement produced by the simple proclamation of the gospel in the good old-fashioned simplicity of unlettered and untaught eloquence.[50]

It is apparent that Campbell was amazed by the response Secrest and his colleagues had on the frontier. Campbell himself did not, at this time, "call upon persons to come forward and be baptized for the remission of sins."[51] While it is not known exactly how Secrest preached "baptism for the remission of sins,"[52] it is clear that his success made a deep impression on Campbell. In fact, it may have been the motivating factor for the next step toward implementing the "Ancient Gospel" in the person of Walter Scott.

b. *The Preaching of Walter Scott.* In 1826 Scott moved to Steubenville, Ohio to teach in a local Academy.[53] That same year Scott attended the annual meeting of the Mahoning Baptist Association at the invitation of Alexander Campbell. In 1827 Scott was again invited to attend the annual meeting which met from August 23-27. Scott was there as a spectator along with several "Christian Connection" preachers (one of whom was John Secrest).[54] At the meeting the Beechville, Ohio church requested that the Association employ an itinerant evangelist to travel among the churches and assist in growth. The need was great since the Association showed only a net growth of 16 for the previous year (and only 18 the year before that). The total membership was only 492. Walter Scott was selected as the evangelist.

In the first several months Scott met with limited success, but November 18, 1827, would be a date that would change Scott's perspective on preaching. William Amend told the story in a letter to Scott:

> Now, my brother, I will answer your questions. I was baptized on the 18th of Nov., 1827, and I will relate to you a circumstance which occurred a few days before that date. I had read the 2d of the Acts when I expressed myself to my wife as follows: "Oh, this is the gospel — this is the thing we wish — the remission of sins! Oh, that I could hear the gospel in these same words — as Peter preached it! I hope I shall some day hear it; and the first man I meet who will preach the gospel thus, with him will I go." So, my brother, on the day you saw me come into the meeting-house, my heart was open to receive the Word of God, and when you cried, "The Scriptures no longer shall be a sealed book. God means what he says. Is there a man present who will take God at his word, and be baptized for the remission of sins?" — at that moment my feelings were such that I could have cried out, "Glory to God! I have found the man whom I have long sought for." So I entered the kingdom where I readily laid hold of the hope set before me.[55]

This event, and the lessons Scott learned from it, was like opening the flood-gates of the city. Within ten days he had baptized 30 individuals.[56] Within three weeks he had baptized 101 (56 in the first nine days of February).[57] In total, Scott and his colleagues baptized 800 persons in six months.[58] The numbers began to grow. Other workers in other fields began to multiply. In six months, Secrest had immersed 530.[59] From November 1, 1827 to May 1, 1828, Jeremiah Vardeman immersed 550; John Smith of Montgomery, Kentucky immersed 339 in the space of 3 months.[60] The "Reformation" was exploding with the introduction of a new perception of "baptism for the remission of sins."

Scott summarized the gist of his preaching in an article for the *Christian Baptist* which appeared in the March 2, 1829 issue.[61] He writes (p. 178):

146

The gospel proposes three things as the substance of the glad tidings to mankind — the remission of sins, the Holy Spirit, and eternal life. . . . In the proclamation of the gospel, therefore, these high matters were ordered thus — faith, reformation, baptism for the remission of sins, the Holy Spirit and eternal life; but how this order has been deranged. . . . Some have substituted sprinkling, some the mourning bench for the baptism of remission. . . . Others will immerse, but not for the remission of sins. . . .

Scott, in effect, put into practice what the Campbells and he had reasoned for several years. The mourning bench is not the way to call sinners to repentance, nor is it the place to seek salvation. Scott perceived that this had been the problem with the Mahoning Association's evangelism. Campbell gives this record of Scott's decision to evangelize with a new zeal and a new message:

He had not been long in the field of labor before he felt the need of something to propose to the alarmed and inquisitive sinner, more evangelical, more scriptural, and consoling, than the mourning bench or the anxious seat of modern revivalists. He had thought much of the ancient or original state of things in the church, but now his attention was specially and practically called to the ancient order of things in the proclamation of the gospel in practical reference to the conversion of the world. He repudiated the mourning bench and the anxious seat, and for these substituted what? *Baptism for the remission of sins!* We had, indeed, agreed that we would say to any person or persons inquiring what they should do just what Peter said, — *"Repent and be baptized in the name of the Lord Jesus in order to the remission of sins."* Nay, that we would "tell the disciples," those desiring to serve the Lord, "to rise in haste and be baptized, and wash away their sins, calling on the name of the Lord."* [*M'Calla's Debate, p. 144.] But it was to him, now, in the actual field of labor, as a new revelation; and, with great warmth and power, he persuaded the people, and many turned to the Lord.[62]

Scott had, however, introduced a new formula to the equation. He was explicitly baptizing individuals in order to receive the remission of sins, and not simply to show that their sins had already been remitted. Campbell alluded to this novelty when he noted that Scott immersed under a *"new formulary,"* i.e., "For the remission of sins and for the gift of the Holy Spirit, I immerse you in the name of the Father, and of the Son, and of the Holy Spirit." He then commented that "this bold style awakened the whole community." Campbell would later adopt this new formula with some modifications.[63]

3. Understanding the "Ancient Gospel."

In the first issue of 1828, January 7th, Campbell began a series of articles which were entitled "Ancient Gospel."[64] The series ran from January 7, 1828 to November 3, 1828 with a total of 10 articles. Reflecting on why he began the series, Campbell wrote that it was in order "to save the true meaning of baptism given in my debate [with Maccalla, JMH] from all excesses and innovations."[65] Apparently, Campbell feared a misinterpretation of his views, or at least that some well-meaning preacher or individual might advocate something which he did not want associated with his name. Consequently, after the first reports of large numbers of baptisms began to come in, Campbell set out to write an extended essay to fully develop his baptismal theology. In fact, though Campbell never mentions it in his writings, Scott visited Campbell in December, 1827 and encouraged him to write the series.[66] Campbell saw the opportunity to mold the movement's thinking on this point as it was beginning to grow at an accelerated rate. It would also be the time when Campbell would move beyond what he said in the Maccalla Debate, and he could, like Scott, now boldly assert "baptism for [in order to] the remission of sins."

Although Campbell would certainly advance a position in the series that was contrary to the Maccalla Debate, he insisted even at the outset of the series that he was not going to say anything more than what he said in the Maccalla Debate though he would say it in greater detail. In fact, Campbell would misstate what he actually said in the Maccalla Debate, reinterpreting it to fit his view of the design of baptism which he now held. In the first paragraph of his series he states:

> In my debate with Mr. Maccalla in Kentucky, 1823, on this topic, I contended that it was a divine institution designed for putting the legitimate subject of it in actual possession of the remission of his sins — that to every believing subject it did *formally*, and *in fact*, convey to him the forgiveness of sins. It was with much hesitation I presented this view of the subject at that time, because of its perfect novelty.[67]

Given the above analysis of the Maccalla Debate, it is clear that Campbell has put a different interpretation upon his words than were readily apparent when they were spoken. Now Campbell can refer to the "actual" reception of the remission of sins at the moment of baptism. Such an expression is absent from the Maccalla Debate. But as if to signal us to a change, Campbell further states that he has recently "been necessarily called to consider it more fully as an essential part of the christian religion" and that he is now "better prepared to develop its import, and to establish its utility and value in the christian religion."[68]

a. *The Order of the Ancient Gospel.* At the end of his third article, Campbell states what the order of the *"ancient gospel"* is: "first a belief in Jesus; next immersion; then forgiveness; then, peace with God; then, joy in the Holy Spirit."[69] This is Campbell's conclusion after three articles of argumentation.

He begins the explanation of the design of baptism by noting its relationship in typology, particularly basing his reasoning upon Hebrews 10:22. He asserts, as a thesis, that "christian immersion stands in the same place in the christian temple, or worship, that the laver, or both [bath] of purification stood in the Jewish: viz. BETWEEN THE SACRIFICE OF CHRIST AND ACCEPTABLE WORSHIP."[70] Just as the High Priest had to wash on the day of atonement before entering the Holiest of Holies, so the believer, before he can worship acceptably, must also have his body washed in the rite of baptism. Calling upon John 3:5, Titus 3:5 and Ephesians 5:26, Campbell concludes that Christian immersion is the antitype of the bath of purification for priests in the Old Testament. This is signaled by the use of the term "washing" itself.[71]

Since baptism corresponds to an Old Testament *"ablution,"* Campbell demonstrates the New Testament "plainly" affirms that "God forgives men's sins in the act of immersion."[72] He argues that disciples were conscious of a particular moment when their sins were remitted, and "a certain act by, or in which their sins were forgiven." That act was the washing which they could remember or forget.[73] Campbell introduces Acts 2:38 to verify this connection between remitted sins and baptism. There Peter "made repentance, or reformation, and immersion, equally necessary to forgiveness," and if no other word were written on the subject, Peter's command here would be "quite sufficient."[74] In consequence of what Peter says here Campbell believes that "in the very instant in which" a person is "put under the water," he receives "the forgiveness of his sins and the gift of the Holy Spirit." Consequently, *"christian immersion is the gospel in water."*[75] After introducing Acts 22:16, Acts 8:40, I Peter 3:21 and Romans 6, Campbell concludes that "christian immersion" has been "designed primarily for *the remission of sins.*"[76]

In the fifth essay Campbell addresses the issue of the "gift of the Holy Spirit." He argues that the Holy Spirit cannot dwell in a heart that has not been purged from guilt. "Before the Holy Spirit can be received," then, "the heart must be purified."[77] Since immersion is required before forgiveness can be bestowed, it follows that immersion is required before the Holy Spirit can be received. If one will not believe and be immersed based upon the promises of God, "there is not one promise in all the Book of God on which they can rely, or to which they can look, as affording ground of expectation for the Spirit of God to dwell in their minds, or to aid them while in unbelief."[78] Campbell's logic is relentless. The gift of the Spirit is the consequent of immersion:

> Because forgiveness is through immersion: and, because, in the
> second place, the spirit of Holiness cannot reside in any heart
> where sin is not absolved. This is an invariable law in the moral
> empire over which the Lord Jesus reigns.[79]

The "ancient order" then is: faith, immersion, forgiveness, reception of the Holy Spirit, and then the believer may be an acceptable worshipper of God. This order, proceeding from faith to the reception of the Spirit, was revolutionary for the early nineteenth century. The normal order, in the Calvinistic context of the frontier, was: regeneration by the Holy Spirit, faith, forgiveness and then immersion.[80] Against that background, many Baptists were shocked by Campbell's presentation in the "Ancient Gospel" series.[81] Campbell, by using this order, necessarily places regeneration in the context of baptism. A consequence of this understanding is that no unbaptized person can be rightly regarded as acceptable before God in the strictest sense. Consequently, Campbell explicitly states that:

> . . . baptism is the first act of a christian life, or rather the
> regenerating act itself; in which the person is properly born again
> — "born of water and spirit" — without which, into the kingdom
> of Jesus he cannot enter. No prayers, songs of praise, no acts of
> devotion, in the new economy, are enjoined on the unbaptized.
> Immersion, next to faith, is a sine qua non, without which nothing
> can be done acceptably. Let no man say this is a position too bold.
> I feel myself more impregnable here than ever did a garrison in the
> castle of Gibraltar. Let him that thinks otherwise try me.[82]

b. *The Foundational Principle.* The great concern of the revivalistic frontier, and, we might say, of theology in general, is: how can I know that I am saved? The struggle on the American frontier was complicated by the presence of the mourning bench in conjunction with Calvinistic theology. The knowledge of salvation in that setting depended upon inward sensations and subjective feelings rather than some objective event. Campbell, and the other Reformers with him, saw baptism as that event which could give the believer objective assurance instead of the subjective assurance he sought at the anxious seat. Thus, baptism gives the believer, what Campbell called, a *"sensible pledge."*[83] Campbell uses "sensible" in the sense of the external senses of the body, that is, the "five senses." Baptism is an objective event. It is visible to the eye, it is performed by the body. It is "sensible" as opposed to mental. Baptism, then, "gives the convert a *sensible pledge* that God, through the blood of Christ, has washed away his sins, has adopted him into his family, and made him an heir of all things through Christ."[84]

Since it is a "sensible" event (or an objective event), it is tied to a particular time and place. The believer can look back to a specific point in time as the precise moment he was saved. This is a key point for Campbell. He summarizes in this statement:

There is an instant of time, and a medium through which the forgiveness of sins is imparted as well as the other blessings growing out of adoption into the family of God. This point is worthy of much investigation, and capable of the clearest demonstration. That there is a definite instant of time in which all former sins are absolved, is generally admitted; but that there is a *sensible* means ordained by which this blessing is conveyed, is not so generally apprehended. . . .

Faith, indeed, is the grand medium through which forgiveness is accessible, but something more is necessary to the actual enjoyment of the blessing than a conviction that it is derived through the blood of Jesus. Hence those who had obtained this belief were commanded *to be immersed for the remission of their sins*, or to arise and be immersed and *wash away their sins*, invoking the name of the Lord.[85]

The choice here is between a subjective ground of assurance and an objective ground of assurance; between a gradual awareness of forgiveness and an instantaneous awareness of forgiveness. Campbell decries the common attitude among the Regular Baptists that assurance is based upon subjective feelings and is only gradually perceived by the believer. "The ancient christians," he argues, "had not to gather the conviction of the pardon of their sins from internal sensations or feelings." They were "derived from the divine testimony" that God had promised them if they would submit to immersion (an objective event), he would remit their sins.[86] In response to a querist regarding this question of assurance, Campbell summarizes his thoughts:

> But our consciousness of forgiveness is not made to proceed from any inward impulses, voices, or operations, either instantaneous or gradual, but from a sure and more certain foundation — the testimony of God addressed to our ears. If operations, impulses, or feelings, were to be the basis for our conviction, it would be founding the most important of all knowledge upon the most uncertain of all foundations. 'The heart of man is deceitful above all things;' and 'He that trusts in his own heart, is a fool.'

> For example, I believe the testimony concerning Jesus of Nazareth in the apostolic import of it. I then feel myself command-ed to be immersed for the forgiveness of my sins. I arise and obey. I then receive it, and am assured of it, because God cannot deceive. Thus I walk by faith — not by feeling.[87]

To some Baptists this smacked of the believer saving himself by the work of baptism. This contradicted grace.[88] Campbell's response is that the believer no more saves himself by being im-mersed than the believer does by believing. Rather, Campbell regards it as an act of grace that God has appointed "some act of ours as a medium of remission, that we might have the assurance of forgiveness, and know when we are forgiven."[89] The believer can look at the objective event of his immersion and enjoy the full assurance of his pardon because he believed the testimony of God and obeyed it in a specific act which was designed to be a "sensi-ble pledge." Baptism, then, is more God's work than man's. Baptism is God's pledge that the sins of the believer have been remitted. This was Campbell's position in the Maccalla Debate, but now Campbell is saying more — he is also saying that baptism is the point at which the sins of the believer *are* remitted.

c. *The Moment of Forgiveness.* Campbell's readers perceived the novelty of his views almost immediately. One reader posed this question, which is the essence of the issue itself: "Is a believer in Christ not actually in a pardoned state, before he is baptized?" Of course, in Reformed theology, the answer would be an unequivocal "Yes," since the believer is saved by faith alone. Campbell's response to the question underscores how far he had actually moved from the position exhibited in the Maccalla Debate:

> Is not a man clean before he is washed!! When there is only an imaginary or artificial line between Virginia and Pennsylvania, I cannot often tell with ease whether I am in Virginia or in Pennsylvania; but I can always tell when I am in Ohio, however near the line — for I have crossed the Ohio river. And blessed be God! he has not drawn a mere artificial line between the plantations of nature and of grace. No man has any proof that he is pardoned until he is baptized — And if men are conscious that their sins are forgiven and that they are pardoned before they are immersed, I advise them not to go into the water for they have no need of it.[90]

Another querist asked him whether or not faith only will entitle one to the heavenly reward. In an extended reply, Campbell begins with the adamant answer: "I answer positively: NO."[91] He calls upon his readers to arise from their Calvinistic slumbers to accept the testimony of God, and be immersed for the forgiveness of sins "and get under the reign of favor that your persons and your works may be accepted, and that the Lord may without equivocation or deceit say to you *well done*. Be assured he will not flatter you with *well done*, unless you have *done well*."[92] Forgiveness is not granted on faith alone, but as a consequent of the act of immersion through faith in obedience to the command of God.

Campbell's answers to these two querists illustrate the distinction between the Campbell of 1823 and the Campbell of 1828. Whereas in the Maccalla Debate, Paul was "really pardoned" before immersion, in the "Ancient Gospel," one is not pardoned until he is immersed.[93] Campbell constantly emphasizes that it is the "very instant" and "act" of immersion in which the believer receives the remission of his sins. For instance, he states, "I do earnestly contend that God, through the blood of Christ, forgives our sins through immersion — through the very act, and in the very instant."[94]

The remission of sins, according to the Campbell of 1828, is received in baptism both actually and formally. In the Maccalla Debate it was received only formally in the act of baptism, and it had been really received at the point of faith. The clearest illustration of the difference here comes during Campbell's written discussion with the Regular Baptist Andrew Broaddus of Virginia.

On July 5, 1830, Campbell issued his "Extra on the Remission of Sins." It was a supplement to the *Millennial Harbinger* intended to answer questions and give a full defense to his views on baptism for the remission of sins.[95] Andrew Broaddus, a leading Baptist in Virginia, replied with a tract entitled *Extra Examined* to which Campbell responded with 48 pages of his own in his "Extra Defended."[96] Campbell's complaint against Broaddus sets the Campbell of 1831 against the Campbell of 1823. He writes:

> Our friend Broaddus gives to baptism no instrumentality at all in the work of salvation. It only indicates, he says, 'that the subject, a *pardoned sinner*, (yes, a *pardoned* sinner) is *openly* and *formally* received into the Lord's service;' and that the pledge is *openly* and *formally* given that he devotes himself to Christ by thus visibly, or externally putting on Christ.' p. 39. This is its moral and religious value on the christian institution — a mutual pledge of an open and formal reception into the Lord's service.[97]

Broaddus' position differs little from Campbell's in the Maccalla Debate except that Campbell relates the formal significance of baptism to the remission of sins explicitly. Broaddus thinks of it as a mutual pledge, but Campbell in the Maccalla Debate thought it primarily as God's pledge to the believer. Yet, the difference between the two men is not substantial. But the Campbell of 1831 objects strongly to Broaddus' position, and argues that in baptism one receives, in that act and at that very instant, the remission of his sins, both formally and actually.

d. *What of the unimmersed?* Since Campbell argues that one is not forgiven before he is immersed, this naturally raises the question of the state of the unimmersed. This question did not escape the notice of Campbell's readers. One querist posed the question in this fashion: "But do you not expect to sit down in heaven with all the christians of all sects, and why not sit down with them on earth?" Campbell's answer became almost programmatic for him. While he answered in the affirmative, he also added:

> But while on earth I must live and behave according to the order of things under which I am placed. If we are *now* to be governed by the manners and customs of heaven, why was any other than the heavenly order of society instituted on earth? There will be neither bread, wine, nor water in heaven. Why, then, use them on earth? But if those who propose this query would reflect that all the parts of the christian institution are necessary to this present state, and only preparatory to the heavenly, by giving us a taste for the purity and joys of that state, they could not propose such a question.[98]

Campbell consistently makes a distinction between the glory and reign of heaven and the kingdom of God on earth (the visible church). When another objector argued that Campbell, by marking baptism as the point of justification (remission of sins) had unjustified "the larger portion of the Old and New Testament worthies,"[99] Campbell replied in this manner: "Many confound the salvation to be revealed at the final consummation, with the enjoyment of the present salvation which primarily consists in a deliverance from the guilt, pollution, and dominion of sin, and which salvation has been, under the Reign of the Messiah, proclaimed through faith and immersion."[100] Campbell does not presume to judge who will be in heaven and who will not. How many God will save "with faith or without it, whether with circumcision, baptism, or the law, or without them," he cannot say though he believes that the intervention of the Mediator can "render their salvation possible."[101] Campbell will only speak with certainty of those who comply with the testimony of God, that is, those who are immersed upon faith in the blood of Jesus.

There are really two questions latent here. The first is: can we expect to see the unimmersed in heaven? The second is: ought we to fellowship, break bread with, the unimmersed upon earth? The second question Campbell answers with an emphatic "No." There is no authority to commune with unbaptized persons.[102] Further, the unimmersed person cannot acceptably worship God, and as a consequence, the immersed cannot acceptably worship God with him. This is a direct implication of Campbell's argument in the first three articles of the "Ancient Gospel" series.

The first question, however, is more difficult. Campbell ambiguously answers: *"We cannot tell with certainty."* But Campbell holds as an opinion that "when a neglect proceeds from a simple mistake or sheer ignorance, and when there is no aversion, but a will to do everything the Lord commands, the Lord will admit into the everlasting Kingdom those who by reason of this mistake never had the testimony of God assuring them of pardon or justification here, and consequently never did fully enjoy the salvation of God on earth."[103] However, Campbell would never teach the unimmersed that they were "safe." Instead, he would encourage them to obey the command of the Lord to receive the full assurance of their pardon.[104]

In summary, then, Campbell holds hope for the unimmersed who are sincere and honest toward God. His hope is that God will pardon them and receive them into eternal glory given their circumstances, ignorance, etc. Campbell compares this hope to the hope of God saving "infants, idiots, pagans, &c" without faith.[105] But just like the pagan who is without faith, so with the unimmersed, Campbell can offer no earthly assurance of heavenly glory. God's testimony only gives assurance on earth to those who have submitted to the ordinance to which he has appointed the remission of sins, that is, baptism. As Campbell states: "There is but one action ordained or commanded in the New Testament, to which God has promised or testified that he will forgive our sins. This action is christian immersion."[106] Consequently, only the immersed may be recognized as Disciples and Christians in the fullest sense. As a result only the immersed are recognized as members of the visible church on earth.

D. Conclusion

We have followed Campbell's baptismal theology from his immersion in 1812 to the beginning of the *Millennial Harbinger* in 1830. By 1830, and the publication of his "Extra on the Remission of Sins," Campbell had arrived at his mature view of baptism.[107] However, his development was a slow one with several major adjustments.

The first adjustment came upon his arrival in America. He had rejected the sectarianism of his Seceder upbringing, and argued that baptism was not a term of communion at all. In his Presbyterian context, he argued that infant baptism was an uncertain institution.

The second adjustment came when his first daughter was born in 1812. After restudying the issue of immersion and believer's baptism, he concluded that all believers were commanded to be immersed. He judged himself an unbaptized person even though he had been baptized as an infant. Upon a simple confession of faith in Jesus as the Messiah, he was immersed by the Regular Baptist Mathias Luce. It is certain, at this point, that Campbell did not regard himself as an unsaved man, just an unimmersed one. The Walker Debate clearly signals us that Campbell did not connect baptism with salvation in any significant sense. There is no evidence that Campbell ever questioned or doubted the salvation of the pious unimmersed prior to the Maccalla Debate in 1823. Consequently, it is certain that when Campbell was baptized in 1812, he was not baptized in order to be saved. Rather, he was simply obeying a command which he had neglected through ignorance. He did not think that "unchristianized" his previous life.

The third adjustment came over a two-year period. From the fall of 1821 until the fall of 1823, Campbell was introduced to and contemplated the idea of baptism for the remission of sins. The Errett tract introduced him to the idea. His first impressions were bolstered by discussions with Scott and his father who had also read the tract. However, it was not until he was preparing to debate Maccalla that he devoted his attention to thoroughly studying the matter. In consultation with both his father and Scott, he determined to try his new understanding in the Maccalla Debate.

Indeed, Campbell did have a new understanding of baptism. He himself called it a "novelty." He distinguished his position from that of his Baptist brethren in the debate. Yet, his position was essentially that of Errett with some differences of emphasis. He argued that baptism was a "formal" and "personal" connection with the remission of sins. Baptism is God's pledge that the believer has had his sins previously remitted by faith. He also insisted that it is the mark of a true disciple — the member of the visible church.

The fourth adjustment came in the fall of 1827 and the winter of 1827-28. After Scott threw away the mourning bench and the anxious seat and began to boldly invite his listeners to the baptismal water for the remission of sins, Campbell began to be more explicit about the connection between baptism and the remission of sins. Now it was no longer considered as a mere symbol, or a sign of something that had already taken place. Instead, baptism was now regarded as the moment, the instant, the very act in which and by which, the remission of sins was bestowed. The baptismal event was the moment of remission. The believer had his sins remitted, not when he believed, but when he was immersed.

This viewpoint called in question one of the most cherished dogmas of the Regular Baptists. It eliminated the mourning bench or the anxious seat (which also disturbed many in the "Christian Connection" and prevented many of them from uniting with Campbell[108]). It eliminated the work of the Spirit in some subjective experience as the ground of assurance. It excluded the gift of the Holy Spirit prior to baptism. It disputed the teaching that one is saved by faith alone without baptism. It was in this context that many Baptist Associations began to withdraw from and censure Alexander Campbell, and all their actions included the issue of "water salvation."[109] The separation from the Baptists in general is directly attributable to Campbell's views on the design of baptism exhibited in the "Ancient Gospel" series.

The Campbell of 1809-1828 was not static in his views of baptism. He moved from Presbyterian (1809), to Baptist (1812), then to modified Baptist (1823), and finally to his mature view of the ancient gospel (1828). It is his mature view, explained as it was at the beginning of the Reformation's explosion in Ohio, Kentucky and Virginia, that dominated the American Restoration Movement. It has become one of its most distinctive features.

Endnotes

1. Campbell wrote two programmatic series in the course of the seven year existence of his first journal, *The Christian Baptist*. The first was entitled "A Restoration of the Ancient Order of Things," and it ran in 30 articles from January 3, 1825, to September 7, 1829. The series was fundamentally a description of the true marks of the visible church. The second programmatic series was entitled "Ancient Gospel" and it ran in 10 articles from January 7, 1828, to November 3, 1828. The series was a discussion of the design of immersion as the point of entrance into the visible church and salvation. (Hereafter, *Christian Baptist* will be abbreviated as CB.)

2. The *Millennial Harbinger* was continued for four years after Campbell's death by his son-in-law Robert Richardson. It ceased publication in 1870. (Hereafter the *Millennial Harbinger* will be abbreviated MH.)

3. MH, 22 (1852), p. 210.

4. See Hillyer H. Straton, "Alexander Campbell's Influence on the Baptists," *Encounter* 30.4 (1969): 355-365. This break was clear by 1830 when Campbell discontinued publication of the *Christian Baptist* and replaced it with the *Millennial Harbinger*. A number of Baptist Associations passed resolutions against Campbell and his followers: The Dover Association (December 31, 1830; see MH, 2 [1831], pp. 76-84); Appomattox Association (see MH, 1 [1830], pp. 261-62); and the most famous of all was the Beaver Creek Anathemas (see CB, 7 [1830], pp. 198-203, 292-294; MH, 1 [1830], pp. 174-177). The one thing all of these had in common was Campbell's view of the design of immersion.

5. All biographical information, unless otherwise noted, is derived from Robert Richardson, *Memoirs of Alexander Campbell*, 2 vols (Philadelphia: J.B. Lippencott & Co., 1868; recently reprinted in Indianapolis, IN: Religious Book Service, n.d.). For a general account of the development of baptism in the early Restoration Movement, see Carl Spain, "Baptism in the Early Restoration Movement," *Restoration Quarterly* 2 (1957), pp. 213-219.

6. See Richardson, *Memoirs*, I:335-347. These early years are meticulously described by William H. Hanna, *Thomas Campbell: Seceder and Christian Union Advocate* (reprint; Joplin, MO: College Press Publishing Co., Inc., n.d.).

7. James Foster was a member of an Independent congregation in Rich Hill, Ireland when the Campbells persuaded him to come to America with them. He heard John Walker and Alexander Carson, two famous Scotch Baptists, preach in Ireland. In fact, Alexander Campbell in a letter to his uncle in 1815 wrote that "I am now independent in Church government; —of that faith and view of the gospel exhibited in John Walker's seven letters to Alexander Knox, and a Baptist in so far as respects baptism" (as quoted by H.C. Armstrong, "Disciples and Scotch Baptists," *The Shane Quarterly* 2 [Apr-Jul 1941]: p. 360). James Foster, as one of the founders of the Christian Association and the Brush Run church, had a significant impact upon the thinking of the Campbells. Just prior to the founding of the Brush Run Church, Campbell had made this comment about infant baptism: "As I am sure it is unscriptural to make this matter a term of communion, I let it *slip*. I wish to think and let think on these matters" (Richardson, *Memoirs*, I:392).

8. MH, 3 (1832), p. 319. For example, concerning the confession of Peter in Matthew 16:16, Campbell writes: "For my own part, I was immersed on this very confession and for that grand object, by special covenant and stipulation with the Baptist who immersed me; and for adhering to this confession alone, we have been separated from that community. They often baptize into the penitent's own experience" (MH, 9 [October 1838], p. 467). See also the account in MH, 19 (1848), pp. 282-283 and CB, 2 (1824), p. 37. Campbell's

concern was simply to obey the will of God. He did not regard this as the point of his own salvation. Indeed, Richardson argues that at this time, immersion itself was subservient to unity (see Richardson, *Memoirs*, I:399).

9. Campbell removed himself from the Redstone Association in 1823 and joined the Mahoning Baptist Association in 1824. He remained a member of the Mahoning Association till it dissolved in 1830.

10. All quotations from the Campbell-Walker Debate are taken from Alexander Campbell, *Debate on Christian Baptism Between Mr. John Walker, a Minister of the Secession, and Alexander Campbell, To Which is Added a Large Appendix by Alexander Campbell. Second Edition Enlarged with Strictures on THREE LETTERS Respecting Said Debate, Published by Mr. Samuel Ralston, a Presbyterian Minister*. Pittsburg: Eichbaum and Johnston, 1822; reprinted by Hollywood: Old Paths Book Club, n.d.). Quotations from the above book will be noted in the text.

For a thorough discussion of the historical background of the Campbell debates and an analysis of them, see Bill J. Humble, *Campbell & Controversy: The Debates of Alexander Campbell* (reprint with additions: Joplin, Missouri: College Press Publishing Company, 1986).

11. Campbell argued that four of these covenants belonged to the "*dispensation of the law*" since they were tied to the particular nation of Israel. These are: the Covenant of Circumcision, Covenant at Sinai, the Covenant of Peace, and the Covenant of Royalty. All the blessings of these four covenants are enjoyed by virtue of "*natural birth*" (p. 166).

12. Note this question and answer in the Appendix (p. 207): "Q. 98. Do the Baptists believe that all *they* receive are born from above? — A. Yes: in the judgment of charity they consider them as *professing* what they possess: hence they are justified in baptizing them." Also, in the debate Walker quoted ancient authors such as Origen and Cyprian, and Campbell responded: "The Infant Baptism of those who first introduced and taught it, was Baptism that washed away all previous guilt: it was, in fact, a purgatorial rite. . . . Even the Baptism of believers they had so far perverted, as to make it purgative of all sins before committed" (Campbell, *Debate*, pp. 119-120).

13. Though the traditional "first meeting" is usually said to have been in 1821-1822, it seems clear to me that the first meeting was in 1820 while Forrester was still alive. Campbell has this recollection (MH, 19 [1848], p. 552): "Some time in 1820 I was first introduced to brother Walter Scott, lately from Scotland, then a Presbyterian, residing with Mr. Forrester, of Pittsburg, a Haldanian, from Paisley, Scotland." Scott confirms this in the *Evangelist*, 1838, p. 268 when he states that "eighteen years ago" he first made his acquaintance with Alexander Campbell. My understanding is that the meeting in 1820 was an incidental one while Forrester was still alive, but that the meeting of 1821-1822 is more significant since it was the first time the two ever discussed "baptism for the remission of sins" with each other.

14. Dwight E. Stevenson, *Walter Scott: Voice of the Golden Oracle, A Biography* (Joplin, Missouri: College Press, n.d.), pp. 37-39; and William Baxter, *Life of Walter Scott with Sketches of his Fellow-Laborers, William Hayden, Adamson Bentley, John Henry, and Others* (Nashville: Gospel Advocate Co., n.d.), pp. 64-68.

15. MH, 19 (1848), p. 467.

16. Scott tells this story along with a small extract from the tract in the *Evangelist* (1838), pp. 283ff. Baxter, pp. 46ff. also contains an extract from the tract. Stevenson, pp. 38-39. Interestingly, Richardson in his *Memoirs* never mentions this particular tract.

17. Baxter, pp. 47-51.

18. Ibid., p. 51.

19. Ibid.

20. Ibid., p. 52.

21. Ibid.

22. Ibid.

23. Ibid., p. 53.

24. Campbell, *Debate on Christian Baptism*, p. 141.

25. MH, 9 (1838), p. 468.

26. It was Walter Scott who persuaded Alexander Campbell to add the name *Baptist* to the title when Campbell himself simply wished to call it *The Christian*. Their hope was that they would attract the attention of the Baptists to their style of Reformation. See Baxter, p. 73; and Richardson, *Memoirs*, II, pp. 49-50.

27. As quoted by Richardson, *Memoirs*, II, p. 135.

28. CB, 1 (1823), p. 35. The article is authored by "T.W." It was known sometime later that "T.W." referred to Thomas Campbell (cf. A.S. Hayden, *A History of the Disciples of the Western Reserve* [Cincinnati: Chase & Hall, Publishers, 1875; reprinted by Indianapolis, IN: Religious Book Service, n.d.], p. 78). Richardson tells us that it was intended for the first issue of the paper, but it was left out due to lack of space, see *Memoirs*, II, p. 83. It is, in my opinion, certain that Thomas Campbell meant nothing more than Errett's tract at this point. Later in the same article he writes: ". . . for such was the import of the gospel testimony, as we have seen, that all who professed to believe it, whether they were intelligent persons or not, understood *at least so much* by it that it gave assurance of pardon and acceptance with God to every one that received it; that is, to every baptized believer: consequently every one that was baptized, making the same profession, he both though himself, and was esteemed by his professing brethren, a justified and accepted person. Hence we do not find a single instance, on the sacred record, of a doubting or disconsolate christian. . . ." (CB, 1 [1823], pp. 36-37).

29. Campbell had received word that he was to be tried for heresy concerning his "Sermon on the Law" delivered on August 30, 1816. In order to keep from being excommunicated just prior to his debate with Maccalla, Campbell moved his membership from the Brush Run Church (which was a member of the Redstone Association) to the Wellsburg Church in Wellsburg, Va. The Wellsburg Church then petitioned to join the Mahoning Baptist Association and was accepted. Consequently, the Redstone Association could take no action against Campbell since he now belonged to a different Association. For a detailed report of these events see MH, 19 (1848), pp. 553-557.

30. Alexander Campbell and W.L. Maccalla, *A Public Debate on Christian Baptism Between the Rev. W.L. Maccalla, a Presbyterian Teacher and Alexander Campbell to which is added An Essay on the Christian Religion by Alexander Campbell* (London: Simpkin and Marshall, 1842; reprinted by Kansas City: Old Paths Book Club, n.d.). All quotations from the debate will be noted in the text. The popularity of the debate is indicated by the fact that within one year nearly 6,000 copies were sold (cf. CB, 2 [1824], p. 40).

31. MH, 9 (1838), p. 468. Campbell strenuously protests that he had not come to this conclusion about the design of baptism until he began his preparation for the Maccalla Debate.

32. Baxter, p. 530.

33. Campbell uses the "church" here in the sense of the visible church or the church on earth. He is not speaking of the universal, invisible church or heavenly glory. His meaning is the same as Errett's on this point. The statement submitted by the Wellsburg Church in August 1823 for admission into the Mahoning Baptist Association expresses Campbell's viewpoint (which is no accident since he was the elder of the church; cf. CB, 2 [1824], pp. 37-38). Interestingly, it corresponds exactly with the above interpretation of the Maccalla Debate: "Every one that believeth by means of the demonstration of the Holy Spirit and the Power of God, is born of God, and overcometh the world, and hath eternal life abiding in him: that such persons, so born of the Spirit, are to receive the washing of water as well as the renewal of the Holy Spirit in order to admission into the Church of the living God" (Hayden, p. 32). Note that one is born of the Spirit before he is born of water in this quotation, and that only one born of water is to be admitted into the visible church.

34. MH, 9 (1838), p. 468.

35. CB, 5 (1828), p. 222.

36. Ibid., p. 256.

A.B. Jones, *The Spiritual Side of Our Plea* (St. Louis: Christian Publishing Co., 1901), pp. 70-192, argues in great detail that Campbell never relinquished this distinction between the "reall" and "formal" remission of sins with respect to baptism. He argues that Campbell always maintained the position exhibited in the Maccalla Debate. However I believe he has misunderstood Campbell on some important points. (1) Jones equates "personal remisson" with "real remission," but Campbell states that personal remission comes at the point of immersion since immersion is the point at which the individual becomes personally assured of his forgiveness. Thus, personal remission is he same as formal remission in the Campbell of 1823. (2) Jones fails to recognize that Campbell used "actual" and "real" remission as synonyms, and that Campbell claimed in 1828 that the actual remission of sins occurs at baptism. (3) Jones' reading of Campbell confuses his statements about the unimmersed. Campbell is not certain of the salvation of the unimmersed, but he does not deny the possibility (even probability in certain cases). If Jones' reading is correct, then Campbell should have no doubt about real forgiveness already belonging to the unimmersed believer. (4) Jones makes the mistake of misreading Campbell's thoughts concerning the intent of the believer's heart (or the "remission of sins in anticipation through faith"). While in the Rice debate Campbell spoke of receiving pardon through "anticipation," it is clear that "anticipation" is not "actual." Campbell remarks: "I believe that when a person apprehends the gospel and embraces the Messiah in his soul, he has in anticipation received the blessing. . . . He anticipates the end of his faith — his actual emancipation from sin" (Alexander Campbell and N.L. Rice, *A Debate Between Rev. A. Campbell and Rev. N.L. Rice, on the Action, Subject, Design and Administration of Christian Baptism* [Lexington, KY: A.T. Skillman & Son, 1844], p. 522). The "actual emancipation" takes place at the moment or instant of baptism. Jones has made the fundamental mistake of reading all of Campbell's writings from the vantage point of the Maccalla Debate. Instead, he should recognize a fundamental difference between the Campbell of 1823 and the Campbell of the 1830s (even 1828). This mistake is still common among the writings of the Disciples, see Stephen J. England, "Alexander Campbell's on Baptism in the Light of the Ecumenical Movement," in *The Sage of Bethany: A Pioneer in Broadcloth*, compiled by Perry E. Gresham (Joplin, Missouri: College Press Publishing Company, 1988), pp. 95-116, esp. pp. 106-107, 114-116.

The Presbyterian minister, N.L. Rice, confronted Campbell with the difference between the Campbell of 1823 and the Campbell of the later years. After quoting the Maccalla Debate where Campbell argued that Paul was "*really* pardoned" when he believed, he quoted from the *Christian Baptist* (5:181) where the Eunuch had been "actually forgiven in the act of immersion" (*Campbell-Rice Debate*, p. 524). Rice comments: "I leave those who can, to reconcile these contradictory views" (p. 524). Campbell did not respond to Rice's charge of contradiction in this specific instance after he quoted the passages from the Maccalla Debate and the *Christian Baptist* in that speech.

In 1851 Campbell published a compendium of his writings on baptism with some original material (*Christian Baptism with its Antecedents and Consequents* [reprint; Nashville: Gospel Advocate, 1951]. This book demonstrates a position in distinction from the Maccalla Debate. Campbell lists three "consequents" of baptism: adoption, sanctification and justification (pp. 220-254).

37. CB, 1 (1824), pp. 176-178. Quotations in this paragraph come from this article. Page numbers of the article are given in the text. For a discussion of the role of baptism in connection with unity, see William D. Carpe, "Baptismal Theology in the Disciples of Christ," *Lexington Theological Quarterly* 14.4 (1979): pp. 65-78.

38. CB, 2 (1824), pp. 61-65, 72-75. All citations in this paragraph are from that article, and are noted in the text.

39. The only reference by the editor, Alexander Campbell, to baptism is found in CB, 2 (1825), p. 225, where he states concerning Colossians 2:12: "But the Spirit of God intended by this phrase to shew that christians in baptism had represented to them their resurrection with Christ to a new life, through a belief of the great power of God, exhibited in raising Christ from the dead." There is nothing here that indicates any change of the viewpoint from earlier statements in 1823 and 1824. Theophilus, on the other hand, had more to say in *Christian Baptist* 2 (1824), pp. 102, 105.

40. CB, 3 (1826), pp. 176-179.

41. Ibid., p. 178.

42. Ibid., pp. 182-183.

43. Ibid., p. 183.

44. Ibid., pp. 197-200.

45. Ibid., p. 203: "for I was once so strict a Separatist that I would neither pray nor sing praises with any one who was not as perfect as I supposed myself."

46. Ibid., p. 204.

47. See chapter 5 of this book for a detailed view of Campbell's mature outlook on the unimmersed.

48. Chapter 7 of this book discusses Stone's movement and his relationship with the "Christian Connection."

49. Hayden, pp. 80-81.

50. CB, 5 (1827), pp. 71-72.

51. *Evangelist*, 6 (1838), p. 275, in a letter from Campbell to Walter Scott dated April 19, 1832.

52. Scott disputes that Secrest actually baptized individuals "for the remission of sins" in the same sense that he would later that year, cf. *Evangelist*, 6 (1838), pp. 277-278. This smacks of "who was first" rivalry, but it is indicative of perception that something *new* happened in 1827.

Campbell even argued that Elder Jeremiah Vardeman had practiced "baptism for the remission of sins" after the Maccalla Debate (MH, 9 [1838], p. 470). Vardeman was Campbell's moderator for that debate.

The resolution to this conflict appears clear to me. There were many who may have practiced "baptism for the remission of sins" prior to 1827 as a result of the Maccalla Debate. Campbell himself claims to have done so (MH, 9 [1838], p. 469). However, the teaching on baptism in the Maccalla Debate is not the same as the teaching on baptism in the 1828 *Christian Baptist*. In 1827 a subtle shift took place. "Baptism for the remission of sins" was now understood, particularly by Scott, to refer to the moment that the remission of sins is actually received. In consequence, some of those that even Campbell had immersed after 1823 were re-immersed after 1827 due to the change in understanding (see *Evangelist*, 6 [1838], p. 276).

Consequently, those who practiced "baptism for the remission of sins" within the Reformation after 1823 did so with the understanding of the Maccalla Debate. That understanding had undergone such a change in 1827 that when Scott began immersing on the Western Reserve, it was not only the practice that was different but the theology as well. This Campbell could never fully recognize, and he may have been blinded by a subtle pride on this point. All his life he would claim that he first preached "baptism for the remission of sins" in

1823, but could not recognize that what he wrote in 1828 was substantially different from what he preached in 1823 (see MH, 2 [1831], "Extra Defended," pp. 2ff. and 9 [1848], pp. 467-469). I believe that Jones, *Spiritual Plea*, was deceived by Campbell's pride on this point since Campbell's perception of never having changed his mind is the foundation of Jones' argument.

53. Interestingly, when Scott moved to Steubenville there were three "reforming"churches there: (1) a Haldane (called "Church of Christ"); (2) a Stonite ("Christian Church"); and (3) a Regular Baptist Church which was a member of the Mahoning Baptist Association. Scott joined the first one. See *Evangelist*, 1 (1832), p. 94.

54. A detailed discussion of the meeting along with the official minutes may be found in Hayden, pp. 54-71. See also Baxter, pp. 83-86. The account given in the text is taken from Hayden unless otherwise noted.

An additional point about this annual meeting of 1827 was the decision to undenominationalize the Association. The Association voted to set aside its denominational character and accept "Christian Connection" preachers into its fellowship. In 1830 it would vote to dissolve itself as an ecclesiastical entity and simply become an annual meeting for fellowship and prayer. For a discussion of how the revival of 1827-1829 affected the unity and communion of the Reformers and the Christians, see Ronald Bever, "The Influence of the 1827-29 Revivals on the Restoration Movement," *Restoration Quarterly* 10.3 (1967): 134-147.

55. Baxter, p. 113. Baxter comments: "This event, which forms an era in the religious history of the times, took place on the 18th of November, 1827, and Mr. Amend was, beyond all question, the first person in modern times who received the ordinance of baptism in perfect accordance with apostolic teaching and usage" (p. 108). John Secrest, and surely Alexander Campbell, would dispute Baxter's claim here.

56. CB, 5 (1828), p. 173, reported in a letter from Scott dated December 4, 1827. Campbell refers to it as "an experiment in preaching the *ancient gospel.*" Campbell became concerned that Scott was abusing the "ancient gospel," or at least felt the need for someone responsible to take a firsthand look at the preaching. He sent his father, Thomas, to be with Scott for several days on the Western Reserve. Thomas Campbell came back with a resounding endorsement, calling it a "bold push," cf. *Evangelist*, 6 (1838), pp. 270ff. and Baxter, pp. 158ff.

57. CB, 5 (1828), p. 200, reported in a letter from Scott dated February 10, 1828.

58. CB, 5 (1828), pp. 271-272.

59. CB, 5 (1828), p. 173. In CB, 5 (1828), p. 130, Campbell remarked that Secrest had baptized 490 up to November 23, 1827, and "it is not more than five months since he began to proclaim the gospel and christian immersion in its primitive simplicity and import." After the Secrest meeting with Campbell in November, 1827, Scott obtained the services of Secrest's companion James G. Mitchell to assist him. Secrest and Mitchell had met Scott when Scott was traveling to see Campbell in Wellsburg. Cf. Hayden, pp. 93-94.

60. CB, 5 (1828), pp. 271-272. The Mahoning Association on the Western Reserve in Ohio would baptize 3,000 through Scott and his colleagues in the next three years where the whole Association had only baptized under 100 in the previous two, cf. MH, 1 (1830), pp. 415, 449. The Mahoning Association of 1830 was six times the size of the same churches in 1827.

61. CB, 6 (1829), pp. 177-179. The author signs his name as "Philip," but this is the name which Scott used. Campbell identified him in CB, 4 (1827), p. 240. Scott used it in honor of Philip Melancthon, Luther's right hand man. Baxter, pp. 117-126, gives a full view of Scott's perspective in preaching the "ancient gospel."

62. MH, 20 (1849), p. 48.

63. MH, 9 (1838), p. 469.

64. CB, 5 (1828), pp. 128-130; 164-168; 179-182; 221-223; 229-232; 254-257; 276-279; and CB, 6 (1828), pp. 14-17; 72-74; 97-100. In addition, Campbell answered questions about the series in two articles entitled "A Catalogue of Queries — Answered," 6 (1829), pp. 164-168, 192-197. In fact, Campbell intended to start this series on the "Ancient Gospel" in the December issue of that paper (see CB, 5 [1827], p. 123), but there was no room for it. The fact that Campbell had prepared an article for the December issue may indicate that Scott's success was a minor part of his motivation in the beginning. Perhaps more weight is to be given to the success of Secrest. Even if Campbell had heard of Scott's success in December, 1827 (which is probable), the success was meager in comparison with Secrest.

65. MH, 9 (1838), p. 489.

66. See Scott, *Evangelist*, 6 (1838), pp. 278-281. In fact, Scott encouraged Campbell to begin his series by discussing faith rather than immersion. Campbell, however, chose to get straight to the point.

67. CB, 5 (1828), p. 128.

68. Ibid.

69. CB, 5 (1828), p. 182. Campbell's more refined order appears in the ninth essay in the series where he sees six points: faith, reformation (repentance), immersion, remission of sins, Holy Spirit, eternal life. He writes that they are not related "as cause and effect; but they are all naturally connected, and all, in this order, embraced in the glad tidings of salvation" (cf. CB, 6 [1828], p. 72). Scott, for the sake of simplicity in preaching (so as to use five fingers), reduced the order to: faith, repentance, immersion, remission of sins, Holy Spirit (cf. MH, 3 [1832], p. 298).

70. CB, 5 (1828), pp. 128-129.

71. Ibid. Also, CB, 5 (1828), p. 166: "We all admit that there is no public outward, or symbolic washing in the name of the Lord Jesus, save christian immersion. To refer to it as a *washing*, indicates that it was an ablution."

72. Ibid., p. 165.

73. Ibid., p. 166.

74. Ibid., p. 167. As he introduces the discussion of Acts 2:38, he makes it clear that *eis* ("for") means "*in order to obtain* the remission of sins" (p. 167).

75. Ibid., p. 168. Earlier in the essay, Campbell had stated that baptism is the "gospel in *water*," just as the Lord's supper is the gospel "in *bread and wine*" since both are external ordinances which exhibit the gospel facts, cf. CB, 5 (1828), p. 164. (Scott was not particularly appreciative of this phraseology, see *Evangelist*, 6 [1838], p. 281). Further, Campbell is insistent upon the fact that it is at the "very instant" of the act of immersion, "in, and by, the act," that one receives the remission of his sins (cf. CB, 5 [1828], p. 167).

76. Ibid., p. 180.

77. Ibid., p. 231.

78. Ibid., p. 232.

79. Ibid.

80. Campbell calls attention to this on numerous occasions. In fact, he set up a chart to illustrate the differences between a Presbyterian, Regular Baptist, Quaker and others on this very point of order (cf. CB, 6 [1828], pp. 72-73).

81. The first visible instance of this kind of reaction in the *Christian Baptist* is a letter from J. in CB, 6 (1828), pp. 23-24. For a more extended response, see the letter from "C.F. of Baltimore, MD" in CB, 7 (1830), pp. 173-176.

82. CB, 5 (1828), p. 231.

83. Ibid., p. 279.

84. Ibid.

85. Ibid., pp. 254-255.

86. CB, 6 (1829), p. 166.

87. Ibid., pp. 165-166.

88. CB, 7 (1830), pp. 173-176. Campbell's response is found on pages 176-181.

89. Ibid., p. 181.

90. CB, 6 (1829), p. 197.

91. Ibid., p. 194. In CB, 7 (1830), pp. 176-177, he responds to another objector: "Not an instance do I know of the pardon of sin by faith only. . . . But under the former economy blood was necessary to forgiveness; and under the new economy water is necessary. — Faith is the principle of action in both — and they are the means, not 'agents,' through which God imparted remission."

92. CB, 6 (1829), p. 195.

93. See CB, 5 (1828), pp. 222, 256.

94. Ibid., p. 277.

95. MH, 1 (1830), "Extra."

96. MH, 2 (1831), "Extra Defended" (appended to the back of the second volume).

Andrew Broaddus (1770-1848) was Campbell's arch-rival among the Baptists in Virginia. According to his son and biographer, "Of all the opponents which Mr. C[ampbell] encountered in the early stage of his Reformation, Elder Broaddus was decidedly the most formidable. . . . in A[ndrew] B[roaddus], Mr. C[ampbell] met 'a foeman worthy of his steel'" (Andrew Broaddus, ed., *The Sermons and Other Writings of the Rev. Andrew Broaddus, with a Memoir of His Life by J.B. Jeter, D.D.* [New York: Lewis Colby, 1852], p. 29). Broaddus and Campbell first met in the late autumn of 1825 (Broaddus, p. 24), and while there was congeniality between them for several years, Broaddus ultimately broke off fellowship with Campbell. His son comments that it was the "Extra on Remission of Sins" that was the final straw: "Mr. Broaddus was one of the last to relinquish the hope of reclaiming Mr. C[ampbell] from what he deemed the path of error . . . but the appearance of the MH Extra, in which his particular and objectionable views were more fully disclosed, put an end to all his hopes" (p. 28).

97. MH, 2 (1831), "Extra Defended," p. 1. Broaddus and Campbell squared off again in the *MH* of 1842 (pp. 145-150). Again Broaddus admits a "sense in which remission of sins is connected to baptism" yet denies that "the actual remission of sins" is "suspended on the performance of a subsequent act," i.e., baptism. He will grant that baptism is a *"visible certificate,"* "the *sensible pledge* of remission — the *formal* washing away of sins." Campbell, however, argues that the actual and the formal are simultaneous in the act of baptism.

98. CB, 6 (1829), pp. 193-194.

99. CB, 7 (1830), p. 174.

100. CB, 7 (1830), p. 176.

101. Ibid., p. 176.

102. MH, 1 (1830), p. 474.

103. MH, 2 (1831), "Extra Defended," pp. 44-45.

104. MH, 1 (1830), p. 474.

105. MH, 2 (1831), "Extra Defended," p. 44; see also CB, 7 (1830), p. 176.

106. CB, 6 (1829), p. 165.

107. Although there may have been further development after 1830, as some have argued (see Joseph Belcastro, *The Relationship of Baptism to Church Membership* [St. Louis, Missouri: The Bethany Press, 1963], pp. 24-27), that is not the concern of this essay.

108. See Dean Mills, *Union on the King's Highway* (Joplin, Missouri: College Press Publishing Company, 1987), pp. 67-68; 146-147.

109. This was a definite change on the part of the Baptists. While there had been some hostility to Campbell before the "Ancient Gospel" series, he was tolerated. In fact, when they did remonstrate against him in the early 1820s, it was not the issue of baptism which motivated them. It was his view of the Spirit, or church order, etc. It was not until after the "Ancient Gospel" series that baptism became the central issue between the Reformers and the Baptists. This indicates that late 1827 and 1828 did actually see a substantive change in baptismal theology and practice on the part of Campbell. The example of Broaddus in note 96 serves to illustrate this conclusion.

5

ALEXANDER CAMPBELL ON CHRISTIANS AMONG THE SECTS

John Mark Hicks

It has been the historical slogan of the American Restoration Movement that they are not the only Christians, but Christians only.[1] While this specific slogan is not present in the writings of Alexander Campbell, the concept certainly is. The purpose of this chapter is to examine the nature of this concept in Campbell in relation to his views on baptism. There are three reasons why such an examination is profitable. First, there has been considerable discussion in recent years concerning Campbell's exact position on this issue. Consequently, historical accuracy demands an examination of the evidence. Second, it forces us to reflect upon the historic goal of the Restoration Movement as it was initially conceived by its most prominent leader. Whether to accept or reject that initial goal is left to the reader; its validity is not the topic of discussion here. Third, a thorough presentation of Campbell's position will enable us to evaluate it with respect to its own intrinsic merit.

Due to considerations of length, this study is limited to the first ten years of the *Millennial Harbinger* (1830-1839). It was during these years that the issues surrounding the concept of "Christians among the sects" became most acute. In particular, these years encompass both Campbell's controversy with Dr. Thomas concerning reimmersion and the infamous Lunenberg letter itself. The controversy which raged in the *Millennial Harbinger* during the 1830s involved three basic questions. This chapter is divided according to the logical development of these three fundamental points. The first section will deal with the reimmersion controversy. Specifically, are there Christians among the Baptists? The second section will deal with the state of the unimmersed. Specifically, are there Christians among the unimmersed (e.g. Presbyterians)? The third part will attempt to systematize Campbell's position on fellowship in relation to these two groups. Specifically, ought the American Restoration Movement to commune with the unimmersed, or those immersed by sectarians?

A. The Immersion of Alexander Campbell

As one approaches the various questions which are the concern of this chapter, it is important to remember the circumstances of Alexander Campbell's own immersion. This is important because it informs his understanding of the state of all those who were once like him or were immersed like him. Consequently, this discussion prefaces the questions of reimmersion, the unimmersed and fellowship.

At the time of his immersion on June 12, 1812, Campbell had not, according to his son-in-law, come to an exact idea concerning the design of baptism. Richardson states that "the full import and meaning of the institution of baptism was, however, still reserved for future discovery."[2] Campbell himself explained that he was not immersed for the explicit purpose of receiving the remission of sins. He placed himself within the category of those who were immersed simply upon a confession of faith in Christ without any explicit knowledge that the immersion was "for the remission of sins." He writes:

> I was immersed by a Regular Baptist, but not in a Regular Baptist way. I stipulated with Matthias Luce that I should be immersed on the profession of the one fact, or proposition, *that Jesus was the Messiah, the Son of God* . . . Brother Spears (who was a Regular Baptist, JMH) accompanied him, and on this profession alone I was immersed; nor have I ever immersed any person but upon the same profession which I made myself.[3]

However, the fact that Campbell was not immersed for the explicit purpose of obtaining the remission of sins does not mean, according to his own thinking, that he did not, in fact, receive the forgiveness of sins at that point. As we will see below, Campbell maintained that one who was immersed upon a Biblical faith received the remission of sins whether he knew he was receiving it at that point or not. Consequently, while Campbell was unaware at the time of his immersion that this was the point at which he was receiving the remission of sins, he nevertheless received it at that point. He was not baptized in the "Regular Baptist way" in the sense that he did not give a testimony of any kind of experience nor was he voted on by the church. Campbell's response to the reimmersion controversy comes from this background.[4]

The only real contrary evidence to this point comes from Campbell's widow in an interview published in the *American Christian Review*. There she states:

> Some of the brethren say that because "remission of sins" was not named at his baptism, he was not scripturally introduced into

Christ's kingdom. Alexander Campbell was baptized into the full faith of the forgiveness of his sins, when baptized into Christ's death, and a full hope of the resurrection unto eternal life; having been planted in Christ in the likeness of His death, that he was assured he should participate in His resurrection, and this burial and resurrection imply a death unto him, and an enjoyment of a new life in Christ, no longer living a servant of sin, nor yielding his members to serve sin. Of course, he was freed from the guilt and pollution of sin, and fully enjoyed a new life, with the pardon of all his past sins, for the promise was to him.[5]

There are several important points to be considered in evaluating this statement. First, she maintains that the "remission of sins" was not named at his baptism, but that he still received it. She does not deny that "remission of sins" was not named, but she only denies that he was not thereby scripturally baptized. This is nothing more than what Campbell had always said concerning any who were immersed upon a Biblical faith, but who were unaware of the specific design of baptism with respect to the remission of sins. Second, she does not state for what purpose Campbell was moved to be immersed, but only what he received when he was immersed. Campbell always argued that one need not understand everything about what God promises in baptism in order to receive all of them. There is nothing in her statement inconsistent with Campbell's own position. He believed that one could be scripturally immersed without the specific knowledge that baptism was for the remission of sins.

In response to the assertion that Campbell was consciously immersed "for the remission of sins" in 1812, it can be argued that Campbell held an essentially Reformed (Calvinist) conception of baptism in his early years. This is indicated by a careful examination of the following statement in the MacCalla debate:

The blood of Christ, then, *really* cleanses us who believe from all sin. Behold the goodness of God in giving us a *formal* proof and token of it, by ordaining a baptism expressly 'for the remission of sins.' The water of baptism, then, *formally* washes away our sins.

174

The blood of Christ *really* washes away our sins. Paul's sins were *really pardoned* when he believed, yet he had no solemn pledge of the fact, no *formal* acquittal, nor *formal* purgation of his sins, until he washed them away in the water of baptism. To every believer, therefore, baptism is a formal and personal remission, or purgation of sins. The believer never has his sins formally washed away or remitted until he is baptized.[6]

The distinction between "real" and "formal" cleansing is nothing more than the Reformed distinction between the "sign" and the "thing signified." Reformed theology admits no instrumental relationship between the "sign" and the "thing signified," but argues that the "thing signified" (salvation) is already possessed when one receives the "sign." Thus, Calvin is able to say that:

baptism should be a token and proof of our cleansing; or (the better to explain what I mean) it is like a sealed document to confirm to us that all our sins are so abolished, remitted, and effaced that they can never come to his sight, be recalled, or charged against us. For he wills that all who believe be baptized for the remission of sins.[7]

Campbell, like Calvin, could speak of "baptism for the remission of sins" and simply mean the symbolic or formal representation of what had already taken place.[8] However, Campbell did not always hold this early position. His extra "Remission of Sins" abundantly demonstrates a change in position. For instance, he states that "this act of faith [immersion] was presented as that act by which a change in their state could be effected; or, in other words, by which alone they could be pardoned."[9]

Campbell exhibits a change in his baptismal theology from the MacCalla debate to the *Millennial Harbinger*. While in the Mac-Calla debate baptism did not convey the forgiveness of sins through faith (though it did formalize or symbolize it), yet in the 1830s baptism actually conveys this forgiveness, both formally and actually. Consequently, if Campbell believed that Paul was already forgiven when he believed before and without baptism in 1823, it is historically certain that Campbell himself believed that he was pardoned when he was immersed. Therefore, he was not immersed "for the remission of sins" in the sense that he was immersed in order to receive the remission of sins. Rather, he was immersed to obey a requirement of God which he had recently learned from studying Scripture. It was almost a decade later when Campbell made the connection between the "remission of sins" and baptism. No doubt he only thought of baptism, at the time of his immersion, as a sign or symbol of the forgiveness he had already received as any good Reformed theologian would argue.[10]

B. *The Reimmersion Controversy*

Who, according to Campbell, is a citizen of the kingdom of heaven? He answers:

> Everyone that believes in his heart that Jesus of Nazareth is the Messiah the Son of God, and publicly confesses his faith in his death, for our sins, in his burial and resurrection, by an immersion into the name of the Father, the Son and the Holy Spirit. Every such person is a constitutional citizen of Christ's kingdom.[11]

1. Faith, the Only Condition of Immersion

Faith in Jesus is the supreme condition for scriptural immersion. Any person who is immersed without faith in Jesus as the Messiah ought to be reimmersed into His death. "They differ nothing from immersed infants."[12] As respects "Christian immersion," that person (the one immersed without faith) "is as one unimmersed." This faith is not based upon some revivalistic experience of the Holy Spirit, but is rooted in God's word. Campbell calls this principle "one of the cardinal items of the present reformation," that is, "none but believers are the proper subjects of baptism; and by *believers* we always intended those who, on

176

the testimony of Apostles and Prophets, receive Jesus as the Son and Messiah of God." Faith in that one fact or proposition is all that is required for immersion into Christ.[13]

Faith does not necessarily entail perfect understanding of all New Testament institutions and neither does it entail a perfect understanding of any one institution. Faith does involve some kind of understanding, but only with respect to the object of faith which is Jesus the Messiah. Consequently, under certain circumstances, Campbell argues that "baptism administered by the Baptists introduces the subjects of it into the kingdom of Christ."[14] The only qualification depends upon the "faith and intelligence of the subject." One may believe that Jesus is the Messiah and "yet not regard immersion for the remission of sins," and still be scripturally immersed. Therefore, Campbell writes:

> But I do think that every one immersed by the Baptist preachers, or "laymen", who really believes in his heart and confesses with his mouth that Jesus is Messiah, *understanding the meaning of what he says* (concerning his confession, JMH), is introduced into this kingdom.[15]

While one who does not understand that baptism is for the remission of sins cannot enjoy the full benefit of assurance, nevertheless, the fact that he did not understand this point does not mean that he does not in fact possess the remission of his sins.[16] It is not uncommon, then, to find Campbell referring to his Baptist friends, even his Baptist opponents, as brothers in Christ. His major opponent in the early 1830s was "brother Andrew Broaddus."[17]

2. Arguments Against Reimmersion

Campbell's fundamental thesis is that faith does not require perfect understanding in order for it to be efficacious. Thus, one may be immersed while lacking understanding of the purposes of immersion and still be introduced into the kingdom. In addition to this premise, Campbell offers several other reasons for his position. First, if the reimmersionist is correct, then the promises of God concerning the existence of the church throughout all ages has failed. Campbell is convinced that though the remnant is small in this "age of apostasy" there is nevertheless a remnant (since the promise of God "has not failed") which "did not commence either in 1827, 1823, or 1809."[18] He dares not place the Baptists, Waldenses and Albigenses "on the same footing with the Papists of the 10th century or with the Mahometans of the 19th."[19] Have the gates of Hades prevailed against the church for "more than 1300 years"? Campbell thinks otherwise:

> Why on *all* your definitions of the kingdom, *supposing*, as you do, that he that is not formally and understandingly immersed for the remission of his sins cannot enter into his kingdom; and it being a fact that before the year 1823, since the fifth century, *baptism for the remission of sins was not preached*, and not until the year 1827 were many immersed with this apprehension of the subject . . . *either the promises of God have failed, or such persons as were baptized as you were the first time, are in the kingdom!*[20]

Second, Campbell argues that one may obey Christ in one of His institutions for a singular purpose (such as, He told me to do it) without a full understanding of its multiple purposes and yet receive all the blessings pertaining to that institution. Campbell uses the analogy of naturalization. Though John Doe became a citizen of the United States in order to hold property, or to stay in this country legally, when John learned of all the other benefits of citizenship (such as to vote, etc.) there was no need for him to be renaturalized. Campbell argues from his analogy in this way:

> When I was naturalized a citizen of these United States, there were certain immunities and privileges attached to citizenship which I had not in mind at the time, nor were they any inducement to be naturalized, any more than to that child now sleeping

in the arms of his mother. But did that circumstance annul my naturalization and leave me an alien?[21]

In the same way, not all understand or realize the tremendous benefits which are attached to immersion. New discoveries do not render the past void. A pure faith (one that sincerely believes in Jesus as the Messiah, not a faith that perfectly understands all of God's will) is all that is necessary for immersion. Campbell explains:

> We proceed upon these as our axiomata in all our reasonings, preachings, writings — 1st, unfeigned faith; 2nd, a good conscience; 3rd, a pure heart; 4th, love. The testimony of God apprehended produces unfeigned or genuine faith; faith obeyed produces a good conscience. This Peter defines to be the use of baptism, the answer of a good conscience. This produces a pure heart, and then the consummation is love — love to God and man.[22]

The motivating factor is faith. One who is immersed upon faith, a faith that understands that Jesus is the Messiah, but may not understand every design of baptism, receives all the blessings which God has attached to baptism. Consequently, Campbell argues that "baptism cannot be repeated unless in its full sense. No person can constitutionally be immersed for remission alone — for the Holy Spirit alone — for coming into the kingdom alone. He must be baptized into Christ, in the whole and full sense of the institution, or not at all."[23]

Campbell only envisions two positions. One position argues that only a singular understanding of the purpose of immersion is necessary. A genuine faith in Jesus as the Messiah will lead one to obey His commands, especially the command to be immersed. This, in Campbell's view, is sufficient. The other position is that one must have a full understanding of all the blessings of baptism in order to receive them. Campbell thinks this is impossible. If one must understand all the blessings involved, then if one

179

misunderstands any one purpose (such as the promised gift of the Spirit), then he must be reimmersed. Therefore, the only immersion is one in the full sense of its meaning. There can be no partial immersion: one for this benefit, another for a different benefit. "It must be in the full sense; that is, for all the purposes for which the institution exists."[24]

How much, then, must one understand about the "full sense" in order to receive all the benefits whether he is aware of all of them or not? Campbell believed that those who were reimmersed because they did not understand baptism the first time "did not understand it the second time" and consequently ought to be immersed a third time![25] To be consistent, every time that they learn something new about benefits of baptism, they ought to be immersed again.[26] Further, it can be argued that even those in the New Testament did not fully understand the purposes of their immersion. Campbell asks whether or not this is the case with the Romans in 6:3,4. Those who argued that we should sin that grace may abound, though Christians, really did not understand the purpose of their baptism.[27]

What, then, must we understand to be immersed, according to Campbell? Only the simple fact that Jesus is the Messianic Savior of the world. There is a difference between believing a fact about the person of Jesus (i.e., that He is the Son of God, etc.) and understanding everything He says. There are many examples of believers in the Gospels who did not understand. For example, the apostles were believers but did not fully understand the implications of their faith.[28] His point may be summarized by this paragraph:[29]

I trust we need not attempt to show that Jesus Christ has not ordained any institution solely for the remission of sins — any rite or observance for expiation. Remission of sins is, indeed, connected with baptism; but so is adoption, sanctification, and all blessings of the new institution. The salvation of the soul, which comprehends every thing which can be enjoyed in the present world, is attached to it. He that believes and is baptized shall be saved. To be baptized for the remission of sins exclusively, is not what is meant by putting on Christ, or by being immersed into Christ.

Since there is more to baptism than simply the remission of sins, Campbell believes it is unjust to single out this purpose as the one which must be understood in distinction from the others. It is unbiblical, in his view, to raise one scriptural blessing of baptism above another.[30]

Third, reimmersion, according to Campbell, is purely an opinionated inference from Scripture. He argues that:

Rebaptism is wholly out of the Record, and is only an *inference* drawn from our own conclusions on the present state of Christianity and the inadequate conception of many professors on the import of the Christian institution.[31]

Since there is no command to reimmerse, and no example of the reimmersion of believers in Jesus as the Messiah, "it is wholly the work of reasoning."[32] Campbell sees all inferences as opinions. To found one's faith upon opinion is to create a sect. In the Campbell-Rice Debate he argued that "faith is *testimony believed*; knowledge is our own *experience*; and opinion is *probable inference*."[33] True unity, however, permits a freedom of opinion. Opinions must be "let alone."[34] No one is to be excommunicated for an opinion. Since reimmersion is based upon inference alone, the one who insists upon it destroys the very foundation of the Restoration Movement. Campbell summarizes his point well:

Few understand all that is comprehended in this; but every new discovery does not render all the past void, nor make it necessary to be born again. And he that insists upon a person being rebaptized in order to fellowship, makes his own inferences a bond of union, and adds to the commands in the book.[35]

Fourth, if the reimmersionist were consistent, he ought to advocate the establishment of a board of inquisition to decide who is required to be reimmersed and who is not. Campbell suggests this should come in the form of a standing committee for the interrogation of candidates for baptism which amounts to the resurgence of the Presbyterian consistory or the Baptist board of deacons.[36] This undermines restoration principles in that some begin to legislate for others. Campbell maintains that the whole issue is not "a matter of discipline or of inquiry."[37] To do so, in Campbell's view, is to destroy the present Reformation:

> I say, to me it appears deserting the proper ground of this Reformation to dogmatize upon this theme. . . . If, then, we must erect a new tribunal to determine *the true believers*, and *the true gospel*, and *the true baptism*, before admission to the Lord's table, we ought to abandon the no-human-creed system, and make christian immersion a church business, and have a vote in the church on all the candidates for immersion.[38]

The only proper procedure for Campbell is to let the individual himself be fully persuaded in his own mind. He argues that a congregation ought to accept a Baptist into fellowship if he himself is "satisfied with his immersion," in which case "the church has no liberty, or is under no precept or obligation to demand reimmersion for its satisfaction."[39] No church council needs to be convened to decide the issue. Campbell is perfectly pleased to "leave this matter to the intelligence and conscience of every individual."[40] As Campbell's son-in-law Richardson states, "All must judge for themselves both of the foundation and the sincerity of their own faith, and act accordingly."[41]

3. Immersion: Merit or Receptacle?

In this whole discussion, however, Campbell is concerned that the act of immersion is often misconceived by the reimmersionists. He fears that the whole controversy belies a view of baptism which sees it as a work of merit or expiation. According to Campbell, those who insist upon reimmersion for the explicit purpose of the remission of sins make "baptism a mere expiatory rite," and regard "it as designed alone for absolution."[42] This kind of attitude which goes to the water for remission of sins is like the Jew who goes to the altar in order to merely receive the remission of sins. This motivation "mistakes the whole matter."[43] Baptism is not to be regarded as the "procuring cause of remission."[44] Fundamentally, the remission of sins is a blessing bestowed by God. Baptism does not procure forgiveness. It receives it upon the condition of faith. Campbell attempts to correct this misconception by this statement:

> Others think that when they have been immersed they have *done* something worthy of praise: nay, verily, they only have *received* something worthy of thanks. He that is immersed does nothing, any more than he who is buried. In immersion, as in being born, and in being buried, the subject is always passive. He that immerses another does something: but he that is immersed has only suffered something. When we talk of the *act* of immersion we have the agent, not the subject, in our eye. He, however, who is acceptably immersed, has been immersed as one that is dead — not as one that is alive. It is criminal to bury a man alive: but virtuous to bury him that is dead.[45]

The point for which Campbell is grasping may be summarized in this question: why does baptism save? Is it because I believe certain things about the institution itself, as in an expiatory rite, or is it because of the object of my faith — Jesus Christ? Baptism is an affirmation of our faith in God's work through the death and resurrection of Jesus. That faith has certain implications for baptism, but it is not necessary to understand those implications. How many who believe in Jesus as the Messiah even understand the nature of the atoning work of Christ, the worship of the church, etc.? For Campbell, baptism is effectual through faith in Jesus as the Messianic Savior, not because of certain things that may or may not be understood about the meaning of baptism.[46]

4. Qualifications

Within the perspective of this broad statement, Campbell

does make certain qualifications. For instance, he does not intend to include within his views those who actively and bitterly attack the ancient gospel. He states that he regards "those Baptists who now directly oppose the ancient gospel and those persons baptized by them in opposition to it" in a different light than "those formerly immersed or those now immersed when the attention of neither the preachers nor people has been called to the meaning of the institution."[47] In particular, Campbell has in mind those disciples who are reimmersed by Baptists as well as those who are specifically immersed in explicit opposition to the true meaning of baptism. He, in fact, regards the baptism of those who "were expressly immersed *because their sins were forgiven*" as at least questionable though he does not go into detail.[48] In another place, he states that those who were immersed in fits of experiential excitement after waiting on the mourning bench ought, perhaps to be reimmersed. But he quickly adds that there is no universal law in this matter — it must be left up to the individual himself.[49] However, Campbell is clear that his position does not imply a blank check for all who have been immersed. If one is immersed upon simple faith, and nothing else, then he ought to be accepted. Yet, if one is immersed, explicitly rejecting and actively opposing the ancient gospel, Campbell raises doubts about his immersion. Nevertheless, it always remains a personal matter.

With these qualifications, Campbell asserts his willingness to extend "the right hand and the whole heart of fellowship as freely and as fully to any one immersed by myself within the last ten years" to the many Baptists who have become "associated under the banners of the Reformation."[50] He argues that anyone who was immersed upon a confession of Jesus as Messiah and Lord "ought, without reimmersion, to be accredited as a disciple and fellow-citizen, and cordially received."[51] In fact, the "only thing which can justify reimmersion . . . is a confession upon the part of the candidate that he did not believe that Jesus was the Messiah, the Son of God — that he died for our sins, was buried, rose again the third day, at the time of his first immersion — that

184

he now *believes* the testimony of the Apostles concerning him, and desires to be buried and rise with Christ in faith in resurrection to eternal life."[52] To do otherwise is to make void the word of the Lord in Mark 16:16 — "He that believeth and is immersed shall be saved."

5. Conclusion

Therefore, Campbell's conclusion is that there are Christians among the Baptists. Though he fears that they "are greatly degenerate, and fast immersing themselves into the popular errors of this age," nevertheless there are some who have not "bowed the knee to the image of Baal, and are as worthy citizens to the kingdom of the Messiah as any of our brethren."[53] However, to accept certain individual Baptists as brothers does not imply an endorsement of the whole sect itself. There is a difference between receiving certain individuals into fellowship and receiving "the whole accredited members of any one sect as citizens of the kingdom of Jesus, and feeling ourselves bound to fraternize with them because they belong to that sect."[54] Though there certainly are many Christians among the Baptist sect, in Campbell's view, he cannot fraternize with the sect as a whole. The third section of this chapter will attempt to clarify his meaning here.

C. The State of the Unimmersed

As Campbell comes to this question, he revises his definition of a Christian. He now writes that a Christian is "everyone that believes in his heart that Jesus of Nazareth is the Messiah, the Son of God; repents of his sins, and obeys him in all things *according to his measure of knowledge of his will*."[55] Campbell compares one who is unimmersed to an imperfect Christian. He cannot bring himself to deny that any person who "is acting up to the full measure of his knowledge," and has not been "negligent, according to his opportunities, to ascertain the will of his Master" is a Christian. In the opinion of Campbell, the only one who is not justified is the one "*who only doubts*, or is not fully persuaded that his baptism is apostolic and divine."[56] He feels that if he were to paganize all the unimmersed simply because they have never had an opportunity to learn about immersion, he would be "a pure sectarian, a Pharisee among Christians." Therefore, he cannot regard all the unimmersed as "aliens from Christ and the well-grounded hope of heaven."[57]

If the answer to the question was left as it now stands, the reader would certainly gain a false impression of Campbell's actual position. It is important to understand that Campbell makes a distinction between the church on earth (the church militant) and the hope of heaven (the church triumphant); between conditions of fellowship in the visible church on earth and conditions of ultimate salvation; between the full enjoyment of assurance by immersed believers and the imperfect hope of unimmersed believers. While the unimmersed are excluded from the former of these, it does not necessarily follow that they are excluded from the latter. While the unimmersed may, by the grace of God, enter heavenly bliss and ultimately be saved, it is impossible for them to enjoy the full fellowship of the church on earth as well as the full assurance of their hope. Campbell's reasoning is rooted in his understanding of the objective value of immersion for the believer.[58]

Campbell insists that anyone who was sprinkled in his infancy ought to be immersed. Since sprinkling is "at best only the fallible inference or opinion of man," the unimmersed ought to be immersed because in it "we have the sure and unerring promise of our Savior and Judge."[59] On this ground, "the present salvation can never be so fully enjoyed, all things else being equal, by the unimmersed as by the immersed."[60] However, anyone who continues to rejoice in his sprinkling or pouring "because of his dislike to, or prejudice against believer's immersion" proves himself to be a self-seeker, and consequently Campbell can have "no favorable

186

opinion" of him.[61]

Consequently, Campbell refuses to make immersion *absolutely* essential to ultimate salvation, though it is absolutely necessary to the full enjoyment of assurance. According to Campbell, everyone who has "obeyed according to their knowledge" and is not "willingly" ignorant of the will of heaven, "although debarred from the full enjoyment of the kingdom of grace here, may be admitted into the kingdom of glory hereafter."[62] There are two situations in which this may be true (and only God knows if there are others). First, each individual must be judged according to his opportunities or circumstances. Anyone who has had no opportunity to be immersed is not subject to the divine command. Campbell made this clear to the Baptist Dr. Fishback who was associated with Barton W. Stone:

> Because, mark me closely, I do admit that a person who believes the gospel, and cannot be immersed, may obtain remission. So that I cannot take the affirmative and say remission is absolutely suspended upon being baptized in water.[63]

In the Campbell-Rice Debate, he reiterates the same sentiment:

> . . . according to our teaching, there is no one required to be baptized where baptism cannot be had. Baptism, where there is no faith, no water, no person to administer, was never demanded as an indispensible condition of salvation, by Him who has always enjoined upon man 'mercy, rather than sacrifice.'[64]

Second, each case must be judged according to the knowledge and devotion of the person involved. Mistakes of understanding, in Campbell's opinion, do not leave men without the hope of heaven. He writes:

> Many a good man has been mistaken. Mistakes are to be regarded as culpable and as declarative of a corrupt heart only when they

187

proceed from a willful neglect of the means of knowing what is commanded. Ignorance is always a crime when it is voluntary and innocent when it is involuntary. . . . I could not, I dare not say that their mistakes are such as unchristianize all their professions.[65]

There is a large difference between one who willfully neglects or ignores the commandments of God, and one who simply mistook the will of God. While the one who neglects to "ascertain the will of the Lord, or to obey his command when he knows it" can never attain immortality, the one who "in all things obeyed according to" his knowledge, may "ultimately" attain it.[66] Consequently, Campbell offers it as his "opinion" that with faith in the sacrifice of Christ and "obedience to Jesus Christ in all things as far as one's knowledge extended, even if one should not have been immersed, it was probable he might be admitted hereafter into the kingdom of glory."[67] Yet, Campbell insists that it is an opinionated inference from Scripture. He cannot make any rules on this point. But it is still his "opinion" that he "cannot make literal immersion in water, *in all cases*, essential to admission into the kingdom of eternal glory; yet I *know* that I believe the Scriptures!"[68]

Campbell's position on the unimmersed may be summarized in this way: the unimmersed can have no concrete assurance in this life, nor are they to be admitted into the fellowship of the church on earth, but it is possible (indeed probable and to be accepted by Christians) that God will admit some of the unimmersed into glory when He takes into account their opportunities and ignorance. This basic perspective reconciles what sometimes appear to be conflicting statements in Campbell's writings. While Campbell may call some of the unimmersed "Christian," he does not mean that he extends to them the right hand of fellowship in the church militant. Rather, he only means that, according to God's gracious accounting of opportunities and ignorances, they may inherit heavenly bliss. He calls them "Christian" in deference to their profession of Christianity as will be shown below.

188

In view of this opinion, Campbell thinks that it is presumptuous to argue that there are no Christians among the unimmersed. He writes:

> There is no occasion, then, for making immersion, on a profession of the faith, absolutely essential to a Christian — though it may be greatly essential to his sanctification and comfort. . . . But he that thence infers that none are Christians but the immersed, as greatly errs as he who affirms that none are alive but those of clear and full vision.[69]

However, there is an exclusivism in Campbell's thought. In his debate with Rice, he argues:

> We are so exclusive, however, that we say to everyone without the fold, you must repent and be baptized for the remission of your sins, if you would enjoy the fullness of the blessing of the gospel of Christ. Still we do not so make conditions of absolute salvation out of conditions of church membership.[70]

In summary, therefore, Campbell sees baptism as "for the church on earth, for the gospel dispensation . . . not the door into heaven."[71] It is not an ordinance which procures the remission of sins, but it is the instrument of the "actual possession and present enjoyment of that remission which God bestows."[72] It is the formal declaration of the appropriation of God's grace. Those who are ignorant of that instrument or never had an opportunity to use that means of grace, though excluded from full assurance and entrance into the visible, earthly church, may yet be graciously received into heavenly glory.

D. Communion with the Sects

1. Christian? In What Sense?

As we have seen, according to Campbell, there are Christians (in some sense of that term) among the sects. The boldest statement of that position came in the Lunenberg letter of 1837.[73] Campbell thought it was well known that this was his opinion. He states that he "gave it as our *opinion* that there were Christians among the Protestant sects; an opinion, indeed, which we have always expressed when called upon."[74] In fact, in his defense he lists numerous quotations from his previous writings in which this was explicitly stated.[75] He complains that his unity movement meant nothing if all Christians are already united within his own fellowship. "Let me ask, in the first place, what could mean all that we have written upon the union of Christians on apostolic grounds, had we taught that all Christians in the world were already united in our own community?"[76] Therefore, as he stated in the Lunenberg letter, "there are Christians among the sects."[77]

However, the issue is a bit more complicated than this mere factual statement. What exactly is the state of these Christians in the sects, and what is their relationship to the Restoration Movement in the thought of Campbell? As will become evident, it is too simplistic to merely assert that Campbell believed there are Christians among the sects as is commonly done.[78]

Campbell draws distinctions between his various uses of the word "Christian." Campbell divides Christendom into three sections. There are (1) the Anti-Christ church, (2) the Apostasy, and (3) the disciples of Christ. This distinction is extremely important for understanding the implications and meaning of Campbell's opinion that there are Christians among the sects.

In Campbell's reply to Christianos, a disciple who wrote a series of articles in the *Millennial Harbinger* (1838-1840) advocating fellowship with the unimmersed, he draws attention to this three-fold distinction of the word Christian:[79]

The *word* Christian has three distinct acceptations in modern times. It has a national, a sectarian, and a scriptural meaning. Nationally it means one who is not a Jew, a Mahometan, a Pagan, an Infidel, but a professor of the Christian faith. In the style of the sects it means something more and something better than a

Romanist, a Churchman, a Presbyterian, a Baptist, a Methodist, etc. It means one who is supposed to be a follower of Christ in the moral virtues of his religion, without regard to his tenets, in comparison with other sectaries.

His categories here are National, Sectarian and Scriptural. In other places, his categories are Anti-Christ, Apostasy and Disciple.[80] The Anti-Christ refers to the whole of the Christian world (i.e., Christendom), but primarily to the Romanists who represent what is basically unscriptural or anti-Christ. The second category refers to the diversity of sects who have severed themselves from the Anti-Christian Church, but are yet apostate. The scriptural use of the term refers to the Restoration Movement as a whole (i.e., undenominational Christianity wherever it exists, including the Scotch Baptists, etc.) wherein Biblical institutions are practiced. More simply, the National use refers to those who though they profess errors, yet "live right"; and the third refers to immersed penitent believers who follow the Biblical pattern.[81]

When Campbell says that there are Christians among the sects, it is important to understand what he means by the term Christian. In the Lunenberg letter, Campbell explicitly states that there are "Christians amongf the sects."[82] Garrison and DeGroot, therefore, argue that in this letter Campbell "insisted that the unimmersed were Christians."[83] This is linguistically correct (i.e., that is what Campbell said) but simplistic, and even misleading since Campbell used the term in different senses. In fact, later that same year (1837), Campbell explained the sense in which he meant the term "Christian." He used it in the sectarian sense, that is, those who make the "profession wrong, but live right," so that "I don't know what he believes, nor how he was baptized, but I know he is a *Christian*."[84] He did not, he declares, use the term in the Lunenberg letter in its "strictest biblical import" but "in the case before us I used it in its best modern application."[85] He explains himself in this manner:

Now in this acceptation of the word, I think there are many, in most Protestant parties, whose errors and mistakes I hope the Lord will forgive; and although they should not enter into all the blessings of the kingdom of earth, I do fondly expect they may participate in the resurrection of the just.[86]

Consequently, while Campbell hopes that these sectarian "Christians" will be saved eternally, he cannot offer any scriptural assurance that they will be. The only one who is correctly called "Christian" in the scriptural, stricter sense is the penitent immersed believer who obeys the institutions of God.

The one who professes Christianity, but does not follow the directives of Scripture may yet (due to either his ignorance or circumstances) receive eternal glory, but he cannot receive the praise of men based on Scripture. According to Campbell only he:

has the praise of God and man, and of himself *as a Christian*, who believes, repents, is baptized, and keeps all the ordinances, positive and moral, as delivered to us by the holy Apostles.[87]

Therefore, no one can be called "Christian" in a Biblical sense except those who resemble the Antiochene Christians "in knowledge and practice."[88]

Are there Christians among the sects? Campbell's seemingly contradictory answer is "yes and no." Yes, in the sense that there are some who may receive eternal life in view of their lack of opportunity to obey or their unwilling ignorance of the divine institutions (such as immersion). This viewpoint, we must remember, Campbell describes as pure opinion. It is only possible, or in Campbell's conception "probable," that these may inherit eternal blessings though they cannot enter the kingdom of God on earth. Yes, also in the sense that there are some who have been immersed upon a profession of faith in Jesus as the Messiah, but remain in the sects. No, in the sense that none but those who teach and practice the Apostolic precepts and examples can be called Christians. Only these may be regarded as fully assured Christians. Campbell himself summarizes his position in this statement:

> And scripturally it means one who has first believed in Jesus as the
> Messiah, repented of his sins, and been immersed in water into
> the name of the Father, the Son, and the Holy Spirit and who
> follows Christ in all his appointments. Such were they who were
> first called Christians at Antioch. Now in the latter sense it can
> never be applied to any but to those who resemble the disciples
> described in the Acts of the Apostles; while in the first and second
> sense of the term (national and sectarian, JMH) there are many
> Christians among the sects, and many that will put to shame (i.e.,
> when they see them in heaven, JMH) those who refuse to award
> to them the style (i.e., the name "Christian") because of their
> mistakes of the ordinance.[89]

As a result, when one affirms that Campbell believed that
there were Christians among the sects, it is necessary to define
what is meant by the term "Christian." For while Campbell may
admit that there are Christians among the sects in an inferior
sense (as defined above), it is also clear that Campbell would not
align himself with nor commune with any sect as a whole.

2. Inter-Body Fellowship?

In the quotation to which the lady from Lunenberg, Virginia
took exception ("we find in all Protestant parties Christians"),
Campbell also makes it clear that the Restoration movement
"cannot form a confederacy with the troops of Satan."[90] He rejects the Baptists, "as a people," since they form part of the
apostasy. Consequently, they "are not of the kingdom of God."[91]
All sects are part of the apostasy since "all religious sects" have a
"human bond of union."[92] Therefore, while there may be individual persons within those sects who may be saved due to their
ignorance (perhaps some who are Christians in the sense that
they have been scripturally immersed), it is nevertheless the case
that sects are sinful and the Restoration Movement cannot unite
with them. Sects as a whole are apostate. They do not constitute

the visible church of God on earth. Campbell is adamant on this point:

> I have already said that I am prepared to admit that the Regular Baptist Institution as a whole, or any other institution as a whole, now existing in the sectarian world, or anterior to the present century for 1200 years, is not identical with the kingdom of Jesus Christ. . . . The Jewish nation has existed, but not *as a nation*, for the last 1800 years. They are scattered among the nations. This may be an analogy to illustrate what we mean by the Lord's people now dispersed through many sects, and yet no where, or in no sect, existing as his kingdom.[93]

No sect can be the kingdom of God on earth, and the kingdom of God on earth can have no fellowship or confederacy with any sect. Yet, there are, according to Campbell, many Christians (in the senses defined above) among the sects. In this way, the promise of God has not failed. Though His kingdom *as such* may not always have existed, He has always had a people among the various sects which have arisen.

This forms the foundation of Campbell's call for union of all Christians. In what may be called the "Campbellite Catechism of 1832" (though Campbell himself disclaimed its catechistic function), an interesting series of questions and answers is found:

Q. 174. Are there, then, no disciples of Christ in these communities?
A. There are, no doubt, many.
Q. 175. How, then, can the communities, as such be in the apostasy?
A. There are republicans in England, and monarchists in America; yet the English community is not a republic, nor the American a monarchy. So there being christians in any sectarian commonwealth, or a sectarian in any christian commonwealth, does not change the nature or character of such a commonwealth.

194

Q. 176. What, then, is the duty of all christians found in these communities?

A. They are commanded to *"come out of them"* Rev. xviii.4. "Come out of her, my people, that you be not partakers of her sins; and that you receive not of her plagues."

Q. 177. From whom are they commanded to come out?

A. From Babylon, the apostasy.

Q. 178. And do all sects constitute Babylon?

A. Yes. Do not the streets constitute every city? What is Rome, or London, but its streets, lanes and houses? And were not the people of God, under the former economy, commanded to come out of Babylon before God destroyed it?[94]

It seems clear from these answers that Campbell rejected all fellowship with the sects and even regarded those who remained in the sects (except for ignorance or lack of opportunity) as heading for destruction. Indicative of this attitude is a statement found in the Campbell-Rice Debate where, while acknowledging that English Baptists commune with the unimmersed, he announced that "we have no such custom among us."[95] Campbell excludes the sects as bodies from the kingdom of God on earth, and does not offer communion to the unimmersed. There is, therefore, an exclusivistic strain in Campbell's thinking.

Whether the Restoration Movement should receive unimmersed persons into their fellowship was a cause of some strife between Barton W. Stone and Alexander Campbell. Stone accused Campbell of being sectarian in that he did not receive the unimmersed into his fellowship.[96] Campbell's response is indicative of his attitude toward fellowship with the sects. Is Campbell's view of immersion as a term of fellowship sectarian? In Campbell's perspective, it is impossible to successfully repel the imputation of being sectarian if "obedience to Jesus Christ be called *sectarian*."[97] If one receives the unimmersed into their fellowship, he has denied the creed of the Restoration movement: the Bible. Campbell explains that:

It is not because of our views of the meaning of immersion (in

195

which he seems to agree with us) but because the 'Christians' (Stonites, JMH) now make immersion of non-effect by receiving persons into the kingdom of Jesus, so-called, irrespective of their being legitimately born; or in brief, regardless of the command, *'Be baptized everyone of you.'* [98]

In a similar vein, responding to William Jones' question about whether Campbell's American fellowship communes with the unimmersed as the English Baptists do, Campbell wrote:

Not one, as far as known to me. . . . Does not this look like making void the word or commandment of God by human tradition. . . . Nay, why not dispense with it altogether, and be consistent . . . we require everyman to pay a courteous and decent respect to Peter — to believe what he preached, and to do what he bade him. With us, in this New World, a Christian means *one that believes what Jesus Christ says, and does what he bids him.* [99]

It is, therefore, beyond doubt that Campbell did not commune with the unimmersed. The reason was not that he did not believe that any of them would enter heavenly glory, but the reason was that none of them were members of the Lord's kingdom on earth. This is an extremely important distinction. Campbell did not, as he saw it, sit as the eternal judge over the unimmersed, but simply acted according to his knowledge of the Scripture. To assign an unimmersed person to heaven or hell was not his prerogative, but he could not, on the basis of Scripture, offer the unimmersed a place in the Lord's kingdom on earth since they had not obeyed the first principles of the ancient gospel.

Stone objected that Campbell should use the same principle that God uses in judging the unimmersed. Since Campbell admitted that it was probable that some of the unimmersed would be eternally rewarded, he ought to accept some of them into his fellowship. Campbell's response to this objection states the main principle of his definition of fellowship:

196

But the question is, are we authorized to make the sincerity and honesty of a person's mind a rule of our conduct? *'Tis God alone who is judge of this*, and surely he would not require us to act by a rule which we can never apply to that case. Neither, perhaps, is it fair to *assume that any man's sincerity or belief will have any weight in the final judgment*; but whether or not, it cannot be a rule for our proceeding in any case. We judge from actions — *God judges the heart*; and therefore, we look for visible obedience; and when we are assured that the Lord has commanded every man to confess him, or to profess the faith and be immersed into his name, *we can never justify ourselves* before God or man in presuming in our judgment of charity to set aside his commandment, and in accepting for it a human substitute.[100]

Men can only judge from the Scripture concerning outward professions and acts — they cannot go beyond this. As Thomas Henley and Temple Walker wrote: "We cannot, we dare not believe or teach any other way than the commission given to the Holy Twelve. We do not, in so doing, limit God; but we do limit ourselves, *and all men now*, to that which it has pleased him to reveal and have recorded and handed down to us as the means of our salvation."[101]

E. Conclusion

The results of this study of the theology of Alexander Campbell may be summarized in four propositions. First, all those who are immersed upon their profession of faith in Jesus as the Messiah for any biblical reason, such as to obey God, or more explicitly for the remission of sins, are Christians even though they may still hold membership in an apostate sect. Second, it is probable that those who are unimmersed or members of an apostate sect due to unwilling ignorance or lack of opportunity will inherit eternal life though they cannot enjoy the full blessings of assurance, nor entrance into the kingdom of God on earth. They are Christians in an imperfect sense. Third, undenominational Christianity

197

has no right to offer the right hand of fellowship to the unimmersed, but ought to do so for all those who have been immersed based upon a faith in Jesus as their Saviour. However, undenominational Christianity has no right to fellowship apostate bodies as a whole even though there may be Christians within those bodies. Fourth, it is the responsibility of all Christians to sever themselves from and come out of the sects since as religious bodies they are apostate.

Endnotes

1. N.B. Hardeman, *Hardeman's Tabernacle Sermons* (Nashville: McQuiddy, 1928), 3:125; James A. Harding, *Harding-Nichols Debate* (Nashville: Gospel Advocate, 1947), p. 94; David Lipscomb, *Questions Answered* (Nashville: Gospel Advocate, n.d.), pp. 176-178, 591-593; F.G. Allen, "Our Strengths and Our Weaknesses," in *New Testament Christianity*, edited by Z.T. Sweeney (Columbus, Ind.: NT Christianity Book Fund, 1926), II, p. 245; F.B. Srygley, *New Testament Church* (Nashville: Gospel Advocate, reprinted 1955), pp. 50, 51, 67, 68. The above works are examples from among the churches of Christ, but they could be multiplied by many other examples from among the other segments of the American Restoration Movement. For a broad survey of the general positions present in the Restoration Movement, see John David Stewart, "The Restoration Movement's Attitude Toward Other Believers," *Restoration Quarterly* 11.3 (1968): pp. 176-183.

2. Robert Richardson, *Memoirs of Alexander Campbell* (Indianapolis, Indiana: Religious Book Service, reprint n.d.), I:405.

3. *Millennial Harbinger*, 3 (1832): 319. The *Millennial Harbinger* will henceforth be abbreviated as MH.

4. In fact, Campbell makes it clear that the first time the true meaning of baptism was connected in his mind was in his debate with MacCalla in 1823, and that it was not preached until 1827. Even in 1823, he later admitted, the connection was not altogether clear to him. See MH, 9 (1838): 86 and MH, 2 (1831), *Extra*, p. 4.

5. *American Christian Review* 22 (1879): 379. It is important to remember that the reimmersionist issue was a "hot" issue in Texas at this time, and the discussion of Campbell's baptism became an important aspect of the discussion. See chapter 8 of this book by Jerry Gross for the background of the reimmersionist issue in the late nineteenth century.

6. Alexander Campbell and W.L. MacCalla, *Campbell-MacCalla Debate*, p. 135. Campbell would in a few years argue that the "formal" and the "real" occur simultaneously (see *Christian Baptist*, 5 [1827]: 222, 256). This is a decisive difference between the Campbell of 1823 and the Campbell of 1827. Chapter 4 of this book treats this subject in greater detail.

7. John Calvin, *Institutes of the Christian Religion* in "Library of Christian Classics," edited by John T. MacNeill and translated by Ford Lewis Battles (Philadelphia: Westminster Press, 1960), II:1304. Chapter 2 of this book, written by Jack Cottrell, gives an exhaustive treatment of the Reformed concept of baptism. Also, chapter 4 discusses in detail the development of Campbell's baptismal theology in relation to Reformed theology.

8. Campbell explicitly stated that Paul's sins were really pardoned before he was immersed, or, to put it another way, Paul already had the thing signified when he received the sign.

9. MH, 1 (1830): *Extra*, pp. 14. The extended article (of 31 pages) is an extra added to the end of volume one. At one point, Campbell was asked this question about his view of immersion's design: "I understand you to assert that immersion, or baptism, is the act of regeneration, and the medium of forgiveness of sins: and that the scriptures do not authorize us to assert or believe that any are regenerated or forgiven until immersed. In other words, that the blood of Christ is never applied but through the medium of baptism. Is this a correct statement of your views?" Campbell replies: "It is very nearly a correct statement of my views" and refers them to his extra (MH, 1 [1830]: 357).

10. This would explain why Acts 2:38 was quoted at his immersion, see Richardson, *Memoirs*, I:397. Baptism was simply a sign of the remission of sins that Campbell had previously received as a believer in Jesus (even though a Presbyterian until 1812).

11. MH, 6 (1835): 419. The reimmersion controversy centered around Dr. John Thomas. Chapter 6 of this book treats this controversy in its historical context and great detail. The purpose here is simply to systematize Campbell's thinking.

12. MH, 6 (1835): 419-420.

13. MH, 7 (1836): 58.

14. MH, 3 (1832): 120.

15. MH, 3 (1832): 120.

16. MH, 3 (1832): 121. In response to the question of whether his position detracts from the importance of the Biblical design of baptism, he states, "Not in the least. It stands true that this is its proper meaning. The not understanding of this institution has prevented many christians from enjoying its benefits; but the not understanding it does not make them aliens from the kingdom of Jesus."

17. MH, 1 (1830), *Extra*: 17. J.A. Harding in his debate with the Baptist Dwight L. Moody referred to his opponent as *"my erring brother"* (*Nashville Debate*, p. 78; cf. p. 240). But in his debate with the unimmersed Methodist Nichols, he refers to him as "Mr. Nichols." Harding, however, did admit that "doubtless there are immersed Methodists who are entitled to the name Christian" (p. 79). Harding's views on rebaptism are summarized by Lloyd C. Sears, *The Eyes of Jehovah: The Life and Faith of James Alexander Harding*

(Nashville: Gospel Advocate, 1970), pp. 177-183.

18. MH, 6 (1835): 418.

19. MH, 6 (1835): 418.

20. MH, 3 (1832): 121.

21. MH, 3 (1832): 119. Campbell uses another example for illustration. In buying a piece of property John was only concerned with the agricultural value of the land, but later he discovered gold on it. Must he now renegotiate the sale? Cf. MH, 2 (1831): 483.

22. MH, 2 (1831), Extra: 4.

23. MH, 3 (1832): 123.

24. MH, 3 (1832): 223.

25. MH, 2 (1831): 483.

26. Interestingly, this was, in fact, practiced by some. For instance, Dasher, one of the leaders of the Restoration Movement in Georgia, was immersed several times on this very basis. Cf. John Mills, *Hans Christian Dasher* (Th.M. thesis, Alabama Christian School of Religion, 1980).

27. MH, 2 (1831): 483.

28. MH, 3 (1832): 318: "Now does it not appear that in your own style, christians may be spoken to as not believing all that Jesus said, and yet not worthy to be unchristianized and treated as aliens."

29. MH, 2 (1831): 482.

30. This whole argument is set forth in a rather detailed fashion by David Lipscomb, "What Constitutes Acceptable Obedience?" in *Salvation From Sin*, ed. by J.W. Shepherd (Nashville: McQuiddy, 1913), pp. 208-234.

31. MH, 6 (1835): 419.

32. MH, 3 (1832): 120.

33. *The Campbell-Rice Debate* (Lexington, KY: A.T. Skillman & Son, 1844), p. 835. This statement by Campbell must be balanced by the fact that he does not disavow the validity of *necessary* inferences, i.e., logical implications.

34. *The Campbell-Rice Debate*, p. 809, cf. pp. 797, 811.

35. MH, 2 (1831): 484, 485.

36. MH, 6 (1836): 59.

37. MH, 3 (1832): 319.

38. MH, 7 (1836): 229.

39. MH, 6 (1835): 565.

40. MH, 7 (1836): 230.

41. Richardson, MH, 7 (1836): 428.

42. MH, 2 (1831): 482.

43. MH, 2 (1831): 481.

44. MH, 6 (1835): 567.

45. MH, 6 (1835): 83, 84.

46. MH, 3 (1832): 123. The other most prominent member of the Restoration Movement, Barton W. Stone, was in agreement with Campbell on this point. Cf. *Christian Messenger*, 7 (July 1833): 140; 8 (January 1834): 23, 24).

47. MH, 3 (1832): 122.

48. MH, 6 (1835): 567.

49. MH, 7 (1836): 58. Here Campbell is answering the writings of Dr. John Thomas. Thomas had wondered whether Campbell believed that Baptist immersions based upon mere "experiences" in a revival would be sufficient faith. See chapter 6 of this book for a detailed discussion of their controversy.

50. MH, 6 (1835): 567.

51. MH, 7 (1836): 63.

52. Ibid.

53. MH, 6 (1835): 418.

54. MH, 3 (1832): 263, 264.

55. MH, 8 (1837): 411.

56. MH, 8 (1837): 563. This may account for the reason why Campbell could regard himself as saved before his immersion.

57. MH, 8 (1837): 412.

58. MH, 3 (1832): 119. Campbell's view of the objective nature of the baptismal event is detailed in chapter 4 of this book.

59. MH, 8 (1837): 563.

60. MH, 8 (1837): 564.

61. MH, 8 (1837): 563.

62. MH, 7 (1836): 62.

63. MH, 3 (1832): 304.

64. *Campbell-Rice Debate*, pp. 519-20. Interestingly, J.W. McGarvey apparently retained this concept. In an article entitled "Justification by Faith" in *Lard's Quarterly*, III:129, he writes: "Faith has never been so imputed, except when it has developed itself in some outward expression. Unless it be in some scriptural cases, like the thief on the cross, where no work of faith could be performed, it has been requisite that some such work should be done."

65. MH, 8 (1837): 413.

66. MH, 7 (1836): 62.

67. MH, 7 (1836): 61.

68. MH, 7 (1836): 62.

69. MH, 8 (1837): 414.

70. *Campbell-Rice Debate*, p. 785.

71. MH, 7 (1836): 62.

72. MH, 7 (1836): 63.

73. MH, 8 (1837): 410ff. What is often ignored must be remembered here. The Lunenberg Letter was an attempt of a pro-Thomas antagonist to put Campbell on the defensive with his own people. (They were, by the way, quite successful.) Campbell knew the letter to have arisen from the Thomas camp, and consequently his response was polemic in nature. This background sets the letter in its original context, and gives a fresh perspective to its contents. See chapter 6 for an extensive discussion of the historical background of this letter.

74. MH, 8 (1837): 506.

75. MH, 8 (1837): 562.

76. MH, 8 (1837): 561.

77. MH, 8 (1837): 411.

78. This has most recently been done by Leroy Garrett, *Stone-Campbell Movement* (Joplin, Missouri: College Press, 1981), pp. 193, 194, who sees a certain inconsistency within Campbell's view. While one may agree or disagree with Campbell, it is possible to view Campbell as internally consistent. See also Garrett, pp. 578-596.

79. MH, 11 (1840): 164.

80. MH, 3 (1832): 360.

81. MH, 8 (1837): 568.

82. MH, 8 (1837): 411.

83. *The Disciples of Christ* (St. Louis, Christian Board of Publication, 1948), p. 389.

84. MH, 8 (1837): 566.

85. MH, 8 (1837): 566.

86. MH, 8 (1837): 567.

87. MH, 8 (1837): 508.

88. MH, 11 (1840): 128.

89. MH, 11 (1840): 164.

90. MH, 8 (1837): 272.

91. MH, 7 (1836): 57, 58.

92. MH, 3 (1832): 362.

93. MH, 3 (1832): 263.

94. MH, 3 (1832): 362-363.

95. *Campbell-Rice Debate*, p. 810.

96. B.W. Stone, *Christian Messenger* 5 (1831): 180-85, 241-57.

97. MH, 2 (1831): 372.

98. MH, 2 (1831): 392. Interestingly, Stone later changed his mind on this question of exclusivism, cf. *Christian Messenger*, 14 (September 1844): 129-134.

99. MH, 6 (1835): 18, 19.

100. MH, 2 (1831): 392, 393.

101. Thomas Henley & Temple Walker, MH, 9 (1838): 88, 89.

6

JOHN THOMAS AND THE REBAPTISM CONTROVERSY (1835-1838)

Roderick Chestnut

Every movement has its heretics. John Thomas (1805-1871), a medical doctor who immigrated to the United States from England in 1832, will long be remembered as one of the Restoration Movement's foremost dissidents. Thomas' hyper-exclusivistic views of baptism and the after-life nearly devastated the fledgling church in Virginia and threatened to divert the course of what was fast becoming the greatest indigenous religious movement in North America. Thomas' teaching, which prompted considerable "in-house discussion" with Campbell during the years 1835-1838, did much to polarize two streams of thought in the Restoration Movement relating to baptism.

Thomas believed that baptism was an expiatory act, that is, baptism, if performed properly, procured salvation. For baptism to be valid the subject, as well as the administrator, had to realize that baptism was for the remission of sins. Baptism, therefore, marked the precise moment of salvation. If that knowledge was lacking it invalidated the rite, leaving the believer in his sins. Campbell differed sharply with Thomas on this. While maintaining that baptism was for the remission of sins, Campbell believed this knowledge could be lacking at the time of immersion and yet not diminish the blessing.

The issue was a particularly sensitive one in Virginia in the 1830's. Here Thomas promoted his exclusivistic teaching. Here the "current reformation" was made up almost entirely of former Baptists. Baptists then, as now, teach that forgiveness of sins comes at the point of faith. Baptism was merely an outward symbol of that inward reality. Thomas' doctrine of rebaptism was to greatly challenge that belief.

The purpose of this chapter is to explore the relationship between Alexander Campbell and John Thomas and to provide an historical study of their controversy regarding baptism. As this is done, the context will emerge for a better understanding of Campbell's Lunenberg Letter. It will be seen that Campbell's teaching regarding what constitutes a Christian were not isolated statements. They were a calculated response to the position taken by Thomas and his followers. Controversies of that sort are shaped by the personalities behind them. The Campbell-Thomas controversy illustrates the ease with which issues can become associated with personalities. Campbell and Thomas did not like each other. That fact was to have a decided effect on the shape of the controversy. What follows is a brief history of their relationship and a statement of their views on rebaptism.

A. *The Relationship Between Campbell and Thomas*

John Thomas came to America from England in 1832.[1] During an unusually difficult and nearly disastrous voyage, Thomas

204

vowed that if he ever reached land he would not rest until he found "the true religion."[2] Circumstances led him to Cincinnati where he met Major Daniel Gano, an influential Reformer, who in turn introduced him to Walter Scott, a noted evangelist for the movement. Scott convinced Thomas of his need of immersion and baptized him "for the remission of sins" in the fall of 1832.[3]

Thomas spent the winter of 1832-33 with the Ganos. In April Thomas left Cincinnati for an as yet undetermined city on the east coast. Cincinnati, it seems, was full of doctors and Thomas hoped to set up practice in a more favorable location. Gano insisted he visit Bethany on his way and gave him letters of introduction to both Campbell and Robert Richardson who was also a medical doctor. Perhaps they could assist him in setting up practice.

Thomas was somewhat surprised at the first sight of Campbell, who was wearing "an old drab coat and slouching white hat."[4] Nevertheless, Thomas felt drawn to him and later wrote concerning his initial meeting:

> We were much gratified with his acquaintance. We became much attached to him. . . . Our visit to Bethany . . . excited in our hearts a friendship for him, which we exceedingly regret should have terminated so unpropitiously; but so it was. For Mr. Campbell, we would have laid down our life if called upon; so much greater was his *personal* than his *literary* influence upon us.[5]

On two occasions Campbell called on Thomas to preach with little or no advance warning. Thomas resented this. On the first occasion Thomas accompanied Campbell on a preaching appointment in Wellsburg. Campbell had spoken in the morning and, following a recess, they were returning for an afternoon service. Campbell informed Thomas that he would be called upon to speak. Thomas records his reaction:

> As may be supposed, we were electrified at this announcement. We expostulated. We urged the suddenness of the call; our unpreparedness; our not having spoken on Christian religion before,

205

and so forth. But all to no purpose; he would take no denial, but insisted, observing that he liked to try what sort of mettle people were made of, or words to that effect.[6]

Thomas did not like having his "mettle" tried in this manner. He wrote that this "hastened our departure from Bethany; for, thought we, we never could stand such impromtuism as this."[7]

Thomas, a twenty-eight year old newly arrived immigrant and novice in the faith was no doubt intimidated by the older Campbell. Campbell, now in his mid-forties, was both a wealthy Virginia landowner and the acknowledged leader of a religious movement that was then taking the frontier by storm. If Thomas felt a little "put down" by his visit to Bethany it would be small wonder. If Thomas harbored the seed of resentment because of it, the tone of the coming controversy would have already been set.

On what was probably Campbell's suggestion, Thomas made plans to open medical practice in Richmond, Virginia, even though he would spend some time in Baltimore and Philadelphia in the meanwhile. After spending a week in Baltimore, where he was once again called upon to speak, Thomas, for unknown reasons, left for Philadelphia where he was to stay eleven months. There, somewhat against his will, he was induced to preach for a small group which met there. While in Philadelphia two significant things happened to Thomas — he married and commenced publication of the *Apostolic Advocate*.

A rapid change had taken place in John Thomas. In less than a year he had gone from being a reluctant, occasional speaker for the movement to the editor of what would soon be an influential journal. He had lost whatever reservations he may have had about preaching and was beginning to develop some rather dogmatic views as the pages of the *Apostolic Review* would soon reveal.

John Thomas arrived in Richmond in May 1834. Here, as in Philadelphia, he planned to practice medicine, edit the *Apostolic Advocate*, and preach as the occasion arose. the church in Richmond (the Sycamore congregation) was without a preacher and asked Thomas to fill the pulpit. Thomas agreed but insisted he do so at his own expense.[8]

Thomas had not been in Richmond long before the first hint of the coming rebaptism controversy arose. In October 1834 he published an article entitled, "The Cry of 'Anabaptism,' " in which he declared for the first time that scriptural baptism demanded a knowledge of the purpose of baptism — remission of sins. When that knowledge is lacking the act is meaningless.[9]

There was no immediate reaction to Thomas' treatise either by Campbell or the brotherhood at large. Though Thomas would print nothing else on the subject for months, the controversy was fanned into flame in the summer of 1835 when Thomas put into practice the ideas he had been putting into print. In late June or early July Thomas rebaptized three of the Sycamore deacons. Three successive entries in the Sycamore Church Minutes reveal the reason for the rebaptisms as well as why the men could no longer serve as deacons:

> June 21, 1835 — "Bro. Jas. Woodson in consequence of his se-
> cond immersion and thereby becoming a babe in Christ, is no
> longer considered a Deacon of this Church."

> June 28, 1835 — "Bro. E. Powell in consequence of having been
> a second time immersed, and thereby having just been introduced
> into the kingdom of Christ is no longer a Deacon. . . ."

> July 5, 1835 — "Wm. M. Carter . . . ceased being a deacon in
> consequence of having recently been immersed the second time
> in order to put on Christ. . . ."[10]

In the September 1835 *Millennial Harbinger*, Alexander Campbell printed a letter from a woman who expressed considerable uneasiness over the recent reimmersions Thomas had performed. Naming herself "Susan," she claimed to speak for "several sisters" who, though not satisfied with their Baptist immersion, could not believe that they had not hitherto put on Christ. She stated that at the time of their immersion they believed they had "remission of sins through faith in his blood" even though they "did not understand baptism as for the remission of sins, or as a sign and pledge from God of our pardon." She asked Campbell if their situation required reimmersion. Campbell's response marked the first time he was to go on record against Thomas.

Campbell was unequivocal in his reply to "Susan."[11] Thomas' actions were comparable to the Jews who bound the Gentiles saying, "except you be circumcised, *according to the manner of Moses, you cannot be saved.*" He was unwilling, in contrast to Thomas, to put the Baptists "on the same footing with the Papists of the 10th century, or the Mahometans of the 19th." Though expressing a "very good esteem" for John Thomas and Albert Anderson (a respected preacher of the reformation who had recently been rebaptized), Campbell was emphatic that their teaching was "wholly ultra (to) our views of reformation; and, in our judgment, wholly unauthorized by the New Testament." Campbell closes his remarks expressing regret that he would ever have to write such a response. He hopes that these "very zealous and excellent young brethren" will not be any more offended with reading his views than he was with reading theirs.

Thomas lost no time in reply. In the next issue of the *Apostolic Advocate* (October 1835) he charges that "Susan" is, in fact, "hermaphroditish," being a man who lacks the courage to challenge him face to face.[12] He accuses "Mr. Susan" and Campbell of using secondhand information and erroneously reporting that he preached the reimmersion of those who were in the kingdom of Christ. If they were in the kingdom of Christ they would not need to be reimmersed. Those Thomas reimmersed were being scripturally baptized for the first time and therefore were entering the kingdom for the first time. Furthermore, Thomas felt Campbell was prejudicing his readers against the reasonableness of his arguments by referring to him as "young and ardent."

> If we have erred, convince us by argument; but do not attempt to
> weaken our position by insinuating the hot headedness of our
> youth. We ask no favors of friend, brother or opponent, but claim
> that argument shall be opposed in argument, reason to reason,
> and proof to proof.[13]

Thomas followed up his reply to "Susan" and Alexander
Campbell with a series of letters to Campbell which he printed in
the *Apostolic Advocate*. He continued to maintain that baptism is
for the remission of sins and must be preceded by an intelligent
faith. On this point, Thomas felt, the very nature of the reformation was at stake:

> If a man is an honest reformer, he will labour first to reform
> himself, and then his neighbours. Does reformation, or coming
> out of Babylon, or preparing to meet the bridegroom, consist in
> nothing more than changing one's place of worship, and in break-
> ing a loaf weekly? And yet this is about the amount of reformation
> we see practiced in many places.[14]

The winter months of 1835-1836 saw both Campbell and
Thomas refusing to lay the issue to rest. Campbell, though seeking to minimize his differences with Thomas, still lamented the
"prominent place" Thomas was giving the rebaptism issue in his
journal.[15] Campbell sought to avoid the discussion for which
Thomas was so obviously pressing:

> Indeed, I do not desire a discussion of such a matter at this crisis. I
> should have to accompany these pieces with strictures, which
> might operate in a direction and to an issue wholly unsuspected
> by our too sanguine friends. Let it be for the time being attributed
> to my cowardice, or to any other cause as probable, which the
> brethren please; but, in my judgment this is not the time nor the
> place for such a discussion, nor is this *the work* to which we are at
> present called.[16]

But Thomas was persistent. He continued to keep the flames of controversy alive by his published pursuit of the matter. In one article he even taunted the "Reformers" for being afraid to "face the inevitable conclusions of the premises they have adopted."[17] Thomas' pertinaciousness moved Campbell to speak more forcefully against him. In the February *Millennial Harbinger* Campbell devoted seven full pages of animated polemic against Thomas' teaching, but relented somewhat as he closed. Once again he mentions Thomas' youth — a ploy which Thomas felt weakened his arguments in the minds of his readers. Campbell condescendingly writes:

> There are but few brethren of whose reasonings and views I could speak so freely; whose errors or mistakes (Oh! that I had a softer name!) I could notice with more freedom and hopes of success. To him I need offer no apology. He is but a stripling in the kingdom — a bold and courageous champion; but like other young converts, of a noble ambition, he aspires to outstrip himself and his years.[18]

By the spring of 1836 both Campbell and Thomas had taken clear stands against each other on the rebaptism question. Each felt his view was vital to the cause of reformation. By this stage of the controversy it was apparent that the movement would not be big enough for the two of them. A showdown was inevitable, although it would be two years in coming. Though Thomas was held in high regard by many brethren in Virginia, the longer he set himself against Campbell on the rebaptism issue the more his influence waned. The issue that really tipped his hand though was his speculative teaching on the soul and the afterlife. This, coupled with his insistent teaching on baptism, caused the brotherhood to increasingly view him with suspicion.[19]

Thomas' view of the afterlife grew out of his belief in conditional immortality. That is, immortality is a gift of God only to those who obey Him. To those who disobey God eternal extinction, not conscious torment awaits them. Anything less than annihilation for the disobedient (even eternal consciousness in torment) was immortality — a gift God reserved only for the obedient. Thomas then, would have three classes of people at the judgment: 1) Those who have obeyed God and thus receive immortality as a gift; 2) Those who reject God and are punished with eternal annihilation; and 3) Those who either have not heard the gospel or are not responsible for obeying it. They will "sleep" forever in a state of undisturbed unconsciousness.[20]

Campbell did not shrink back from challenging Thomas on this new matter. Indeed, beginning in 1836, treatment of Thomas' errors involved both his speculative teaching and the rebaptism issue. Campbell attacked Thomas' eschatology directly and indirectly. Directly in a series of articles entitled, "Materialism"; indirectly in a column called "Father Goodal's Family Circle."[21] This was an occasional feature of Campbell's paper which discussed issues, sometimes humorously, through a group of characters. In the "Materialism" articles, which followed the Goodal satire, Campbell said that heretofore he had dealt with Thomas' error in "a very mincing and palliatory style . . . presenting hints rather than seriously and gravely arguing any question."[22] Now he pulled out both barrels. In these articles Campbell produced seventeen arguments from scripture showing the absurdity of Thomas' views.

The strong personal element, which had characterized the controversy so far, was not absent from this discussion. An example of this is found in Campbell's second installment on "Materialism." Campbell, now willing to discuss Thomas' theories without the aid of "Father Goodal," reproduced a portion of Thomas' June article, "Dialogue between Three Friends," a response to Campbell's satire. Thomas, through the mouth of "Tomaso," stated that Campbell, an Irishman by birth, was unable to objectively consider the matter of flesh and spirit because he had hopelessly been influenced by "traditions" of "ghosts and witches."[23] "Tomaso" then goes on to state that Thomas, because of his non-theological background, was immune to tradition and was therefore able to receive truth from scripture "like a blank sheet (receives) the impression of the printer's type." Campbell angrily and sarcastically pointed out Thomas' faulty logic:

> To throw this into a logical laboratory and draw it off after fermentation subsides, it reads logically as follows: — To be born in Ireland, to be educated in Scotland disqualifies a person from perceiving some truths. But the Editor of the Millennial Harbinger was born in Ireland and educated in Ireland and Scotland; therefore the Editor of the Millennial Harbinger cannot perceive certain truths.

> To be born in England and to be educated in a private boarding house, and to spend seven years among bottles and dead bodies, makes a man's mind a blank sheet, and prepares him for the discovery of every truth. But the Editor of the Apostolic Advocate was born in England, educated in a private boarding-house, and spent seven years among bottles and dead bodies; therefore the Editor of the Apostolic Advocate has a mind fair as a blank sheet, prepared for the discovery of every truth.[24]

In the discussion of Thomas' latest speculations the ever-widening rift with Campbell became most apparent. Thomas at this point was accusing Campbell of treating him in an "unbrotherly" and "unfriendly" way.[25] He likened Campbell's action to those of Pope Leo X as he sought to deal with a young Martin Luther. When all efforts to win him back had failed, Leo X banned the reading of his books. In effect, Thomas claimed, this is what Campbell had done as he sought to diminish the influence of the *Apostolic Advocate*.[26]

As the controversy regarding Thomas' new theories raged, the rebaptism question was gradually pushed to the back burner. With the exception of the Lunenberg correspondence, the Campbell-Thomas controversy would now center on Thomas' eschatological speculations. Thomas felt his antagonists were relieved to have this new issue to attack rather than pursue all the implications of the rebaptism question. Regarding the appearance of thirty-four questions, Thomas said: ". . . these questions came as a god-send to these preachers, who preached baptism for the remission of all men's sins but their *own*."[27]

The last straw for Campbell came after the Thomas-Watt debate in August 1837. John Watt, a Presbyterian, debated Thomas at a Lunenberg County, Virginia, site on what had come to be known as Thomas' "peculiar views." The debate received considerable exposure. James Hunnicutt, a local Methodist preacher, wrote a report for the Methodist *Virginia and North Carolina Journal*. His report in both the *Apostolic Advocate* and the *Millennial Harbinger* formed the most extensive eyewitness account of the meeting. It was not a very flattering treatment of Thomas.

Thomas' latest defense of his theories proved to be the impetus for decisive action by Campbell. Thomas had done considerable internal harm to the movement and now his renegade teaching was becoming an embarrassment to denominationalists. "*The Rubicon is passed in the late discussion*," wrote Campbell.[28] He could no longer hold Thomas in fellowship and unreservedly called on others to sever their ties with him. In the strongest words Campbell had used to date, he declared:

> I can have no more fellowship with these pernicious doctrines, nor with those who believe and teach them, than I can with Mormonism and those who teach it. . . . I regard the author of them as an incorrigible factionist, and the new doctrines as now avowed positively subversive of the Christian faith.[29]

Campbell made his statement of disfellowship with "great reluctance" for fear of being charged with usurping authority over the brotherhood. Yet, "the present crisis elevates me above all this squeamishness," he said. Campbell called upon the church of which Thomas was a member to take action against him, and for other churches to follow suit. Campbell's call was not to go unheeded.

The next several months saw many churches go on record against Thomas. These included most of the churches in Virginia north of the James River and other churches, such as the one in Philadelphia with whom Thomas had previously been associated. Churches south of the James River were nearly unanimous in their support of Thomas. The elders of the Paineville congregation, of which Thomas was a member, voiced a determination to remain loyal to Thomas in spite of the consequences:

> Although we may hazard the loss of fellowship with many, yet we feel bound to risk that loss; rather than sever from our communion one whose walk is so exemplary, and whose devotion to the truth is so ardent as that of Bro. Thomas.[30]

Tension between the opposing forces reached its height in 1838. Although Thomas had his strongest support in churches south of the James River, nearly every congregation had at least a few members who were willing to keep the controversy alive on the local level. By the end of 1838 men on both sides of the issue were pressing for a "summit" of some kind between Campbell and Thomas, hoping this would avert the widespread division which seemed inevitable.

Campbell remained adamant in his censure of Thomas. In May 1838, Campbell, having already denied fellowship with Thomas, denied even a mention of him in the *Millennial Harbinger*. "I am . . . resolved that his name shall never again appear on our pages, until he reforms."[31] In October of the same year Campbell set out on an extended tour of the South. Passing through Virginia and observing the state of the church, he was moved to speak out against what he had previously chosen to ignore. Determined to settle the matter once and for all, Campbell sent word to Thomas that he was coming to Paineville the second week of November and would like to meet with him either publicly or privately to discuss his views. Thomas and a number of his supporters were there.

214

When members of both parties met, a formal debate was agreed upon. The propositions were to concern immortality, the resurrection, and the annihilation of the wicked. Campbell was insistent that no public record be made of the meeting so as to prevent even further shame to the movement.[32] Three days of debate followed. By the third day the discussion had not left the first point — the mortality of man! It was determined that since the men were at an impasse, further discussion would be fruitless. Therefore a committee of twenty-three men, comprising members of both parties, met to arbitrate the outcome of the meeting. They met for five hours and came out with a statement agreeable to both men. It declared that "all difficulties" between Campbell and Thomas had been resolved, and that "perfect harmony and co-operation" had been mutually agreed upon between them.[33]

The most significant thing to come out of this meeting was the resolution adopted by the participants. It reads as follows:

Resolved, that whereas certain things believed and propagated by Dr. Thomas, in relation to the mortality of man, the resurrection of the dead, and the final destiny of the wicked, having given offense to many brethren, and being likely to produce a division amongst us; and believing the said views to be of no *practical* benefit, we recommend to Brother Thomas to discontinue the discussion of the same, *unless in his defense, when misrepresented.*[34]

The Paineville agreement was effectively Thomas' last stand. He and Campbell had come eyeball to eyeball and Thomas had blinked. It was evident that the vast majority of the brethren, even those sympathetic with Thomas, wanted to avoid division at all costs. Thomas, having lost both face and credibility, could never be the same. In April 1839, he left Virginia to inspect land in Illinois. Finding it favorable, he returned to Amelia County in July and by the following December he and his family were on their way to the "far west."[35]

Thomas returned to Virginia for a brief visit in the summer of 1843 and moved back to Richmond in the fall of 1844. Here he reopened old wounds and sought again to sow the seed of discord. He was not as successful this time around. Thomas ultimately renounced all connection with the reformers, but not before he had been almost universally disfellowshipped.[36] Former friends and supporters were now coming to see Thomas' legacy of hate and division. Having been shut out of the movement, Thomas saved face by declaring non-fellowship with it. Since the reformers were no longer tolerant of his views, he was no longer tolerant of them.

Thomas apparently spent the rest of his life in Richmond, where he continued to preach, publish and practice medicine. Thomas travelled extensively during the later part of his life, both in the United States and abroad. His efforts at making converts produced weak results, but were not without some effect. Thomas' religious heirs today, the Christadelphians, trace their roots directly to Thomas' influence and teaching.[37] Thomas died on a preaching tour in New York City on March 5, 1871. He had survived his nemesis by only five years.

B. Thomas' Position on Rebaptism

Thomas' greatest impact on the American Restoration Movement was not his teachings on the soul and the afterlife, but his teachings regarding rebaptism. Thomas articulated an ultra-conservative position on baptism that was to affect the movement long after his disassociation from its ranks. Thomas, drawing on his own experience of being baptized by Walter Scott "for the remission of sins," and alluding to Campbell's earlier writings in the *Christian Baptist* and *Millennial Harbinger*, felt that his teachings were but "a consistent application of Campbellite principles."[38] His arguments are strong ones and worthy of consideration.

216

In "The Cry of 'Anabaptism,' " Thomas' first statement on the subject, Thomas made a distinction between baptism and immersion that was to form the basis for all his future arguments. Basing this distinction on a definition of *baptizo* found in Schrevilius' Greek lexicon, Thomas became convinced that the basic idea of *baptizo* was to dye, therefore *baptisma* was simply "a dyeing by immersion."[39] Immersion, therefore, was a generic term referring to the dipping of something into *any* liquid. Baptism, however, was a specific term referring only to the dipping of something into a certain *type* of liquid — that containing a dye.

Thomas felt this definition of *baptizo* had great implications for Christian baptism. Since *baptizo* meant to dye, the English word immersion was only a partial definition of baptism: "A man may be immersed, and yet not baptized; a man, however, cannot be baptized without being immersed."[40]

What, then, made the difference between Christian baptism and merely getting wet? Thomas said "the eye of faith" of the baptismal candidate must see the "crimson dye" of Jesus' blood flowing through the waters of baptism.

> If a man confess Jesus to be the Son of God, and apprehend his bloodshed for the remission of sins, and he be immersed . . . the eye of faith can see those waters dyed around him with the blood of Jesus. The eye of faith, however, must be open in the person baptized or dyed, as well as in the dyer or baptizer. A dyer accustomed to look upon coloured fluids may imagine water in his vat to be so; his imagination, however, will not dye the cloth; so may an administrator of baptism imagine that the subject recognizes the blood of Jesus, but his imagination will not supply the defect thereof. No! the subjects must believe and confess for himself, or his dipping will be mere immersion and not baptism.[41]

Knowledge of certain facts, therefore, at the time of the immersion determined the validity of the act. Following Campbell's lengthy "Reimmersion and Brother Thomas" in February 1836, Thomas stated this conviction as clearly as he would ever put it in print:

> A man, I conceive, may believe that Jesus is the Son of God, *in the scripture sense*, and that he arose from the dead, and upon this belief be immersed, and yet not be baptized . . . it is clear, that there is one thing lacking . . . *a belief in the sin-remitting efficacy of the blood of Jesus. . . .* It is not belief in certain *general* facts or truths; to which Jesus referred, when he said, 'he that believes and is baptized shall be saved' or have the remission of his sins. *Believes* WHAT *for salvation or the remission of sins?* . . . I answer, with deference to age and wisdom, in the paraphrase of the text — *He that believes in my blood, the blood of the New Institution, shed for many, for the remission of sins, shall be saved or pardoned* — how? *By what means?* BY BEING BAPTIZED FOR THE REMISSION OF SINS.[42]

Thomas used I Peter 3:21 — ". . . this water symbolizes baptism that now saves you" (NIV) — as support for his view that baptism is an expiatory, or intrinsically redeeming act. Commenting on this verse, Thomas stated that "anyone who knows anything of the true genius and spirit of the gospel of Christ" will realize that it is the blood of Jesus "in the holy ordinance of divine baptism"[43] that brings about the remission of sins. "He who says it is not, gives lie to the Holy Spirit, who declared by 1 Peter iii, 21 that '*we are saved by baptism.*' "[44]

Thomas derived further testimony regarding the efficacy of baptism from Ephesians 5:26-27. Speaking of Christ's sacrifice for the church, Paul writes: "To make her holy, cleansing her to himself as a radiant church, without stain or wrinkle or any other blemish, but holy and blameless" (NIV). Thomas had this to say about this passage:

> It is clear to my mind, from all Paul's writings, that he teaches, that as soon as a person is subjected to the INFLUENCE OF THE 'BATH OF WATER WITH THE WORD,' (emphasis mine — RMC) he is wholly sanctified, and cleansed, having neither spot, wrinkle, nor any such thing, that he is holy and without blemish; as free from actual transgression as a child unborn.[45]

218

Thomas uses I John 5:8 and Acts 19:1-6 to substantiate his claim that certain facts must be known by the one receiving baptism for that act to be valid. Citing I John 5:8, Thomas said scriptural baptism consisted of three elements — the water, the blood, and the Spirit. The water and blood are present in the ordinance of baptism. This is Thomas' "divine dye" necessary for salvation. The one to be baptized, therefore, must be led by the witness of the Spirit contained in Scripture to a knowledge of the faith necessary for baptism — "faith in the blood of Jesus and immersion."[46]

> Hence, then, two things are essential to constitute baptism, namely, *blood* and *water*. Four things are likewise necessary before a person can enjoy the benefits which flow from blood and water. First, *belief*; second, *repentance*; third, *confession*; and fourth, *immersion*.[47]

The event of Acts 19:1-6 should be regarded as a biblical precedent for rebaptism, Thomas maintained. Anyone baptized with a misunderstanding of the nature of Jesus and His redemptive work, as were these disciples of John, should be reimmersed for the right reason. Baptist immersion, for example, is "in almost all cases unscriptural" because it immerses people into a "declaration of falsehoods" — that pardon has been received prior to baptism, which is contrary to what the Scriptures teach.

> Our argument is this, that the *premises upon which an immersion is predicated characterizes the immersion, and that if these premises do not harmonize with those laid down in the Scriptures of truth, the immersion is not Christian immersion or baptism.* The twelve disciples of John were re-immersed for this very cause. . . .[48]

Thomas applied his view of the necessity of an "intelligent faith" in published correspondence with the elders of the Baltimore church, a congregation with whom he had previously

219

been associated.[49] Thomas had learned from two brethren who had visited Baltimore that the church there did not unconditionally accept Baptists into their fellowship, but required a public confession of faith in Christ at the time of admission. Although Thomas would have rebaptized the former Baptists, he was delighted that the Baltimore church "recognized the principle" he was advocating — *"that the terms of admission into a Baptist Church are not adequate to a reception into a Church of Christ."*[50]

Thomas still maintained that the Baptists were immersing on the basis of a counterfeit faith. To prove his point Thomas cited the case of Michael Quin, a Baptist missionary in Cape May, Maryland, whose story appeared in the *Religious Herald*, a Baptist paper published in Richmond. Quin, who reported thirty-one baptisms, described his successes and the emotional revivalistic techniques he used to bring them about. This is the ground of Baptist immersion, Thomas said. Sinners are immersed into their experiences rather than on the basis of an intelligent faith in Jesus Christ. They are "terrified" into obedience rather than edified. Theirs was a washing of water *without* the word rather than with it (Eph. 5:26), therefore it was invalid. Thomas even went so far as to say that "in nine hundred and ninety-nine cases out of one thousand members of popular Baptist churches *both confession and re-immersion* are necessary for their admission into the Church of Christ."[51]

In their response to Thomas the Baltimore elders declared that they receive none from the Baptists who have not previously believed "the message of salvation *as taught by their preachers.*" The confession they asked of prospective members was to satisfy themselves of *"the ground* on which . . . *their whole Christian movements rested."* The elders then set forth a line of reasoning that Thomas would hear again — one need not have full knowledge at the time of baptism for it to be considered valid:

If you would *re-baptize* every one who knows less of the 'one

220

faith, one Lord, and one baptism' than you now do, it might so happen (for who is perfect in knowledge) that some years hence, some disciples may excel your present knowledge, and call upon you to submit a second time to immersion, and in this way, we would, instead of the *one baptism*, have every one who is diligent in acquiring knowledge, immersed every year.[52]

From the very beginning Thomas' view of baptism received a mixed response. Some came out in full sympathy with Thomas,[53] while others, such as "Susan," Campbell, and the Baltimore Elders, had grave reservations. Anti-Thomas sentiment gained momentum following publication of speculative teachings concerning the afterlife. The rebaptism issue ceased being the focus as attention turned to Thomas' latest novelty. In fact, as time wore on it appears that some ambiguity developed over what Thomas' true views were concerning baptism. Therefore certain brethren sought to find out. Following repeated attempts throughout 1837 to have Thomas clarify his view,[54] Thomas Henley and John DuVal, former Baptists and prominent Virginia evangelists, called on Thomas to "declare explicitly" whether "we are *christians* or not, *without re-immersion*. You have studied the subject well, and known many of us for several years. We desire a *short* and *unequivocal* answer."[55]

Thomas' answer was neither "short" nor "unequivocal." At the end of a six-page article Thomas evasively stated that it would be impossible for him to make a determination. "My faith upon the matter is, that I do not believe, that one is a Christian who has not obeyed the gospel." Each individual must examine himself to see if his conversion was "identical" to that of the early Christians. If it is not, Thomas said, "I would not die in his state for a thousand worlds."[56]

Thomas' answer was, not surprisingly, unacceptable to Henley and DuVal. In May 1838 DuVal wrote Thomas stating "a few conclusions he had reached concerning him." In what was later known as "The DuVal Anathema," DuVal claimed Thomas was both a "deceiver" and a "corrupt man" and was merely using the movement to his own selfish ends.[57] DuVal's disfellowship was significant as he and the Tidewater brethren he represented had once been among Thomas' strongest supporters.

Thomas' conservative view of baptism found an enduring place in the Restoration Movement.[58] His position is essentially the one held by many in the mainstream and conservative churches of Christ (non-instrumental). The issue has periodically surfaced for debate. Thomas' position, requiring express knowledge of the remission of sins that takes place at baptism, continues to be embraced by the more conservative elements of the movement.

C. Campbell's Position on Rebaptism

As Alexander Campbell spoke out against John Thomas' practice of rebaptizing immersed Baptists, he was, in fact, defending his own baptism. In 1812, when faced with a decision of whether or not to baptize his new-born daughter, Campbell commenced a study of the subject and concluded that Scripture does not authorize infant baptism. So convinced was he that on June 12 of that year he and seven others (including his wife, a sister, and mother and father) were immersed at the hand of Matthias Luce, a local Baptist minister who had been called in for the occasion.[59]

Alexander Campbell was not knowingly baptized for the remission of sins. The connection of baptism with remission of sins did not become apparent to him until just before his debate with the Presbyterian W.L. MacCalla in 1823.[60] Nevertheless, Campbell always maintained that ignorance of this one feature or blessing of baptism in no way invalidated an otherwise scriptural act. Campbell always maintained that a simple profession of faith in Christ at the time of immersion was an ample basis for scriptural baptism.

While Campbell was not aware at the time of his immersion

that baptism was for the remission of sins, the question remains — did he believe his sins were already forgiven prior to June 12, 1812? More than likely, yes. Campbell held to a "Reformed" concept of baptism at least until his debate with MacCalla in 1823.[61] What this means is he believed baptism was a "sign" (outward representation) of the "thing signified" (salvation). The "thing signified" is a present possession when one receives the "sign." Consider the following excerpt from the Campbell-MacCalla debate:

> The blood of Christ, then *really* cleanses us who believe from all sin. Behold the goodness of God in giving us a *formal* proof and token of it, by ordaining a baptism expressly 'for the remission of sins!' The water of baptism, then, *formally* washes away our sins. The blood of Christ *really* washes away our sins. Paul's sins were *really pardoned* when he believed, yet he had no solemn pledge of the fact, no *formal* acquittal, no *formal* purgation of his sins, until he washed them away in the water of baptism.[62]

Although Campbell's thinking on the purpose of baptism was slowly evolving, it is clear that he thought his sins were already forgiven. When he discovered the true import of baptism he felt no need to be reimmersed.[63]

Campbell routinely opposed Thomas' efforts to promote the rebaptism of former Baptists. Campbell felt this was without biblical basis and "wholly ultra [to] our views of reformation."[64] Faith in Jesus was the sole prerequisite for baptism. This formed the burden of Campbell's argument. To require more than a simple faith in Christ was to bind where Scripture does not bind, and to make a mockery of 1800 years of Christian history.

Campbell was quick to label Thomas' view of reimmersion as legalism. In the opening paragraph of his reply to "Susan" (his first public response to Thomas' position) Campbell, quoting Acts 15:1, compared Thomas' actions to the Jews who taught the Gentiles that "except you be circumcised, *according to the manner of Moses, you cannot be saved.*"[65]

Characteristic of Thomas' legalistic approach was his distinction between immersion and baptism. This was the basis for his teaching and Campbell felt it was a flimsy one. Baptism and immersion were synonyms — "the one means not immersion with faith, and the other immersion without faith; for they equally mean immersion, with or without faith, so far as either the original language or New Testament usage is concerned."[66] In a later article Campbell came more to the point:

> Is not this a *lusus verborum*, a mere play of words? A tyro may know what the Doctor means, but no learned man will affirm that the words are correctly applied. Is it not as good sense to say, Baptism is not immersion, neither is re-baptism re-immersion? Is baptism both faith and immersion!! Well, then, 'he that believes and is baptized,' is bad divinity. It should read, He that is baptized shall be saved![67]

To carry Thomas' dogmatism further, Campbell, with tongue-in-cheek asserted that to be consistent a council ought to be held to pass judgment on every Baptist's immersion.[68] Such a committee could then determine the motive which prompted them to first be immersed and discern whether or not they ought to be rebaptized.[69] Campbell strongly believed that sectarianism would be the result.

> If, then, we must erect a new tribunal to determine *the true believers*, and *the true gospel*, and *the true baptism*, before admission to the Lord's table, we ought to abandon the no-human-creed system, and . . . vote in the church on all the 'candidates for immersion.'[70]

Instead of councils and tribunals Campbell said he would follow Paul's injunction in II Corinthians 13:5 — "Examine yourselves, whether you are in the faith." Thomas' view would change the verse to read "Examine one another whether you are in the faith."[71] Campbell was content to "leave this matter to the intelligence and conscience of every individual," accepting those who felt their baptism conformed to New Testament teaching, and "cheerfully re-immersing" those who felt it did not.[72]

Thomas' sectarian view of baptism was a slap in the face to all in previous centuries who have sought the Lord to the best of their knowledge. Campbell felt that Thomas' call for believers to "nullify their former profession" that they might be "baptized for the remission of sins" was to "paganize all immersed persons, and to place the world, the whole world, Jew, Gentile and Christian, just as it was on the day of Pentecost."[73] He was unwilling, in contrast to Thomas, to put immersed persons outside the pale of the reformation "on the same footing with the Papists of the 10th century, or the Mahometans of the 19th."[74]

The force of Campbell's argument against rebaptism lay in his belief that "he that believes and is baptized shall be saved."[75] The faith scripture speaks of, Campbell declares, is not in baptism, but in Jesus Christ and His sacrifice which gives baptism meaning. Therefore Campbell could boldly assert:

Who is a citizen of the kingdom of heaven? I answer, every one that believes in his heart that Jesus of Nazareth is the Messiah the Son of God, and publicly confesses his faith in his death for our sins, in his burial and resurrection, by an immersion into the name of the Father, the Son, and the Holy Spirit. Every such person is a *constitutional* citizen of Christ's kingdom.[76]

While Campbell believed that sins were ultimately washed away at baptism, he felt that knowledge of this fact at the time was not material to the faith necessary for immersion. The faith Scripture speaks of in connection with baptism is not the understanding of a list of *facts* but *trust* in a person (Jesus Christ) and what He has accomplished. One does not need to clearly understand everything about baptism at the point of immersion, otherwise Paul would have to rebaptize the Christians in Rome, Galatia, and Corinth, for in his letters to Christians in each of these places he had to explain the meaning of baptism.[77]

Campbell had addressed this point earlier in a series on baptism in the *Christian Baptist*, the forerunner of the *Millennial Harbinger* printed in the 1820s. Using the analogy of a marriage, Campbell likens baptism to a wedding ceremony. Just as a bride puts on the name of her husband at the altar, a believer "puts on Christ" in baptism. Just as a bride receives all kinds of rights and privileges as a result of her new name, so also the baptized believer receives all that is Christ's (I Cor. 3:21-23):

> Because we are Christ's, we have all things. . . . Among these 'all things' we can easily find the forgiveness of sins. . . . Some persons have thought that because they did not understand the import of christian immersion, at the time of their immersion, they ought to be immersed again in order to enjoy the blessings resulting from this institution; but as reasonably might a woman seek to be married a second, a third, or a fourth time to her husband, because at the expiration of the second, third, and fourth years of her marriage, she discovered new advantages and blessings resulting from her alliance with her husband, of which she was ignorant at the time of her marriage.[78]

Long before Thomas appeared on the scene Campbell had been forced to deal with the issues of faith, remission of sins, and baptism. In July 1830 Robert B. Semple, a prominent Virginia Baptist, wrote Campbell asking his view of baptism. Semple wanted to know if Campbell believed baptism was "the act of regeneration" without which sins could not be forgiven and that "the blood of Christ is never applied but through the medium of baptism." Campbell, referring Semple to his "Extra on Remission" (MH, 1830) said, "It is very nearly a correct statement of my views."[79] It is easy to see how Campbell could be misconstrued as believing baptism was an expiatory rite.

Misconstrued it was. In 1831, following Campbell's "Extra on Remission," Andrew Broaddus, another prominent Virginia Baptist, published a tract entitled, "Extra Examined," in which he accused Campbell of taking the very extremes Thomas would take about four years later. In his defense, Campbell, though not denying the connection remission of sins has with baptism, did deny that baptism is an expiatory rite, saying he that views it as such "mistakes the whole matter."[80] Baptism is far more than a "mere outward bodily act" as Broaddus had accused him of maintaining. "The soul of the intelligent subject is as fully immersed *into the Lord Jesus*, as his body is immersed *in the water*. His soul rises with the Lord Jesus, as his body rises out of the water. . . ."[81]

In his defense to Broaddus, Campbell stressed that remission of sins was not the only blessing connected with baptism. It is impossible to be baptized for the remission of sins "apart from all other blessings."

> We do not insulate the remission of sins as the only blessing connected with baptism, nor as the only thing necessary to salvation; but . . . we regard baptism as securing to the believing subject all the blessings of the new covenant, and especially the remission of sins, on which we *emphasize* when we address the penitents, or those who make baptism a mere ceremony.[82]

It is not necessary to understand all of these blessings to receive the benefit of them. Rebaptism, therefore, besides being "without command, precedent, or reason from the New Testament," is an inference of man and is without authorization. The very nature of baptism demands it to be a one time experience. The one who comes to baptism with a sincere faith in Christ, has the full assurance of salvation when he obeys God by being immersed. Subsequent revealing of the blessings he has obtained in Christ Jesus will only make him more appreciative of what God has done in Christ.[83]

Barton W. Stone, like Campbell, believed baptism was the means of salvation but was not the source of salvation. Stone writes:

> Baptism saves us and washes away our sins, in the same manner that the waters of Jordan washed away Naaman's

leprosy. . . . None are so ignorant as to think that the literal water washed away his leprosy; but that it was Naaman's obedience to the divine order. So in baptism, none are so ignorant as to imagine that water washes away sins or saves; but it is the grace of God through obedience to his ordinance.[84]

Campbell's view of baptism formed a biblical middle ground between two extremes. On one hand, baptism, as viewed by Thomas and others, was merely a legalistic formula for procuring remission of sins. On the other hand lay the equally dangerous view that Broaddus and others held — baptism is merely an external bodily act, detached from God's plan of salvation. Faith in Jesus and the willingness to conform one's life to His image formed the only prerequisite to baptism. "He that believes and is baptized shall be saved."

D. The Lunenberg Letter and the Thomas Controversy

No treatment of the Thomas controversy would be complete without a treatment of the famous Lunenberg Letter. One woman's question regarding what constituted a Christian and Campbell's answer to her has become a focal point for all subsequent discussion in the Restoration movement on the fellowship question. The Lunenberg Letter was a direct response to Campbell's controversy with Thomas regarding baptism. This is a perspective many historians fail to consider when treating the letter and its related comments. "Shelemiah," as the lady from Lunenberg styled herself, wrote to Campbell at the height of his controversy with Thomas. She wrote to Campbell from the heart of a region favorable to Thomas. She was obviously in sympathy with what Thomas taught in regard to baptism. These considerations were to have a decided effect on how Campbell responded to her question.

The place of the Lunenberg letter incident in the sequence of the Campbell-Thomas controversy is significant. The letter, which was dated July 1837, came during a lull in the on-going feud. Campbell and Thomas' positions regarding rebaptism had been established during 1835 and early 1836. The *Gospel Advocate* incident, in the fall of 1836, brought feeling for Thomas to an all-time high, but, in early 1837, pro-Thomas sentiment had clearly begun to wane. The first half of 1837, which brought no major developments in the controversy, was largely a silent period in which Thomas, having just moved to the Virginia countryside from Richmond, became adjusted to his new surroundings. "Shelemiah" addressed her letter to Campbell near the end of this period, just before Thomas' crucial debate with Watt.

Campbell's response to the Lunenberg letter brought considerable alarm to many of his supporters in Virginia. The letter was obviously intended to put Campbell on the defensive. His frank discussion of the issue played right into the hands of the Virginia Thomasites. Although it may have been calculated to elicit support for Thomas' position, the letter had little effect as far as Thomas was concerned because by this point other factors had sealed Thomas' fate in the mind of the movement. Attention in the Lunenberg letter incident would be focused wholly on Campbell.

"Shelemiah's" letter appeared in the September 1837 *Millennial Harbinger*. In it she expressed concern over recent statements by Campbell assuming that there were Christians in Protestant denominations:

> Will you be so good as to let me know how any one becomes a Christian? At what time did you become a Christian? At what time did Paul have the name of Christ called upon him? . . . Does the name of Christ or Christian belong to any but those who believe *the gospel, repent*, and are buried by baptism into the death of Christ?[85]

In his reply to "Shelemiah," Campbell said it is imposible to believe that there are "no Christians in all the world except ourselves." Such a claim implies that Christ's people had been extinct for centuries and that *"the gates of hell have prevailed against his church!"*[86] There are, therefore, Christians among the sects.

But to advance the "one point" to which "this conscientious sister" was leading, Campbell declared:

> But who is a Christian? I answer, Every one that believes in his heart that Jesus of Nazareth is the Messiah, the Son of God; repents of his sins, and obeys him in all things according to the measure of knowledge of his will. *A perfect man in Christ*, or a perfect Christian, is one thing; and "a babe in Christ," a stripling in the faith or an imperfect Christian is another.[87]

Campbell's assertion that one is a Christian who obeys God to the full extent of his knowledge was a startling one indeed coming from one who had in the past decade done so much to restore a proper understanding of baptism. His statement *seemed* to negate everything he had taught on the subject. What if one's knowledge did not include baptism as taught in the New Testament? "Is not that the time we are born of water and spirit?" the lady from Lunenberg asked.

Campbell clearly stated one could be a Christian, although an imperfect one, without scriptural baptism. In doing so he seemed to be reacting against the Thomasite emphasis on the external nature of baptism and not the change in character the action was to symbolize.

> I cannot, therefore, make any one duty the standard of Christian state or character, not even immersion into the name of the Father, of the Son, and of the Holy Spirit. . . . It is the image of Christ the Christian looks for and loves; and this does not consist in being exact in a few items, but in general devotion to the whole truth as far as known.[88]

Having clearly answered "Shelemiah's" question, Campbell concludes with an important qualification:

But to conclude for the present — he that claims for himself a license to neglect the least of all the commandments of Jesus, because it is possible for some to be saved, who, through insuperable ignorance or involuntary mistake, do neglect or transgress it; or he that willfully neglects to ascertain the will of the Lord to the whole extent of his means and opportunities, because some who are defective in that knowledge may be Christians, is not possessed of the spirit of Christ, and cannot be registered among the Lord's people.[89]

Campbell's response sent a shock-wave of excitement through the brotherhood. In the coming months Campbell's reply would be discussed by restorationist and non-restorationist alike. Many would express puzzlement when Campbell's reply to the Lunenberg letter was compared with earlier writings. In the November *Millennial Harbinger* Campbell was forced to further clarify his position.[90]

Campbell claimed to have used the term "Christian" in a limited sense. Just as Paul spoke of inward and outward Jews, Campbell asks, "May we not have the *inward* and the *outward* Christians?" Baptism is more than a mere ritual — it is a submission of both the will and the intellect to Christ. It is possible, Campbell declares, for someone to be scripturally unbaptized, yet exhibit the change of character which is wholly pleasing to God. Such a person is indeed a Christian, though in an imperfect sense.[91]

In December Campbell again felt compelled to speak out on the issue. He particularly wanted to defend himself against the charge of inconsistency. Speaking of his present view, Campbell said, "It is with us as old as baptism for remission of sins," referring the reader to the first two issues of the *Christian Baptist* and the days of his debate with MacCalla. Campbell then gives excerpts from his writings which clearly show he affirmed Christians among the denominations. He claimed he could produce many more.[92]

Campbell believed the sheer logic of the movement supported the idea of Christians among the denominations. Why plead for unity of all Christians, he asked, if it is believed that all Christians were already united in one religious body? Why has the movement so often "quoted and applied" passages such as Revelation 18:4 — "Come out of her, my people" — to "apostate Christendom" if it is not believed that some of God's people yet remain in Babylon?[93]

The fact that there are Christians among the sects in no way invalidates the need for scriptural baptism. This was Campbell's contention. He declared:

> There is not on earth a person who can have as full an assurance of justification and remission of sins, as the person who has believed, confessed his faith, and been intelligently buried and raised with the Lord. . . . [It is] the duty of all believers to be immersed, if for no other reason than that of honoring the divine institution and opening a way for the union and co-operation of all Christians.[94]

Although Campbell's response to the Lunenberg letter did not satisfy all of his readers, either ancient or modern, an underlying consistency seems to run through his writings on the subject. Campbell realized that what he was giving was opinion and therefore he did not want to appear too dogmatic.[95] Nevertheless, his views have influenced the movement to this day.

E. Conclusion

Perhaps the most enduring lesson to emerge from a study of the Thomas controversy is the need of the Restoration Movement to define the limits of Christian fellowship. May only the immersed be accepted, and if so, on what conditions? This was the basic issue of the Thomas controversy and one that has begged the movement's attention ever since.

Two extremes present themselves. There are those who

would extend Christian fellowship to any who profess the name of Christ whether they are immersed or unimmersed. This is an unbiblical extreme because the New Testament knows nothing of unimmersed Christians. The speculative possibility that God may eventually save unimmersed persons for reasons of His own does not authorize fellowship with the unbaptized. Within the Restoration heritage the Disciples of Christ denomination has followed this approach as they actively seek union with other religious bodies.

On the other extreme are those who would claim fellowship only with those who have been immersed with the express knowledge that it was for the remission of sins. It was John Thomas who first articulated and practiced this extreme in the Stone-Campbell movement. He represents an extreme that historically has been associated with the more conservative elements of the movement. Proponents of this view place an over-emphasis on the remission of sins aspect of baptism. Since the New Testament reveals a variety of blessings that result from the act, it is erroneous to restrict valid baptism to the knowledge of just one of these blessings. Consistency would demand full knowledge of all the blessings rather than the arbitrary focus upon just one. For example, many who hold this position would rebaptize all who were immersed unaware that baptism was connected with the remission of sins, but accept all those who may have been unaware that baptism was connected with the receipt of the Holy Spirit (Acts 2:38; I Corinthians 12:13).

Is there a middle ground? Between these two extremes are those who avoid the unbiblical position of the left by asserting that fellowship can only be extended to the immersed. Yet, on the other hand, they avoid the extreme of the right by maintaining that baptism is valid if it is done with faith in the person and sacrifice of Jesus Christ. Alexander Campbell represents this moderating view. In response to Thomas he made remarks which may have over-stated his case, yet the fact remains that Campbell nowhere advocated full fellowship with the unimmersed. Only those immersed with a genuine faith in Christ have the assurance of salvation. Only to the immersed can fellowship conscientiously be extended. This has not always been a popular view in the Restoration Movement. Advocates of the extremes have always been easier to find. Yet it is the tenet on which the movement began. It may also be its best hope for the future.

Endnotes

1. The principal source for biographical information on Thomas has been Robert Roberts' *Dr. Thomas: His Life and Work* (Birmingham, England: C.C. Walker, 1911). This work was first published by Roberts, a Christadelphian and close associate of Thomas, in 1884.

2. John Thomas, Richmond, Virginia, 17 November 1834, to Alexander Campbell in *Millennial Harbinger* 6 (February 1835): 87. (Hereafter designated as MH).

3. Roberts, *Dr. Thomas*, p. 15.

4. Ibid., p. 18.

5. John Thomas, "Reformation in Richmond, Chapter 2," *The Advocate or the Testimony of God* 5 (July 1838): 87. *The Apostolic Advocate* (1834-39) ran variously as the *Apostolic Advocate* (vols. 1-2), the *Apostolic Advocate and Prophetic Interpreter* (vol. 3), and the *Advocate for the Testimony of God* (vols. 4-5). (Hereafter designated as AA, AAPI, and ATOG.)

6. Ibid.

7. Ibid.

8. Ibid., pp. 92-93.

9. John Thomas, "The Cry of 'Anabaptism,' " AA 1 (October 1834): 121-29.

10. Richmond (Virginia) Sycamore Church, Minutes of Meetings, 1832-1851 (Photocopy). In Virginia State Library, Richmond, Virginia. These were not the only rebaptisms Thomas performed during this same period. (See Thomas, "Reply to Albert Anderson," AA 2 [1 August 1835]: 88.)

11. "Susan" (pseud.?), Fredericksburg (prob.), Virginia, 1 August 1835, to Alexander Campbell, in MH 6 (September 1835): 417-20.

12. John Thomas, " 'Susan' and Brother A. Campbell," AA 2 (1 October 1835): 130. Thomas says "Mr. Susan" was from Fredericksburg, Virginia as the initial "F" indicates. He evidently has someone specific in mind.

13. Ibid., p. 133.

14. John Thomas, Richmond, Virginia, 20 December 1835, to Alexander Campbell, in AA 2 (1 January 1836): 202.

15. Alexander Campbell, "Re-baptism," MH 6 (December 1835): 619.
See also "Reimmersion and Brother Thomas," MH 6 (November 1835): 565.
16. Ibid.
17. John Thomas, "Rising with Christ in Baptism," AA 2 (1 January 1836): 215.
18. Alexander Campbell, "Reimmersion and Brother Thomas," MH 7 (February 1836): 58-59. This article is not to be confused with a previous one by the same name (MH November 1835).
19. In the August 1836 *Gospel Advocate* an article by "Plain Dealing" appeared entitled, "Dr. John Thomas of the Apostolic Advocate, a Factionist." (GA 2, pp. 123-24.) Attacking Thomas as a divisive spirit, the pseudonymous author called for Thomas' immediate disfellowship. A number of Reformers rose in Thomas' defense (cf. Robert Richardson, Bethany [W.] Virginia, 29 September 1836 to Benjamin F. Hall and John T. Johnson, in GA 2 [October]: 145-47), thus indicating that the brotherhood as a whole was still tolerant of Thomas and his views. Thomas held Hall and Johnson, the editors of the paper, personally responsible. Johnson disavowed all responsibility for the piece (cf. AAPI 3 [1 November 1836]: 157.) In his remarks to Johnson's letter, Thomas said he expected a similar explanation from Hall. It never came.
20. Thomas' first indication of his unorthodox eschatology appeared in the form of thirty-four questions in "Information Wanted," AA 2 (1 December 1835): 177-80. He elaborated his views in " 'The Spirits of Just Men:' — The Resurrection," AA 2 (1 February 1836): 218; "Enoch and Elijah: Animal and Spiritual Bodies; the Judgement; Thief on the Cross; Stephen; Souls; Religion in the Blood," AA 2 (1 March 1836): 241-46; and "Future Punishment: Not Eternal Life in Misery, but Destruction," AA, supplement (1 April 1836): 1-12 (i.e., 285-296).
21. Alexander Campbell, "Materialism — No. 1-4," MH 7 (September 1836): 396-403; (October 1836): 451-57; (November 1836): 520-25; (December 1836): 556-60. "Conversations in Father Goodal's Family Circle at Thomas Goodal's. [:] Ghosts — Sleeping Spirits — Paradise," MH 7 (April 1836): 169-74; "Conversations in Father Goodal's Family Circle, on a visit to Paynesville at the House of Mr. Payne," MH 7 (September 1836): 407-11.
22. Campbell, "Materialism — No. 1," p. 397.
23. Thomas, "Dialogue between Three Friends on Men and Things," AAPI 3 (1 June 1836): 28.
24. Campbell, "Materialism — No. 2." p. 454.
25. Thomas, "Matter and Manner, or Spiritualism as defended by Brother Alexander Campbell," AAPI 3 (1 September 1836): 105.
26. Thomas, "The Harbinger on 'Materialism,' No. 2," AAPI 3 (January 1837): 209.
27. Roberts, *Dr. Thomas*, p. 76. Roberts cites *Herald of the Future Age* 3 (1847): 125.
28. Campbell, "Remarks on the Preceding Documents," MH 1, n.s. (November 1837): 514. Campbell reprinted both Thomas' and Hunnicutt's

235

reports of the debate.

29. Ibid., p. 512.

30. Thomas, "The Church at Paineville and the Harbinger," ATOG 4 (January 1838): 302-303.

31. Campbell, "The Richmond Letter and Dr. Thomas," MH 2, n.s. (May 1838): 226.

32. Campbell, "A Narrative of My Last Interview with Dr. John Thomas," MH 7, n.s. (May 1843): 225.

33. Ibid., p. 226.

34. Ibid.

35. Roberts, Dr, Thomas, pp. 153-156.

36. Apparently Thomas' formal renunciation of the Reformers took place in March 1847. James Wallis, editor of the British MH affirms this in the October 1848 edition of his paper. This information appears in Dr. Thomas, p. 259.

37. For additional information on Christadelphianism, see Frederick J. Powicke, "Christadelphians" in Encyclopedia of Religion and Ethics, ed. James Hastings (New York, N.Y.: Charles Scribner's Sons, 1955), 3:569-71; and Alan Eyre, The Protesters (Birmingham, England: The Christadelphian, 1975), pp. 166-90.

38. Roberts, Dr. Thomas, p. 34. (See also John Thomas, "Rising with Christ in Baptism," AA 2 [1 January 1836]: 215).

39. Thomas, "The Cry of 'Anabaptism,' " p. 122.

40. Ibid.

41. Ibid.

42. Thomas, "Brother Campbell's Ultimatum or the 'Stripling' and the 'Giant,' " AA 2 (1 April 1836): 245-75.

43. Thomas, "The Cry of 'Anabaptism,' " p. 125.

44. Ibid., p. 126.

45. Thomas, "Re-immersion," and "Remarks," AA 2 (1 September 1835): 104.

46. Thomas, "The Cry of 'Anabaptism,' " p. 123.

47. Ibid., pp. 123-24.

48. Thomas, "Re-immersion" and "Remarks," p. 102.

49. John Thomas, Richmond, Virginia, 10 June 1835, to Baltimore Elders, in AA 2 (1 July 1835): 65; "Re-immersion" and "Remarks," pp. 97-105. This last piece included the Baltimore Elders' reply to Thomas' letter followed by his remarks.

50. Ibid., p. 65.

51. Ibid., p. 66.

52. Baltimore Elders in "Re-immersion" and "Remarks," p. 99.

53. See James M. Bagby, Louisa, Virginia, 14 August 1835, to John Thomas, in AA 2 (1 October 1835): 139.

54. Thomas M. Henley and John DuVal, King and Queen, Virginia, 11 January 1838 to John Thomas, in ATOG 4 (February 1838): 343.

55. Henley and DuVal, Letter, p. 344.

56. John Thomas, "To All 'In the Pursuit of Truth and Christian Unity,' " ATOG 4 (February 1838): 349-50.

57. John DuVal, King and Queen, Va., 23 May 1838, to John Thomas, in ATOG 5 (July 1838): 82-83.

58. An enlightening example of the long-standing acceptance of the conservative position is seen in the writings of Tolbert Fanning. See "Remission," *Christian Review* 2 (September 1845): 195-197, and "Dr. John Thomas and His Cause," *Gospel Advocate* 4 (January 1858): 30-31. See chapter 8 of this book for later controversies.

59. Robert Richardson, *Memoirs of Alexander Campbell* (Indianapolis, Indiana: Religious Book Service, reprint ed., 1976), pp. 391-98. As a Presbyterian, Campbell had been sprinkled as an infant (p. 395).

60. This fact is well attested by Campbell in "Dr. Thomas — Again," MH 2, n.s. (February 1838): 86. In "The Extra Defended: Being an Examination of Mr. A. Broaddus' 'Extra Examined,' " MH 2, Extra (10 October 1831): 4, Campbell credited his father with drawing the connection between baptism and remission of sins (See letter by "T.W." [Thomas Campbell] in the *Christian Baptist* for September 1823.) Campbell confessed that although he preached baptism for the remission of sins as early as 1823, its full import did not become apparent until much later ("Remission of Sins," MH 1, Extra [5 July 1830]: 50).

61. I am indebted at this point to John Hicks in a privately circulated paper, "Alexander Campbell and Christians Among the Sects." (Editor's Note: See chapter five of this book for a revised version of that paper.)

62. Alexander Campbell and W.L. MacCalla, *A Public Debate on Christian Baptism* (London, England: Simpkin and Marshall, 1842; reprint ed., Kansas City, Mo.: Old Paths Book Club, 1948), p. 116. Emphasis is Campbell's.

63. Campbell's distinction between "formal" and "actual" forgiveness of sins was less apparent by 1828. In the *Christian Baptist* for that year he maintained that baptism "did formally, and in fact, convey . . . the forgiveness of sins" ("Ancient Gospel — No. I [:] Baptism," *Christian Baptist* 5 [7 January 1828]: 401). In the same series of articles Campbell affirmed "that in, and by, the act of immersion, so soon as our bodies are put under water, at that very instant our former, or 'old sins' are washed away" ("Ancient Gospel — No. II [:] Immersion," *Christian Baptist* 5 [4 February 1828]: 416). Campbell's extra on "Remission of Sins" at the close of the first volume of the *Millennial Harbinger* reflects this change of thought.

64. Alexander Campbell, " 'Reply' to Susan," MH 6 (September 1835): 418.

65. Ibid.

66. Campbell, "Re-immersion and Brother Thomas," MH 6 (November 1835): 565.

67. Campbell, "Re-immersion and Brother Thomas," MH 7 (February 1836): 61. Both this article and the one printed in November 1835 had the same title.

68. Campbell, "Re-immersion," (November 1835): 566.

237

69. Campbell, "Re-immersion," (February 1836): 59.

70. Campbell, "The Apostolic Advocate," MH 7 (May 1836): 229-30.

71. Campbell, "Re-immersion," (November 1835): 566.

72. Campbell, "Apostolic Advocate," p. 230.

73. Campbell, " 'Reply' to Susan," p. 418.

74. Ibid.

75. Campbell alludes to Mark 16:16 in "Apostolic Advocate," p. 229.

76. Campbell, " 'Reply' to Susan," p. 419.

77. Ibid.

78. Campbell, "Ancient Gospel — No. VI [:] Immersion," *Christian Baptist* 5 (2 June 1828): 447. Campbell did admit, however, that someone who was "expressly immersed *because their sins were forgiven*" may be "ignorant of the gospel" and need to "confess their presumption and reform." ("Re-immersion" [November 1835]: 567.)

79. Robert B. Semple, 5 July 1830, to Alexander Campbell and Campbell's reply in MH 1 (2 August 1830): 352, 357.

80. Campbell, "Rebaptism," MH 2 (7 November 1831): 41.

81. Campbell, "The Extra Defended," p. 11.

82. Campbell, "Rebaptism," p. 485.

83. Ibid., p. 482-483.

84. Barton W. Stone, "Reply," Obadiah Seward, Rushville, Ind., in *Christian Messenger* 2 (May 1828): 153. Stone, while believing in the necessity of baptism, does admit the possibility of being saved without it. Citing the case of Cornelius he says, "This proves that he has not bound himself to a plan from which he cannot depart" (p. 154). Stone and Campbell held similar views both on when sins were forgiven (*Christian Messenger* 3 [July 1829]: 217) and on the silence of the New Testament regarding Christian rebaptism (*Christian Messenger* 3 [July 1829]: 224).

85. "Shelemiah" (pseud.), Lunenberg, Va., 8 July 1837, in "Any Christians Among Protestant Parties," MH 1, n.s. (September 1837): 411. Campbell did not publish "Shelemiah's" letter in full. One year after the appearance of the Lunenberg letter in the MH, Thomas printed correspondence from Louisa A. Anderson, who, claiming to be "Shelemiah," produced an unedited copy of the now famous letter. This, with a cover letter, appeared in "The Celebrated Letter from the Lunenberg Sister," ATOG 5 (September 1838): 155-157.

86. Campbell, "Any Christians Among Protestant Parties," p. 411.

87. Ibid.

88. Ibid., p. 412.

89. Ibid., p. 414.

90. Campbell, "Christians Among the Sects," MH 1, n.s. (November 1837): 506. In this latest article Campbell revealed his answer to the Lunenberg sister had been decidedly shaped by her pro-Thomas perspective. (See also "Any Christians Among the Sects?" MH 1, n.s. [December 1837]: 564-66.) This underscores the need to look at Campbell's reply to the Lunenberg letter in light of the Thomas controversy.

91. Campbell, "Christians Among the Sects," pp. 507-08.
92. Campbell, "Any Christians Among the Sects?" pp. 561-63.
93. Ibid., p. 561.
94. Ibid., p. 564.
95. Campbell, "Christians Among the Sects," p. 506.

7

BARTON W. STONE AND BAPTISM FOR THE REMISSION OF SINS

Michael D. Greene

A. Biographical Background

Barton Warren Stone was a unique figure among the early leaders of the American Restoration Movement of the nineteenth century. He was the only one of the early leaders who was born in America. His early life in the late seventeen hundreds gave him opportunities to see the physical and ideological struggle for freedom, both political and religious, that we know as the American Revolution. This gave him a unique perspective on religious freedom and greatly affected his later thinking especially in the areas of unity and religious controversy.

Stone was also unique in that he was one of the first of the

241

early leaders of the Movement to begin his journey back to the Bible. His decisions to leave sectarianism and denominationalism were made several years before Alexander Campbell, who is generally accepted as the greatest leader in this movement, came to America. In many ways Stone was the precursor of Campbell and his work.[1] This is seen no better than with the subject this treatise covers: Stone's struggles for a complete understanding of what Bible baptism was all about, a struggle which began for Stone in 1807 and continued until his death in 1844. In order to understand Stone's pilgrimage some knowledge of his early life is necessary.

1. Exposure to Liberty

Stone was born near Port Tobacco, Maryland on December 24, 1772. His father died when he was very young. His mother, Mary Warren Stone, raised him and a large family alone. In 1779, they moved into Virginia. It was during this time that Stone was exposed to the fight for freedom. The revolutionary war was still raging and Stone was exposed to all the horrors of war. Religion was ignored and sin and every vice reigned. About this time, Stone later remembers:

> From my earliest recollection, I drank deeply into the spirit of liberty, and was so warmed by the soul-inspiring draughts that I could not hear the name of British, or tories, without feeling a rush of blood through the whole system. Such prejudices, formed in youth, are with difficulty ever removed. I confess their magic influence to this advanced day of my life.[2]

The effect of Stone's love for liberty can no doubt be seen in how he approached the matter of religion. Having learned early to hate all that called to mind oppression and despotism, he carried the same feeling into religion. Stone came to loathe anything that had an appearance of oppression and despotism in religion as he sought the ideal of "gospel liberty." This, as will be seen, affected how he approached religious controversy and differences

242

even among brethren.

Early in life Stone was also exposed to tyrrany in the classroom. His early exposure to education was through a teacher whom Stone called "a very tyrant of a teacher" who whipped and abused his students for every trivial offense. Stone remembered that when he was called upon to recite his lessons, he was stricken with fear and trembling and so confused in his mind, he could say nothing.[3] Again, the effects of such incidents early in life cannot but color one's attitudes, feelings and actions later in life.

2. Spiritual Liberty

Mary Warren Stone was too busy rearing her children to have what could be called a devout home. The climate of war and its attendant evils also worked to mitigate the effects of religion in Stone's early life. However, in his later education, the Bible was used as a text and Stone read from it often. He also loved to hear converts to religion tell their experiences, as was required of Calvinists of the day. This Stone accepted as the way of God, at this time knowing nothing better.

After the war, interest in religion began to grow and Stone's concern for spiritual matters also grew. Most in that day were Baptist or Presbyterian. But on an occasion a few Methodists appeared on the scene. These he remembered as being "grave, meek, plain and humble . . . and their zeal was fervent and unaffected." But the Baptists and Presbyterians resisted and opposed them.

> They publicly declared them to be the locusts of the Apocalypse and warned the people against receiving them. Poor Methodists! They were then but few, reproached, misrepresented, and persecuted as unfit to live on the earth. My mind was much agitated and I was vacillating between these two parties.[4]

Again, we see how Stone's concepts of liberty and hatred of

oppression in all things, including religion, were formed early in life and stayed with him throughout.

3. His Spiritual Pilgrimage

When Stone reached the age of fifteen or sixteen, his father's estate was divided between him and his three older brothers. Stone decided to invest his share in an education and entered Guilford Academy in North Carolina. This log cabin school was under the direction of David Caldwell. Caldwell was an ordained Presbyterian minister, trained at Princeton, who, along with many others like him, established these log cabin schools throughout the land to educate and train ministers. Stone at this time had no intention or desire to be a Christian, much less to preach. Although not openly hostile to religion, he was more intent on getting an education and becoming a lawyer.

When he arrived at Caldwell's school, he discovered a great deal of religious fervor among the students. This atmosphere had its effects on the tender mind and heart of Stone. He finally decided to "live and let live" and pursue his studies with all diligence. This succeeded for a time until a preacher named James McGready appeared, preaching as only a Calvinistic revivalist in the mold of Jonathan Edwards could. At his preaching Stone said "such was my excitement, that had I been standing, I should have probably sunk to the floor."[5]

From this point, Stone began a personal struggle that without doubt affected his mindset toward others who might also be struggling with truth, religion and their relationship with God in a very profound way. When one experiences a thing that affects him deeply, he develops great empathy toward others in a similar situation. Thus, Stone's personal travails with religion gave him a unique perspective and attitude toward others who were also unsettled in religion and questioning truth. This empathy is manifested often in Stone's later conflicts over many subjects including baptism and its relationship to salvation.

Now Stone is subject to a sometimes violent inner conflict.

Should he embrace religion or be content with his present state? At first he decided to reject religion and pursue the course he had set. But, if that was the case, it meant he would find himself among the damned, subject to all the terrors McGready had spoken of. That would never do! He decided then to seek religion, in the only way he knew. He began to look for God's coming, his work of grace, that experience which would, according to Calvinism, mark him as one of the elect. "For one year," Stone writes, "I was tossed on the waves of uncertainty — laboring, praying, and striving to obtain saving faith — sometimes desponding and almost despairing of ever getting it."[6]

At the close of that year, McGready came again to the environs of Caldwell's log cabin academy to preach. Again, his labors left Stone in a melancholy and "gloomy state, without one encouraging word." In this state he remained for some days more, during which time his strength failed him and "sighs and groans" filled his day. After a few days with his mother in Virginia, Stone returned to school and attended another meeting to hear a man named William Hodge preach. Hodge had been trained by Caldwell and had been preaching only a short time. He, however, was able to reach Stone, not with the fiery descriptions of hell and the fate of the damned, but with an emotional description of the love of God and what that love had done for sinners. Here Stone yielded, and threw himself on the mercies of this loving God that had been proclaimed. "My heart warmed," Stone wrote, "with love for that lovely character described and . . . hope and joy would rise in my troubled breast."[7] Thus Stone was "converted" around 1791 or 92.

One should not underestimate the effect of the sermon and the ministration of William Hodge on his young convert. This "new" concept and its significance was not lost on Stone, either at that time or in later life. E.E. Snoddy observed:

The sermon greatly moved him and from its influence he never escaped. The thought of the sermon became an anchor of his soul

245

throughout his period of doubt and uncertainty, and was the formative factor on his attitude toward all men. He could very appropriately be called "An Ambassador of the Love of God."[8]

Stone now desired to preach and pursued that new direction in his life. But even now, Stone's life was filled with emotional turmoil.

His religious life even for a while after his conversion suggests the tracings of a seismograph, showing now deep emotional stirrings and now, states of quiescence. His was a "tortured" soul, seeking religious satisfaction, finding it momentarily, only to plunge into some temporary despair. . . .[9]

In 1793 Stone became a candidate for the ministry from the Orange Presbytery in North Carolina. He received his license to preach in 1796 from that same presbytery. During these years the emotional turmoil continued. The turmoil was generated by his uncertainties about the Calvinistic doctrines which he had been taught and which he now preached. Stone saw the contradictions of urging men to believe when, according to Calvinism, they had no power to believe, and they must wait on God's power to act to mark them as one of the elect. Then and only then could they be empowered to believe.

Often when I was addressing the listening multitudes on the doctrine . . . my zeal in a moment would be chilled at the contradiction. How can they believe? How can they repent? How can they do impossibilities? How can they be guilty in not doing them? Such thoughts would almost stifle utterance, and were a mountain pressing me down to the shades of death.[10]

4. He Turns to the Word

Where was he to go for a solution? What was the answer? From this came an insight which affected Stone in a most profound way and paved the way for his future. He saw the only solution as being in the Word of God. Surely it would answer his questions; surely it would clear up his confusion.

> From this state of perplexity I was relieved by the precious Word of God. From reading and meditating on it, I became convinced that God did love the whole world, and that the reason he didn't save all was because of their unbelief; and the reason they believed not, was not because God did not exert his . . . power . . . but they neglected his testimony, given in the Word concerning his Son. . . . I saw that the requirement to believe on the Son of God was reasonable, because the testimony given (in the Word) was sufficient to produce faith in the sinner. . . . This glimpse of faith — of truth was the first ray of light, that ever led my distressed, perplexed mind from the labyrinth of Calvinism and error, in which I had so long been bewildered. It was that which lead me into the rich pastures of gospel liberty.[11]

The die was cast, the decision made, the Rubicon had been crossed. From this point on, Stone would find himself repeating this pattern of going to the Word for answers to religious questions and solutions to problems again and again. It soon became apparent to Stone that the solution to the problems facing the religious world was, as he had done, to go back to the Bible in all matters of faith and practice. Thus, he began to preach the universality of the gospel and the need of all men to hear the evidence God has given in the Word and believe it. Faith on the part of the sinner became the condition on which salvation was granted. All who heard were urged to believe and comply with the teachings of the glorious gospel of Christ.

Stone knew that his new pattern, this new approach to solving religious problems, as well as his new emphasis on the sinner's need and responsibility to believe the gospel, would cause him problems when it came time to be ordained, for at that time they would ask if he accepted the Confession of Faith, the creed of the Presbyterian church in which the doctrine of Calvinism was taught. Stone knew not how to respond, for if he spoke his conscience he would not be ordained. But to accept the creed would violate his conscience. When the occasion for his ordination came, he at first wanted to postpone it until he was "better informed and settled." But at the urging of his fellows he proceeded. When asked if he was willing to accept the Confession of Faith, Stone replied, "I do, as far as I see it consistent with the Word of God." No objection to this position was voiced and Stone was therefore ordained as a minister by the Transylvania Presbytery in the fall of 1798. He immediately became the minister for the Concord and Cane Ridge Presbyterian churches near Lexington, Kentucky where he was living at the time. One might think Stone's trials and tribulations would have abated, but it was not to be.

5. Introduced to Unity

In 1801 Stone was caught up in the revivals that occurred in the frontier state of Kentucky. The first occurred in Logan County, Kentucky, and was soon followed by one at Cane Ridge. During these revivals, men of every religious group worked in preaching the gospel in order to save the souls of men. Stone later said the "effects of these meetings (and preaching) through the country were like fire in a dry stubble driven by a strong wind." He further noted: "Yet the good effects were seen and acknowledged in every neighborhood, and among the different sects it silenced contention and promoted unity for a while."[12]

This unity was also a new concept. When set in contrast to the bitter controversies that raged in the religious community with "zeal and bad feeling," it is no wonder that it quickly captured Stone's mind and ultimately became his "polar star."

> The revival had opened to him the doors of a new idea through which he did not, apparently, pass until later: if men of many denominations can be united in a revival, there is no reason why they shouldn't be united all the time. Stone's idea of Christian unity unquestionably had its genesis in the revival experiences where many denominations worked together.[13]

248

For Stone, unity soon became more than a worthy goal to be pursued; it became a passion, a dominant passion in his life. He then began to labor for unity as though his life depended on it: for Stone, all was measured in terms of how it might affect that unity. In all of Stone's efforts, a spirit of conciliation was manifested, because for Stone, the basis of unity is the spirit (i.e. attitude) of Christ, and Christian love and forebearance were essential ingredients of that spirit.[14]

6. Conflict with Creeds

It was only a matter of time before the conflict between Stone's teaching and the Confession of Faith would be brought before the Presbytery. In 1803 Stone's close friend and compatriot, Robert McNemar, was brought before the Synod on charges of heresy. Stone, McNemar and four others[15] saw the ultimate outcome and resolved to withdraw from the Presbyterian church.

> This act of Synod (attempting to expel McNemar) produced great commotion and division in the churches; not only were churches divided, but families; those who had before lived in harmony and love, were now set on hostile array against each other. What scenes of confusion and distress! not produced by the Bible; but by human authoritative creeds, supported by sticklers for orthodoxy. My heart was sickened, and effectually turned against creeds, as nuisances of religious society, and the very bane of Christian unity.[16]

These six men went together to form the Springfield Presbytery which existed only in form and for only one year. They soon realized they were also "savoring of a party spirit." They threw the party name overboard, took the name Christian and, trusting in the Word of God alone, they divested themselves of all party creeds and names. From this period Stone dated "the commencement of that reformation which has progressed to this day,"[17] albeit with tribulation and opposition.

To announce this decision to all concerned parties, Stone and the others published the Last Will and Testament of the Springfield Presbytery dated June 28, 1804, and signed by Stone and his five fellows. This document consisted of an introductory statement and twelve items. It served as both an explanation of their actions and a guideline for their future course. In it they expressed their desire for unity of all believers, free recourse for all Christians to the scriptures, freedom from creeds and the oppressive church governments they empower, the need to follow only the Bible and an urging for the day that preachers and people cultivate a spirit of mutual forbearance, and the need to pray more and dispute less.[18]

7. Summary

From these lengthy introductory matters, we see the picture of a man who at age 30 had seen enough of oppression, wrangling and disputes in religion, and therefore wanted peace. We see a man with great emotional capabilities, who, being himself given to feel so deeply both pain and happiness, often found it easy to follow his feelings to overcome and override what his mind knew to be true, and display a spirit of compromise, forbearance and longsuffering that was unequalled in the Restoration Movement. Yet, he was a man who was driven by the goal of unity based on the teachings of scripture, a unity he knew would never be achieved until the shackles of the creeds, party names and ecclesiastical power and oppression were cut asunder by the power of the Word of God. No doubt he knew that these two parts of him would often be in conflict. These conflicts kept Stone in the center of religious controversy for the next forty years. In 1824 he wrote in a letter to James Blythe:

> God knows I am not fond of controversy. A sense of duty has impelled me to advance it. In the simplicity of truth is all my delight. To cultivate the benevolent affections of the gospel shall employ my future life.[19]

Indeed controversy raged in Stone's life. In no area did it do

250

so more than in the controversy about baptism. To that matter attention is now turned. The ensuing discussion will follow these natural divisions: (1) from 1800 to 1826, during which time Stone's movement and influence spread throughout the region of Kentucky and its environs; (2) from 1826, when Stone began to publish the monthly periodical *The Christian Messenger*, on the pages of which Stone and others hammered out a theology of baptism and many kindred subjects, to 1832, when the union of Stone's Christians and Alexander Campbell's Disciples (or Reforming Baptists) was consummated; and (3) from 1832 until Stone's death in 1844.

B. Early Problems

When Stone and the others decided to take the Bible as the only rule of faith and practice, they had little realization of how far reaching that decision was and how many of their cherished and accepted practices would have to be modified or given up entirely. One can see that by the time of the signing of the Last Will and Testament of the Springfield Presbytery in 1804, Stone had allowed the scriptures to greatly modify his view of church government.

But earlier than this, the Bible's teaching had already modified his views on baptism somewhat. Near 1800 Stone became concerned because Robert Marshall, a fellow-worker and signer of the Last Will and Testament of the Springfield Presbytery, had a flair for the Baptist practice of immersion.[20] Stone became fearful that Marshall would unite with the Baptists and become lost to the cause. He then wrote Marshall trying to convince him of what he believed was error. In reply, Marshall "so forcibly argued in favor of believer's immersion and against pedobaptism, that my mind was brought so completely to doubt the latter, that I ceased the practice entirely." From this it is obvious that Stone was, at this point, willing to accept what he perceived was the teaching of

251

God's word, because of cost or changes it necessitated in his beliefs or practices. During the revivals of 1801 and following, the subject was almost forgotten. But it did revive in a few short years.[21]

1. David Purviance

During the year 1805, David Purviance, a close friend and ally of Stone, began to study the matter of baptism. It was brought about at the birth of his last child on June 6, 1805. He wondered whether she would be baptized, that is, sprinkled in the tradition of the Presbyterians. He went to the New Testament and studied

> as though I had all yet to learn on the subject of baptism. I accordingly proceeded until I read Acts 2:41. . . . That passage struck my mind with weight and decision. It appeared to me that baptism was the introductory ordinance by which they were added or joined to the church. . . . But it seems that only those were baptized who received the word.[22]

Purviance proceeded to study diligently the conversion stories in the book of Acts, as well as how Christian baptism related to the covenant of Abraham and John's baptism. At the close of his examination his conclusion was

> that had I rightly understood the subject when I was received into the church, I must and would have been initiated by baptism. But I did not realize the obligation or necessity at that time; moreover, as we had experienced many difficulties, ... I did not wish to incur a new difficulty, or kindle another fire, should it even be done by water. I therefore thought it best to be cautious, and measurably silent on the subject.[23]

Here Purviance rested until 1807. It must be noted that Purviance realized that he was never properly baptized, but did not "realize the obligation or necessity at that time." Whether he had reference to his own obligation or necessity to submit to immer-

252

sion or to the later understanding they reached of the relationship between baptism and salvation is not known. It seems that he had reference to his own obligation due to his actions of 1807, which will be noted in due course. It is also interesting to note that despite his new found understanding of a Bible subject, he was willing to remain silent for a time rather than create controversy or problems, thereby exercising what he called moderation and forbearance.

> In general, moderation and forbearance were exercised. We seldom preached on the subject: but recommended to the people coolly and deliberately to search the scripture — and thus the work progressed, until baptism generally prevailed, without serious injury to the cause. Whereas, had we been pressing and urgent, and had we charged our opponents with bigotry and adherence to human tradition, I have no doubt much mischief would have ensued.[24]

2. Stone Baptized

The problem resurrected in 1807 when a young woman presented herself to Stone to be baptized. The pulpit had been silent on the matter and we must assume that the woman came to desire baptism from private study.

Stone recalled that it was about this time that he himself had become dissatisfied with his infant sprinkling. Stone, the brethren, elders and deacons came together to discuss the subject, for they "had agreed previously with one another to act in concert, and not to adventure on anything new without advice from one another."[25] But Stone and the rest needed to make some decisions.

It was becoming increasingly apparent that none of them had ever been scripturally baptized, for all had been sprinkled as infants. All the ramifications of this were no doubt unclear in their minds at this time, for they were not yet sure of the relationship of baptism to salvation, and were only now coming to a full understanding of the relationship of baptism and membership in the church. What course could they follow? Should they be immersed? If they are, does that mean they really were not "in the church" all these years? What about others who knew not this new found truth, yet regarded themselves as faithful Christians? If they are immersed, what effect will that have on "the cause" in which they were now engaged? However, the commitment to follow the Word where it led had been made. Would they follow it into the water?

As each individual pondered these matters and their condition before the Lord in light of this new found understanding of the Word, a more practical question arose: "Who will baptize this young woman?" It would not seem right to call in a Baptist preacher to do so. They finally reasoned that if they were authorized to preach, they were authorized to baptize.[26]

A meeting was scheduled for the purpose of baptizing the woman.[27] The word spread, the crowds came and the woman was baptized by Stone. During the meeting, Ruben Dooley preached and others were baptized. Purviance realized his need and asked Stone to baptize him, to which Stone consented. Purviance mentioned that the only thing he regretted was hurting the brethren's feelings, to which Dooley replied, "The best way to please the brethren is to please the Lord."[28] Before being baptized, Purviance addressed the congregation giving his views. He later said, "It was the first time the subject had been publicly named among us." They went into the water and Dooley said to him quietly, "As soon as you are baptized, I shall want you to put me under the water," to which request Purviance willingly acquiesced. Stone was not baptized that day. Purviance later remembered:

None of us urged the matter. We exhorted the people to search the scriptures, and act according to their faith, and to forbear one another in love. And, in general, peace and harmony continued to prevail. Stone studied the peace of the church; and his character for candor and honesty so well was established, that by

254

pursuing a prudent course, he preserved the people in the unity of the Spirit, and retained their confidence.[29]

Stone was baptized later in 1807, exactly when and where is not now known. Soon his congregations generally submitted to baptism, but the pulpit was silent on the matter.[30] There is no record that these baptisms were "for the remission of sins." In fact, years later on two occasions, Stone reminded those who felt fellowship was dependent on immersion for the remission of sins that they could not fellowship him, for he was not immersed with this understanding.[31] However, Stone remembered that in the ensuing discussion, "which engaged the attention of the people very generally, some, with myself, began to conclude that it was ordained for the remission of sins, and ought to be administered in the name of Jesus to all believing penitents."[32]

3. Stone Preaches Acts 2:38

Near this time, at a great meeting at Concord, Kentucky, Stone had labored with a group of penitent mourners before the stand with none of them being comforted. When he thought what could be the cause, he thought of Peter's words on Pentecost as recorded in Acts 2:38. If Peter were present, thought Stone, he would address these mourners in the same words. He arose and addressed them in the same language and "urged them to comply."[33] This seemed to chill the audience, so he let the matter drop.[34] He was not led into the spirit of the doctrine of baptism for remission of sins until it was revived some years later by Alexander Campbell.[35] But for the present in 1807, it was determined "that every brother and sister should act freely, and according to their conviction of right — and that we should cultivate the long neglected grace of forbearance towards each other — they who should be immersed, should not despise those who were not, and vice versa."[36]

Again, Stone's conciliatory attitude can be easily seen. It is here apparent that when a conflict arose that might threaten the unity they had achieved, even if the truth of scripture was perceived by all and agreed to, patience and forbearance as they perceived it was extended for the sake of that unity.

It must here be noted that from this time on, neither the mode of baptism, nor the proper candidate for baptism was subject to much discussion. It seemed all agreed and were willing to stand fast on the Bible truths of baptism as immersion and believers being the only fit subjects to receive it. The question that becomes the center of discussion and remains so for 37 years is the design of baptism. Is it or is it not for remission of sins and therefore necessary for salvation?

Baptism for remission of sins next surfaces in 1821. John Rogers was in Millersburg, Kentucky to attend a meeting conducted by Stone. He writes:

> Many professed religion, and many more, who were at the mourners bench, refused to be comforted. After laboring with the mourners until a late hour of the night, without being able to comfort them, Brother Stone arose and thus addressed the audience: "Brethren, something must be wrong; we have been laboring with these mourners earnestly, and they are deeply penitent; why have they not found relief? . . . the cause must be that we do not preach as the apostles did on the day of Pentecost. Those who 'were pierced to the heart' were promptly told what to do for the remission of sins. And 'they that gladly received the word were baptized, and the same day about three thousand were added to them.' " . . . When Brother Stone sat down, we were all completely confounded. . . . I thought our dear old brother was beside himself. The speech was a perfect damper on the meeting. The people knew not what to make of it. On a few other occasions, Brother Stone repeated about the same language, with the same effect. At length he concluded the people were by no means prepared for this doctrine and gave it up.[37]

About this same time, a man by the name of David Jamison became disturbed about the condition of his soul. He had been "seeking pardon" for a long time without relief. He began to study the word for light on the subject and became convinced that one could not claim the promise of pardon until he was baptized. Stone, Dooley and others "held a conference" on the matter. They decided that Jamison was a fit subject for baptism but that he had "doubtless received pardon, but was not conscious of it" before baptism. They baptized him, however, and he went on his way rejoicing.[38]

It should be noted that Stone's practice in the years 1821-22, though not completely free of Calvinistic concepts and practices such as the mourners bench, was to immerse those who had been led to a point of faith by the evidence in the Word but not to press the matter of baptism either in theory or practice. In his biography, he simply states that he preached and baptized daily, and that those who were baptized were added to the Lord. The following incident will further illustrate his practice.

> One day, after having preached, I started alone to another appointment. On my way, a gentleman who was returning home from the same meeting, came up; we rode on together. I introduced the subject of religion, which I found not to be disagreeable to him, though he was not a professor. I urged him by many arguments to a speedy return to the Lord. His mind, I saw, was troubled, and vacillating as to his choice of life, or death. At length we came to a clear running stream; he said, "See, here is water; what doth hinder me to be baptized?" I instantly replied in Philip's language, "If thou believest with all thine heart, thou mayest." He said, "I believe that Jesus Christ is the Son of God, and am determined hereafter to be his servant." Without anything more we alighted and I baptized him. We rode on in our wet clothes until our ways parted.[39]

It is clearly seen that Stone's notion of conversion had undergone significant change since he himself sought religion in the early 1790's. One might conclude that his practice was very close to the Baptist practice of the day, but without the "work of the Spirit" to mark a person as "one of the elect" that the Baptists sought. Stone saw the plan as faith upon hearing the word and then being baptized to obey God and to be added to the church. This writer is convinced that Stone probably believed in his mind that baptism was for the remission of sins, and was therefore in some way necessary to salvation, but was not convinced in his heart and therefore was not willing to press the matter for the sake of unity and the cause in which he was engaged. This can be seen by a careful consideration of subsequent events as well as arguments Stone later advances in the *Christian Messenger*, as will be seen in due course.

4. Stone and A. Campbell Meet

In 1824, another significant event transpired. Alexander Campbell made one of his many sojourns into Kentucky, and in Georgetown Stone and Campbell met for the first time. Each had been aware of the other's efforts for some time. This acquaintance was mutually beneficial and they were drawn together in deep affection over the years, although they had their points of disagreement. Of the occasion of their meeting, Stone writes:

> When he came to Kentucky, I heard him often in public and in private. I was pleased with his manner and matter. I saw no distinctive feature between the doctrine he preached and that which we had preached for many years; except on baptism for remission of sins. Even this I had once received and taught . . . but had strangely let it go from my mind, till brother Campbell revived it afresh. . . . In a few things I dissented from him, but was agreed to disagree.[40]

In 1825 a co-worker named B.F. Hall became concerned because the mourners who presented themselves did not receive consolation under their ministration, a thing that never happened under the apostles' preaching. In the New Testament conversion accounts, comfort was immediately obtained and the people went on their way rejoicing. He concluded something was wrong. Then in 1826 he obtained a copy of the Campbell-MacCalla debate on baptism, its mode, subject and design. Having read this, he became firmly convinced that baptism was for remission of sins and therefore necessary for salvation. In the summer of 1826, Hall and Stone were working together. Hall then

> spoke of the idea to him. He told me that he had preached it early in the present century (1807), and that it was like ice water thrown on the audience; it chilled them, and came near driving vital religion out of the church; and that, in consequence of its chilling effect, he had abandoned it altogether. I (Hall) insisted that it was God's truth, nevertheless, and that I felt compelled to preach it at a meeting at Sulphur Well, to which we were then going. He begged that I should not preach it while he was present, but he said he would leave after meeting Lord's day morning; then I could do as I saw proper.[41]

Why Stone "strangely let it go from" his mind, and why he urged Hall not to preach this doctrine must be discussed. One cannot but wonder why a man so dedicated to the scriptures could willingly ignore what he knew to be the teaching of the scripture. Again, he did so, no doubt, to preserve the unity which he had achieved and promote its expansion.

Further, throughout this time period, it seems, the whole matter was regarded as a matter of opinion. Lines of fellowship, at least for Stone, were not drawn with baptism, but with "vital piety" and holiness of life. Stone was determined not to bind what he felt was an opinion on anyone else, but rather, he would be motivated by love and forbearance. Although beyond the scope of this work, it is interesting to note the influence of Alexander Campbell. Stone was immersing two years before Campbell came to America. But the controversy over baptism for remission of sins "was revived by Brother Campbell some years after." If the Campbell-MacCalla debate affected B.F. Hall as it did, no doubt it affected others, many of whom were in the Stone movement. This difference in attitude toward the subject later becomes one of the primary differences between the Christians, as Stone's followers came to be known, and the Reforming Baptists, as Campbell's followers were known.

C. The Christian Messenger 1826-1831

1. 1826

In Stone's first year of editing the *Christian Messenger*, little was said of a controversial nature respecting baptism. The only mention of it is in one of Stone's articles dealing with the early history of his work. In discussing the events of 1807 he states: "The far greater part of the churches submitted to be baptized by immersion, and now there is not one in 500 among us who has not been immersed."[42] But there is, nevertheless, an awareness shown of the controversial nature of the subject. He writes further: "From the commencement, we have avoided controversy on this subject, and directed people to the New Testament for information on this matter. . . . Some (of the preaching brethren) began to urge the necessity of making a stand upon the truth we had already learned and desist from further search. It was understood that we should have some other bond beside the Bible and brotherly love."[43]

But this would never do. Stone saw no need for anything other than God's word. Anything beyond this would be a creed and Stone would have no part of it. Although Stone disliked controversy, he was acutely aware of the need and right of freedom for all men to study the Bible and let it lead them where it will. To eliminate inquiry into any subject, even one as hot as baptism, was an abridgement of that right. Stone would not, at this time, tolerate that.

2. 1827

In a letter to Stone, Obadiah Seward challenged Stone's views of baptism, saying Stone's views would make it a term of communion. He suggested that he was not alone in this understanding, and called upon Stone to defend himself.[44]

In Stone's reply, we see for the first time a contemporary statement of his beliefs respecting baptism. Seward's problem, as Stone perceived it, was that Seward could not accept baptism as "a means of grace to the salvation of the believer." He then reasons from Mark 16:15-16 that none would deny that "faith in the gospel is ordained as the means of salvation." How then can any deny that "baptism is also a means of salvation, seeing it stands immediately connected with faith?" Then from Acts 2:38, 22:16 and I Peter 3:21 he reasons that "remission of sins . . . to be received through baptism . . . is in perfect accord with the commission given to the apostles." Further, "baptism saves in the same manner as the waters of Jordan wash away Naaman's leprosy . . . (through) obedience to the divine order," and that in baptism "believers are buried and risen" with the Lord. Baptism then is the "very answer, representation, or image of the resurrection of Christ."

He reviews the conversion accounts in Acts and shows that the norm is baptism before and as a means to salvation. He notes that the only exception to this rule was Cornelius, who, Stone says was saved before baptism which was evidenced by his receiving the Holy Spirit. This was, he admits, an unusual case, for this was to remove any objection to taking the gospel to the Gentiles by Peter. Stone then anticipates the objection "can any be saved who are not baptized?" To which he answers:

God did save the Gentiles (Cornelius) . . . prior to their being baptized. This proves that he has not bound himself to a plan from which he cannot depart.

Ignorance is seen as the reason for Cornelius not being baptized and God winked at that ignorance, but he now commands all men everywhere to repent and obey His ordinance. Should baptism be made a term of communion? "No more so than it should of salvation," Stone would answer. If God can save in ignorance, we can fellowship in ignorance.[45]

Further evolution in Stone's thinking about this matter can now be perceived. It is obvious that Stone's practice and teaching implied to Seward and others that he believed there was more to baptism and salvation than the baptists of the day believed. Further, his thinking is coming more in line with that of Campbell, although Stone is never able to go as far as Campbell with respect to withholding fellowship from the pious unimmersed. For Stone at this point, three thoughts keep him from doing so: 1) God has not limited Himself to saving by only one plan; 2) God saved Cornelius in his ignorance, surely He can save others in ignorance, and if God can save in ignorance, one can fellowship in ignorance; and 3) the only test of fellowship are faith in Christ and "vital piety." These three notions become mainstays in Stone's defense of his enigmatic position.

3. 1828

In 1828 the flood gates opened in reference to baptism. There were twelve articles written, an average of one an issue, on baptism, with eight of these dealing specifically with the design of baptism. In this group of articles were two series of articles that demand our attention.

The first series was three articles by James E. Matthews.[46] In the first article Matthews shows that the ordinary practice of the apostles was baptism for remission of sins. Since they were under the influence of the Spirit, this must be the plan of heaven! This example then is a sufficient warrant for their practice.[47] In the second he adds that the conversions were much quicker, i.e., in one hour in apostolic days, where it often took days and weeks of mourning under contemporary "modern preaching." He added that if baptism saves, then one cannot be saved before it (I Peter 3:21).[48] In the third, Matthews concludes:

I and others in this country have acted on the above plan, and we have never yet known it to fail. If we had but *one* apostolic exam-

262

ple on which to found our practice, we believe we would act safe-
ly. But we think we have many examples as well as precepts.
Should any yet dispute its correctness, we should be glad that
they would introduce *one* precept or example from the scriptures
showing that it is wrong. We should be glad also, (if possible), that
they would cite to us *one* authority in the book of God, for requiring "an experience of grace" to be related, antecedent to
baptism.[49]

A John O'Kane takes up Matthews' articles and attempts to
reply. His reply suggested that: 1) Peter never said baptism was a
means to forgiveness of sins or that baptism is the only channel of
regeneration or new birth; 2) the Greek preposition *eis* in Acts
2:38 means on account of or because of; 3) the promise of baptism is the Holy Spirit; and 4) the blood is not mentioned in Acts
2:38.[50]

Stone then takes up O'Kane's reply arguing that none could
doubt repentance as necessary to remission of sins, yet Peter joins
repentance and baptism "in the very same relation in Acts 2:38."
Then he makes an enigmatic statement for Stone: "Did Peter tell
them that Baptism was the only channel of regeneration? No.
Neither Peter *nor the most stupid ignoramus amongst us* ever
spoke such a sentiment" (emphasis mine, M.G.). He then shows
that *eis* is used with the meaning of unto or for (Matthew 26:28;
Matthew 9:13, et al).[51]

Does the fact that Stone did not attempt to question anything
that Matthews wrote, but rather defended Matthews' thoughts,
suggest that he was in agreement with Matthews? This is probably
basically true. Yet it can be seen that while Stone agreed with the
plan, he was not yet willing to carry his knowledge to its logical
conclusion of fellowshipping or acknowledging as Christian only
those immersed for remission of sins. Matthews' writings show
that others had. Was Stone here hedging on his commitment to
follow the Bible where it led him? And if so, why?

What he had to say about this written discussion needs to be
noted just here:

We are always pleased to see the gift of inquiry on subjects of importance. To express freely, humbly and meekly our ideas, is a good way of arriving at truth. But any expression of a harsh and arrogant spirit will produce bad effects. Such it is humbly hoped will be avoided by our correspondents.[52]

Because the subject was important and Stone was receiving so much correspondence concerning it, to print it all would fill the pages of the *Messenger*. Because he did not want "to make it a subject of controversy, but of calm investigation," it was determined that he and Thomas Adams would conduct a written discussion of the matter.[53]

This discussion was begun. Adams wrote two articles which never did get to the point of discussing baptism for remission of sins. However, he did raise three questions: "Has God more than one plan for forgiveness of sins?" If He has more than one, why contend for one over the other, both would be equally effective. But if He had not given more than one plan, "have we any authority for believing that any ever has been, or ever can be, in the gospel age forgiven out of that plan?"[54] Due to an illness to Adams, no more than two articles appeared.[55] But in one of his replies, Stone did respond to Adams' questions. He suggested that God has one plan for saving sinners. The Lord instituted the plan of faith, repentance and immersion as a means of the remission of sins and salvation. He goes on to say:

God has but one fundamental plan under the gospel. . . . The blood of Christ leads to repentance and remission of sins follows repentance. . . . To keep in view this foundation and repentance and forgiveness, that is, the death, burial and resurrection of Jesus, the Lord instituted baptism or immersion in connection with faith and repentance as a means of remission of sins and salvation. . . . God has but one plan under the gospel, and this plan includes all these things already named, as faith, repentance, confession, prayer, baptism and obedience. . . . All are necessary to salvation. . . . Yet we are far from saying he will forgive no other. This would cut off all the heathen, who have not heard the gospel, from forgiveness, however penitent they might be. . . . This would contradict a matter of fact, recorded of the Gentiles in Acts 10. . . . But should this encourage us in disobedience to his plan, because he has in pity blessed us out of it? No.[56]

Stone is holding fast to the plea of ignorance and Cornelius as reason to believe God would save some without baptism. To this he adds a third, that is, an emotional appeal. If one excludes the penitent unimmersed, then what happens to the multitudes of ignorant heathen? Notice also that he suggests that God in pity had blessed them out of the plan. Yet if Stone's understanding of the scriptures is right, where was his evidence that God had blessed him or anyone else with forgiveness of sins outside the plan, that is, prior to immersion? For Stone, that evidence would be the Christian life and Christlike spirit of the believer.

4. 1829

In the last issue for 1828, Stone suggested that he and his patrons and friends felt enough had been written on baptism and nothing more could be said. Therefore, nothing more would be printed. He encouraged all to search the scriptures and "act according to conviction." But because it was important and many were interested, he left the door open for more discussion: "We do not promise to say nothing more on the subject. Circumstances may hereafter make it necessary."[57] No doubt this was done because Stone saw this controversy as becoming so heated that it threatened the unity and life of the church. This was a convenient way to at least make an effort to put a damper on the controversy. He managed to keep the discussion out of the *Messenger* for seven months.

He then received some questions from two readers, Jo. Baker and Js. Kinkennon, among which was, "Is any one lawfully a subject of the kingdom of Christ, before he is immersed into his name?" Stone replied:

None are lawfully subjects of Christ's kingdom until they are baptized . . . but (with reference to those who are accepted as
members who were not immersed, there are many among the
sects that) are bright examples of piety whom we love and enjoy
the fellowship of the spirit, and hope to dwell with them in
heaven. In this as in other things we believe such pious persons
honestly err.[58]

In response to this, James Henshall takes Stone to task. He
asks, "If one is not in the church before he is baptized, how can
Pedobaptists be Christian seeing they are not immersed?" He further challenges that Stone is using the logic of the sectarians: "We
go on the footing that nothing is an article of faith but what is
clearly revealed in the scriptures of truth, and where is it said the
disobedient shall be saved?"[59]

To this Stone replies:

I will not contend that unbaptized persons are Christians in the full
sense of the term: nor was this intended when I wrote the article.
That men may be holy and pious without being baptized in water,
is a sentiment cherished with pleasure by me. I must believe that
the household of Cornelius were made holy and received the Holy Spirit previous to their baptism; yet before they were baptized
they were not Christians nor united with the church of Christ.[60]

Stone here modifies his position somewhat with respect to
Cornelius. He now admits he was not a Christian, just that he was
holy and pious, and although such were not Christians and not in
the church, Stone still hoped to see them in heaven. He further
argues that if fellowship is marked at baptism, that would "make
baptism *sine qua non*, it would exclude from heaven . . . the poor
penitent thief, and millions more, who had no opportunity to be
baptized; and were ignorant of the ordinance as ordained by
Jesus; yet they were pious and holy men."[61] Thus he appeals
again to emotion and ignorance. He continues: "But to denounce all not immersed as lost, and to cut them off from salvation, however holy and pious they may be, appears to dethrone

266

charity and forbearance from our breast. If I err, let it be on the side of charity."[62]

Henshall responds by saying we are not demanded to be so charitable, and that even if it seems uncharitable, he "will still contend for the honor of my Savior's character, both as a legislator and a king in his own kingdom, both for the reasonableness of his laws, and of the awful state of those who despise his government."[63] He challenges Stone on his terminology of "Christians in the full sense of the term" and shows that to be pious and holy and disobedient involves a contradiction. If one believes the Bible, he must believe all of it, not part of it. He then makes an appeal:

> Where is the champion, who will step forward and draw the line of demarcation, between what is, and what is not necessary to be believed in order to salvation? Obedience is better than sacrifice and to hearken than the fat of rams. . . . I would not take my pen, brother, to write a word against you; but I do it in sincerity, believing it more cruel to tell people all is well, when they are living in rebellion against God, than to tell them plainly the test of Christian character.[64]

In reply, Stone again makes an emotional appeal which is much more personal:

> None but the few, who lately have been immersed for the remission of sins (are Christians); all the rest are unbelievers. The greater part of my yokefellows in the gospel are cut off, if you are correct; for though we have been immersed, it was not with the understanding we now have, that immersion, connected with faith and reformation was for the remission of sins. My dear bro(ther): zeal for a favorite sentiment has carried many beyond the boundaries of truth, charity and forbearance.[65]

This ended the discussion between Henshall and Stone. It would be enlightening to know if it ended because Stone chose to print nothing more from Henshall or because Henshall wrote no more. The latter is more probable because, as we shall see, Stone planned a further discussion on the subject.

In the same issue of the *Messenger* (the last for 1829), Stone responds to some things put forward in Campbell's *Millennial Harbinger*, among them baptism for remission of sins:

> I both contend for it in theory and practice it, from a firm conviction of truth. . . . Between Mr. C and myself I see no difference on this subject, in theory or practice. The only apparent difference is, that I am not yet prepared to reject from fellowship all not immersed for remission of sins. If I understand him, he does. Should I reject all not immersed for remission of sins, I should reject the greater part, even of the reforming Baptists; for very few of them were baptized for remission of sins. I should myself be rejected, for when I was immersed it was not with this understanding.[66]

To this article he adds a postscript which suggests that in future numbers "we shall pay particular attention to the subject of immersion, for the remission of sins, and endeavor to remove every objection to it. This we feel impelled to do, as indispensible duty at the present crisis."[67] Of what magnitude this crisis was we can only surmise, but no doubt this controversy was having its effect on Stone and his work. However, this attention to the problem would have to wait for at least a year, for there was no *Messenger* in 1830 for reasons which Stone felt unnecessary to give.

5. 1831

Attention was paid to the matter in the 1831 *Messenger*, but Stone was not as active in the controversy as before. Perhaps the year's rest and reflection had cooled his interest and vigor for the subject, but the matter appeared nevertheless. In an article on opinions, Stone seems to lament the controversy, suggesting that opinions have always been divisive due to the importance men place upon them.

Stone felt that because so many opinions of truth existed, a man must obey what he knows and understands to be the truth and let God deal with anything lacking. If a man is truly a Christian, it will show in his godly, reformed life, not in his doctrinal opinions or whether or not he is baptized. We then can unite with them on their godly life and belief in Jesus. Stone places baptism among opinions and makes the following plea:

> (opinions about baptism have) long been the cause of sore contention, and unnatural division among Christians. We have looked and hoped for an end, but it now appears further off than ever. . . . The case I shall leave . . . till a satisfactory determination be made. Till then would it not be better, and would not the cause of Christianity more gloriously advance, if all would cultivate brotherly affection towards each other, and bear with each others weaknesses and errors which affect not their pious and holy life?[68]

Yet it seems that Stone was really missing the point. It is up to the Lord where the boundaries of the kingdom lie, and no doubt He has revealed such in the scripture. If that be the case, has any man the right to say a man is in the kingdom if he hasn't done all the scriptures say he must do to get in that kingdom, no matter how pious or holy a life he may lead? Stone admitted the force of the argument, but appealed to the fact that if it were true, then many who were living pious godly lives, who believed in Jesus and who were working in the churches were lost. This Stone just could not accept.

> How many honest, pious, godly souls are there among the different sects, who have not, till lately, ever thought seriously on these subjects; of this we are assured, because we speak from experience. But the time is come, when the minds of all sects are roused to inquiry. Let truth be exhibited in all its clearness . . . let tenderness, brotherly love, and forbearance be exercised towards the other — let piety, justice and mercy be cultivated by us all. Then will be effected the union of Christians in the truth.[69]

He then proceeded to use the case of Cornelius as his justification for his stance. Cornelius was a devout man and accepted by God before his baptism. "Cornelius had the kingdom of righteousness in him," but "not the fulness of it." If God could do so with Cornelius, then why not with Stone and others?

> Let us still acknowledge all to be our brethren, who believe in the Lord Jesus, and humbly and honestly obey him as far as they know his will, and their duty. Let us not reject whom the Lord has received. "By their fruits shall ye know them." Let us not reject experience, as good evidence of our acceptance with God. We know we have passed from death unto life, because we love the brethren. etc. Religion without experience is nothing better than a body without the spirit.[70]

It is seen then that Stone saw as the measure of one's Christianity his pious life (vital piety as he called it), and whether he loved the brethren. As compelling as those thoughts may seem, it still fails to extricate Stone from his dilemma. If baptism is indeed for remission of sins unto salvation, then one is not a Christian without it, regardless of the piety of his life. But Stone saw as the implication that the many are lost, and because it was an unpopular doctrine, the unity of believers would be threatened.

Under the pseudonym of Archippus, a James Fishback wrote a series of seven articles on baptism for remission of sins. He invited Stone to reply. In his reply, Stone added nothing new to the discussion but did say: "I begin seriously to fear that too much of late is spoken and written on the subject of baptism. . . . Hence may have proceeded that great dearth of religion, which is so visible in societies, where this subject is commonly agitated."[71]

He then offered the pages of the *Messenger* to the service of any who wished to reply further.[72] Alexander Campbell replied to Archippus in the *Millennial Harbinger*. Stone reprinted these articles in the *Messenger*, but made no comment on them. Later, an Elder C. Sine sent Stone a question relating to baptism for remission of sins. Stone did not answer the question, hoping it would be answered by a qualified correspondent in another number.[73] This correspondent was not forthcoming, so Stone himself answered the question, though adding nothing worthy of note to the discussion.[74]

D. 1832 to Stone's Death in 1844

1. The Union of 1832
During the years of 1804 to 1831, Stone's influence and movement had grown throughout the regions of Kentucky, Ohio and environs. Congregations of the Christians or Christian churches, as his group was known, could be found throughout the area. Stone was also part of what was loosely known as the Christian Connexion. This loose association of churches that had taken the name Christians and sought to throw off creeds included several churches in the East that also went by the name Christian. Alexander Campbell's influence and movement was also growing. He, too, was seeking to bring Christians together on the Bible by seeking what he called the "Ancient Order of Things." Campbell's group, known as the Reforming Baptists, Reformers or Disciples, also had congregations throughout Kentucky, Ohio and Virginia. The circumstances were such that in many places there would be congregations of Christians and Reformers in the same community. In the late 1820's, much discussion ensued as to whether these congregations should be united or remain apart.

When the subject began to be discussed, it became obvious that there were basically two issues where substantial differences in the two groups existed. The first was the name to be worn. Stone and his group preferred Christian; Campbell and his followers preferred Disciple. The other issue was the role of baptism for the remission of sins and whether one could fellowship the pious unimmersed. In August of 1831, Stone wrote an article in the *Messenger* addressing the question: "Why are you and the Reforming Baptists not united?" Stone replied that in spirit they were united, and that no reason existed from Stone's perspective as to why they should not be united in form. The Reformers were teaching the same doctrines taught by Stone and his followers for thirty years, i.e., rejection of creeds, that all should be united, and the freedom of man to believe and obey the gospel. Thus, Stone saw no reason why they should not unite.

He went on to say that differences of opinion on some points existed. Stone did not object to these as a term of fellowship, but if he had understood correctly, the Reformers objected to some of the Christians' opinions and saw them as hindrances to the unity. These he listed as: (1) the unwillingness of Stone to reject from fellowship those not baptized for remission of sins; and (2) the different names each had chosen. In defending his position on fellowshipping the pious unimmersed, Stone says:

> For if the immersed only, receive the remission of sins, all the millions that have died, being unimmersed, have died in their sins, or unwashed from their sins. . . . Why were they sent to hell? For disobedience to the one command of being immersed. . . . On earth, says he (the pious unimmersed), in obedience to the King whom I loved, whose laws I lived, whose family I loved, I denied myself, took up my cross and followed him. I was taught that baptism meant to be sprinkled with water, in the humble spirit of obedience I submitted. . . . But now, alas! for my ignorance of the right way of performing one command, I must be forever banished from God into everlasting punishment.[75]

Stone then wondered how we would react to an earthly king who would deal with his loving subjects so. We would "reprobate his conduct." He again stated that his belief is that baptism was ordained as a means of receiving remission of sins.

> We therefore teach the doctrine, believe, repent, and be immersed for the remission of sins; and we endeavor to convince our hearers of its truth; but we exercise patience and forbearance towards such pious persons, as cannot be convinced.[76]

Stone stated that he and the Christians stood "ready to meet with and unite with these brethren, or any others, who believe in, and obey the Saviour according to their best understanding of his will, on the Bible, but not on opinions of its truth." It is seen then that the basic difference between the two groups on these issues was not so much one of belief, but of practice. Stone believed the same as Campbell, but practiced differently, and what Stone regarded as a matter of opinion, Campbell regarded as a matter of faith.

In spite of these differences, Stone and representatives of the Christians met with representatives of the Disciples (Campbell was not among them) on New Year's Day, 1832, to effect a union of the two great brotherhoods. In a very emotional service that day, the union was effected.[77] John T. Johnson of the Reformers agreed to serve with Stone as co-editor of the *Messenger*. John Smith of the Reformers and John Rogers of the Christians would ride together through the country visiting the churches to bring the union to a more widespread fruition. By and large, these efforts were successful, in spite of opposition by many. This union, Stone regarded as the "noblest act of my life."[78]

Now that the union of the two groups had, for all practical purposes, been effected, the nature of the discussion of baptism on the pages of the *Christian Messenger* changed. Stone found himself in an unenviable position. He must defend himself to the Christians in the East as well as some of his own followers who accused him of "selling out to" or "going over to" the Campbell position on baptism. So to these he must defend, from the scriptures, his belief that the Lord's plan for saving man included baptism, a position both he and Campbell occupied. At the same time he must also defend to the reformers his belief in baptism for remission of sins unto salvation and the apparent contradiction between that belief and his practice of continuing to fellowship the pious unimmersed. Many attempts were made to convince Stone that he could not have it both ways, but Stone continued to occupy this position and extend what he called forbearance and patience for the sake of unity. Stone was, at this point, in a "can't win" situation. If he didn't take a stand one way or the other, he would be (and was) charged with compromising the truth. If, on the other hand, he took a consistent stand and said those not baptized were lost, he would lose his influence with the Christians in the East and many of his own followers, and the unity he worked so hard to attain would be threatened. But, on the other hand, he could not reject the plain teaching of the scriptures that baptism is the means by which men in the Christian age receive forgiveness of sins and are received as members of the church.

Until his death twelve years later, Stone would spend much time in the unsuccessful effort to extricate himself from this dilemma.

2. 1832

Early in 1832, Stone received a letter from Stephen Roach, which lamented the dashed hopes of a moral reformation and millennial glory. Instead, after all the expectations, the ears "are astounded by the grating sound of immersion in water for regeneration." Roach then posed the question, "Who is in the kingdom?" Stone was called on to defend his belief that baptism was essential to salvation and entrance into the kingdom. This he did by drawing an analogy. If a man immigrates to this country from another and develops the spirit of a citizen, loves the government and respects its laws and subjects, but has not qualified himself as a citizen by our constitution, is he a citizen? Only by obeying the law, and taking the oath of allegiance does he become a citizen, for the oath is the "constituted door of entrance" into citizenship.

In like manner, professed Christians believe that the "divinely instituted door of entering the church is baptism." This act, Stone said, changes the state of a man, not his heart. His heart must be reformed prior to baptism (i.e., repentance) before he is a fit subject for baptism. But, before baptism he had not been legally a member of the church, or fellow citizen with the saints in the kingdom, "because he had not been born of water."[79]

Some months later, J. McGilliand of Ohio posed the question to Stone: "When does God forgive sin? When the sinner gives up his whole heart? or after he is baptized?" At this point Stone must defend his belief in the doctrine of baptism for the remission of sins. Stone replied:

> Who are forgiven? This I have already answered. The believing, repenting, obedient soul, that submits to be immersed in the name of Jesus. This we observe is God's revealed plan of forgiveness; yet I dare not confine his grace of forgiving to only who are immersed. . . . So God's plan under the Gospel is to forgive thro' faith in Christ crucified with repentance and immersion; yet he may forgive without immersion, such as neglect it in ignorance. But should any know it to be his duty to be immersed, and neglect it, to him it is sin; he cannot receive, remission or forgiveness. . . . When are they forgiven? Whenever they believe, repent, and are immersed in the name of the Lord Jesus Acts 2,38. This none can deny. They may say, at some other time than this they are forgiven. It may be so; yet proof is hard to be obtained — proof direct — I mean; proof from the holy scriptures. It is easier to cavil and object than to prove.[80]

In the September 1832 issue, Stone wrote an important article entitled, "An Address to the Churches of Christ." This article was more or less a statement paper wherein Stone tried to show where he stood on a number of issues, such as creeds, union and baptism. He began by showing that creeds could be both written and unwritten, but either way they are divisive and serve only to exclude, and either way an affection for the "creed" generates an intolerance toward those who dissent. Some held as part of their unwritten creed (no doubt the Christians in the East) that none should be baptized who have not been saved and had their sins forgiven.

> These . . . oppose zealously those who would act up to the old commission, "preach the gospel to every creature. He that

believeth and is baptized shall be saved — and repent and be baptized for the remission of sins, etc." Do they preach that a man must be saved from his sins, and must have his sins remitted before baptism? This is their creed; and the plain scripture to the contrary must be frittered away, in order that their creed may stand securely.[81]

He asked that the contending brethren would "cordially attend to an old servant and brother, while he pleads for reconciliation." He proceeded to show that a change of heart must take place prior to baptism, i.e., a man must repent, for baptism cannot and does not change a man's heart. But his sins are not at this point remitted or forgiven. "He submits to be baptized, and now the pardoning act of God is passed, he is forgiven, wrath and guilt are removed." He then anticipated the objection, "Can God forgive none but the immersed?"

We are assured he will forgive the immersed penitent, because his word has assured us he will. We cannot be so sure that he will forgive the unimmersed penitent. Could a person be brought by doctrine to believe that faith and repentance were only necessary to remission, and that baptism was entirely unnecessary to this effect, he might receive this word with gladness, and this he might take for evidence of remission; but we should ask the important question, what saith the scripture?[82]

In each of these articles Stone forcefully argued the truthfulness of his position. He also made the significant observation that there was no proof (hard proof from the scriptures) that men are forgiven or admitted to the church at any other time but at the point of baptism, and that in order to justify any other position, "the plain scripture . . . must be frittered away." He also observed that the doctrine that leaves off baptism or promises forgiveness at any other point may produce gladness in the heart of the believer, which might be taken for evidence of pardon, but, that is not consistent with scriptural teaching. From these statements one would quickly infer that Stone accepted as saved only those who believe, repent and are immersed, for that surely is implied by what he has said. But to continue the above quote:

> We have no doubt that multitudes have been changed, are pious, and will ultimately be saved with an everlasting salvation who have not been immersed. We are far from saying, that God has so bound himself by his plan, that he cannot pardon an humble penitent without immersion! Far from us be this sentiment.[83]

How Stone could call others to account in such a forceful way, and then ignore his own advice is hard to understand. It seems that in order to make the last statement, Stone was guilty of doing the very things he accused others of doing, that is, failing to produce "proof direct" from the scriptures and "frittering away" plain scripture teaching. The how may be answered by noting that Stone regarded what he had plainly shown was the teaching of scripture, i.e., that the purpose of baptism was forgiveness of sins and the rite of admission to the kingdom, was but an opinion, and opinions are not tests of fellowship. Further, one can quickly see that Stone felt that if he gave up his position that many are saved in ignorance, the unity he so desired would never be achieved. He urged all to accept one another in disagreement.

> Our opinions we wish no man to receive as truth, nor do we desire to impose them on any as tests of fellowship. This is the principle on which we as Christians commenced our course many years ago, and I cannot but view those as departed from this principle, who will not bear with their brethren, because they believe in baptism for the remission of sins. . . . O brethren, these are subjects concerning which many of us differ, but for this difference we ought not to separate from communion, and Christian fellowship. All believe that immersion is baptism — why should they who submit to the one baptism contend and separate because they do not view every design of it alike?[84]

3. 1833

In the first issue for 1833 Stone addressed his readers and gave his perception of the state of the movement. He noted that the "Sects of Christians are crumbling to pieces" in the face of the "grand principle of Christian union." He felt that this union could not be achieved until all gave up their creeds as authoritative, their names of distinction and its party spirit, for no unity could be obtained based on the creeds of men. Unity must be founded on the New Testament alone. Yet, Stone admitted, opposition was great. The oppositon was no doubt from within and without as has been shown. However, when the truth is taught in the spirit of meekness, and when in meekness the objections are met with scriptural arguments, "we are in the way of doing good to our fellow men in error." Though he recognized the diversity of opinions in the groups, he did not see these as challenging the union, for it was based on the New Testament and not on a system of opinion (a creed) as were other churches. Still, Stone admitted, some were fearful that the union was in danger

> because of a supposed diversity on the subject of baptism; not on the act of baptism, for we all immerse — not on the subjects for we immerse none but such as believe and repent — and I may add, not on the design, for I know but few among us that deny baptism to be a divinely instituted means for the remission of sins, and for the gift of the Holy Spirit. Where then is the difference between us? A says immersion only is baptism — B agrees to this truth. A says, baptism introduces us to the kingdom — B agrees. A says by baptism we put on Christ — B agrees. A says, by baptism we receive the remission of sins and the gift of the Holy Spirit. B still agrees. Where is the difference between A and B? B says, I hope there are many Christians in the kingdom, who are saved, and who have received the remission of sins, who have never been immersed — and that these persons shall be admitted into heaven at last. A indulges all good hopes, but confesses that he has not sufficient scripture evidences for an unwavering faith. This diversity of opinion ought not to excite bad feelings towards each other; but forbearance and brotherly love should prevail.[85]

He then urged the brethren to dwell less on "doctrinal disquisitions" and give more time to "practical piety" which for Stone was much more the test of Christianity and acceptance with God than one's doctrinal concepts. Because of his position

278

Stone expected "contempt, hard speeches and persecuting slander . . . but this we will cheerfully suffer for the truth's sake."

Again, it seems Stone is missing the point and the force of his own arguments for his position. If baptism for remission of sins is the "divinely instituted means for remission of sins" and there is nothing more than one's indulgent "good hopes" for salvation without it, how can he continue to maintain such a position? Certainly, it is, again, because of his ardent desire for the union of believers. But, would a union that is achieved by setting aside a divinely instituted ordinance be beneficial, long lived or pleasing to the Lord? These are questions that evidently never occurred to Stone.

In order to understand his notion of union better, consideration is given to an article which appeared in the October, 1833 *Messenger*. The article was a description of four types of union: book union, head union, water union and fire union. Book union was a union founded on the book or creed or confession of faith. However, wherever a creed had been introduced, even with the goal of union, it had been "the unhappy cause of disunion." He looked for the day all such would be banished from the Christian community. Head union was a union founded on opinion. Many who seek such denounce the creeds, but exalt their own opinions of what the Bible teaches into an unwritten creed, which in practice is as authoritative and divisive as a written one. Water union was union based upon immersion in water. All three of these Stone saw as inadequate to the task of uniting God's people.

Fire union, on the other hand, was what Stone called the unity of the spirit, i.e., a "union founded on the spirit of truth." That spirit comes through faith and submitting oneself to Christ's teaching. This spirit of Christ is the only means that will ever unite God's people. He concludes:

So must we be first united with Christ, and receive his spirit, before we can ever be in spirit united with one another. The members of the body cannot live unless by union with the head nor can the members of the church live united, unless first united to Christ the living head. His spirit is the bond of union — Men have devised many plans to unite Christians — all are vain. There is but one effectual plan, which is, that all be united with Christ and walk in him.[86]

Here we see what was a significant difference between Stone's pursuit of union and that of Alexander Campbell. Campbell had a modus operandi for achieving that noble goal. He saw unity as being an inherent characteristic of the early church. Therefore, if one could go back and capture in modern days the essence of the early church, it would have to be united. But how do you do so? Campbell saw the solution in restoring what he called "the ancient order of things." Thus, Campbell's plan was to restore the early church thereby restoring the pristine unity of that body. Stone, on the other hand, did not have a well-thought-out plan of attack. He saw unity as more of a state of mind and even of heart; doctrinal unity or purity was not as important to Stone as to Campbell. Stone's concept of the union being based on the spirit of Christ[87] allowed him the latitude to unite with those who had not fully understood or obeyed as long as they had the dual qualities of "vital piety" and the "spirit of Christ." Stone's notion then was more emotional whereas Campbell's was more rational. For Stone, unity was the compelling passion, the "polar star"; for Campbell, and in time his followers, the notion of restoring the church became primary as the only rational and workable means to unity.

One can quickly see that Stone's method, while sounding appealing in the abstract, becomes a very impractical concept. Stone himself was caught in the dilemma already mentioned, from which he could never extricate himself as long as he held that the basis of union was the way a man lived or the way he felt in his heart. It was possible that one could live right and have the right emotional disposition to extend forbearance, love and patience, qualities Stone would say exhibited the spirit of Christ, while holding to a doctrine which might go contrary to some very basic concept of Christianity. To be consistent, Stone would have to be in fellowship with such a one. Campbell's concept, however, would be more concerned with the practical question of "what saith the Lord" and would not allow unity or any other worthwhile goal or hope set aside from what the Bible taught, for this alone was the course to Biblical unity.

4. 1834

As has been suggested, the nature of the discussion about baptism had by this time in Stone's life changed. A correspondent from Ohio wrote to challenge Stone that baptism was not essential to salvation and that in so affirming the doctrine, Stone had abandoned the ground he occupied twenty years before. Stone forcefully argued from Acts 2:38, 22:16 and I Peter 3:21 that baptism is scripturally connected with remission of sins and salvation. The querist had suggested he could produce ninety-nine experienced Christians who received forgiveness out of the act of baptism to prove his point. To this Stone replied,

> Had you brought one thus saith the Lord in the new institution, which says that sinners obtain forgiveness out of the act of baptism, it would have produced more certain conviction to my mind, than 10,000 fallible witnesses. I did expect that proof from scripture would alone be brought to upset a doctrine proved to be taught in the scripture in plain unequivocal language.[88]

Stone still held out the hope, in the name of charity, that many have been and would be saved in their ignorance without baptism. This, however, did not excuse those who knew to be baptized and refused. Again, Stone, by some mental exercise, failed to see that by his own words demanding scriptural proof, his own position on the pious unimmersed was left without foundation.

In answer to the challenge that he had forsaken the ground of twenty years previous, he stated:

You wish to know whether I preached the same doctrine I now

preach, twenty years ago, when you heard me in Ohio. I cannot recollect what I then preached when you heard me, but if I have advanced no farther in knowledge for twenty years, I must be a very dunce. Would you have me preach nothing more than I preached twenty years ago? Must I make no improvement? If any are tremblingly afraid to leave the ground occupied twenty years ago, and to adventure into the ocean of truth, I envy not their lot; — I am determined to follow where the truth may lead me.[89]

One cannot but feel that the last statement would need to be amended to say that he was willing to follow the truth where it would lead, as long as it did not jeopardise the unity he had achieved!

5. 1835

In the 1835 volume of the *Messenger* the discussion continued on basically the same lines previously mentioned. However, three articles included statements which gave further insight into the mindset of Stone.

To urge this doctrine (of baptism for remission of sins) . . . has already done irreparable harm to the peace, harmony and growth of the church, and will do more, if persisted in. Those opposed to the doctrine; and those who advocate it have been too sensitive and indulged in hard feelings and speeches. Instead of attempts to heal the wound, they have caused it to bleed afresh, till division has been the result. We cannot but deplore the weakness of man.[90]

In a very brief article simply entitled "Remarks" Stone writes:

The scriptures will never keep together in union and fellowship members not in the spirit of the scriptures, which spirit is love, peace, unity, forbearance, and cheerful obedience. This is the spirit of the great Head of the body. I blush for my fellows (the Reforming Baptists? M.G.), who hold up the Bible as the bond of union yet make their opinions of it tests of fellowship; who plead for the union of all Christians; yet refuse fellowship with such as dissent from their notions. Vain men! Their zeal is not according to knowledge, nor is their spirit that of Christ. There is a day not far ahead which will declare it. Such antisectarian-sectarians are doing more mischief to the cause, and advancement of truth, the unity of Christians and the salvation of the world, than all the skeptics in the world. In fact, they make skeptics.[91]

In a reply to Will S. Gooch, Stone stated that they were agreed that baptism was for remission of sins, and that all were agreed that when a penitent, reforming believer was baptized, he did receive the remission of sins.

Your *Opinion*, deduced from this truth, is, that no unimmersed person, however penitent or believing, can be saved, or have his sins remitted . . . you deny present and future salvation to all that have not been immersed. . . . These are your *opinions* — opinions I call them, and am happy in the thought that they are not Bible-truths. . . . Though we agree in the doctrine of baptism for remission, I dissent from your opinions.[92]

To justify his belief that this was merely an opinion and not the true implication of the doctrine, he referred to his own personal religious history. He stated that nothing was added to him when he was immersed save the "satisfaction received" from having complied with his duty. He remembered when he relinquished his will to God as a hopeless sinner. At that time he became conscious of being a son of God because he loved God, the brethren and kept His commandments as far as he understood them! "Had I then known it was the will of God to be immersed, I would with all readiness, all humility of soul have submitted." This former experience, especially his feeling he was saved, was all a delusion if the *only* means of salvation is baptism unto remission.

I, with the millions of the fairest Christian characters on earth, will be doomed to hell forever; why? Because we had not been immersed; and this we did not have done, because we were ignorant of it as a duty! Had I such views of God's character, I could not serve him with cordial love.[93]

He proceeded to give additional reasons as follows: (1) it allows no mercy to those who in ignorance do not understand and perform every command of God; (2) those who profess the doctrine show no more the fruits of the spirit than those who do not accept it, that is, it does not make people live any better; and (3) the teaching of it has produced a flood of opposition against the precious truth. It is interesting that there is no scriptural justification for Stone's position given. It becomes clear, though, that Stone's major objection continued to be on subjective, not objective grounds.

6. 1836-1840

In the 1836 volume of the *Messenger*, the discussion of baptism seems to have lost its vigor. Only one article of importance appears in it. Stone added nothing of significance to the discussion. He consistently defended his belief in the scriptural doctrine of baptism for the remission of sins as being the "esteemed doctrine of Christ" and as being, in fact, a part and parcel of being born again. However, he stood firm on his rejection of the implication of that doctrine by extending "much charity" to the "honest worshipper" who through ignorance failed to be baptized. "They are in the hands of a merciful and righteous God, who will do right. The obedient spirit would do whatever the Lord required if he knew his master's will. This is, we hope, accepted for the deed."[94]

The *Messenger* for 1836 contained fewer pages and fewer articles than any of the previous years, and at the close Stone stated this could possibly be the last ever published. He and his family had been sick some time and Stone himself, now sixty-four years old, was at death's door. What he was able to write concerned his favorite theme of unity. Stone's prophecy concerning the end of the *Messenger* was true to a point. There was no *Christian Messenger* for 1837-1839. It was resurrected in 1840 at the urging of those in the "far West" and only with the assistance of Thomas M. Allen and Jacob Creath, Jr., both of Missouri. Again, for reasons unknown, the issue of baptism for remission of sins did not appear on its pages.

7. 1841

After the close of the 1840 *Messenger*, Stone was stricken with a paralysis which continued with him until his death. In the opening issue for 1841, issued some six months after the close of the 1840 volume, he stated that he was unfit for any other employment and so without the aid of Brothers Allen and Creath, set out to issue yet another volume of the *Christian Messenger*.

In this year, his sixty-ninth, Stone entered into a lengthy disputation with Brother Marsh, editor of the *Christian Palladium*. The *Palladium* was issued by the Christians in the East who had refused to enter into the union with the Stone and Campbell movements some eight years before. They accused Stone of "selling out" to Campbell on baptism for the remission of sins, saying that Stone had renounced his former views in favor of Campbell's. Marsh sent Stone a copy of the October, 1841 *Palladium* with an article by Thomas Carr marked for Stone's perusal. In that article, to which Stone replied in two articles in the *Messenger* for November and December of 1841, Carr first challenged that in order to have union with the Disciples, one had to accept the doctrine of baptism for remission of sins and give up the ground held for years. As a result, people had been "disgusted," many brethren had left and gone back to the denominations and "the cause for which we plead has been thrown back more than ten years." It is clear that Carr, Marsh and the Christians in the East still held to the doctrine that remission of sins was given upon faith, repentance and prayer and the evidence of forgiveness and the vindication of the doctrine is found in "experimental religion," i.e., the manner of life and subjective, emotional state of the convert.

To this point, Stone responded by asking who it was that

demanded they give up or renounce any teaching in order to have union. Stone certainly had not; whether any others had is unknown. But he went on to point out that it was the Bible that brought him to give up his former views, not any man. No doubt Campbell is implied here. It is only natural that the Bible would lead one to give up his former views that were not consistent with scripture. "Why boast of the Bible alone, if we must believe no more of it than what were our former views? In fact, did we all agree in our first views? And have we all, or any, remained in them all, without renouncing some. . . . We hold up the Bible as the only criterion to test the rectitude of our feelings or experience, as well as our faith."

The article by Carr continued and challenged Stone in no uncertain terms to accept the implication of his stand on the doctrine of belief, repentance and baptism as the divinely ordained means for remission of sins. Carr writes,

> Now if this system be true everything else must be false; consequently very many of those whom we always recognize as Christians have not been immersed, and cannot be regarded by them (Stone and the Reformers, M.G.) as Christians! . . . Hence the Disciples must regard us, at least, as brethren walking disorderly and ought in all conscience to withdraw themselves from us. . . . The honest and undesigning among them do not fellowship any but the immersed. Others, for the sake of advantage, seemingly fellowship all. Now what is such friendship but dissimulation?
>
> The Editor of the *Christian Messenger* (whom I highly esteem) says, "in his parts they commune with Methodists, Presbyterians, etc. Such a course, to say the least of it, is doubtful. The Lord says 'come out from among them, and be ye separate.' To embrace as brethren those whom they know are not such, shows a want of moral honesty, and a disregard of God's word."[95]

Carr goes on to say that only if the Disciples renounce this unwritten creed can unity be obtained, and that he had more respect for those who rejected fellowship from the unimmersed "because

I think them honest, not hypocrites." For these reasons and others, he felt it best that the Christians in the East seek no more to be united with the Disciples, for that, he perceived, required all to bow down to the creed of the "Ancient Order as taught by A. Campbell."

No doubt this correspondence cut the old and venerable Stone to the quick for at least three reasons: (1) he again is accused of bowing down to A. Campbell; (2) the unity with the Christians in the East and the West for which he had worked for years seems all but lost; and (3) Carr in no uncertain terms calls Stone a hypocrite and dishonest.

In reply, Stone proceeded to show that the scriptures do indeed teach that baptism is for remission of sins, and there is no other plan in the New Testament for saving man. "If this teaching be the cause of strife or confusion, who is to blame for it? the teacher or the taught?" If Carr were present at Pentecost and heard the words of Peter, he would have refused union and withstood even the apostle, and consequently the Lord Himself! "He should be careful lest he be found fighting against God."

Stone went on to defend his contradictory stance by again appealing to ignorance. A man would be lost if unimmersed but still knew that God required immersion and still did not obey. Ignorance of duty excused him.

> Yet these same people have the spirit of obedience, and did they know that immersion is required, they would obey. For twelve years I thus lived without immersion, and believe that I lived under the smiles of heaven. But when I became acquainted with my duty, I submitted to it. How then should I act? Should I teach the world that baptism was unnecessary for salvation, because I experienced salvation without it? Should I labor to comfort people in their ignorance or teach them their duty and urge them to obey?[96]

He accused Carr and others of showing a sectarian attitude

because they would not agree to extend charity to those pious unimmersed and refused union because of their acceptance of what the Bible taught. Again Stone defended his belief in the divine origin of baptism for remission of sins, without accepting the implication of it, even when called upon to do so. He continued to appeal to his own personal experience, his concept of charity, and ignorance of duty as reasons why he could not.

In a later article written in reply to a letter by D. Long published in the *Palladium*, Stone reminded those who accused him of leaving the original ground of the movement that he was brought to this position because he *followed* one of the basic principles they had set out on many years before: taking the Bible as the *only* rule of faith and practice. It was because he had studied his Bible on this matter of baptism that he believed and taught as he now did. He had changed because he "knew not then that the Bible taught it." Surely he could not be regarded as having left those principles, when it is, in fact, the putting of those principles into practice that brought him to a new understanding of baptism and a union with the Reformers.[97]

Several more articles appeared by Stone on this subject in the 1841 volume of the *Messenger*,[98] none of which added anything new to the discussion. Stone simply maintained his positions just as he had for years. In the last article Stone said that nothing more would be written about the subject unless he was called upon to defend himself.

8. 1843-1844

There was no *Christian Messenger* published for eight months. When it reappeared in May of 1843, the name of D.P. Henderson joined that of Stone as editor. Stone wrote that the absence of the periodical was caused by financial difficulties, infirmities of the flesh (Stone was now seventy-one years of age), and inability to obtain paper for printing.

In the last two volumes of the *Messenger* the ardor for the discussion of baptism cools considerably. This is no doubt attributable to Stone's advancing age, and is evidenced by a statement by Stone preceding a letter from a preacher he had not seen for forty years:

> We have received a lengthy communication from an old friend and brother, in Arkansas, on the subject of baptism. He wishes for it a place in the Messenger. We grant his request; but have to say, that his opinions have been so often the subject of our animadversions, that we should have been better pleased to receive a dissertation on any practical subject, yet his years, and long standing as a Christian, demand our respectful attention.[99]

In the letter, the old friend, George Gill, suggests that the Gentiles are not subject to the ordinance of baptism for remission of sins. He argued that in the New Testament only Jews were told to be baptized for the remission of sins, whereas the Gentile convert Cornelius was not. In his reply, Stone argued that John's baptism was for the Jews, whereas Christ's baptism was universal (Mk. 16:15,16). Also both the baptism of Pentecost and the baptism of Cornelius were consistent with the commission of Christ. The conclusion was that all are subject to that baptism.[100] Later in this same volume Stone, in answer to a question, stated there was only one revealed plan for getting into Christ and therefore receiving forgiveness. That was through baptism (Rom. 6:1-4). However, he restated his hope that "innumerable hosts" have been saved and put on Christ without baptism "being wrongly instructed and ignorant of their duty."[101]

In the final volume of the *Messenger*, the seventh issue contained the notice that the beloved Barton W. Stone had passed from this life on November 9, 1844 at the age of seventy-one years, ten months and sixteen days. Just a few weeks prior, in the September issue, Stone responded to the question, "Do you admit into communion and into the church" those who have "engaged in obedience to all God's commands but one, which is immersion?" In his reply Stone admitted that one may be a good man but that, according to the scriptures, one was not properly a Christian until he was baptized into Christ. He admitted the force of the statement: "This plainly implies that no unbaptized person was a member of the church, according to the order of heaven, in the time of the apostles."

Nevertheless he proceeded to argue that a man may be ignorant of a portion of God's will and still be accepted. He cites as proof the apostles who lived in disobedience to the command to preach the gospel to every creature, including Gentiles for eight to ten years. There were Christians still observing the Law in apostolic times (Acts 21:20). From these things he reasoned it is improper for unbaptized people to partake of the privileges of Christians or exercise an office in the Lord's church, but to "unchristianize" by breaking fellowship is contrary to scriptural principles. He outlined a three-step course "though acknowledged to be clogged with difficulties" that would remove the difficulties and unite the brethren.

First, hold up the Bible alone as the foundation of the church, "to believe what it says, and do what it enjoins." Second, if any refuse to give up their creed, "reject them not" . . . if they do not impose them on others as authoritative. Third, let each be kindly and affectionately treated in brotherly love. If this were done, "a great cause of offense would be removed, and Christians would begin to flow together in love, and be of one soul and heart."[102] It is again observed, that while Stone was moved closer to accepting the implication of his belief, an implication which he himself admitted, he still refused to break fellowship with the pious unimmersed, holding out the hope that such a course would in some way unite the brethren.

E. Conclusions

What conclusions should be drawn from this study of Stone's enigmatic position on this controversial issue? It is clear that Stone held true to his commitment to hold the Bible as the only rule of faith and practice and as the only creed needed to effect unity, to a point. Over the years he continued, often in heated exchanges, to change his views on baptism to bring them more in line with his changing perceptions of Bible teaching. Yet his inability to accept the implication concerning the pious unimmersed remained with him throughout his life. The reasons for this can be summed up as follows.

First, Stone's early experiences with oppressive situations, both religious and secular, created in him a powerful resentment of anything that even appeared to be oppressive. This combined with his notion of the love of God versus the judgment of God forged, no doubt, out of his experiences in his own struggle with religion and the teachings of McGready and Hodge refused to allow him to judge others in matters he clearly considered opinions. This was surely reinforced by the efforts of the Presbytery to expel him and his fellows in 1803 along with the continued efforts of the clergy to defeat his work over the years.

Second, Stone's own spiritual pilgrimage became normative for all who were working their way out of a man-made religion into the light of gospel liberty. He remembered that when baptism for remission of sins first began to be discussed, no one pressed the issue. As a result, the majority of his converts and followers, in time, submitted to baptism and ultimately accepted the truth of the Bible doctrine of baptism for remission of sins. He further felt that if the issue had been pressed, or if a strong stand was taken, that due to the unpopular nature of the doctrine, few would have accepted it and the great cause in which they labored might be dealt a death blow. Therefore, Stone refused to press the matter, hoping that by extending forbearance and patience all could be won to the Biblical truth on baptism, and unity would follow.

Thirdly, Stone's dominant passion and pursuit in life was the unity of all believers. While Stone had no well-thought-out modus operandi to bring to fruition this noble goal, he persisted in measuring all things in terms of unity or how it might affect unity. In this, Stone's efforts fell short of others of his day. Campbell and others had a practical and workable plan that had a scriptural basis and precedent in the Old Testament as well as the New.

291

Stone's was a unity based more on subjective grounds; Campbell's was more rational. To Campbell, a unity that was not based on clear scriptural teaching, or which compromised that teaching was unacceptable and undesirable. But not so for Stone; he could simply agree to disagree. Doctrinal purity was subordinate to unity. Such a unity, when achieved, could not be long lived, and one must wonder whether it would be approved by God.

Finally, it must be acknowledged that Stone's emotional make-up and approach to problem-solving would place him in the psychological category of intuitor and/or feeler. This type of person is much more emotional, relationship-centered and visionary. This type of person is not persuaded as much by logic as by how he feels. It is easily seen how Stone's background reinforced this personality characteristic. Therefore, he was led by his heart more than his mind, and his heart led him to refuse to accept what his mind saw as truth. Yet, this type of personality has the ability to get close to people and feel what they feel. In this, Stone provided a needed counter-balance to the cold logic of others in the movement. Had it not been for Stone and others like him, in spite of his doctrinal and other shortcomings, it is doubtful that the movement of the 19th century, known as the Restoration Movement, would have reached the heights of success that it did.

Endnotes

1. In later years, who was "first" in the movement became quite an issue for Campbell, but it was not nearly so important with Stone.
2. John Rogers, *Biography of Elder Barton Warren Stone* (Cincinnati: J.A. and V.P. James, 1847), p. 3.
3. Ibid.
4. Ibid., p. 5.
5. Ibid., p. 8.
6. Ibid., p. 9.

7. Ibid., p. 10.

8. Charles C. Ware, *Barton Warren Stone, Pathfinder of Christian Union* (Bethany, West Virginia: The Bethany Press, 1932), p. xiv.

9. William Garrett West, *Barton Warren Stone* (Nashville, TN: Disciples of Christ Historical Society, 1954), p. 5.

10. John Rogers, pp. 30-31.

11. Ibid., pp. 32-33.

12. Ibid., p. 42.

13. West, p. 46.

14. Ibid., p. 110.

15. The others were Robert Marshall, John Dunlavy, John Thompson and David Purviance. Of these five, only Purviance remained with Stone. Marshall and Thompson returned to the Presbyterians and Dunlavy and McNemar went over to the Shakers.

16. John Rogers, p. 48.

17. Ibid., p. 50.

18. Taken from the "Last Will and Testament of the Springfield Presbytery" as quoted in John Rogers, *Biography of Elder Barton Warren Stone*, pp. 52-53.

19. Ware, p. 210.

20. Ibid., p. 173. Ware places these events at eight years before the Christians began immersing, which was in 1807. Stone, in his biography edited by Rogers (p. 60), says it was while he was yet a Presbyterian preacher, and before the great excitement (the revivals of 1801) began.

21. John Rogers, p. 60.

22. Levi Purviance, *The Biography of Elder David Purviance* (Dayton, Ohio: B.F. and G.W. Ellis, 1848), pp. 148-51.

23. Ibid., p. 151.

24. Ibid., p. 152-153.

25. John Rogers, p. 60.

26. Ibid.

27. The location is given as about seven miles from the Cane Ridge meeting house near Paris, Kentucky where a bridge crosses Stoner's Creek, according to a Captain James M. Thomas who claims William Rogers as his authority. James H. Rogers, *The Cane Ridge Meeting House* (Cincinnati: The Standard Publishing Co., 1910), p. 70.

28. Purviance, pp. 151-152.

29. John Rogers, pp. 127-28.

30. Ibid., p. 60.

31. See notes 65 and 66 below.

32. John Rogers, p. 61.

33. Ibid.

34. John I. Rogers, ed., *Autobiography of Elder Samuel Rogers* (Cincinnati: Standard Publishing Co., 1880), p. 58.

35. John Rogers, p. 61. Alexander Campbell later held two debates with

293

Presbyterian preachers on various aspects including the design of baptism. In June of 1820, he debated John Walker at Mount Pleasant, Ohio. In October, 1823, he debated W.L. MacCalla near Washington, Kentucky. In the MacCalla debate, Campbell argued that baptism was for the remission of sins, and since an infant is incapable of sinning, he cannot be a fit subject for baptism. It may be these debates and earlier articles in the *Christian Baptist* which are referenced here.

36. Ibid., p. 60.
37. John I. Rogers, pp. 55-56.
38. Ibid.
39. John Rogers, p. 75.
40. Ibid.
41. John I. Rogers, p. 58.
42. Barton Warren Stone, ed., *The Christian Messenger* 14 vols. (Volumes 1-7 by the author at Georgetown, Kentucky; Volumes 8-14 by the author at Jacksonville, Illinois, 1826-1844), 1:267. Hereafter references to *The Christian Messenger* will use the symbol CM follow by the volume and page number(s).
43. Ibid.
44. CM, 2:151-52.
45. CM, 2:152-53.
46. John I. Rogers, p. 60, informs us that these articles were written at the urging of B.F. Hall. In 1827 Matthew and Hall were in a meeting together when Tolbert Fanning was immersed for remission of sins. "Brother James E. Matthews embraced the sentiment at or soon after that time, and at my (Hall's) insistence, wrote several articles on the subject, addressed to B.W. Stone, which were afterward published in his Christian Messenger."
47. CM, 3:126.
48. CM, 3:150.
49. CM, 3:213.
50. CM, 3:213-16.
51. CM, 3:217.
52. CM, 3:216.
53. CM, 3:219.
54. CM, 3:220.
55. CM, 3:279.
56. CM, 3:223-24.
57. CM, 3:279.
58. CM, 4:160-62.
59. CM, 4:233-35.
60. CM, 4:235.
61. CM, 4:236.
62. CM, 4:237.
63. CM, 4:268-69.
64. Ibid.
65. CM, 4:271.

66. CM, 4:272.
67. CM, 4:276.
68. CM, 5:20.
69. Ibid.
70. CM, 5:21.
71. CM, 5:105.
72. CM, 5:109.
73. CM, 5:209.
74. CM, 5:223.
75. CM, 5:180-81.
76. Ibid.
77. John A. Williams, *Life of Elder John Smith* (Nashville: Gospel Advocate Co., 1956), pp. 367-78.
78. John Rogers, *Biography of Stone*, p. 79.
79. CM, 6:209-10.
80. CM, 6:209-10.
81. CM, 6:264.
82. CM, 6:265.
83. Ibid.
84. CM, 6:266.
85. CM, 7:3.
86. CM, 7:315-16.
87. Ibid.
88. CM, 8:136.
89. CM, 8:140.
90. CM, 9:153.
91. CM, 9:180.
92. CM, 9:221.
93. CM, 9:222.
94. CM, 10:26.
95. CM, 12:33-34.
96. CM, 12:38.
97. CM, 12:112-116.
98. CM, 12:75 (cf. 143, 180, 228).
99. CM, 13:209.
100. CM, 13:210-14.
101. CM, 13:220.
102. CM, 14:129-34.

8

THE REBAPTISM CONTROVERSY AMONG CHURCHES OF CHRIST

Jerry Gross

The controversy over rebaptism that led to the establishment of the *Firm Foundation* in 1884 was a controversy that had been smoldering ever since the Campbell-Thomas controversy in the 1830's. In an article in response to Austin McGary in the *Gospel Advocate*[1] in 1884, Lipscomb stated that, for 20 years, he had a controversy over this issue with people he esteemed highly. However, in the 1870's and 1880's the debate heated up in earnest between Lipscomb, Harding, and J.T. Poe of the *Advocate* and McGary, J.W. Jackson, John T. Durst and others who later became associated with the *Firm Foundation.*

The controversy actually issued out of the success that the restoration movement was having among the denominations

(chiefly the Baptists). In the earliest days of the Campbell movement the principles of the movement to restore the ancient order
of things were adopted by individuals. But, with time, whole
churches began to come over to the movement. In the decade
between 1820 and 1830 the movement began to have a powerful
impact even upon whole associations of Baptist churches.[2] Initially, preachers who advocated the restoration plea could move
freely among the Baptist churches. But as the movement swept
through the Baptist churches in Kentucky, Ohio, and Pennsylvania, stiff opposition developed in the Beaver, Tates Creek, and
Dover associations. But the effect of the Reformers upon the
Baptists was so great that, in an entry in the New York Baptist
Register, it was estimated that one half of the Baptist churches in
Ohio had embraced the movement while even more in Kentucky
had done so.[3]

After these initial, widespread successes the restoration
preachers continued to appeal to individuals to come over and
take their stand on the Bible along with those seeking to be Christians only. Quite frequently it would be reported in the papers
that, at a gospel meeting, several had been baptized and a few
others had come over from the Baptists.

Some preachers began to question the practice of "shaking
in" the Baptists without requiring them to accept a "scriptural baptism." Hence, the question that came to be hotly debated was,
"What shall be done with those who seek to unite with us who
have been immersed among the sects?" This issue generated a
number of written debates among brethren as well as a decades
long battle between two religious papers, the *Gospel Advocate*
and the *Firm Foundation*.

In this chapter we will survey the history of this debate among
churches of Christ after the Campbell-Thomas controversy. Our
main focus will be upon the running debate between David
Lipscomb of the *Gospel Advocate* and Austin McGary of the *Firm
Foundation*. However, we will also consider the development of
this controversy during the twentieth century. We will begin with

the chief opponent of rebaptism, David Lipscomb.

A. *David Lipscomb and the* Gospel Advocate

Without question, the most prominent voice among the churches of Christ in the South during the last half of the 19th century was David Lipscomb. As an editor, preacher, and educator, Lipscomb's influence upon the post-civil war churches of Christ was deep and wide.

David Lipscomb was born in Middle Tennessee on January 21, 1831, to Granville and Nancy Lipscomb. When he died in 1917, at the age of 86, Lipscomb had lived through one of the most critical periods in our nation's history. No single individual did more to stabilize these southern churches during this most trying time.[4]

Lipscomb's earliest years were profoundly shaped by the Christian convictions of his father, Granville, and his teacher at Franklin College, Tolbert Fanning. His commitment to the scriptures was learned early and remained with him, guiding his thoughts and actions, all of his days.[5]

The *Gospel Advocate* was begun in 1855 by Tolbert Fanning and Lipscomb's older brother, William. However, when the war began it was impossible to continue publication. The *Advocate* was reborn in January of 1866 with David Lipscomb replacing his brother as co-editor. For the next fifty years, David Lipscomb's influence would guide editorial policies of this paper.

The editors did not intend for the *Advocate* to be an exclusively southern paper. Yet, the strong sectional loyalties after the war, as well as the editor's position against instrumental music and the missionary society, prevented the *Advocate* from being widely accepted in the North. However, these factors helped it to be the leading journalistic voice among the churches of Christ in the South.

The editors intended to provide a forum for the open and

candid discussion of all scriptural questions. Thus, it soon became obvious that Lipscomb's view on the rebaptism question was not universally shared.

1. Lipscomb and Rebaptism

No doubt Lipscomb's experience with his own baptism greatly influenced the position which he later took. At the age of fourteen, Lipscomb was recovering from typhoid fever when he sent for Tolbert Fanning to come and baptize him. In the *Gospel Advocate* in 1883, Lipscomb recounted the event of his baptism.

> I was baptized quite young by Brother Fanning. He asked me why I wished to be baptized. I responded "to obey God." He explained it was to bring me into a condition that God would forgive me and accept me as a child of God. I responded, "I wish to be baptized to obey God." I have studied the question for forty years, and I do not yet know how to improve the answer I made.[6]

With that reply, Lipscomb was baptized by Fanning in a box.

Years later Tolbert Fanning, then editor of the newly established *Gospel Advocate*, was asked a question about rebaptism.[7] The questioner observed that it was "the practice of the brethren to receive members from the denominations without rebaptism."[8] However, the querist observed that the Baptists baptized *because* a person's sin was remitted, whereas the brethren baptized *for*, or *in order to*, the remission of sins. Fanning stated that "The only point to be determined is, what is the design of baptism?"[9] So, "in baptism the subject must clearly understand the objects and action, which constitute the obedience of faith."[10]

Fanning insisted that:

> We know every acceptable act of worship must be with the Spirit and understanding. If persons are taught they are forgiven before baptism, and are really and spiritually in Christ, or are Christians, and they are baptized because they have passed from the state of death into the state of life, in order to become members of the

same party, we think they must either discredit their teaching to obey God in the act of baptism or we must admit the service can be acceptably performed in ignorance of the design of the institution.[11]

Fanning, though, went on to write that, in such cases, each person must decide for himself.[12]

A few years later, William Lipscomb responded to a series of questions regarding the issue of re-immersion. William Lipscomb replied that, "No service is acceptable to Heaven which is not performed with a full understanding of its purposes. No individual who goes through the form of immersion without understanding its meaning is in the least profited thereby."[13] He granted that many people were baptized in unscriptural bodies while believing that baptism was for the remission of sins. "Yet," he argued, "the authority of the Scripture is for re-immersion where the intention of act (sic) was not clearly understood."[14] But, again, it was conceded that it would be up to the individual to decide for himself whether the baptism was valid.

In 1869, John Durst, who later was to be such a strong ally of Austin McGary, asked David Lipscomb about the reports of gospel meetings that were published in the *Gospel Advocate*. Durst noted that mention was made of several persons being received from the sects without re-baptism. Durst suspected that most, if not all of them, believed they were pardoned before they were baptized and were baptized because they were Christians.[15] David Lipscomb observed that he had answered this question so often that he could only respond in the following brief fashion:

The first prime design of baptism is to honor God by submitting to his appointments. The remission of sins is one of the fruits that flow from a submission to God in baptism. There are many other fruits. We have never found where it was required that a man should understand all the fruits flowing from an act of obedience in order to render it valid. If so, we fear we have never obeyed acceptably a single command.

301

> A man who believes in Christ, repents of his sins, and is baptized
> in order to honor God, by obeying his commands, we would cer-
> tainly say was baptized with a valid, susceptable baptism, even
> though he did not know at what point of his obedience God
> would bestow his blessing.[16]

This response continued to be Lipscomb's answer for the next
four decades. Over the years, Lipscomb wrote page after page
explicating and defending these brief remarks. But the thrust of
the response never changed. There was great consistency in
Lipscomb in his controversies with the re-baptists through the
years. By 1913, Lipscomb had effectively retired from his labors.
However, in the *Gospel Advocate* of September 25, 1913,
Lipscomb had submitted an article titled, "The Revised Testament and Re-baptism." In this article, Lipscomb argued that the
Revised Version corrected an expression that had promoted an
important misunderstanding about the design of baptism.
Lipscomb had constantly argued that the expression suggested
"the idea that baptism is to pay for remitting the sins as a man
pays for a horse. It is giving value received; that we are entitled to
it for the service we have rendered."[17] Lipscomb had always
maintained that the better translation was "unto the remission of
sins" or "into the state of a remission of sins." The rebaptists (as
Lipscomb called them) had maintained that the command to be
obeyed was "be baptized for the remission of sins." Lipscomb
now felt some vindication of his view that the expression "for (or,
better, into) the remission of sins" was a promise concerning
God's part of salvation.

2. Lipscomb and McGary

By 1876, Lipscomb could say that he had "written and written and rewritten on it (i.e., rebaptism — JG) until we have
grown just a little tired of repeating things that will never give any
one trouble if they will lose their sectarianism and study the
Bible."[18] However, the controversy was not to rage full force until

Austin McGary founded the *Firm Foundation* with the main intent of giving his position on rebaptism a fuller airing. Although Lipscomb had been generous in giving McGary space in the *Advocate* to argue his case, McGary felt compelled to provide a stronger means to express his views. So, in 1884, McGary founded the *Firm Foundation* for the explicit purpose of attacking the views expressed by Lipscomb in the *Advocate*. "When McGary resigned as editor in 1900, the controversy waned and ceased within a few years."[19]

Although Lipscomb and McGary were not the only combatants, they certainly represented the strongest advocates of their respective sides. First of all, "What David Lipscomb was to the church of Christ in Tennessee, Austin McGary was to the church in Texas."[20] Secondly, both were editors of influential papers in their respective regions. Thirdly, their personal commitment to the seriousness of the issue was equal in intensity. Each of them was completely devoted to being faithful to the word of God without regard for the contrary opinions of others.

3. Austin McGary

Austin McGary was born on February 6, 1846, at Huntsville, Texas. His father had fought at the battle of San Jacinto and had guarded Santa Anna the night after he had been captured. For several years, Austin McGary lived a rugged and dangerous life first as a sheriff and then as a transporter of convicted prisoners.

McGary was a skeptic until he became serious about religion at the age of thirty-five. During this year of his life he began reading the Campbell-Owen Debate. About this same time he heard an English immigrant named Harry Hamilton preach the gospel in Madisonville, Texas. After continuing his religious investigation, McGary was baptized on December 24, 1881. Shortly thereafter he began to preach as the opportunity arose.

For years before McGary's conversion it had been the practice of the churches of Christ in Texas to accept immersed believers into their churches without requiring baptism. Eckstein has observed that records indicate that in Texas "over a twenty-seven year period eleven different preachers of the churches of Christ accepted forty-seven candidates on the basis of their former immersion."[21]

McGary expressed his concern with the practice in the pages of the *Gospel Advocate* in a series of articles in the early months of 1884. In September of 1884, McGary published the first issue of the *Firm Foundation*.

4. The *Firm Foundation*

There is no question but what McGary began the *Firm Foundation* in order to combat the practice of "shaking in the Baptists." However, there were other concerns that prompted the publication of this paper. In 1889, McGary explained how he decided to publish the paper at a state meeting in June, 1884.

> Just before we began the publication of this paper we attended the Bryan State meeting, where we realized the sad fact that many innovations upon apostolic Christianity were being ushered in upon us. There we carefully noted Brother J.W. McGarvey's lectures and saw that the chief art in the theological science that he was dispensing, was the art of manipulating congregations, so as to give the pastor that place and power that modern pastors now occupy in our city congregations which is so unlike anything found in the New Testament, and which is so fast destroying all apostolic features in the churches and precipitating discord and derision upon the disciples of Christ. Hence, when we returned home from that "State Meeting" we soon determined to begin the publication of this paper, to oppose everything in the work and worship of the church, for which there was not a command or an apostolic example or a necessary scriptural inference.[22]

McGary had 250 copies printed. Of these, he mailed copies free to as many friends and acquaintances as he could think of; then, as J.D. Tant later put it, "he pushed the rest under the bed as he had no one to send them to."[23] McGary began the project by himself, although later Elijah Hansbrough financially supported the venture. The paper began as a monthly and rose to a circulation of 5000 after five years. In February 1888, the paper became a semi-monthly, and then on March 7, 1889, it became a weekly. In 1900, McGary resigned after sixteen years as editor.[24]

In late 1884, David Lipscomb had the following to say about McGary's new effort:

> We gave Brother McGary space in the *Advocate* to discuss this question. He occupied several pages, mostly of a rambling nature. The last two of them were repetitions of the former. We suggested this repetition was useless. He quit. He is now publishing a paper that misrepresents me and his brethren, and generally persists in saying I defended Baptist baptism, which he knows is not true. I never wrote an article nor referred to the subject, that I did not carefully draw the distinction between a baptism in obedience to the command of Christ, and one for the purpose of satisfying the requirements of Baptists.[25]

B. McGary's Arguments for Rebaptism

In his writings and debates, McGary offered a variety of arguments against the practice of accepting those immersed among the Baptists and other denominations.

1. The "Campbellism" Argument

The first major article to appear in the first issue of the *Firm Foundation* was an article by McGary titled, "Campbellism — What Is it?"[26] McGary knew that the term "Campbellism" was used in derision against those who sought to restore New Testament Christianity. However, McGary used the term to refer to "that very large class of my brethren who are practicing, against the protest of their brethren in the minority, things instituted by Brother Campbell, for which he, nor they, have ever shown a 'thus saith the Lord.' "[27] What McGary specifically had in mind was Campbell's plea, which he labeled "our plea," "for the union into one body of all who have been immersed, regardless of their failure to understand the design of baptism or their having omitted making the good confession before compliance with that ordinance."[28]

In a series of six articles during the first months of the *Firm Foundation*, John S. Durst confronted head-on the theme of "Our Plea for Christian Union."[29] Durst represented this plea as the popular view so that the writers of the *Firm Foundation* might be seen as extremists. He described this plea as the view that

> Christians are scattered all through Sectdom, notwithstanding they were taught and baptized according to sectarian usages. That all are in the church of God who have been immersed, whether they have scripturally confessed that Christ is the Son of God or not. If they were immersed to honor God in His appointments they are Christians; and if Christians they are children of God; and if children of God they have been so acknowledged by the Father, and hence should be acknowledged by us.[30]

McGary believed that "our plea" provided the source for this widely practiced error of receiving people from the sects on the basis of an invalid baptism.

2. The Good Confession

Another critical issue for McGary was the good confession. McGary and his companions insisted that the erroneous confession made by Baptists prior to baptism was proof that their baptism was unscriptural. The true confession to be made prior to baptism was that "Jesus is the Christ, the Son of God." Baptists, on the other hand, offered confessions such as "I believe that God for Christ's sake has pardoned my sins." Consequently, anyone who had been baptized without making the scriptural confession had not been baptized properly.

McGary frequently quoted Alexander Campbell to show that Campbell himself was on record in contradiction to his own plea for Christian union. For example, in his written debate with

306

James A. Harding, McGary quoted Campbell's words from *Campbell on Baptism* regarding Peter's confession of Jesus in Matthew 16:16: "This confession must be made by every applicant for Christian baptism in order to his being constitutionally built upon the divine foundation."[31]

3. Ignorance of the Design

A third argument that McGary raised in behalf of rebaptism was based on the subject's ignorance of the design of baptism. According to McGary, the design of baptism was what it was "for," and it was "for the remission of sins." McGary frequently quoted Campbell to substantiate the orthodoxy of his hard line on this issue. In quoting from the *Christian Baptist*, p. 521 (one volume edition), McGary cited Campbell's words about the benefits of the sacrifice of Jesus.

> Knowing that the efficacy of this blood is to be communicated to our consciences in the way which God has pleased to appoint, we 'stagger not at the promise of God,' but flee to the sacred ordinance which brings the blood of Christ in contact with our consciences. Without knowing and believing this, immersion is as empty as a blasted nut.[32]

McGary's point was that, for baptism to be effectual, the recipient must "know and believe" that it was through baptism, this "sacred ordinance," that the blood of Christ was brought in contact with one's conscience.

It is evident that the rebaptism controversy was generated partly because there was considerable confusion as to the importance of knowing the design of baptism. At first, some writers who shared Lipscomb's views seemed to be saying that it was not essential for a person to understand the purpose or design of a command in order to obey it acceptably. For example in 1883, the *Gospel Advocate* quoted a writer named Ely from the pages of the *Christian Evangelist* with the following words: "A knowledge of the importance and design of baptism is not necessary to its validity and acceptance. If so, whose baptism is valid?"[33]

That same year, in his column, "Texas Work and Workers," John T. Poe wrote:

> Salvation is predicated on obedience, and the soul that from love to God obeys, even when he does not see the reason why, will reap the blessing as surely as do those who know all the whys and wherefores. His faith is even greater than those who have a reason for their obedience beyond the fact that God commanded it.[34]

In the first issue of the *Firm Foundation*, McGary quoted the following statement of T.R. Burnett in the *Christian Messenger*:

> Ignorance of the design of an act does not invalidate the act, else Abraham's journey out of his own land would have been a failure. He went out, "not knowing whether he went." If we hire a man to build a house, and he builds it, the act is performed, whether the builder knows the design of the building or not.[35]

In the January 1885 edition of the *Firm Foundation*, Elijah Hansbrough presented an article titled, "What Is the Gospel? Of What Is It Composed?" In this article, Hansbrough argued that it was necessary to understand not only the commands but also the designs of the commands entailed in the gospel.[36] In the May 1885 issue, Hansbrough reported that he had received a letter from J.W. McGarvey in response to his own letter asking McGarvey to point out any wrong position he may have taken. Hansbrough was astonished to learn that McGarvey objected to Hansbrough's position on understanding the design of baptism. McGarvey was quoted as saying,

> In regard to the validity of baptism when it is not understood to be for remission of sins, I think you are wrong. My reason for thinking so is brief. It is because God has not made the blessing attached to baptism dependent on our understanding the design of

the ordinance. The blessings of eating or taking proper medicine follows whether we understand it or not. So, if God promised pardon to the penitent believer, who is baptized, the blessing comes whether the sinner expects it or not.[37]

McGarvey had earlier discussed this issue in an article titled "What Is A Valid Immersion" in the *American Christian Quarterly Review* in 1862 (reprinted in the January 16, 1941, issue of the *Gospel Advocate*). McGarvey wrote:

As for the design of immersion, which expression means merely the blessing promised to those who are immersed, it involves no duty either of the immerser or of the immersed. It belongs to God and not to man.[38]

McGarvey went on to observe that "while a knowledge of the design of the institution is not made a condition of the fulfillment of that design, it was the duty of the administrator to inform the recipient of the blessing promised to him."[39]

Later, it would be argued that while one ought to understand something of the purpose of baptism, there was not just one design that had to be understood. Rather, there were many purposes or designs of baptism and one could be baptized acceptably for any one of these designs.[40]

Furthermore, Lipscomb maintained that:

To be baptized for the remission of sins as the only design — that is if we do it, moved only by the desire of securing the remission of sins, the design is wholly a selfish one. I do not believe that men baptized by a design purely selfish are acceptably baptized.[41]

McGary was convinced that this ambivalent attitude toward the design of a command was effectively compromising the true nature of obedience and was filling up the church with unconverted sectarians. For McGary and his companions an act of obedience required submitting to the form of the act while understanding and affirming the end or purpose for which the act was ordained.

Very often the case of Alexander Campbell was drawn into the controversy. Lipscomb and his adherents argued that Alexander Campbell was baptized without a knowledge that baptism was for the remission of sins. They reasoned that he came to that awareness some years later in his debates on baptism. However, McGary frequently quoted Campbell's words on the design of baptism from Campbell *On Baptism* (p. 253):

> Evident then it is, that there is no *specific design* on account of which any one can constitutionally be baptized, except it be for the remission of sins previously committed.[42]

McGary was convinced that either Campbell understood the design at the time of his baptism, or else he later corrected it.[43]

4. The Authority Issue

Another argument that McGary advanced in support of rebaptism was the argument on behalf of proper authority. In his debate with Harding, McGary summed up the issue with a question: "Does the Lord authorize the immersion of such persons as do not know for what He has commanded them to go 'down into the water?' "[44] McGary noted that all would agree that it was right to teach candidates for baptism that baptism was for the remission of sins and baptize them for that purpose. Yet, he objected, Lipscomb, Harding, and the rest were saying that it was permissible to baptize other people as well — people who have not been taught the truth on baptism. McGary contended that there was no authority for baptizing this class of people.

C. Lipscomb's Position

David Lipscomb was born in Franklin County, Tennessee, on

January 21, 1831. At the age of fourteen in 1845, David was baptized by Tolbert Fanning, as Lipscomb put it, "to obey God."[45] Some twenty-five years later, in the early years of the republication of the *Gospel Advocate*, Lipscomb commented that he had so often responded on the rebaptism question that he was inclined to answer queries regarding the issue in the briefest of fashions.[46] Nevertheless, Lipscomb found himself, over the next forty years, devoting numerous articles, editorials, and responses to the issue. In spite of numerous challenges to his position from Tennessee to Texas, Lipscomb maintained a consistent position as he met his critics head on.

Lipscomb always believed that the desire to honor God was the noblest motive with which one could seek baptism. When a person did his part by being baptized to honor God in obedience to His command, then God did His part in providing the blessings that He had promised. Among these blessings was remission of sins. Lipscomb always insisted that it was not essential that a person understand when the blessings were going to be bestowed for him to receive them. As a matter of fact, a person could be mistaken as to when the blessing would be bestowed, but that mistake did not prevent God from bestowing the blessing anyway. For instance, if a person mistakenly believed that God had pardoned him of his sins at some time prior to baptism and yet was baptized out of faith in Jesus and a strong desire to obey God, then God would pardon him of his sins in spite of that mistaken belief. Such was the case, Lipscomb believed, because remission of sins was God's part based on man's obedience. And man's obedience entailed being baptized in penitent faith with a desire to honor God with such obedience.

Lipscomb insisted that the expression "for the remission of sins" in Acts 2:38 was not part of the command. If it were, then one would have some problem in explaining the design for that command. If "be baptized for the remission of sins" is the command, then how could "for the remission of sins" be the design? Obviously, "be baptized for the remission of sins for the remission of sins" is nonsense.

Lipscomb sometimes asked what one must believe in order to be saved. Jesus said in Mark 16:16 "He that believeth and is baptized shall be saved." What was it that a person ought to believe in order to be saved? Obviously, thought Lipscomb, a person had to believe that Jesus was the risen Savior. Yet, the rebaptists were concluding that one also had to believe that baptism was for the remission of sins. Lipscomb argued that such a contention was tantamount to adding to the Word of God. He could find nowhere where it was stated that to be saved one must believe that baptism is for the remission of sins. Furthermore, Lipscomb wondered why, since they were making such an issue of it, the rebaptists did not insist that a candidate confess that he believed baptism to be for the remission of sins. If one must believe that baptism is for the remission of sins, and that one was being baptized for that specific purpose, then it would appear that a preacher would find it necessary to ascertain these facts prior to performing the act. Yet there was no example of such an interrogation in the New Testament.

Lipscomb maintained that the emphasis upon remission of sins in the examples of conversion in Acts occurred only where a strong sense of guilt was prominent in the mind of the converts. In Acts 2, the Jews on Pentecost were stunned with the realization that they had crucified the Messiah. In Acts 22, Saul of Tarsus was laboring under the pain of a convicted conscience for having persecuted the church. However, in the other examples, the need for providing relief for a conscience agonizing over personal sin was not so pronounced (e.g., the Ethiopian treasurer in Acts 8). In these other cases, the emphasis shifts to baptism in the name of Christ. Lipscomb felt it extremely important to point out that the expression "in the name of Jesus" was connected more often with baptism in Acts than the expression "for remission of sins."

Lipscomb in no way was supportive of Baptist baptism. A person who was baptized to get into the Baptist church was submitting to an invalid baptism. But a person who was baptized to get into the church of Christ was just as mistaken. For nowhere do we "read of anyone ever having been baptized into the church of Christ."[47] Lipscomb understood that there were all kinds of errors being taught about baptism. But the acceptance of error did not always nullify obedience. For instance, one writer asked Lipscomb about a woman who had been taught that she could not understand a word of the Gospel until she was quickened by the Holy Spirit. She had been encouraged to be baptized and had done so. The writer maintained that she could not have done so with proper faith in Jesus. Lipscomb argued that "the fact that she was taught that she could not believe without first being quickened by the Spirit is not clear evidence that she did not believe."[48] The problem with that false doctrine was not that it prevented belief, but that it prevented acting on that faith.

Lipscomb cited another case wherein mistakes in understanding did not hinder obedience.

> Years ago in Kentucky I was preaching, and an intelligent man made the confession; he had been raised under strong prejudices in favor of Baptist teaching. After much hearing and comparing of teaching, he became satisfied he ought to obey the Lord. As I took his confession, a Baptist preacher who was present asked the privilege of a question. "Do you believe God for Christ's sake has pardoned your sins?" He responded, "I believe he has, so far as I have submitted, and will as I still submit to him." It was hard to give up entirely the old idea that in believing he received forgiveness. But he wished to obey God and honor him in all his appointments, and I baptized him.[49]

Lipscomb insisted that it was a mistake to suggest that one could not learn the truth that was necessary for baptism among the Baptists. Although there was much error taught, still it was possible for one to learn the gospel and obey it in the sects. The responsibility one would then have would be to leave sectarianism and join with those who were seeking to practice New Testament Christianity. But Lipscomb always insisted that the ad-

313

ministrator of baptism was irrelevent. Even though his opponents granted this point, they implied the opposite by their other arguments. Since the Baptists taught and practiced error with respect to the confession and baptism, McGary and the others insisted that it was highly improbable that anyone could be properly obedient while a part of such bodies. For Lipscomb, this position strongly indicated that people coming from the sects had to satisfy some mere man before they could be accepted.

Frequently, the case of the twelve disciples in Acts 19 was presented to Lipscomb. Obviously here was a group of men who had been baptized out of a desire to obey God; and yet they had to be rebaptized. Lipscomb countered that they had *not* been baptized to obey God since God had not given the command to which they were obedient. (That is, the baptism of John was no longer a command of God. In other words, the two situations were not parallel. The twelve disciples had been baptized into John's baptism after the baptism of John had ceased.)

Lipscomb often called attention to the significance of the preposition *eis* when it was used with the verb for baptize. After citing several passages (Acts 8:16; I Cor. 12:13; Gal. 3:27), Lipscomb concluded, "The word *eis*, or its English into, denotes object or end. These Scriptures explicitly declare that the great end or object, or design, or purpose of baptism, is to put men into Christ."[50] And remission of sins is but one of the fruits, or blessings, of being in Christ.

In Lipscomb's mind, it was essential that the one baptized be the one who decided whether his baptism was valid. When someone else had to be satisfied, then the baptism was not essentially different from infant baptism. To his credit, Lipscomb was consistent in yielding to the conscience of those who decided that rebaptism was necessary. In 1875, he wrote:

We have baptized a second time a number of persons — we are of the conviction that not one of them ought to have been baptized again. It is a matter though that we cannot decide. It is for them to

314

decide. When done with . . . anxiety to serve God we suppose it to be pardonable, but still we have never attended to it without misgivings. We found these grow stronger as we grow older.[51]

D. The Controversy Continued:
J.D. Tant and F.B. Srygley (1927)

After the decline of Lipscomb's health, other key men at the *Advocate* addressed the rebaptism issue from time to time. For example, E.G. Sewell aggressively challenged the rebaptist position in a series of articles between 1911 and 1913. Years later, F.B. Srygley reaffirmed the same position that Lipscomb and Sewell had defended in the pages of the *Advocate*. In 1927, an interesting exchange took place between F.B. Srygley and J.D. Tant that reflected the continuing role that the *Advocate* had taken in this debate.

1. J.D. Tant

Jefferson Davis Tant was born on June 28, 1861, to William and Mattie Lloyd Tant in Paulding County, Georgia. In the fall of 1876, William Tant moved his family to a farm near Austin, Texas. Young Jeff had joined the Methodist Church at the age of fourteen, while still in Georgia, and began preaching for the Methodists at age nineteen.[52] Tant had been immersed in the Methodist church while in Georgia and, as a Methodist preacher, had sprinkled babies without questioning the scripturalness of this practice. During 1881, Tant had had the opportunity to hear some "Campbellite" preachers set forth the principles of non-denominational Christianity. On August 14, 1881, Tant came forward in a gospel meeting in Buda, Texas, and was received into fellowship on the statement that he was satisfied with his baptism.[53]

Tant did not question the validity of his Methodist immersion until he met J.F. Grubbs in 1885. Tant had bitterly condemned McGary's position as set forth in the *Firm Foundation* from its inception in 1884, and he "waded into" Grubbs "with all the arguments and sophistry at hand."[54] But the next time he met with Grubbs, Grubbs met every argument that Tant made. Years later, Tant confessed.

> In 1886 when J.F. Grubbs showed me that I could not make a Bible argument in favor of sect baptism, I then deserted those brethren who held to it and rode a Texas pony one hundred and twenty-seven miles to get John Durst to baptize me.[55]

In 1895 Tant visited the office of the *Gospel Advocate* and met Lipscomb for the first time. Lipscomb persuaded Tant to serve as field editor which he did until the end of 1898. In the spring of 1899 Tant preached for seven weeks in Nashville. In commenting upon the spirit of unity and cooperation among the churches in Nashville, Tant had the following to say about the rebaptism controversy.

> I found that Harding and Lipscomb condemned Methodist and Baptist baptism as bitterly as I do. Here is where the great trouble has been and how the breach has been greatly widened: we have tried to force these brethren to accept and hold a position they have never believed, neither do they advocate the same. Both were as willing as I to affirm that baptism as held and practiced by Baptists and Methodists is unscriptural; but they claim that all Christians belonging to these churches are in there through obedience to God's word, not in obedience to the sectarian doctrine. In this matter I thought these brethren inconsistent in their doctrines to save any one; but they thought I was extreme in not giving Baptists and Methodists credit for the good they do. In all these differences I am now convinced, as I have been for a number of years, that had all on both sides exercised more patience, and been more careful in words that expressed our differences, the bitterness, envy, and strife which have existed to a great extent would have been unknown. Our differences have never been so great as our writings convey to the world they are, when we understand one another properly. While it is considered that Lipscomb and Harding are extreme on the one hand, and I

on the other, yet, after my association with them, I think they both love me more than before and I can truthfully say that after having more knowledge of the zeal and godliness and work of these dear brethren, my love for them is far greater than ever in the past; and I am sure that many who regard those brethren today as enemies of the cause and not in accord with the word of God, are greatly mistaken.[56]

Furthermore, Tant went on to say:

I often think of what a noted Texas preacher said to me some years ago: that the best way to bring about an understanding between Lipscomb and McGary would be to work up a big meeting somewhere, select the two to hold it, and at the close of the meeting they would find they were so near in accord on almost all things that they would be ashamed to claim a difference.[57]

In 1901, Tant engaged in a written debate with James A. Harding on the rebaptism question. The debate was carried in the *Firm Foundation* and the *Gospel Advocate* with both papers carrying Tant's article one week and then Harding's response the next.

Yater Tant, J.D.'s son, saw this debate as one of the factors that kept the issue from finally dividing the churches of Christ.

Probably this discussion did as much to promote harmony and to resolve the "rebaptism question" as any single thing throughout the entire controversy. Tant was a recognized champion of the "rebaptizers"; while James A. Harding, co-founder of Nashville Bible School, and one of the greatest evangelists in all the church, was held in utmost esteem and veneration by all. Those who held to his position would have been as willing to trust their cause to his hands as to any man whom they might have found.

While the controversy was to continue for many years (and even now, more than half a century later, is occasionally referred to), yet this discussion probably turned the tide, and assured that there would be no general division over the matter. Tant and Harding

317

demonstrated that brethren could differ, could discuss their differences as Christians, and still fellowship one another. The bitterness and acrimony which had marked the Lipscomb-McGary debate a dozen years previously was markedly absent this time. Perhaps the brethren were growing up.[58]

2. Tant and Srygley

In September 1927, J.D. Tant submitted a report to the *Gospel Advocate* about his recent activities and plans. In passing he made the following remarks:

> My observation in forty years' preaching is, if a man preaches the gospel, the denominations do not come satisfied with their baptism; and if my preaching brethren had courage enough to preach a complete gospel and not call on the sects to lead in prayer and fool them by making them believe they are children of God, none would come satisfied. I never see H.M. Phillips or R.E.L. Taylor reporting their meetings and telling how many came "satisfied with their baptism."[59]

F.B. Srygley took strong exception to Tant's implications. Srygley said, "Brother Tant is trying to make fun of me for asking if he is satisfied with his baptism."[60] Srygley took Tant to task for sitting in judgment of others' baptism. "One who would refuse to fellowship a man who had been baptized to honor and obey God, though he may have been mistaken as to when God pardoned him, needs baptism worse than the one he has thus refused."[61]

A few weeks later, Tant submitted a very conciliatory response, expressing deep concern that Srygley, by labeling him as a hobby rider, was undermining Tant's influence.[62] To clarify the matter, Tant stated concisely what he believed. In the same issue, Srygley questioned Tant's view that "sinners must hear and understand the gospel."

> I think a sinner must understand all of it that he has to obey. He is not required to understand God's side of it, but his side. "For the remission of sins" is God's side of the gospel, and no one is re-

quired to obey "For the remission of sins." It is a deep design of baptism, and it is God's design, not the sinner's.[63]

Srygley chided Tant for casting aspersion upon the practices of preachers associated with the *Advocate*. "Brother Tant knew my position, and he knew the position the *Gospel Advocate* has occupied for half a century."[64]

So, it is appropriate to notice that, even though the heat of the controversy diminished after the decline of Lipscomb and McGary, the basic positions had not changed. Lipscomb's position remained the *Advocate*'s position from its rebirth in 1866 until well into the third decade of the twentieth century.

E. G.C. Brewer and the Advocate

In the 1930's, 40's and early 50's, the rebaptism issue was again discussed in the pages of the *Advocate*, this time by G.C. Brewer. G.C. Brewer was born in Giles County, Tennessee, on December 25, 1884, and died in Searcy, Arkansas, on June 6, 1956. He graduated from the Nashville Bible School (David Lipscomb College) with a B.L. degree in 1910. He was an able writer, preacher, and debater.

In the *Gospel Advocate* of April 27, 1950, Brewer reviewed his involvement in the rebaptism controversy.

In the long ago there was a serious issue among the brethren on whether or not people are ever baptized scripturally by denominational preachers. The controversy was not without some bitterness, and brethren in some instances disfellowshipped each other because of their differences. Those who care to consult the files of the *Gospel Advocate* and of the *Firm Foundation* will find a great deal written by both sides upon this issue. Also the names of tracts that discussed these points may be listed in the catalogues of these two publishing companies. I was myself involved in the controversy to some extent when I was a much younger man than

319

I am now, and there may be found in the files of the *Gospel Advocate* things I wrote in this controversy long, long ago. [However, about eighteen years ago, after the controversy had died, I wrote a series of articles entitled "Denominational Baptism." This series was published on the editorial page of the *Gospel Advocate*, the editor giving his space to my articles.] I had a department in the paper at that time called "Topics for Thought," but these articles, as stated above, were transferred to the editor's space. It was the effort of these articles to avoid controversy rather than to renew it. The articles also endeavored to show that there are limits to which any of us can go in the matter of teaching God's word and getting people to obey it.[65]

The basic question that fewer addressed was, "Are people scripturally baptized by denominational preachers?" Brewer answered in the affirmative. In the first of a series of articles on "denominational baptism" published in the *Advocate* around 1932, Brewer outlined the issue with the following questions:

1. Is there any room for controversy on this point?
2. In what sense do we accept or reject people on their baptism or on any other condition?
3. Does the fact that people are satisfied with their baptism have any weight in determining the scripturalness of their baptism?
4. Is the expression "for the remission of sins" a part of the command to be baptized?
5. Does one have to understand that baptism is for the remission of sins before one can be baptized scripturally?

Brewer reminded his readers that, while the denominations do teach some truth regarding baptism, they also teach some things contrary to the truth. But, he noted, it is possible for a sincere person to learn the truth about baptism while a part of a denomination. Consequently, "from the mere statement that a man was baptized by a denomination we cannot say whether he was or was not baptized scripturally."[66]

However, Brewer concluded that since a particular denomination can be known to teach error on baptism, the presumption should be that the individual's baptism was not scriptural. Therefore, the preacher's task is to set forth the New Testament teaching on baptism and contrast it with the denomination's teaching. But if the individual insists that "he knew and understood the New Testament teaching at the time he was baptized, and that he obeyed the teaching of the New Testament and not the teaching of the denomination,"[67] then there would be nothing left to do but to accept the person's baptism. "The whole point, then, turns upon the individual's attitude — his motive, his faith, his repentance, his obedience."[68] So, it is not possible to settle the matter by debate. Each case has to be decided on its own merit.

In answer to the second question, Brewer was curious to know who exactly does the accepting or rejecting of a person's baptism — the preacher or the whole church? Our task, he concluded, was to teach the Word and help others to understand it.

In response to the third question, Brewer cautioned that we have to be very careful about such subjective matters because "the mere fact that a man is satisfied with his attempt to obey the Lord does not prove that his obedience has been acceptable to the Lord."[69] But, it is the individual himself that must be satisfied in his own conscience as to whether he has been obedient.

The fourth question addressed a key issue in the decades long controversy: Is the expression "for the remission of sins" a part of the command to be baptized? McGary and his comrades had argued that the command to be obeyed was "be baptized for the remission of sins." If one was not baptized specifically for the remission of sins then one was not being obedient to the command. Lipscomb had responded that the expression "for the forgiveness of sins" was a blessing (not *the* blessing) promised by God for obedience to the command to "be baptized." Brewer came down on the side of Lipscomb.

To make "for the remission of sins" the one and only end of the command to be baptized is certainly to rob the command not only of some of its importance, but of some of its beauty, and it takes away some of the highest inducements to obey the command. This expression, "for the remission of sins," cannot be overemphasized if it is emphasized for what it teaches, but it certainly can be wrongly emphasized. We have heard brethren use such an expression as: "Baptism for the remission of sins is a condition of salvation." As an example of tautology or redundancy this could hardly be excelled since remission of sins and salvation mean exactly the same thing. Therefore to say that baptism is a condition for salvation is sufficient, or to say that baptism is a condition of the remission of sins is sufficient, and either one of these would be equivalent to saying that baptism is for the remission of sins.[70]

The fifth question raised the matter that was the central concern in the controversy. "Does one have to understand that baptism is for the remission of sins in order to be scripturally baptized?" At that point, Brewer was less than helpful. In fact his answer seemed to contradict what he had previously stated just the page before. Notice the inconsistencies in these two sections.

To make "for the remission of sins" the one and only end of the command to be baptized is certainly to rob the command not only of some of its importance, but of some of its beauty, and it takes away some of the highest inducements to obey the command. This expression, "for the remission of sins," cannot be overemphasized if it is emphasized for what it teaches, but it certainly can be wrongly emphasized.[71]

It is difficult to see how anyone could learn enough about baptism to attempt to obey the command at all without learning the purpose of the command. If such a person has learned that baptism is required in the word of God, it is certain that the person would have learned at the same time something of the blessing promised to those who are baptized, had he not been misled by denominational teaching. Furthermore, if anyone learns that the Lord has required him to be baptized, and is therefore baptized in order to meet the Lord's requirements, he certainly must have learned from the same Scriptures that salvation, remission of sins, and spiritual blessings were promised to those who obey the command, and to those only.[72]

In the second section, Brewer spoke of "*the* purpose of the command" and "*the* blessing promised. . . ." If "end" and "purpose" mean basically the same thing, then Brewer was being inconsistent in saying that remission of sins was not the one and only end of the command while saying that it was *the* purpose of the command. Brewer summarized his view in a somewhat confusing fashion by stating:

> Our conclusion is, therefore, *that anyone who is baptized as the Scriptures teach that he should be baptized must have known that baptism was unto the remission of sins or was a condition of salvation. If he did not know this, there has been some misreading or some misleading somewhere.*[73]

With this response, Brewer effectively ignored the chief points that Lipscomb had so laboriously laid out in the pages of the *Advocate* over a span of nearly fifty years. No one ever denied that baptism was a condition of salvation, or that it was for the remission of sins. Furthermore it was agreed that everyone should be taught that baptism was for the remission of sins. It also was agreed that anyone who thought otherwise was in error. However, Lipscomb's point was, "How much error is allowable?" Lipscomb contended that when the error prevented obedience then the error was critical. But when a person had been baptized to obey God, then in Lipscomb's he was obedient regardless of the confusion in his mind about the proper exegesis of Acts 2:38. Lipscomb would have readily agreed that baptism was a condition of salvation. He denied that understanding that baptism was for remission of sins was a condition for salvation.

Brewer's position seemed to be that a candidate for baptism should be aware that baptism was for the remission of sins. But it was possible for a person in a denomination to come to that knowledge and thus be scripturally baptized. Thus, Brewer occupied a mediating position between McGary and Lipscomb.

Brewer agreed with Lipscomb that the practice of demanding

a proper, formal confession prior to baptism had been pushed too far. In response to a question about confession prior to baptism, Brewer quoted with approval from Lipscomb in the book *Queries and Answers* edited by J.W. Shepherd. He said, "Brother Lipscomb's position was the position of the *Gospel Advocate*, and on most points his position is still the position of this paper."[74] The following lengthy quote by Brewer well represents the position that the *Advocate* had taken.

What Confession Does One make Before Baptism at the Hands of a Baptist? In discussing the points involved in the re-baptism issue, brethren frequently say that a man could not be baptized by the Baptists and think that he was doing so in order to be saved because the Baptists require him to confess before baptism that he believes that God for Christ's sake has pardoned his sins. It must be observed now, however, that all Baptists do not require this confession. I have personally heard them take the confession just as we do, and then baptize the man on that confession after the vote of the church has been secured. But in order to help us in evaluating any case, I wish here, at the risk of making this article too long, to relate something that I have never before committed to print:

My father-in-law, Mr. E.G. Hall of Huntingdon, who died some thirty years ago, was a faithful member of the church and an elder in his home congregation. He was a well-informed man; he knew the Bible from cover to cover, and he read the religious papers and was thoroughly acquainted with the controversy on rebaptism. He read both sides without bias. He however, was never baptized except by the Baptists. He admitted that he confessed, "I believe that God for Christ's sake has pardoned my sins," before he was baptized by the Baptists, and yet he said he had no thought of being saved before and without baptism. He did not know that the Baptists taught that immersion is because of remission or that it is a door into the church. When he learned that the Baptists teach this, he turned from the Baptists. He said he always believed that baptism was a condition of pardon, and that salvation is enjoyed only after one is baptized into Christ. In explanation of his confession, we have a viewpoint that no one would

324

ever suspect unless he had heard some man express such a view. Brother Hall said that what he understood by the confession was that God had made adequate atonement for his sins in the death of Christ: that God had provided the pardon for his sins when Christ died on the cross. He means to express implicit faith in the atonement of Christ and in the plan of God that had made this provision for his salvation. He believed his sins were pardoned on the cross in the sense that the debt was paid then and there. He did not think that he, personally, enjoyed the pardon before his baptism. He was being baptized in order to come into the fullness of salvation. He never changed his view and never entertained a doubt as to the scripturalness of his baptism, and yet he was such an informed and outspoken opponent of the Baptists that they feared him more than they would fear a dozen preachers.

This is related in the hope that brethren may see that sometimes a man may even confess that which seems to them to be in error and yet the man himself is not in error.[75]

F. The Significance of the Rebaptism Controversy

A superficial evaluation of the rebaptism controversy would indicate that it was not one of the most significant controversies of the Restoration Movement among churches of Christ. After all, even though it captured that attention of a wide segment of this brotherhood for several years, it never resulted in a rupture of fellowship between the two positions. However, the controversy is important in understanding the later thinking of the churches of Christ as reflected in their two leading journals. For example, although the *Advocate's* position was basically that of Lipscomb for seventy years or more, it appears that McGary's view has now become that of both the *Advocate* and the *Firm Foundation*, as we shall later demonstrate. Consequently, there are some more serious issues reflected in the transitions in thinking that have occurred since the debate began in earnest. In this evaluation we will examine two related issues: (1) Who is a Christian? and (2) What is the nature of obedience?

1. Who is a Christian?

One of the enduring questions of the Restoration Movement was the question, "Who is a Christian?" It is evident that Alexander Campbell did not begin by redefining the essence of being a Christian. Rather, it was his ambition to see the union of all Christians take place. In 1826 he wrote, "I labor to see sectarianism abolished and all Christians of every name united upon the one foundation on which the apostolic church was founded."[76] In the following years, through his debates, Campbell hammered out a more fully developed theology of baptism. However, in his paper the *Millennial Harbinger* in 1837, Campbell had the following comments in response to a lady from Lunenberg, Virginia, comments that precipitated much discussion of the issue of the connection of baptism with being a Christian.

> We would indeed, have no objections to cooperate in these matters with all Christians, and raise contributions for such purposes as, in our judgment, are promotive of the Divine glory or of human happiness, whether or not they belong to our churches: for we find in all Protestant parties Christians as exemplary as ourselves according to their and our relative knowledge and opportunities.[77]

Although Austin McGary felt deeply indebted to Campbell for his own conversion, McGary strongly opposed the notion of a union of those who had been immersed among the sects. McGary's view more than suggested that no confidence could be placed in a baptism at the hands of a denominational preacher. In his view, no one was a Christian who had not been properly baptized, and no one had been properly baptized who had not been immersed with a full understanding that it was "for the remission of sins."

The natural outgrowth of this latter opinion has resulted in the suggestion that more is entailed in becoming a Christian than a belief in the simple gospel facts. Consider, for instance, a recent article in the *Gospel Advocate*.

> To deny that one must understand at least enough concerning the kingdom of God to identify the Kingdom of God in contrast to the Kingdom of Satan (the world including denominationalism) and to leave and/or discontinue worship and/or religious fellowship with the kingdom of Satan upon baptism is to reject clear apostolic teaching. Said rejection advocates one may receive scriptural baptism without having received proper and adequate instruction and flies in the face of the truth, harmony, and consistency of scripture.[78]

This article, as well as a number of other articles and editorials in the *Gospel Advocate*, suggest that the *Advocate* has adopted the position of McGary, namely, that one is not a Christian unless one has been baptized acording to the proper design of baptism, which is for the forgiveness of sins.

In a recent issue of the *Gospel Advocate* a long time student of the Restoration Movement simply provided a series of quotations from Lipscomb, Srygley, Harding and McGarvey (nearly all of which had appeared on the editorial pages of the *Advocate*) articulating the historic view of the *Advocate* relative to the rebaptism question.[79] Following the publication of that article there has been a series of articles strongly challenging the historic position, while no articles or editorials supporting the historic view have been published.

It is evident, therefore, that McGary's basic contention seems to have prevailed.

2. The Nature of Obedience

The rebaptism controversy endured as long as it did because there was obvious disagreement over a more basic issue. As one reads the numerous exchanges over the issue of rebaptism, it becomes clear that agreement could not be reached on this topic, because the parties involved held different views about obedience.

McGary argued that obedience was not acceptable unless a person obeyed with the right motive and understanding. One had to understand the purpose and design of the command in order to obey it. Lipscomb responded that, if that were the case, hardly anyone had been obedient. Indeed, Lipscomb countered that the biblical model for obedience was Abraham who "went not knowing whither he went." Lipscomb maintained that a person should obey as soon as he knows what is expected of him. If people wait until they understand the full range of blessings and purposes of the command, then they will be remiss. In Lipscomb's mind, the heart of obedience was submission to the will of God. Lipscomb was once asked by a person who was baptized at six whether he should be rebaptized because he now understood the real meaning of baptism. Lipscomb replied as follows.

> We have no appreciation of the order to rebaptizing people because they learn this or that about baptism. This is putting the virtue of the saving in our knowledge, not in our submission to God. The act of baptism is a declaration of our faith in God through Christ Jesus and of a willingness to give ourselves up to him as our guide and ruler. When a person has faith that leads to this submission to God, that submission is acceptable, no matter how much or how little else he may know of the will of God. When one trusts Christ as the Lord and leader, he as a learner is baptized into Christ as his leader and Lord, yet to learn and do his will.[80]

Furthermore, Lipscomb noted that much of the debate had come to hinge on "learned distinctions and differences of translations of which the greatnesses of the people know, and can know, nothing."[81]

> The very men who are loudest in demanding the validity of the service depends on the understanding of these distinctions themselves do not understand the distinctions and differences in the use of the word. Jesus thanked his Father that he had hid his way of salvation "from the wise and prudent," and "revealed it

unto babes." One fitted to enter the kingdom of heaven must become as a little child, willing to obey the commandments of God without knowing the why and wherefores or when he will be entitled to this blessing or that. It is a perversion of the Scriptures and a misrepresentation of the character of God to insist obedience depends upon the understanding of nice distinctions.

If we make baptism depend upon what man understands about it, its purpose and meaning, he will never know when he is baptized. It has been told of Dr. John Thomas, who started out to be baptized when he learned new truth about the purposes of baptism, that he was baptized over twenty times. I do not know whether this is true; but what we understand of the purpose of baptism is not the proper ground for being baptized. But the ground is, God has required it as an act of fealty to him, and we do it to obey him; and when we do this, we enter into him, that in him we may enjoy all blessings and favors. I have been disposed to be very forbearing to the position, because when young I was strongly inclined to the position, and believe that a faithful study of God's word, and especially a more complete drinking into the Spirit of Christ, will lead us to a clearer understanding of God's dealings with men.[82]

Lipscomb and the other opponents of rebaptism had warned of this tendency toward placing undue emphasis upon the administrator and the detailed knowledge of the candidate. Eckstein indicates that this tendency reached its fruition in McGary himself.

To make the administrator important in addition to the design evidenced the uncertainty in McGary's own mind. Although baptized by Harry Hamilton in 1881, McGary later questioned the validity of the rite and asked W.H.D. Carrington to rebaptize him. However, it was purported that he had lost faith in Carrington by 1884 and the question was asked, "What will he do next? Will he get Brother Poe to rebaptize him?"[83]

Endnotes

1. "Rebaptism," (April 16, 1884), p. 246.

2. See Errett Gates, *Two Early Relation and Separation of the Disciples and Baptists* (Chicago: Christian Century, 1904).

3. Ibid., see Chapters 8,9.

4. Earl Irvin West, *The Search for the Ancient Order* (Indianapolis, Indiana: Religious Book Service, 1950), 2:6.

5. Robert E. Hooper, *Crying in the Wilderness* (Nashville: David Lipscomb College, 1979), pp. 13-43.

6. David Lipscomb, "Re-baptizing Baptists," *Gospel Advocate* XXV (April 23, 1883).

7. Tolbert Fanning, "Re-baptism," *Gospel Advocate* I (October 1855), pp. 112-114.

8. Ibid., p. 112.

9. Ibid.

10. Ibid.

11. Ibid., p. 113.

12. Ibid.

13. Walter Lipscomb, "Re-immersion," *Gospel Advocate* IV (June, 1858), p. 187.

14. Ibid., p. 188.

15. John Durst, (untitled), *Gospel Advocate* XI (May 13, 1869), p. 447.

16. David Lipscomb, (reply), *Gospel Advocate* XI (May 13, 1869), pp. 447f.

17. David Lipscomb, "The Revised Testament and Rebaptism," *Gospel Advocate* (September 24, 1913), p. 922.

18. David Lipscomb, (reply), *Gospel Advocate* 18 (September 28, 1876), p. 936.

19. Stephen D. Eckstein, Jr., *History of the Churches of Christ in Texas, 1824-1950* (Austin, Texas: Firm Foundation Publishing House, 1963), p. 251.

20. West, II, p. 397.

21. Eckstein, p. 254.

22. Austin McGary, *Firm Foundation*, September 5, 1889, p. 4, quoted in Lane Cubstead, "The *Firm Foundation*, 1884-1957 — The History of a Pioneer Religious Journal and Its Editors," (Austin: University of Texas, 1957), Unpublished Masters Thesis, p. 21.

23. J.D. Tant, *Firm Foundation*, January 17, 1933, p. 2.

24. See Lane Cubstead, "The *Firm Foundation*."

25. David Lipscomb, "Did They Sin," *Gospel Advocate*, 1884, p. 754.

26. Austin McGary, "Campbellism — What Is It," *Firm Foundation*, Vol. I, No. 1, (September, 1884), pp. 2-5.

27. Ibid., p. 2.

28. Ibid., pp. 3-4.

29. John S. Durst, *Firm Foundation*, Vol. I.

30. John S. Durst, "Our Plea for Christian Union," *Firm Foundation* I (November, 1884), p. 59.

31. J.A. Harding and A. McGary, "A Debate Between J.A. Harding and

330

A. McGary on the Baptismal Question," (Austin, Texas: McGary and Hansbrough, 1888), p. 35.

32. McGary, 'Debate," p. 21.

33. *Gospel Advocate* XXV (June 27, 1883), p. 408.

34. John T. Poe, "Texas Work and Workers," *Gospel Advocate* (June 6, 1883), p. 362.

35. A. McGary, "Brother Burnett for Plunging Anyhow, Design or No Design," *Firm Foundation* I (September, 1884), p. 15.

36. Elijah Hansbrough, "What Is the Gospel?" *Firm Foundation* I (January, 1885), pp. 5-9.

37. Ibid., p. 9.

38. Quoted in a tract by I.M. Crum, "Reflections on Valid Immersion," (no date), p. 7.

39. Ibid., p. 8.

40. David Lipscomb, "Rebaptism," *Gospel Advocate* (January 2, 1884), p. 6.

41. Ibid.

42. A. McGary, "Our Reply to Brother D. Lipscomb," *Firm Foundation* I (February, 1855), p. 8.

43. Ibid., p. 9.

44. A. McGary, "Debate," p. 7.

45. David Lipscomb, "Re-baptizing Baptists," *Gospel Advocate* 25 (April 23, 1883), p. 1.

46. David Lipscomb, *Gospel Advocate* (May 13, 1869), p. 447.

47. David Lipscomb, *Questions Answered* (Nashville: Gospel Advocate, n.d.), p. 49.

48. David Lipscomb, "Rebaptism," *Gospel Advocate* 16 (November 19, 1874), p. 1094.

49. David Lipscomb, "Rebaptizing Baptists," *Gospel Advocate* 25 (April 23, 1883), p. 1.

50. David Lipscomb, "Rebaptism," *Gospel Advocate* (January 2, 1884), p. 6.

51. David Lipscomb, *Gospel Advocate* 17 (October 14, 1875), p. 978.

52. Fanning Yater Tant, *J.D. Tant — Texas Preacher* (Athens, Alabama: C.E.I. Publishing Co., 1958), p. 26.

53. Ibid., pp. 30-37.

54. Ibid., p. 60.

55. J.D. Tant, *Firm Foundation* (January 17, 1933), p. 2. See also, *Texas Preacher*, pp. 59-61.

56. Yater Tant, *J.D. Tant — Texas Preacher,* p. 219.

57. J.D. Tant, "Our Nashville Meetings — No. 1," *Gospel Advocate* XLI (June 6, 1899), p. 427.

58. Yater Tant, *J.D. Tant — Texas Preacher*, p. 240-41.

59. J.D. Tant, "Forthcoming Debate," *Gospel Advocate* (September 15, 1927).

60. F.B. Srygley, "Satisfied With His Baptism," *Gospel Advocate* (December 1, 1927).

61. Ibid.

62. J.D. Tant, "Am I a Hobby Rider?" *Gospel Advocate* (December 29, 1927), p. 1233.

63. F.B. Srygley, 'Reply to Brother Tant," *Gospel Advocate* (December 29, 1927), p. 1239.

64. Ibid., p. 1240.

65. G.C. Brewer, "Questions About Rebaptism," *Gospel Advocate* (April 27, 1950), p. 268. This article was reprinted in Brewer, *Autobiography of G.C. Brewer* (Murfreesboro, TN: DeHoff Publications, 1957), pp. 107-116.

66. G.C. Brewer, 'Denominational Baptism — No. 1" in *Contending for the Faith* (Nashville: Gospel Advocate, 1941), p. 166.

67. Ibid. p,. 167.

68. Ibid.

69. Ibid., "Denominational Baptism No. 2," p. 171.

70. Ibid., "Denominational Baptism — No. 3," pp. 174ff.

71. Ibid., p. 174.

72. Ibid., p. 175.

73. Ibid., p. 175f.

74. G.C. Brewer, "The Formal Confession," *Gospel Advocate* (September, 1944), p. 2. Reprinted in *Autobiography*, pp. 102-106.

75. G.C. Brewer, "Questions About Rebaptism," *Gospel Advocate* (April 27, 1950), pp. 269-70.

76. Alexander Campbell, "Reply to T.T.," *Christian Baptist* III (February 6, 1826), p. 146.

77. "Letter to England," *Millennial Harbinger* VIII (1837), p. 272.

78. B.A. Clayton, "Unto What Then Were Ye Baptized?" *Gospel Advocate* (March 15, 1984), p. 182.

79. J.M. Powell, "The Baptismal Question," *Gospel Advocate* (September 19, 1985), p. 564.

80. Lipscomb, "Rebaptism," *Gospel Advocate* (1906), p. 793.

81. Lipscomb, "Rebaptism," *Gospel Advocate* (November 15, 1906), p. 728.

82. Ibid.

83. Eckstein, p. 258. Cf. *Gospel Advocate* 29 (February 16, 1887), p. 110.

9

THE OPEN MEMBERSHIP CONTROVERSY AND THE CHRISTIAN CHURCHES

James B. North

Baptism has always occupied a key place in the thinking and practices of the churches of the Restoration Movement. The mere fact of this book underlines that. Several of the other chapters point to problems or issues dealing with baptism in the early years of the Movement, and the significance of the issue continues down to the present. But the focus of this chapter is to deal specifically with concerns over the thinking and practice of baptism in the period approximately 1890-1930. To properly understand these issues in this context, however, some background becomes necessary.

A. Background of the Issue

The Restoration Movement, or the group known variously as

the Christian churches, the churches of Christ, or the Disciples of Christ, began in the early years of nineteenth century America with two major concerns. First, the early leaders such as B.W. Stone, Thomas and Alexander Campbell, and Walter Scott were concerned that the Bible and the Bible alone be the authority for the thought and practices of the churches. This led in turn to the commitment to abandon man-made creeds and articles of faith as binding on Christian fellowship. Specifically, these leaders rejected the Westminster Confession of Faith and the Philadelphia Confession of Faith as inimical to the life, fellowship, and identity of the churches and individual Christians. "Where the Bible speaks, we speak," announced Thomas Campbell, and "Where the Bible is silent, we are silent." There is a clear and consistent appeal to the Bible alone as authoritative in the early years of the Movement.

The second major concern, however, was an equally clear appeal to the unity of all believers in the one Body of Christ. Stone, the Campbells, and others came out of a background of denominational divisions marked by partisan strife and sectarian bitterness. They were deeply desirous of getting the various branches of Christendom back together in order to exemplify the unity for which Christ prayed in John 17: "I pray that they may be one." Many felt that the process of world evangelization could not be accomplished unless the church was united. Evangelism was the ultimate goal, unity the immediate goal, and an emphasis on exclusive biblical authority the means. Only if the churches could agree on the basis of church authority could they ever become united. The origin of most of the divisions in the church was the failure to follow the Scriptures fully, or the addition of human teaching to the Word of God. If all agreed to follow the Scriptures alone as the guide to the church, the church could be united on that basis.

Thus the Restoration Movement would restore the unity of believers in the one body of Christ, a united church. This dual emphasis on unity and Biblical authority also created a problem with reference to an appropriate name. Ever since the Stone Movement began in 1804 its members had called themselves Christians, or churches of Christ. Alexander Campbell did not like that label; he preferred Disciples of Christ, with individuals known as disciples (normally with a lower case "d"; later a capital "D" became more standard). When the Stone and Campbell movements joined in 1832, this confusion over names continued. Many were still Christian churches, or churches of Christ, but the bulk of Campbell's followers preferred "Disciples of Christ." Because Campbell's influence was the largest of any single leader, this term became somewhat standard, both within and without the Restoration Movement. In the nineteenth century the term "Disciples of Christ" generally stood for the entire Restoration Movement in all its branches. By the 1920's, however, this term was being restricted to those churches and individuals who were still actively identified with the national agencies which we will talk about later. But it is necessary to point out that prior to the 1920's, references to "Christian Churches" or "Disciples of Christ" are completely identical.

The Movement's early teaching on Biblical standards for the church led to an examination of the Biblical teaching on salvation. Walter Scott is most identified with the "five-finger" plan of salvation which presented Biblical baptism as immersion for the remission of sins. The early leaders acknowledged baptism as a key issue in the developing intellectual commitment to a united, restored, and Biblical church.

In the next several decades baptism continued to be one of the most distinguishing characteristics of the Christian churches, or the "Cambellites." Many denominations attacked this as "baptismal regeneration." Numerous Christian church speakers debated on the subject, mode, and purpose of baptism. Members of the Restoration Movement became famous for their impassioned and often hostile defense of believer's immersion for the remission of sins. The result, again, was to focus attention and rivet identity to this particular issue. Throughout the century their

335

baptismal theology and practice remained the key identifying mark for the churches of the Movement.

B. Development of Liberalism

However, this univocal position of baptism eroded significantly by the early twentieth century. The advent of theological liberalism was the major cause of this. Under the influence of liberalism, many within the Christian churches saw baptism in a different light, holding a different position within the scheme of things. This transition produced some explosive confrontations within the Christian churches in the next couple of decades, most of them focused on the issue of baptism.

Four basic components of liberalism can be identified: (1) Friedrich Schleiermacher countered the ideas of the rationalistic Enlightenment by calling attention to the place of religious feelings and emotions. His appeal to experience as a standard removed theology from a dependence upon Bible or creed to an examination of self consciousness and religious experience. (2) Albrecht Ritschl emphasized ethics, both individual and corporate, paving the way for the Social Gospel. Again, this tended to take the place of any emphasis or concern with biblical theology as such. Jaroslav Pelikan says that a preoccupation with the empirical and a concern for ethical results are the two features which identify American Liberal theology.[1] (3) Charles Darwin's theory of evolution was accepted by the liberals and applied toward almost every aspect of theology. Daniel Day Williams even identified Liberal theology in terms of bringing Christian thought into organic unity with the evolutionary world view.[2] This undermined the traditional supernaturalism of Christian orthodoxy, questioning both the authority of scriptures and the possibility of miracles. (4) The field of biblical criticism was perhaps the most significant aspect of the growing liberalism. A mutually influencing relationship existed between the new biblical criticism and the field of evolutionary theory. Biblical critics felt confident in denying the miraculous because the scientists discounted it also. The scientists felt reinforced by the biblical critics who were arguing most of the miracle stories in Scripture came from editors centuries after the facts anyway and thus could not be taken literally. The Graf-Wellhausen theory of various sources for the Pentateuch eliminated any integrity in the stories of the patriarchs in Genesis or other miracles in the Pentateuch. Additional critics charged that Isaiah was of multiple authorship, and that Daniel was written in the Maccabean period, and thus its prophecies could also be discarded.

New Testament scholars discovered different writing styles in the Four Gospels and rejected "verbal inspiration." Scholars of the Tubingen school discovered "Petrine" and "Pauline" "schools" within the New Testament itself. Influenced by theories of evolution, biblical critics saw the Bible not as an inspired revelation from God, but a record of man's upward quest for religious meaning. They saw here the evolution of man's developing religious sensitivity, but certainly not a God-given deposit of dogma or lifestyle. The Bible became a book of religious devotion, with no ultimate normative authority.

Various denominations in America reacted differently to these developments. Baptists and Congregationalists, with their traditionally loose organization and congregational freedom, offered the least resistance to the newer ideas. Since the theological seminaries were also independently organized, there was little hope of united and effective action against a school whose faculty adopted such views. By the end of the century all Northern Baptist seminaries were firmly in the liberal camp, even though a couple of professors had been fired in the process. Methodist bishops seemed to have no interest in heresy hunting, and the Episcopal Church's only heresy trial came in 1906. The Lutherans managed to avoid most of the liberalism at the time.

The Northern Presbyterians had the most significant heresy trials of the period. David Swing was tried for heresy by a presbytery in Chicago in 1874,[3] but the real test came when Charles A. Briggs made his inaugural address at Union Theological Seminary in New York in 1891 and roundly denounced the doctrine of verbal inspiration. When he was put on trial for heresy, the presbytery acquitted him, but the General Assembly reversed the verdict. The Seminary withdrew from the Presbyterian church to keep Briggs from being fired.[4] Henry Preserved Smith of Lane Seminary avoided heresy charges only by leaving the Presbyterians and becoming a Congregationalist.[5] This all indicates that the problems that were soon to beset the Restoration Movement were not unique to them; similar problems afflicted virtually every significant religious affiliation in the country. The only difference was that given the unique perspective of the Christian churches, it would affect them in a different spot. Through a series of developments, that spot tended to be baptism.

One of the first representatives of liberalism among the Christian churches was L.L. Pinkerton. He is significant not because he was influential, but because he was such a lone voice.[6] The minister of a church in Midway, Kentucky, in 1868, Pinkerton advocated receiving unimmersed persons into local church membership if they were already members of some kind of a church (this practice is known as open membership) and were known locally as pious.[7] In addition, in a magazine he edited in 1868, the *Independent Monthly*, he openly renounced plenary inspiration of the Scriptures, focusing particularly on Psalm 137:9 where the Psalmist urges infanticide against Israel's enemies. Pinkerton said he was satisfied with a Bible that contained only the Synoptics, Romans and Corinthians. For him belief in Christ was more important than belief in inspiration.[8]

A second incident ocurred in London, England, in 1885 when W.T. Moore, a missionary under the Foreign Christian Missionary Society, began to work with a local British church of Christ that practiced open membership. Americans protested subsidizing a missionary who did not rightly represent the cause

he was sent to represent. But the president of the Foreign Society, Isaac Errett, called for an end to controversy over the issue
and asked that the whole matter be left to the executive committee of the Foreign Society.[9] Because people were willing at that
point to trust the missionary executives, they left the issue with
them. However, some thirty years later, such trust was no longer
present, and similar pleas would be of no avail.

A third incident of early liberalism revolved around R.C.
Cave, minister of the Central Christian Church in St. Louis,
Missouri. In 1889 he preached a sermon stating that the Old
Testament patriarchs were grossly ignorant of God's true
character; Cave denied the virgin birth and the resurrection,
described the Bible as an evolution rather than a revelation, and
concluded that there were no "conditions" to salvation.[10] Within a
week he also presented the congregation with a series of resolutions, the thrust of which was to allow any one to become a
church member there who felt he was following his own conscience.[11] Under heavy pressure from one of the elders, J.H.
Garrison, editor of the *Christian-Evangelist*, Cave finally resigned
some months later.

It is interesting to observe that in these three early ap-
pearances of liberalism, two of them had to do with biblical integrity, but all three of them had to do with baptism. Indeed, this
would continue to be the focus of concern within the Christian
churches.

However, the significant exposure of liberalism into the Christian churches did not come through occasional references in the
pulpit or even practices on the mission field. It came through involvement in higher education on the part of several young men
preparing for the ministry in the Christian churches and securing
graduate education through some of the leading universities and
divinity schools in the country: Yale, Harvard, Union Theological
Seminary in New York City, and the University of Chicago
Divinity School. The young men who went to these liberal institutions soon absorbed the liberal perspective presented there and

339

brought that perspective to bear on the commitments of the Restoration Movement. The University of Chicago Divinity School became the most significant institution in this process, mostly because it was located in the Midwest where most of the young men came from, and thus was more geographically convenient than schools on the Atlantic coast which were several hundred miles from home, and located in areas where there were few churches in which to secure a part-time preaching ministry. W.E. Garrison, H.L. Willett, and E.S. Ames all started out at Yale but soon transferred to Chicago, where they were joined by C.C. Morrison, A.W. Fortune, Hiram van Kirk, Finis Idleman, Burris Jenkins, and dozens of others.

Once these men adopted a liberal perspective, it made some significant impact upon their understanding of the *raison d'etre* of the Restoration Movement itself. The Movement began as a dual commitment to Christian unity and the authority of the Bible alone for the churches. But the liberals saw the Bible merely as an evolutionary process of man's developing quest for God. The Bible was no longer a normative, authoritative book, either of faith or practice. Liberalism's interest in ethics and the Social Gospel replaced any concern for biblical theology or orthodox Christian doctrine. Biblical authority was one of the two key foundations of the Restoration Movement; for the liberals who denied this foundation, the only thing left by which to maintain an identity in the Christian churches was a commitment to Christian unity. The original leaders of the Movement were committed to practicing unity on the basis of biblical teachings; but the current liberals were not interested in restricting unity to biblical standards. They had no such standards. Christian unity became an end in itself.

C. Focus on Baptism

One of the early applications of this new perspective was open membership. Traditionally the Christian churches practiced baptism by immersion for remission of sins. But under the liberal presupposition that the Bible is not normative for either doctrine or practice, the New Testament teaching on baptism became quite relative. Liberals could continue to practice traditional Christian church baptism if convenient, or they could also adapt (continuing the evolutionary development of the biblical record itself) to a changing culture and accept the baptism of individuals who were already members of denominational churches, even those who had been sprinkled as infants. Thus again baptism became a symbol of the liberal perspective, and open membership was its application.

Hugh C. Garvin became professor of Biblical Literature and Modern Language at Butler University in Indianapolis in 1889. He had studied in Germany for a while where he became acquainted with biblical criticism and some of the current trends in theology. He set high standards for his students, expecting them to read the whole Bible in its original languages and also know church history, theology, and other disciplines applied to biblical interpretation. Such methods raised the cry that Indiana wanted preachers, not scholars, and a number of ministers jointly wrote a letter to Garvin asking him to resign from the Bible department at Butler.[12]

Butler University defended its professor, and both the *Christian Standard* and the *Christian-Evangelist* denounced the efforts to have him fired. In an effort to defuse the situation, Garvin tried to explain his position, but his answers seemed vague and evasive. Apparently Garvin himself was still trying to think through his own position, for in one of his explanations he raised the question of the pious unimmersed. The *Christian-Evangelist* chided him with emphasizing "how much one may leave undone" rather than conforming to the facts of the New Testament.[13]

The public relations impact of his case worsened in 1896 when one of his students, George E. Hicks, introduced the practice of receiving the unimmersed into the membership of the church where he was preaching in Indianapolis. This practice soon split the little congregation, and Hicks himself left the Christian churches within a few years.[14] Hicks' actions were blamed on "Garvinism," and the *Christian-Evangelist* blamed the professor for "teaching a view of the gospel that is antagonistic to and subversive of the principles of the Reformation for which we have contended from the beginning."[15] In the mind of many it also showed the relationship of open membership to the new liberal teachings about the Scriptures. Remove the authority of the Bible as a God-given revelation, and there is no authority for maintaining believers' immersion.

A similar incident, but with wider institutional impact, occurred in Cleveland at about the same time. Harris R. Cooley, the minister of the Cedar Avenue church, began the practice of open membership. The secretary of the Ohio Missionary Society discovered this in late 1895, and early in 1896 the Cleveland Disciples Ministerial Association formally requested the Cedar Avenue elders to discontinue the practice. The elders refused.[16] In March Cooley mentioned to a news reporter that the Disciples missionary organizations would not refuse their offerings, but the Foreign Christian Missionary Society did that very thing.[17] Secretary F.M. Rains returned the money, explaining that the Society could not let itself be placed in a position where it appeared to endorse open membership.[18] Twenty years later, there will be significant variation from this pattern.

Two years later J.M. Philputt, minister of a church in Harlem, New York, adopted a procedure where unimmersed persons attending the church could become "members of the congregation" rather than "members of the church." Numerous individuals throughout the brotherhood denounced the development,[19] and Philputt was unsuccessful in convincing J.H. Garrison of the validity of the distinction.[20]

H.L. Willett brought a new focus to the subject of baptism in 1898. That year he began writing the background material for the Uniform Lesson Plan Sunday School material in the *Christian-*

342

Evangelist. The first lesson for 1898 dealt with John the Baptist. In the process of discussing the text, Willett remarked that baptism by immersion was used by the Jews before the Christian era to initiate proselytes from heathenism to Judaism.[21] J.B. Briney, a leading conservative from Kentucky, denied the existence of Jewish proselyte baptism prior to A.D. 70. Willett referred to several references in the Talmud,[22] and the argument degenerated into a lengthy discussion of the reliability of that Jewish document, much of which was oral tradition written down after the beginning of the Christian era.[23] The point of the dispute was the concern that if immersion were a religious rite prior to the Christian era, did this not erode the uniqueness of Christianity? Liberals could then argue that Christianity was simply continuing a borrowed practice, perhaps even representing an aggressive syncretism of Near Eastern religions. Conservatives were concerned lest Willett's contention undermine the uniqueness of the Christian institution and thus compromise divine authority.

Another instance of compromise on baptism occurred early in the twentieth century in Oakland, California. The minister there, Frank A. Powell, was also a student at Berkeley Bible Seminary where he had studied under Hiram Van Kirk. Van Kirk held a Ph.D. from the University of Chicago Divinity School, and thus any suspicion about Powell was automatically thrown also upon Van Kirk. According to reports, Powell rejected the idea of a blood atonement, biblical miracles, the inspiration of Scripture, and the necessity of baptism.[24] Van Kirk was further charged with denying inspiration, with stating that the gospel was an evolution from the law, and that the New Testament was "an uninspired record gathered by uninspired writers."[25] While most of the controversy focused on Van Kirk and his alleged liberalism, it is no accident that this theological suspicion was the base for Powell's entrance into open membership.

The conservative attention caused by this incident in California in 1902 quickly shifted to a similar but even clearer incident in Chicago which occurred in 1903. E.S. Ames had received his

Ph.D. degree from the Department of Philosophy of the University of Chicago in 1895, taught for two years at the school, went to Butler University in 1897, but in 1900 returned to Chicago as the minister of the Hyde Park Christian Church, in the university neighborhood. At the same time he also became an instructor in the Department of Philosophy of the University, ultimately becoming full time professor and late chairman of the Department.

In 1903 Ames introduced open membership into the University church. He developed a plan of "associate membership" for those individuals who wanted to become members without being immersed.[26] Ames denied that Disciples had ever rigidly believed that immersion was essential to salvation, though it was true that they regarded it as essential to church membership. He also stated that the New Testament knew of no situation of a person claiming to be a Christian without immersion. Therefore there was no explicit New Testament precedent with regard to the "pious unimmersed." Ames concluded that receiving such persons into associate membership was scriptural, reasonable, and consistent for Disciples.[27]

Reactions to Ames' innovation were varied. H.L. Willett, the leading editor of the liberal *Christian Century*, was a member of the Hyde Park Church. He and the other editors of the *Century* expressed their deep regret that Ames saw fit to make such an issue out of open membership, but they refused to condemn him. "As long as he is loyal to the divinity of Christ and the mind of Christ revealed in the New Testament we must accord him the liberty of doing what we deeply deplore."[28] The *Christian Standard* not only deplored Ames' actions, they desired to run him out of the brotherhood. A lengthy editorial called Ames a Unitarian because he denied Christ's divinity as traditionally understood. The *Standard* also suggested that Ames be ejected from the Chicago Christian Minister's Association, and the Hyde Park church removed from the Chicago Christian Missionary Society. The journal concluded, "We must regard Mr. Ames as having departed from the gospel faith, and separated himself from his fellow-disciples. Henceforth, we are compelled to regard him as alien, . . . an antagonist of the truth which we are to support and defend."[29]

Ames denied he was a Unitarian, and he insisted, "I believe with all my heart that Jesus is the Christ, the Son of God and my Savior," even though it was the perfected humanity of Jesus that made Him divine.[30] Meanwhile the church refused to be placed outside the fellowship of other Disciples churches.

J.H. Garrison, editor of the influential *Christian-Evangelist*, referred to Ames' belief that "Jesus is the Christ, the Son of the living God, and my Savior" and commented that a man who could make such a statement and seek to be loyal to it in his personal life and public ministry could never be an "alien" to other Christians.[31] Just a couple of years earlier Garrison had said that the practice of open membership would "create general confusion, alarm the brethren in many quarters, precipitate strife and produce much misunderstanding of our positions."[32] He stated that any churches that practiced open membership had cut themselves off from full cooperation with the rest of the Disciples.[33] Yet now he refused to apply this principle to the Hyde Park church and Ames. He pleaded for liberty and understanding, but conservatives wondered where it would all end.

One new implication came up late in the year 1904. The Disciples in Chicago had some years previously created the Chicago Christian Missionary Society to plant new churches and missions in the area, support them financially, secure ministers for them, and generally organize the disciples through the city and suburbs. One of the major problems was securing adequate funds for its work. In 1902 they entered into an agreement with the American Christian Missionary Society whereby the ACMS would contribute twice the amount raised by Chicago Disciples for mission work within the city.[34] Under this two-for-one agreement, the ACMS sent the money directly to the CCMS which in turn disbursed it to mission churches by paying ministerial salaries, building rental, and other expenses.

But late in the year 1904 the ACMS learned that open membership churches in Chicago were represented on the CCMS board helping to decide how to spend the money from the ACMS, and that some of the money was in fact being sent to support missions practicing open membership. The American society thus resolved to stop sending its contributions to the city board, but send them directly to certain mission stations approved by them. In effect this would seriously curtail the activity and usefulness of the Chicago society.

Thus several members of the Chicago group traveled to Cincinnati to discuss the issue with the executives of the ACMS.[35] They affirmed their loyalty to the principles of the Disciples and also explained the details of the Chicago situation. From the explanations it seems that two of the mission works had indeed been practicing open membership, but had now stopped. Hyde Park was still practicing it, but was receiving no money from the society, and had no representation on the board helping decide how to spend the missionary money. According to the city society, no member of the city board was in sympathy with the practice of either "associate membership" or open membership.[36] Thus the ACMS decided to continue its practice of channeling its money through the Chicago society.[37]

But this arrangement came under risk again in 1906 when one minister in the city reported that the mission work in Austin was again practicing open membership, contrary to the 1904 agreement.[38] To settle the problem this time, a delegation from Cincinnati went to Chicago. After some discussion, the city board voted that the 1904 agreement had not been violated. William J. Wright, the Superintendent of Evangelism of the ACMS, suggested that the ACMS simply supply the salary of a City Superintendent of Missions for Chicago rather than designate a certain sum of money for the mission works in particular.[39] Therefore, as long as the City Superintendent remained orthodox, the ACMS would not feel responsible for individual churches' practices. This was in spite of the fact that two of the local churches were now clearly open membership (Hyde Park and Austin), and that representatives from both churches were on the board of the CCMS. In this entire incident, the ACMS had a clear opportunity to refuse to support open membership finacially; instead they decided to look the other way and allow the situation to continue as long as the ACMS name was not embarrassed in the process. This kind of incident convinced numerous conservatives that the missionary societies could not be trusted to act with integrity with regard to theological implications or the issue of open membership.

C.C. Morrison added to the increasing discussion and practice of open membership. He had been preaching for the Monroe Street Christian Church in Chicago while taking occasional classes at the University of Chicago, but in 1902 he left the church, took a heavier class load, and commuted to Springfield, Illinois, on weekends to preach for the prestigious First Christian Church there. In 1904 he became full-time minister at Springfield. But his attempts to introduce open membership there brought controversy and discontent. Attendance dwindled to about fifty and finally in 1906 Morrison was fired.[40] He returned to Monroe Street in Chicago, and that church adopted open membership before the year was over. In openly announcing the development, Morrison stated that two churches in Denver and one in Kentucky were currently receiving the unimmersed as "associate members," while Hyde Park was receiving them as "members of the congregation." But Monroe Street removed all such qualifications and accepted them as full members, thus being the first church to do so.[41]

In 1910 C.C. Morrison, now the editor and owner of the *Christian Century*, began a series of editorials on baptism. His conclusion was that the Disciples were making too much of the *dogma* of immersion. He perferred to present immersion as the basis for future unity without insisting that other forms were wrong. This meant open membership for now so that all might practice immersion in the future.[42] Errett Gates argued that the "baptism conscience" of the Disciples pulled them toward an exclusivist policy, while the "union conscience" must move them toward a *rapprochement* with all children of God. He suggested that a united church was more pleasing to Christ than an immersed one.[43] Perry J. Rice agreed, but added his fears that an attempt to develop the "union conscience" would only agitate the "baptism conscience."[44]

In the 1912 Disciples Congress C.C. Morrison read a paper entitled "The Essential Plea of the Disciples in the Light of Their Origin and Aim," in which he developed the thesis that the adoption of immersion was an abandonment of the original aim of Thomas Campbell for unity. J.H. Garrison led the formal response to the paper, defending immersion and predicting that receiving the unimmersed would only produce division. O.F. Jordan disagreed, denouncing the fears that "the Disciples were going to split" as "utterly inadequate and false reports."[45] History would bear out that Garrison was a more accurate prophet than was Jordan.

Open membership was still spreading among the Disciples churches. Its next appearance was in Berkeley, California in the spring of 1911. The minister, H.J. Loken, had been a student under Hiram van Kirk at Berkeley Bible Seminary.[46] Interestingly, the trustees of Berkeley Bible Seminary in May of 1912 dismissed the entire faculty of the Seminary, apparently for the liberalism of its faculty and their alleged sympathy with the open membership plan of Berkeley church which most of them attended.[47] The connection between the alleged liberalism of the school and the advent of open membership in the church they attended is significant. As we have consistently seen, open membership was simply an application of the theological liberal presuppositions increasingly coming into vogue among the Disciples.

A development in 1916 showed just how far the Chicago Christian Missionary Society had gone. In March Ames requested that the city board send twenty five dollars per month to the struggling Monroe Street church, the same amount to be guaranteed by the Hyde Park church.[48] The Monroe Street church had adopted the association membership plan the previous year. In May the CCMS unanimously recommended that the ACMS send the Monroe Street church twenty-five dollars per month, to be paid through the ACMS by the Hyde Park church.[49] This is an open indication that the directors of the ACMS had also adopted a sympathetic view toward liberalism and open membership for they accepted the arrangement. Nothing could be clearer about the growing liberal developments in Chicago.

In 1919 a small church in Corydon, Indiana, resolved to drop immersion as a requirement for membership, and agreed to leave the form of baptism up to the candidate for membership.[50] The *Christian Century* applauded the church for dropping immersion as a membership requirement, but it mildly protested the agreement for the church itself to practice other forms of baptism than immersion. Apparently it was one thing to accept persons who had earlier been sprinkled; it was something else to practice sprinkling.[51] The church at Corydon disagreed, charging the *Century* and its editor with inconsistency.[52]

In the same year the Hyde Park church dropped its "membership in the congregation" category and granted full membership to the unimmersed.[53] Also in 1919 the East End Christian Church in Pittsburgh began practicing open membership. The idea developed out of discussions with a local Baptist church and a local Presbyterian church concerning church union. The merger of the three congregations did not occur, but open membership did.[54]

A whole new focus opened on the discussion of open membership in August of 1920 when R.E. Elmore released several letters from a China missionary dealing with the subject. In light of the fact that a union church of the major Protestant denominations was being discussed, Frank Garrett asked the Foreign Christian Missionary Society about open membership. In his letters he stated that he and all other China missionaries would approve of open membership if the Foreign Society approved.[55] Morrison of the *Christian Century* raised the level of controversy when he indicated that open membership was in fact already being practiced in "most if not all of the mission churches of Disciples in China," basing his information on letters from another China missionary, George B. Baird.[56]

The Foreign Society officially denied that open membership was being practiced but refused to recall Frank Garrett merely because of his opinion that he would practice open membership if approved by the Society.[57] This led to a great deal of discussion at the 1920 convention in St. Louis which resulted in the Medbury Resolution. This document plainly stated that the Executive Committee of the Foreign Society expected missionaries to act "in consonance with the teaching and practice of the disciples of Christ in the United States" and specifically stated that the committee did not approve "of the advocacy or practice of open membership." In addition the resolution called for all missionaries to give either "open avowal of loyal support" of the committee's stand against open membership, or else "a prompt cessation of service as representatives of the disciples of Christ."[58] The Medbury Resolution passed easily in the convention.

When the 1921 convention met in Winona Lake, Indiana, the next summer, the most important question was to learn how the Medbury Resolution had been applied by the Executive Committee of the now United Christian Missionary Society. (The American Christian Missionary Society, the Foreign Christian Missionary Society, and the Christian Women's Board of Missions were recently merged to become the United Christian Missionary Society.) The China missionaries expressed their loyalty to the wishes of the brotherhood and denied the existence of open membership in China, but they explained that since the terms of the Resolution bound them to American practices rather than the Bible, they respectfully had to refuse obedience to it.[59] Frank Garrett was himself present at the convention and explained that there was really no open membership in China; the churches were simply practicing "open fellowship," that is, allowing the unimmersed to attend their services.[60] After a great deal of discussion, the convention adopted the report of the Executive Committee, a report that included the refusal of the China missionaries to accept the Medbury Resolution.

So many of the conservatives were dissatisfied with this decision that many of them began to cut support to the organized missionary work of the various societies. It did not take long for this to become quite a financial squeeze upon the United Society, and everybody knew that the reason for the reduced funds was that many churches feared the Society was endorsing open membership. In January of 1922 the Board of Managers of the Society responded with the Sweeney Resolution. This emphasized that the missionaries were to grant church membership only to "those who are immersed, penitent believers in Christ," and no missionaries would be appointed or continued in the service of the Society who were not "in sincere accord" with this policy.[61]

The key, of course, was how this resolution would be interpreted by the Society officers. Things got very interesting at the 1922 convention returning to Winona Lake, Indiana. John T. Brown, a conservative from Kentucky, had just traveled to the Orient to see for himself whether there was or was not open membership on the mission field. He found it in the Philippines, where E.K. Higdon in Manila was practicing it at the Taft Avenue church; some of these unimmersed were even deacons in the church.[62] Yet the missionary executives concluded that they were not interested in violating the sanctity of a person's private belief. They stated that the phrase in the Sweeney Resolution "in sincere accord" meant that a missionary should be "willing to earnestly carry on the work in the manner suggested" and need not sacrifice his own personal opinion that open membership was a good thing.[63] Tied in with this Higdon Interpretation, the Sweeney Resolution and the report of the Society was overwhelmingly accepted by the convention.[64]

Brown also offered detailed evidence for open membership in

China. Talking with native Chinese through an interpreter, Brown discovered all he needed to document the case. Now standing before the convention in Winona Lake, Brown listed the mission stations, the missionaries, and the Chinese by name.[65] Unfortunately, however, the missionaries present from China as well as the Society officials discounted his evidence. They pointed out that the Chinese are a very polite people, always willing to tell foreigners what they believe the foreigners want to hear. Brown asked leading questions, the Chinese discovered what he wanted to hear and thus told him in full detail all Brown wanted. The only problem, explained the missionaries, was that it was not true. It was just the Chinese trait of being hospitable to a foreigner and not wanting to disappoint him after travelling half way around the world to discover open membership in China. Most conservatives were dissatisfied with these explanations and discounting of Brown's evidence, but there was nothing they could prove. But the previous experience with earlier deceit on the part of the missionary societies convinced them not to be too trustful of these explanations now.

Conservative disenchantment with the missionary societies now again took a financial form. With the adoption of the Higdon Interpretation and the virtual abandonment of the intention of the Sweeney Resolution, conservative churches again cut funds to the missionary societies. First Christian Church in Canton, Ohio, was representative of this. In 1921 the Canton church cut off support to the Society.[66] In September, 1922, after the adoption of the Sweeney Resolution, it reinstated its support, but only to designated missions, not to the general United Society budget.[67] In March of 1924, however, the church cut off all support to the missionary society, claiming that the only solution to the problem was the complete dissolution of the United Society.[68]

In 1924 Peter Ainslie became the center of some controversy. He was the minister of Christian Temple in Baltimore, a large congregation that had also established ten branch churches in the city. Two or three of these branch churches were "community

352

churches" since there were no other Protestant churches in their neighborhood; these particular churches were also practicing open membership. The other branches, and the Christian Temple itself, were located in areas among other Protestant churches, and for them open membership was thus unnecessary.[69] Then in 1924 Ainslie established open membership at the Christian Temple itself. He stated it was the logical step for Disciples who had already established the traditions of the open pulpit and open communion.[70]

Ainslie was also the president of the Association for the Promotion of Christian Unity, an agency of the Disciples churches formed in 1910 and answerable to the convention. When the convention met in Cleveland in 1924, the conservatives openly attacked him. For some time he had been suspected of compromising the position of the Disciples in his official dealings with other denominations, but he had always escaped censure. Now, however, the Committee on Recommendations of the convention received a resolution calling for the dissolution of the Association because its teachings were not in accord with the New Testament.[71] The editor of the *Christian-Evangelist* pointed out that much of the animus of the resolution was caused by Ainslie's new role as an advocate of open membership.[72] Ainslie contended that the Association had taken no position on open membership, but the *Christian-Evangelist* charged that the influence of the Association had been to encourage open membership, consciously or not. The Association and its president, therefore, had become divisive elements in the Disciples — ironic for an agency designed to promote Christian unity.[73] Unity with the denominations at the expense of undermining immersion meant division from Christians who wanted to adhere to New Testament teaching.

The convention at Cleveland also received a resolution that called attention to the "serious misunderstandings" that existed between the Disciples' "organized agencies" and other brethren and churches that opposed these agencies. The resolution did not specifically mention open membership, but for the first time in the history of the convention, it did openly admit the problem and desire to do something about it candidly. The resolution further called for a committee of five members to make a complete review of the disagreements and formulate constructive recommendations to remedy the situation by the next convention.[74] This became known as the "Peace Committee," and it would report at the convention in Oklahoma City in 1925. An article in the *Christian-Evangelist* openly stated that those practicing open membership and denying biblical miracles should not even be counted among Disciples. If such were done, the "disagreements" would be healed easily.[75]

When the convention met in Oklahoma City, the report of the Peace Committee was of utmost interest to most of those in attendance. In its report, the Committee pointed out the large measure of distrust among many Disciples because they believed the United Society employed missionaries who were committed to open membership. They did not say that in fact the missionaries *were* committed to such, but they did admit that many people *believed* the missionaries were. Thus the committee proposed that no one be employed or retained in employment by the United Society who was committed to "belief in or practice of" open membership.[76] On the floor of the convention numerous men spoke for and against the proposals. Those opposed, and this included several United Society officials, based their arguments on the "creedal" aspects which restricted an individual's belief. The chairman of the Peace Committee denied that the recommendations set forth any creed, saying these were simply working relationships between employer and employee. When it came to a vote the convention adopted the recommendations and C.C. Morrison sorrowfully admitted the vote was at least four to one, if not ten to one.[77]

The question then was how the proposals, known as the Peace Resolution, would be "interpreted" by the leadership of the society. The *Christian Standard* insisted that the resolution be enforced in its obvious intent, not emasculated as were the Medbury and Sweeney Resolutions.[78] The *Christian Century*, however, advised that there was doubt as to what was meant by the phrase "committed to belief in."[79] A number of liberals took action to try to influence the decision of the Society. Within three weeks after the convention, a number of "open-minded men" met in Philadelphia and planned a meeting to be held in Columbus, Ohio, in December. Attendance at Columbus included such names as W.E. Garrison, E.S. Ames, Peter Ainslie and several missionary society officials. W.E. Garrison read a paper in which he contended that the real issue was not open membership, but the question of creating a series of authoritative doctrines. Garrison believed the genius of the Disciples movement was its free inquiry into the principles of the religion of Jesus and its application to the needs of a sinful and suffering world, and thus the Disciples ought not to accept any limitation on their feedom to interpret the spirit of New Testament Christianity. In particular they ought to refuse to allow missionaries to be hounded by an inquiry into their beliefs.[80]

As it turned out, these men in Columbus need not have worried. The Board of Managers met six days before the Columbus Conference and decided the phrase "committed to belief in" was "not intended to invade the right of private judgment, but only to apply to such an open agitation as would prove divisive."[81] The *Christian Century* greeted this news with evident relief, even though it admitted that the Peace Resolution plainly called for no less than an "inquisition into the private beliefs of missionaries on the question of open membership," though the Board now took that to mean a discharge of only those missionaries who believed in open membership so strongly that they insisted on its implementation, thus causing trouble on the field.[82]

This interpretation of the Peace Resolution would come up for approval at the next convention, in Memphis in 1926. Conservatives were convinced that there was a mounting array of evidence which indicated that the United Christian Missionary

355

Society was adament in its determination to espouse and support open membership, both at home and abroad, and was acting in utter defiance of clear resolutions from the annual conventions to stop the practice. The credibility gap between the conservatives and the United Society was too great for the conservatives to believe the Society denials that open membership was in fact being practiced on the field. They went to Memphis determined to break the back of the Missionary Society.

Unfortunately, the conservatives did not win any of their rounds at the convention. The convention adopted the Board of Managers' interpretation of the Peace Resolution with scarcely a negative vote. This collapse of a promised major protest may need some explanation. The *Christian Century* explained that the vote in support of the Board's interpretation was not a vote for liberal theology, but a vote for liberty of opinion.[83] Disciples who were adamantly against open membership (as admittedly most of them were) were also keenly sensitive about any charge of encroaching on another man's conscience. Even though the Peace Resolution clearly stated that all missionaries who believed in open membership should be recalled, when the Board of Managers interpreted it in phraseology which defended Christian liberty, the convention could do nothing other than accept that interpretation. Disciples' hatred for creeds simply would not allow otherwise.

This 1926 convention in Memphis was quite significant, for it marked the last time the conservatives mounted a serious challenge to the direction of the United Christian Missionary Society or even the International Convention itself. The conservatives continued to struggle for control over the various state conventions for the next decade or more, but they never again fought over the national convention. They lost faith in both the Convention and the Society and no longer felt they were genuinely united with those Disciples who continued their loyal support of these agencies. The next year they simply planned a national gathering of their own, which became the North American

Christian Convention, first held in Indianapolis in October, 1927. For all practical purposes, the conservatives and the liberals divided. Because the name "Disciples" was consistently used for the organized agencies taken over by the liberals, the conservatives consistently dropped use of that label, calling themselves simply Christian churches, or churches of Christ.

In retrospect it is easy to see the events of 1926 and 1927 as the definitive break between the conservative Christian churches and the liberal Disciples of Christ. Actually, of course, it was not that clear-cut. For some time there was continued contact across the theological lines. Some churches and institutions did not position themselves clearly in one camp or the other until the 1950's. For a while the *Christian Evangelist*, the official organ of the International Convention, approved of the existence of the North American Christian Convention. This way the International Convention could handle the business items of the brotherhood, while the North American could represent the preaching, the fellowshipping, and the evangelistic concerns of the churches.[84] But very few people attended both conventions. It was not long before there were in fact two different constituencies. Things continued to polarize until the 1950's when the dividing seemed to have become complete.

ASSESSMENT

Throughout most of this discussion, our attention has centered on baptism and its affiliated problem, open membership. It is easy to believe that different practices and applications of baptism are the root of the problems that led to serious division. Yet this is misleading. In spite of all the focus on baptism, this was not the real problem. In discussing a 1929 attempt to reunite the two groups, George A. Campbell remarked that there were two causes for the disturbances: one was theological and the other organizational.[85] The organizational cause was directly related to the United Society and conservatives' fears that the

357

Society would control policy for supposedly autonomous churches. Since its very beginnings with Thomas Campbell and B.W. Stone, the Restoration Movement had been leary of ecclesiastical organization. Twentieth century conservatives were extremely reluctant to create any sort of agency that might later assume authority over churches and individuals. Conservatives counted their freedom more precious than organization efficiency.

The other cause of Disciples disturbances was much more complex. Ostensibly it was the issue of open membership. Yet most knowledgeable leaders of the time realized that open membership was but the symptom of theological divergence, as indicated by a *Christian Standard* editorial which proclaimed that open membership was but a screen for the entry of "the liberalistic philosophy of religion." The real enemy was "the disposition to treat Christianity as an evolution rather than a revelation."[86]

It was not just biological evolution that the *Standard* was referring to here. It was the application of evolutionary thought to the development of religious consciousness, that saw the Bible as a continuing record of men's developing quest for religious sensitivity, but not as a received revelation of God or from God. Closely allied with an evolutionary view supplementing the theories of religious development was the issue of higher criticism. Higher criticism and the theories of religious development aided each other in their common task of understanding the New Testament period. In 1927 the *Standard* claimed that a recent case of open membership in East Orange, New Jersey, was "the fruit of the tree that ought to have been uprooted at Pittsburgh in 1909."[87] What was this "tree at Pittsburgh"? It was the willingness to use the liberal H.L. Willett to speak at the Centennial Convention — a higher critic who was "sound" on baptism, but who had already suggested that much of the traditional understanding of the New Testament would have to be revised.

Previously Disciples had had a fairly uniform authoritarian and literalistic interpretation of Scripture. Now, however, modern scholars began to suggest that the Bible was an historical document, not purely a revelation from on high. The New Testament was a document (or a series of documents) from the early Christian era, but it was no longer authoritative as a standard for the twentieth century. Disciples liberals could agree that immersion was the practice of the early church while also adapting open membership to the needs of twentieth century Christianity.

Conservatives were caught in the dilemma of having no creed that defined how the New Testament could be used. Disciples had never even formulated a generally accepted theory of inspiration. The Campbells had relegated all such matters to non-essentials. However satisfactorily that might have worked in the early nineteenth century, the intellectual developments and biblical scholarship of the twentieth century had destroyed the univocal perspective of the early Restoration Movement. Conservatives knew they could not make a test case out of New Testament interpretation. All they could dare was a fight over open membership. It was but a symptom of the underlying conflict, but the battle had to be fought there. In essence the conservatives won that battle. The International Convention consistently refused to accept the outright adoption of open membership. All three of the Resolutions — Medbury, Sweeney, and Peace — came down hard against open membership and threatened unemployment to any missionaries who did not agree. But the conservatives could never command a majority when the issue became one of liberty of conscience, as the outcome of all three resolutions also proved.

Again, the individuals at the time realized the distinction between the symbolic battle being fought over baptism and the underlying battle being fought over the authority of the Scriptures. In an article in the 1926 *Christian Standard*, P.H. Welshimer, the nationally known minister of First Christian Church of Canton, Ohio, said this:

> If you remove the authority of Jesus, you destroy the meaning

of baptism. If you eliminate the inspiration and the all-sufficiency of the Scriptures, you take away the meaning and sacredness of baptism, and hence it would be of no importance to practice anything and call it baptism.

This is a fight for more than an ordinance. It is a fight for loyalty to Jesus Christ and for an appreciation of His authority, the inspiration of His word, and the compliance with stipulated conditions that remission of sins may be granted.[88]

Both conservatives and liberals claimed to stand at the center of the historic position of the Disciples of Christ — liberals standing for freedom of Christian conscience and a commitment to Christian unity; the conservatives standing for the historic practices of the early church as understood by the Campbells and their early followers. Ironically, however, liberal Disciples and conservative Disciples were not compatible to each other. The difference lay in a completely different view toward the New Testament (or the authority of early Christian precedents) and the modern world. Conservatives were convinced that the original pattern of the New Testament church should be duplicated in all ages. Liberals were convinced that within a very general framework of commitment to Christian ideals each generation (and culture) should work out its own concepts of Christian identity.

It is also important to note that this failure to maintain a univocal hermeneutic in the light of the liberal developments did not require some kind of fatalistic flaw in the basic design or purpose of the Restoration Movement. It was not a simple case of the absence of a creed causing an untenably loose theological relativism. If that were so, then the denominations that did have such a creed would have been spared similar conflicts. In fact, none of them escaped the problem. We have already noticed in the beginning some of the fights the Presbyterians experienced over the issues and implications of higher criticism. They did not fight over baptism, because that issue was not so essential to them. But the results were the same.

This similarity to the experience of the Restoration Movement in the years 1890-1930 is even more graphically displayed in the history of the Northern Baptists. In his book, *A History of Conservative Baptists*, Bruce L. Shelley points out the development of religious liberalism among the Northern Baptists in the first third of the twentieth century. He demonstrates the application of these liberal presuppositions in problems with liberalism in the Baptist schools, conflicts with comity agreements with regard to mission work, and the problem with open membership.[89] It is somewhat difficult to imagine Baptists practicing open membership, but that is exactly what happened, given the same pattern of liberal influence that affected the Christian churches. Furthermore, Chester E. Tulga in his work *The Foreign Missions Controversy in the Northern Baptist Convention, 1919-1949: Thirty Years of Struggle* chronicles the difficulty the conservatives had in controlling the missionary societies and the national conventions once these agencies took on liberal leadership.[90] Again, the similarities between the Baptist experience and the Christian churches is amazing. It is the same problem, working out in the same way, in two different religious groups. The history of the Disciples of Christ with liberalism has its counterpart in virtually all religious denominations in the country at the time. The Missouri Synod Lutherans may be a little different only in the fact that their crisis came in the 1960's rather than three decades earlier as it did for the Disciples and the Northern Baptists. The Southern Baptists just now are going through exactly the same problems. Their situation may have a somewhat different application given their particular context, but the principles and development are distressingly similar.

With regard to the Christian churches of the Restoration Movement, this whole issue represents the basic cause of the current division between the Disciples of Christ on the one hand and the conservative Christian churches on the other. The Disciples sometimes refer to this latter group as the Independents, because of their refusal to work with the organized missionary societies of the Disciples and their insistence upon sending out missionaries independent of such societies. Such churches also use musical instruments in worship and are not to be confused with the non-instrumental churches of Christ.

It is tragic that a movement that began with the goal of unity now exists with these subdivisions. What it represents, however, is a failure within the last century to agree on the prime goal of the Restoration Movement and how to achieve that goal. As we stated in beginning, the Movement began with twin goals — Christian unity and biblical authority. The Disciples of Christ have chosen to emphasize Christian unity and have abandoned any meaningful emphasis on biblical authority because of their acceptance of theological liberalism. The whole issue of open membership is but the application of that choice. Without an authoritative Scripture and the desire to follow the precedents and teaching of the New Testament church, the Scriptural pattern of baptism by immersion became an option for the Disciples rather than a standard. The conservative Christian churches were not willing to compromise their commitment to the biblical teaching on baptism and thus separated themselves from the increasingly liberal Disciples of Christ. For them the practice of open membership is not at all an acceptable alternative. Given this difference in perspective, the division between the two groups was inevitable.

In 1915 the Christian Churches in Chicago divided over the liberalism issue some dozen years before the schism became apparent nation-wide. Chicago had been going through problems locally with the liberal influence coming out of the University of Chicago Divinity School and its attendant Disciples Divinity House established there in 1894. Open membership in the Hyde Park, Austin, and Monroe Street churches had focused attention on the problem there early. Disagreements about missionary responsibility with regard to the work of the American Christian Missionary Society and the Chicago Christian Missionary Society also saw the question of missionary society integrity in sharp light in Chicago before it became a national item of significance. In the midst of these troubles and discussions, J.F. Futcher, minister of the Ashland church in Chicago stated:

> It is all summed up in one word, "theology." Not until we get together from a theological point of view, will we become one. These financial and church problems are going to continue to come upon us just as long as we are divided in our theology.[91]

Futcher could not have stated the issue more succinctly. The problem was not over baptism; baptism was but the symbol. The problem was that liberals and conservatives had a different view of theology — particularly a different view of biblical authority and the basis for theological epistemology. Once liberalism made its inroads in the Disciples of Christ, it was inevitable that division occur; that it occurred over baptism and open membership was but a commentary on the soteriology of the Restoration Movement and what its members regarded as essential.

Endnotes

1. In the "Introduction" to Kenneth Cauthen's *The Impact of American Religious Liberalism* (New York: Harper & Row, Publishers, 1962), pp. vii, viii.

2. Quoted in Lloyd J. Averill, *American Theology in the Liberal Tradition* (Philadelphia: The Westminster Press, 1967), pp. 22-23.

3. Winthrop S. Hudson, *Religion in America*, Third Edition (New York: Charles Scribner's Sons, 1981), p. 281.

4. See Max Gray Rogers, "Charles Augustus Briggs: Heresy at Union" in *American Religious Heretics: Formal and Informal Trials in American Protestantism*, edited by George H. Shriver (Nashville: Abingdon Press, 1966), pp. 89-147.

5. Hudson, p. 282.

6. Winfred Ernest Garrison and Alfred T. DeGroot, *The Disciples of Christ: A History* (St. Louis: The Bethany Press, 1969), p. 419.

7. John Shackleford, Jr. (ed.), *Life, Letters and Addresses of Dr. L.L. Pinkerton* (Cincinnati: Chase & Hall, Publishers, 1876), pp. 108ff.

8. Ibid., p. 113.

9. Garrison and DeGroot, pp. 391-392.

10. Ibid., pp. 386-387.

11. *Christian-Evangelist*, December 26, 1889, p. 825.

12. Henry K. Shaw, *Hoosier Disciples: A Comprehensive History of the Christian Churches (Disciples of Christ) in Indiana* (St. Louis: Bethany Press, 1966), pp. 265-267.

13. Shaw, p. 269; *Christian-Evangelist*, January 23, 1896, pp. 50-51.

14. Shaw, pp. 271-272.

15. *Christian-Evangelist*, March 26, 1896, p. 194.

16. Henry K. Shaw, *Buckeye Disciples: A History of the Disciples of Christ in Ohio* (St. Louis: Christian Board of Publication, 1952), pp. 288-290; Alfred Thomas DeGroot, "The Practice of Open Membership Among Disciples of Christ" (Unpublished B.D. Thesis at the College of Religion, Butler University, Indianapolis, 1929), p. 20.

17. *Christian Standard*, January 18, 1896, p. 194.

18. Ibid., March 21, 1896, pp. 369-370.

19. Herbert Lockwood Willett and Lillian Reynolds Philputt (eds.), *"That They May All Be One": Autobiography and Memorial of James A. Philputt, Apostle of Christian Unity* (St. Louis: Christian Board of Publication, 1933), pp. 65-66.

20. *Christian-Evangelist*, February 17, 1898, p. 103.

21. Ibid., December 23, 1987, p. 816.

22. Ibid., January 20, 1898, p. 38.

23. Ibid., February 10, 1898, pp. 120-121.

24. *Christian Standard*, November 29, 1902, p. 1660.

25. Ibid., February 21, 1903, pp. 254-258.

26. Edward Scribner Ames, "Associate Church Membership," A Sermon at the Hyde Park Church of the Disciples, Chicago, October 4, 1903, pp. 8-11.

27. Edward Scribner Ames, "Christian Union and the Disciples," A Sermon at the Hyde Park Church of the Disciples, Chicago, January 11, 1903, pp. 11-14.

28. *Christian Century*, March 31, 1904, p. 308.

29. *Christian Standard*, April 9, 1904, pp. 525-526.

30. *Christian Century*, April 14, 1904, p. 364.

31. *Christian-Evangelist*, April 21, 1904, p. 515.

32. Ibid., January 23, 1902, p. 52.

33. Ibid., July 18, 1901, p. 910.

34. Chicago Christian Missionary Society Minutes, May 31, 1906. These minutes are kept in the library of the Disciples Divinity House of the Universty of Chicago.

35. C.C.M.S. Minutes, November 12, 1904; *Christian Century*, December 8, 1904, p. 1134.

36. C.C.M.S. Minutes, p. 61; *Christian Standard*, December 24, 1904, p. 1828.

37. *Christian Standard*, December 24, 1904, p. 1832.

38. C.C.M.S. Minutes, n.d., p. 142.

39. Ibid., March 4, 1906, pp. 153-154.

40. *Christian Standard*, December 31, 1921, p. 3058; June 17, 1922, pp. 3647-49.
41. *Scroll*, Vol. IV, No. 4 (1906), p. 6.
42. *Christian Century*, January 13, 1910, p. 27; January 20, 1910, p. 51.
43. Ibid., February 24, 1910, pp. 178-179.
44. Ibid., p. 181.
45. *Christian Century*, April 25, 1912, pp. 297, 403, 406-407; see also *Christian-Evangelist*, May 9, 1912, p. 637.
46. *Christian-Evangelist*, December 21, 1911, p. 1805; *Christian Standard*, December 23, 1911, pp. 2130-2131.
47. *Christian-Evangelist*, June 6, 1912; *Christian Standard*, June 15, 1912, p. 971.
48. C.C.M.S. Minutes, March 14, 1916.
49. Ibid., May 8, 1916.
50. *Christian Century*, February 13, 1919, p. 20.
51. Ibid., February 13, 1919, p. 5.
52. Ibid., February 27, 1919, pp. 13-14.
53. A.T. DeGroot, *Disciple Thought: A History* (Fort Worth: published by the author, 1965), p. 188; Van Meter Ames, (ed.), *Beyond Theology: The Autobiography of Edward Scribner Ames* (Chicago: The University of Chicago Press, 1959), p. 82.
54. *Christian Century*, May 22, 1919, pp. 7-8; July 3, 1919, pp. 7-8.
55. *Christian Standard*, August 7, 1920, pp. 1107-1110.
56. *Christian Century*, August 26, 1920, p. 7.
57. *Christian-Evangelist*, September 16, 1920, p. 929.
58. *Christian Standard*, October 30, 1920, p. 1433.
59. Ibid., September 17, 1921, pp. 2667-2668.
60. Ibid., p. 2668.
61. *Christian Century*, February 23, 1922, p. 243.
62. *Christian Standard*, September 9, 1922, pp. 3947-3949.
63. Ibid., pp. 3949-3950; *Christian Century*, September 14, 1922, pp. 1139-1140.
64. *Christian Standard*, September 9, 1922, p. 3951.
65. Ibid., pp. 3947-3949.
66. Ibid., December 3, 1921, p. 2941.
67. Ibid., September 30, 1922, p. 4020.
68. Ibid., March 29, 1924, p. 667.
69. Ibid., November 17, 1923, p. 154.
70. *Christian Century*, July 1, 1924, p. 895.
71. *Christian-Evangelist*, October 30, 1924, p. 1407.
72. Ibid., p. 1382.
73. Ibid., February 26, 1925, p. 262.
74. *Christian Standard*, November 1, 1924, p. 111.
75. *Christian-Evangelist*, November 13, 1924, p. 1465.
76. Ibid., October 15, 1925, p. 1336.

77. Ibid., pp. 1337-1338; *Christian Century*, October 22, 1925, p. 1315.

78. *Christian Standard*, October 24, 1925, p. 2239.

79. *Christian Century*, October 22, 1925, p. 1322.

80. In the Garrison Papers, located in the Disciples of Christ Historical Society, Nashville, Tennessee.

81. *Christian-Evangelist*, December 10, 1925, p. 1599; *Christian Century*, December 17, 1925, p. 1582.

82. *Christian Century*, December 17, 1925, pp. 1565-1566.

83. Ibid., November 25, 1926, p. 1462; *Christian-Evangelist*, November 25, 1926, p. 1495.

84. *Christian-Evangelist*, October 27, 1927, p. 1426.

85. *Christian Century*, August 28, 1929, p. 1071.

86. *Christian Standard*, October 5, 1919, p. 946.

87. Ibid., April 9, 1927, p. 347.

88. Ibid., December 4, 1926, p. 655.

89. Bruce L. Shelley, *A History of Conservative Baptists* (Wheaton, Illinois: Conservative Baptist Press, 1971).

90. Chester E. Tulga, *The Foreign Missions Controversy in the Baptist Convention* (Chicago: Conservative Baptist Fellowship, 1950).

91. C.C.M.S. Minutes, May 3, 1915.

10

THE DESIGN OF BAPTISM IN THE NEW TESTAMENT

David W. Fletcher

The Restoration Movement suffers from a limited theology of baptism. Early controversies left the movement with a strong emphasis on baptism "for the remission of sins."[1] This emphasis often neglects or at best subordinates other important truths about baptism. For example, how frequently do we hear of baptism "for the gift of the Holy Spirit"? When did you last hear a sermon about baptism "into the death of Jesus"? We have produced a warped doctrine of baptism by making other truths subservient to the phrase "for the remission of sins." So on our part the argument continues. But the message lacks relevancy to a generation of people with little or no knowledge of baptism dogma of the early restoration. Furthermore, to the surprise of naive brethren and to the chagrin of stubborn brethren, certain Baptists, Methodists, Congregationalists, Independents, etc., express beliefs on baptism similar to or identical to what we thought all along to be "our" teaching. They have broken loose from their denominational mold. Why can't we? It is time for us to wake up, to open our eyes to the fullness of the doctrine of baptism that is taught in God's word.

The biblical teaching on baptism is not monolithic. New Testament authors describe Christian baptism with various images. It is death and resurrection (Romans 6:3-4). It is donning the Messiah (Galatians 3:26-27). Baptism is circumcision of the sinful nature (Colossians 2:11-12). It is rebirth and renewal, bringing forgiveness of sins and the gift of the Holy Spirit (Titus 3:4-6; Acts 2:38). It is an appeal to God for a clear conscience (I Peter 3:21). These images are vivid and powerful. They are exciting. They depict God's effort to rescue a perishing world. They also portray baptism as something which effects a new beginning. God intervenes by sending His *monogenes* ("only-begotten") Son as a remedy for the desperate human situation. God establishes a new order of things, a new creation through Him (II Corinthians 5:17). God conquers death and brings life. He discards the old and brings in the new. He clothes His people with the righteousness of Jesus and empowers them with the strength of His Spirit. He effects a new beginning through Jesus His Son, and He uses baptism as an important means to accomplish this. This work of God via baptism in effecting new beginnings will be the theme of this chapter.

A. *The Importance of Baptism*

Jesus affirmed to rabbi Nicodemus the change needed for entrance into God's kingdom. "Unless a man is born again (or, from above, *anothen*), he cannot see the kingdom of God" (John 3:3). This change takes place in Christian baptism. Jesus defined this change as a birth "of water and the Spirit" (v. 5). Baptism is truly a new birth; it is spiritual transformation; it is the occasion for the working of God's Spirit, and so baptism is one birth with two aspects, water and Spirit.[2] Furthermore, this change does not take place because of a person's own righteousness; it is solely accomplished by God's mercy.

> He saved us, not because of righteous things we had done, but because of his mercy. He saved us through the washing of rebirth and renewal by the Holy Spirit, whom he poured out on us generously through Jesus Christ our Savior, so that, having been justified by his grace, we might become heirs having the hope of eternal life (Titus 3:5-7; cf. Ezekiel 36:25-27).

Here, "baptism is qualified as a cleansing bath; but then as a cleansing that is to be understood in the context of the saving, eschatological activity of God ('the appearing' of his mercy, etc.)."[3] Beasley-Murray observes,

> God saved us "not by reason of works . . . but in accordance with his mercy" (v. 5). A two fold contrast is here drawn between deeds that earn and faith that receives, and the power of God that mercifully achieves what man cannot do for himself. This, we observe, is related to baptism; the emphasis on the powerful operation by the Spirit in the "washing" underscores this very fact that God does for us what we are powerless to perform — he makes us anew and gives us new life. . . . No statement of the New Testament more unambiguously represents the power of baptism to lie in the operation of the Holy Spirit.[4]

So what is worked in this "washing of rebirth" is worked by God's mercy. The main actor is God, and man passively receives God's gift of renewal, the Holy Spirit. But man receives in faith and he receives via God's appointed means of baptism.

> The washing with water of baptism represents the new birth as the transition from the old mode of existence dominated and

qualified by sin to that which derives its character from the Spirit as the eschatological gift of salvation. . . . Baptism is the means in God's hand, the place where he speaks and acts. . . . It is God who gives baptism its power, on the faith of the one baptized.[5]

Yet this work of God and his Spirit in baptism does not eliminate the need for the physical element of water. The text itself suggests that God does not work his saving mercy among mankind without formal means. God uses physical means to effect spiritual consequences. Note the important phrase "through the washing of rebirth" (*dia loutrou palingenesias*; cf. Ephesians 5:26; Hebrews 10:22; majority text of Revelation 1:5; Acts 22:16; I Corinthians 6:11). *Washing* "may mean the *water used for washing*, or *the process itself of washing*."[6] *Rebirth* "defines the nature of the 'washing' which God employs as his instrument in effecting the salvation of man; not any 'washing' whatever, but that of the new birth."[7] This washing in water is the outer dynamic of Christian baptism, but in this washing the inner dynamic of the Spirit's renewal clearly predominates (cf. I Corinthians 12:13; John 3:5-8). Yet the Spirit works his change upon the sinner "through the water, and with the water, and not without the water."[8] The two aspects are closely intertwined. So it is by these two dynamics, water and Spirit, one outer and one inner (which corresponds to man's body and spirit), that God transforms sinful man.

However, some believers disagree with this connection between baptism and salvation. "How can something physical like water baptism produce spiritual results like salvation?" they ask. The objection, however, stems from a philosophical basis that denies the full reality of the physical.

Of course the Bible itself never presents a physical element or act as in itself being the source of a spiritual effect. See John 3:6; 6:63. Only God, who is spirit, can bestow such blessings. But the inabililty of flesh to produce spiritual effects is not due to some kind of inherent antithesis between matter and spirit. The inability

370

is due simply to the inherent impotence of anything less than God himself to effect the kind of spiritual changes which are in view. Though God alone is the source of all spiritual blessings, material elements or acts are regarded as proper and appropriate means of bestowing these blessings.

For the first 1500 years of Christian history, very few questioned the propriety of the use of a physical element as a necessary part of ceremonies which were essentially spiritual in their result. Zwingli, however, denied both the causal and the chronological connection between the material and the spiritual. John 6:63 was his proof-text, but Platonic dualism was the philosophic basis of his objection. Thus, beginning with Zwingli in the 1520's a large element of Christendom has continued to deny any necessary causal or chronological connection between physical acts [and spiritual results]. The sacramental elements are limited to symbolical and psychological significance. This is the basic principle of sacramental theology in all Reformed groups, and in all groups which have adopted the Reformed approach to the sacraments (e.g., most Baptist and most Wesleyan groups).[9]

Because of this Platonic dichotomy between the physical and the spiritual, many modern believers neglect the due import of Christian baptism. Some see baptism as wholly unnecessary. For instance, many recent and otherwise excellent works on evangelism completely fail to mention Christian baptism. Most of these opt for the "praying-through" method of salvation.[10] Others recognize the need of baptism but place it in a subordinate or secondary role as regards salvation. One writes, "Although water baptism is always closely related to the time of forgiveness in the New Testament, it is not a requirement or a work necessary for salvation."[11] This attitude toward baptism is common. But believers neglect Christian baptism to their spiritual jeopardy. The lack of any tangible means of God's grace as regards salvation leaves many believers questioning their status with God. It leaves them with "deep dissatisfaction" in not knowing "the specific day on which they crossed over the line to be on the Lord's side."[12] What is needed to remedy this lack of assurance is a healthy appreciation of the apostle Peter's assertion, ". . . baptism now saves you" (I Peter 3:21). With the proclamation and obedience of such a concrete act as Christian baptism, believers can experience the assurance that God desires to grant them. With baptism as their starting point, believers can go forward with confidence. They can know that the foundation of their spiritual journey is of the Lord's doing. They will have no need to trust their own subjective reasonings.

B. Before the Descent of the Spirit

Arguments for various Jewish or pagan antecedents for Christian baptism have not proven conclusive. While a discussion of the Mosaic lustrations, circumcision, pagan initiation rites, Jewish proselyte baptism, the Essene baptisms, etc. might prove useful,[13] such would not change the essential design of Christian baptism in the NT. Christian baptism is qualitatively different from all of the above, because Christian baptism is baptism "in the name of Jesus Christ."[14] Whatever particulars it might possess in common with other contemporary practices, be it Jewish or pagan, Christian baptism has the distinction of being the only "initiation rite" in the name of a historical figure. In baptism, the "initiate" experiences intimate identification with decisive historical events, the death and resurrection of Jesus of Nazareth (see Romans, chapter 6). So radical is this identification in baptism that the "initiate" is stamped, as it were, with the name of Jesus. He now wears the name "Christian," and he shares his new life with brothers and sisters in an intimate, family-like community of fellow-believers who are also called "Christians." Nothing exactly like this is found in Jewish practice. Nor do pagan religions provide an exact parallel.[15] Christian baptism is unique.[16] So the NT must be allowed to speak for itself concerning the design of Christian baptism.

1. The baptism administered by John [Matthew 3:6,7,11;

372

21:25; Mark 1:4,5,8; 11:30; Luke 3:3,7,12,16; 7:29,30; 20:4; John 1:25,26,28,31,33; 3:22,23,26; 10:40; Acts 1:5,22; 10:37; 11:16(?); 13:24; 18:25; 19:3].

One valid antecedent of Christian baptism found in the NT, however, is John's baptism. That John's baptism represented a decisive break with sectarian (e.g., Pharisaic and Sadducean) order and tradition seems obvious from the combined testimony of Matthew, Mark, and Luke. John came on the scene suddenly, and his work was detached both geographically and sacramentally from the Jerusalem temple cult. He came "baptizing in the desert region and preaching a baptism of repentance for the remission of sins" (Mark 1:4). Like the prophets before him, John preached a cutting away of the old and a bringing in of the new (see Matthew 3:9-10). Significantly, the gospel of Mark identifies this coming of John as "the beginning of the gospel about Jesus Christ," and both Matthew and Luke begin their narratives about Jesus with the work of John (after telling the birth stories). Luke also notes the beginning of John's ministry with the customary chronological data. The gospels depict the work of John as a very important starting point. The book of Acts does the same. When selecting a replacement for Judas, Peter limits possible replacements to those "who have been with us the whole time the Lord Jesus went in and out among us, beginning from John's baptism . . ." (Acts 1:21-22; cf. 10:37; 13:24). This emphasis on John's work as an important starting point is highly significant, for it is precisely the baptism of John that provided the embryonic nucleus of the Messianic community. "John came baptizing . . ." and he introduced something new.

In response to his preaching John called for an action which was wholly novel — baptism in the Jordan River. It has been conjectured that John's baptism was derived from the Jewish practice of baptizing proselytes, or from the rites of initiation practiced at Qumran. No clear line of dependence can be shown in support of these theories. Baptism appears rather as a unique activity of the prophet, a prophetic sign so striking that John became known simply as 'the Baptizer'.[17]

His baptism was quite different from ceremonial cleansings and proselyte baptisms. John's baptism was administered by John himself, or perhaps by his disciples;[18] it was not performed by the recipient himself. John's baptism was performed only once; it was not repeated. John's baptism initiated covenant relationship with God; it was not administered merely to retain the purity of that covenant relationship. John's baptism was "for the forgiveness of sins" (Mark 1:4; Luke 3:3).[19] Note that his baptism was "repentance baptism" or "turning baptism" (cf. Acts 13:24; 19:4). It was a call for Israel to flee "the coming wrath" by turning to their Lord, specifically their Messiah Lord.[20] Rather than "an outward symbol of the inward change," John's baptism effectually completed the recipient's repentance or turning unto God. Those who were baptized by John "acknowledged that God's way was right." But those who refused John's baptism "rejected God's purpose for themselves" (Luke 7:29-30). This text in Luke clearly distinguishes between "all the people and the tax collectors" and "the Pharisees and the lawyers" on the basis of John's baptism. Note the typical antecedent use of the aorist participle (e.g., "having been baptized . . . not having been baptized"). The former group ackowledged God; they were God's people; they had experienced a change via the baptism of John. The latter group rejected God; they were not God's people; they had not experienced this change through John's baptism. [21] So John's baptism clearly marked a decisive break with the past and a new beginning in the lives of those individuals receiving it.

2. The baptism administered to Jesus [Matthew 3:13ff.; Mark 1:9; Luke 3:21; John 1:29ff.].

The baptism of Jesus also marked a new beginning. The synoptic gospels record Jesus' baptism with extreme brevity and simplicity. No explanation seems necessary; yet the terseness of the records makes the interpretation all the more difficult. Note

374

the importance of the event. "Jesus came from Galilee to the Jordan" (Matthew 3:13; Mark specifies "Nazareth of Galilee," 1:9). If John was baptizing in the wilderness region of Judea near the Dead Sea,[22] then Jesus came a distance of over fifty miles. Jesus came this lengthy distance for the express purpose "to be baptized by him."[23] Note John's reluctance. With prophetic insight he confesses, "I need to be baptized by you, and you come to me?" (Matthew 3:14). The reluctance is based upon Jesus' sinlessness. John administered "a baptism of repentance for the forgiveness of sins." But Jesus needed no forgiveness of sins, because he had no sin. This coming of Jesus perplexed and puzzled John.[24] Note also Jesus' response. Jesus was not surprised at John's reaction, nor does he rebuke John for feeling the way he does. Calmly, with conviction, Jesus reassures John, "Let it be so now."[25] Confidently he shares with John the reason, "It is proper for us to do this to fulfill all righteousness" (Matthew 3:15). Jesus comes to John with an intimate understanding of the Father's will, a knowledge that leads Him to the waters of the Jordan river to be baptized by John "to fulfill all righteousness" (*plerosai pasan dikaiosunen*). What does it mean "to fulfill all righteousness"? Different interpretations have been offered, for example "to fulfill God's purpose," "to identify himself with sinners," "to leave nothing undone that had been revealed in the righteous will of God," etc.[26] Perhaps the best explanation lies in Matthew's use of the word "righteousness" (*dikaiosune*). John came to Israel "in the way of righteousness" (Matthew 21:32). His message and his baptism were "from heaven" and not "from men" (Matthew 21:25). He came preaching and baptizing to prepare a remnant for the coming kingdom of God and his righteousness (Matthew 6:33). He came also to prepare the way for the righteous king himself. As Malachi and Isaiah foretold,

I will send my messenger ahead of you,
who will prepare your way—
a voice of one calling in the desert,

375

'Prepare the way for the Lord,
make straight paths for him' (Mark 1:2-3).

So John came, and Jesus came to John to usher in the righteousness of God in its fullness (i.e., in his own person as Messiah; cf. Colossians 2:9).[27] It is not unimportant that the only place where Jesus and John ever meet is the Jordan river. Herein lies the greatest significance of the baptism of Jesus. John prepared for the coming Messiah king. John revealed to Israel the Messiah king. Then John relinquished to the Messiah king. Compare the crude illustration of a relay race. The first man runs, he passes the baton, and then he stops running. The baptism of Jesus, so to speak, is the passing of the baton. John himself confesses, "I myself did not know him, but the reason I came baptizing with water was that he might be revealed to Israel" (John 1:31).[28] Before the baptism, John did not recognize Jesus (i.e., as Messiah, as Son of God). After the baptism however, John could confess, "I have seen and I testify that this is the Son of God" (verse 34). God planned that Jesus should be revealed to John in the act of baptism, when the Holy Spirit descended from heaven in dove-like form (verse 33). In addition to being God's sign of confirmation and approval to John, the descending Spirit resting upon[29] Jesus at baptism marked the beginning of the "already but not yet" new dispensation. Barrett aptly remarks.

Jesus has the Spirit in order that he may confer it; and it is the gift of the Spirit that pre-eminently distinguishes the new dispensation from the old; it belongs neither to Judaism nor even to John.[30]

Jesus had the Spirit, but He had not yet given the Spirit to His followers.[31] That would come later. So John could say of Jesus "He *will baptize* you with the Holy Spirit."[32] In anticipation of that time, John could now tell his disciples, "Look, the Lamb of God, who takes away the sin of the world!" (verses 29, 36). But John must now decrease so that Jesus might increase.[33] At the baptism of Jesus a new beginning had taken place. The Spirit of the Lord had come upon Jesus (cf. Luke 4:1,18); God's righteous Messiah king had come.

3. The baptism administered by the disciples of Jesus [John 3:22,23; 3:26; 4:1,2].

Another possible antecedent to Christian baptism in the NT is the baptism administered by the disciples of Jesus. Unfortunately, the NT preserves very little information about this baptism. The narrative in the gospel of John simply states, "Jesus and his disciples went out into the Jordan countryside, where he spent some time with them, and baptized" (3:22; cf. 4:1-2). Given the strong comparison with John's baptism,[34] this baptism evidently paralleled John's baptism in design. Only the administrators were different. This is the point of difference that engendered an argument ("who" rather than "what"), and the point of difference noticed by the Pharisees.[35] The whole incident serves to demonstrate the growing popularity of Jesus and the gradual decrease of John's ministry. John came to testify to the superiority of Jesus. The fact that Jesus increasingly baptized more shows that John did his work well.

4. The baptism sayings of Jesus [Mark 10:38,39; Luke 12:50).

Two baptism sayings of Jesus deserve brief treatment at this point.[36] Undoubtedly, both sayings refer to Jesus' suffering and death. Both speak of a future baptism to be experienced by Jesus. In Luke 12:50, Jesus says, "I have a baptism to be baptized with; and how I am constrained until it is accomplished!" (RSV). In Mark 10:38, He asks His disciples, "Are you able to drink the cup that I drink, or to be baptized with the baptism with which I am baptized?" (RSV). The "cup" as a metaphor for suffering occurs often in biblical literature.[37] But what does Jesus mean when He calls His death a baptism? Plummer remarks, "Regarding troubles as a flood in which one is plunged is also common in [biblical] literature."[38] But the "trouble" of Jesus ran very deep.

He came to pour out His life unto death, to be numbered with the transgressors, to bear the sin of many (Isaiah 53:12). He had no sin, but God made Him "sin for us" (*hamartian huper hemon*, II Corinthians 5:21). Jesus could not give a more potent description of this great burden than "baptism." It was a baptism of death. Initially, with John's baptism, Jesus had offered Himself to the Father to fulfill all righteousness; now He would complete that task. He had come by water, now He would come by blood (I John 5:6). The baptism of water, which inaugurated His ministry, anticipated the baptism of death, which crowned His ministry.[39] Furthermore, this baptism of death was a baptism unto resurrection and glorification. It marked a new stage in the ministry of Jesus and in His relationship with both the Father and His followers. So this baptism likewise marks a very important new beginning. For this reason Jesus would not avoid this baptism of death; He would do the Father's will!

C. After the Descent of the Spirit

An important change takes place in the meaning of baptism after the descent of the Holy Spirit. This does not mean to suggest a lack of continuity between John's baptism, the baptism of Jesus, and Christian baptism, but it is to say that another new beginning has occurred.

> This new baptismal gift of the Holy Spirit is imparted neither by Jewish proselyte baptism nor Johannine baptism. It is bound up with the person and the work of Christ. . . . The outpouring of the Holy Spirit 'on all flesh' (Acts 2:17) presupposes the resurrection of Christ and follows on Pentecost.[40]

Of this Pentecostal descent of God's Spirit, Peter affirms, "This is what was spoken by the prophet Joel. . ." (Acts 2:16). Later he refers back to this time as "at the beginning" (*en arche*, Acts 11:15). God's "last days" had been ushered in. Jesus had kept

378

His promise. The Holy Spirit had come.[41] The kingdom of God had come with power from on high. But the "extraordinary" means used by God on this occasion for the sending and the reception of the Spirit are not permanent. "Ordinary" immersion in water becomes God's means of bestowing forgiveness of sins and the gift of the Holy Spirit.

> *Christian* baptism is only possible after the church is constituted as the locus of the Holy Spirit. . . . What happened in a collective manner at Pentecost is in future to take place for each individual in the sacrament of the transmission of the Spirit. . . . Pentecost represents the decisive turning point. . . . The church is constituted here as the locus of the Holy Spirit, as the body of Christ crucified and risen. Thus the baptismal death of Christ completed once for all on the cross passes over into church baptism.[42]

1. Baptism in the growing church [Acts 2:38,41; 8:12,13,16,36,38; 9:18; 10:37,47,48; 11:16; 13:24; 16:15,33; 18:8,25; 19:3,4,5; 22:16].

Peter's message on Pentecost provoked a response from the hearers. Peter answered their question "What shall we do?" with, "Repent, and be baptized every one of you in the name of Jesus Christ for the forgiveness of your sins, and you shall receive the gift of the Holy Spirit" (RSV, Acts 2:38). Peter did not tell his inquirers "to await the Holy Spirit in a second Pentecost event with wind, fire and tongues."[43] Rather, Peter offers his audience Christian baptism. Note the strong imperatives, "You repent, and let each of you be immersed. . . ."[44] The appeal of the apostle is urgent. "With many other words he warned them; and he pleaded with them, 'Save yourselves from this corrupt generation' " (Acts 2:40). "Waiting" would be totally inappropriate. As Bruner remarks, "The apostolic wait in Jerusalem applied only to that unusual period in the apostles' career between the ascension of Jesus and his gift of the Spirit to the church at Pentecost."[45] Waiting was no longer necessary, because the Spirit had already been given.[46] What was necessary was the receiving of God's gift through the humble rite of baptism. The connection between verse 40 and verse 41 must not be overlooked. The emphasis in Peter's exhortation is not "save *yourselves*" as most of the English translations seem to imply. Rather, the emphasis is "*save* yourselves." The text simply reads *sothete*, "be saved. . . ."[47] "Peter is urging them to submit to God's way of salvation which he has just explained."[48] Those who accepted Peter's message to "be saved" *were baptized (ebaptisthesan)*, that is, they were saved. In consequence, no longer were these 3000 souls part of a "corrupt generation." They accepted God's means of salvation, and God added them to the number of His people.[49]

Luke explains that the Lord Himself added these believers to the number of His people. He had granted to them "forgiveness of sins" and "the gift of the Holy Spirit." Such had been accomplished through "baptism in the name of Jesus Christ." Bruner rightly remarks,

> The baptism in the name of Jesus Christ, according to Luke's account, includes both the forgiveness of sins *and* the reception of the Holy Spirit — together. This single two-fold benefit corresponds exactly to the Old Testament promise of the coordinate forgiveness of sins and gift of the Spirit (Jeremiah 31:31-34; Ezekiel 36:24-27). The baptism is, in the careful formulation, "for the forgiveness of sins, *and* you shall receive the gift of the Holy Spirit."[50]

"Forgiveness of sins" indicates the release that comes with the canceling of man's debt to God. Man's failure to keep God's righteous law incurred a debt, namely, "the certificate of debt consisting of decrees against us which was hostile to us" (NAS, Colossians 2:14). Man was unable to keep the former law; the flesh was too weak by itself without the Spirit. So God sent His Son Jesus to "condemn sin in the flesh," to render satisfaction to the just demands of God's law, and to "cancel out the certificate of debt" by granting to mankind forgiveness of sins (see Colossians 2:13ff.; Romans 8:1ff.). Furthermore, God sent His Spirit to enable men and women to put to death the deeds of the body and to live (Romans 8:13)! This "gift of the Holy Spirit" indicates the new power that comes with the renewing of man's life to God. Taking away the old ("the law of sin and death"), God establishes the new ("the law of the Spirit of life in Christ Jesus"). In the words of Paul in II Corinthians 5:17, "The old has gone; the new has come," and the time of this release and renewal is Christian baptism.

Another indication of the saving power of Christian baptism comes from the immediacy of the administration of this ordinance by the first proclaimers of good news. Other preachers like Peter attached immediate importance to the rite of baptism. Ananias of Damascus told Saul of Tarsus, "Get up, be baptized and wash your sins away, calling on his name" (Acts 22:16; cf. 9:18).[51] This devout believer had just told the persecutor God's plan for his life (Acts 22:14-15). Then he exhorted him to be baptized by asking, "What are you waiting for?"[52] The cause for immediacy in baptism is obvious. Saul must first experience forgiveness himself before he can witness to others. He must first wash away his own sins and call upon the name of the Lord via baptism. Then he can witness to others concerning salvation through Jesus the Messiah. Strikingly, the turning point of Saul's career from persecutor to Christian preacher comes precisely at the time of his baptism (see Acts 9:17ff.).

Some argue that Paul's conversion occurred at the time of his heavenly vision. But the time of the inception of faith must not be confused with the concrete expression of that faith in baptism. Just as planting a seed does not guarantee a new plant, so the germ of faith within any human heart does not guarantee new spiritual life. Both must await the death of the outer shell, and for the believer this death occurs when the old man is crucified and the new man is resurrected with Jesus in baptism. However, the distinction between faith and baptism must not be drawn too sharply. On the one hand, baptism without faith (i.e., an *ex opere operato* initiatory ceremony) is unthinkable. On the other hand, faith without baptism (except for those waiting the opportunity of baptism, such as Paul) is equally unthinkable.

> In the church of the NT, faith and baptism belong together, like soul and body in biblical thought: the one cannot exist without the other. To regard sincere faith as adequate to salvation apart from baptismal incorporation into Christ's body is sheer 'Christian Science' by the standards of NT theology; by ignoring the reality of the body it makes salvation a subjective affair, a disembodied soul-salvation of individuals who have 'enjoyed' a certain 'experience'. The profession of faith without the bodily action of submission in baptism is not the obedience of the whole man; a mental act which has no outward embodiment is a mere phantom of the full-blooded, full-bodied wholeness of biblical thinking. Believing while dispensing with the act of baptism, is a kind of docetism, and is thus not belief in the NT sense at all. The action — or rather, the passion — of being baptized, is itself part of the act of believing, since to believe means to obey.[53]

So Paul's faith in Jesus as Lord probably had its beginning at the time of the heavenly vision. But the completion of his faith in obedience to his Lord did not occur until he was baptized by Ananias.[54] When the importance of baptism is rightly understood (i.e., the completing or making whole of one's faith), the exhortation of Ananias to Paul is easily understood (i.e., "get up now and do it!").

Similarly, Lydia of Thyatira, a Roman jailer of Philippi, and Crispus of Corinth received baptism soon after hearing and believing the message of Jesus. Crispus heard Paul, believed, and was baptized (Acts 18:8). Possibly he listened to Paul's message for some time before making his commitment (see v. 11), but the language of verse 8 suggests that once Crispus and others believed, then baptism followed immediately. Lydia also accepted Paul's message and received baptism (Acts 16:13-15). Like Crispus, she confirmed her faith in Jesus in the act of baptism. She herself saw this response to Paul's message as "being faithful to the Lord" (pisten to kurio einai; v. 15). Of course, some time could have elapsed between the teaching and Lydia's baptism ("we stayed there several days," v. 12; cf. v. 18), but the narrative appears to recount events of one day, that is "on the sabbath" (v. 13). Regardless of the exact time sequence, her confirmation of faith in baptism occurred soon after her hearing of the message. There was no delay of months or years. In like fashion the Roman jailer was baptized "immediately" or "at once" (parachrema) after Paul and Silas spoke the word of the Lord to him ("the same hour of the night," Acts 16:33). Marshall even conjectures that the jailer and his family were baptized "in the prison itself."[55] This immediacy with regard to baptism indicates the seriousness of the matter to these early Christian preachers. Delay in proclamation of the word and the obedience of baptism was out of the question. The jailer, like Lydia and Crispus, needed salvation (Acts 16:20-31), so salvation was offered and accepted via baptism. Afterwards the jailer's family rejoiced. They "had believed in God" (pepisteukos to theo, Acts 16:34). Notice the perfect tense of the verb. Basically, the perfect tense expresses a "punctiliar event in the past, related in its effects to the present."[56] The past event referred to by the verb pepisteukos ("had believed") seems to be the family's baptism. Baptism confirmed their faith in Jesus as Lord, just as an ancient seal would complete and ratify an ancient document.[57] The man and his family had trusted in God's promise to save them by accepting His mercy in baptism. In consequence of this, God granted to them joy and new life. For them it was a new beginning.

For twelve disciples of John at Ephesus, baptism became a source of joy and new life in the Lord Jesus and in the Holy Spirit (Acts 19:1-7). These disciples apparently had been taught by Apollos. Like Apollos they "knew only the baptism of John" (Acts 18:25). They had received limited instruction in "the way of God," and therefore they suffered from limited benefits.

> Apollos taught the things of Jesus accurately, but he did not yet
> know how to apply or end his teaching by offering baptism into
> the name of Jesus Christ. . . . [Consequently] Apollos' converts
> were inadequately initiated.[58]

By accepting John's baptism, these disciples had accepted a life
of faith towards God. But they needed something more, and
Paul sensed this deficiency. He asked them, "Did you receive the
Holy Spirit when you believed?" (v. 2).

> Some scholars would translate, 'Did you receive the Holy Spirit
> *after* [*since* in KJV] you believed?' with the implication that recep-
> tion of the Spirit is a gift subsequent to belief in Jesus. This
> is . . . undoubtedly a wrong understanding of the phrase here in
> context; it . . . goes against the constant NT association of the
> Spirit with conversion.[59]

The aorist participle "having believed" (*pisteusantes*) denotes an
action corresponding in time to the action of the main verb "you
received" (*elabete*).[60] The members of the group should have
received the Spirit at the time of their conversion (i.e., when
belief was confirmed at baptism).[61] In other words, one cannot
become a true believer in Jesus without receiving the Holy
Spirit,[62] and the means of receiving the Spirit is baptism "into the
name of the Lord Jesus." The text holds no promise for the two-
stage initiation theory of water baptism followed by Spirit baptism.

> Baptism then, and not baptism plus a subsequent confirmation or
> 'baptism with the Spirit' is what marks a man as a Christian. It is
> the unrepeatable sacrament of Christian beginnings. . . . Baptism
> is *the* mark of Christian belonging, the badge which all God's peo-
> ple have in common whatever their differences. The NT knows
> nothing of believers in Jesus who do not get baptised. Neither
> does it know anything of Christians who get themselves rebap-
> tised. For baptism is the sacramental expression of Christian initia-
> tion.[63]

This is why Paul immediately questioned them about their baptism ("what baptism did you receive," *eis ti oun ebaptisthete*, v. 3; cf. Hebrews 6:2, "instruction about baptisms," *baptismon didaches*).

> As they knew John's baptism, they might have been expected to know John's teaching, that his baptism of repentance prepared the way for the coming of One who should baptize *en pneumati hagio* ["in the Holy Spirit"], but this, apparently, they did not know.[64]

"Men unsure of the gospel and not possessing the Spirit need Christian baptism, whatever has gone before; Paul ensured that they received it."[65] After further instruction as to the preparatory function of John's baptism, these disciples "were baptized into the name of the Lord Jesus" (v. 5).[66] Formerly disciples of John, they now become disciples of the Lord Jesus. Formerly ignorant of the Holy Spirit, they now become empowered with God's gift and speak in tongues and prophesy (v. 6).[67] So Christian baptism secures a new beginning for these people. In this *new* baptism (not rebaptism!), they acknowledge Jesus as Lord and Savior, and they receive the Holy Spirit. It is these two foundational experiences of Jesus as Lord and the Holy Spirit as helper that make baptism so essential for any believer.

The baptism of Samaritans and Gentiles likewise meant new life in Jesus for these groups, but these baptisms also marked an explosive and exciting new period for the corporate life of God's church. God wanted to make an undisputable point when He decided to extend the boundaries of His church from Jews to Samaritans to Gentiles, and He made His point through special workings of His Spirit. "Who has understood the Spirit of the Lord, or instructed him as his counselor?" (Isaiah 40:13). The events at Samaria (Acts 8:4-25) and Caesarea (Acts 10:1-48) are not typical! Maybe this is why Luke records these events, because they are different and very important to the story of the history of the church!

The story in the eighth chapter of Acts "records the reception of the gospel by the Samaritans, a people whom the Jews hated and regarded as heretical."[68] Green rightly notes, "However you choose to interpret chapter 8, it leaves you with problems."[69] The persecution led by Saul scattered the Christians "throughout Judea and Samaria" (v. 1). Missionary activity increased because of greater adversity! Philip, one of the seven servants of the church (Acts 6:1-7), travelled to the region of Samaria and preached Christ there.[70] The message brought about a good response, with signs, exorcisms, healings, and great joy (vv. 6-8). Even the sorcery of Simon, which had held the people spell-bound for some time, could not stop the progress of the gospel. The power of the "good news of the kingdom of God and the name of Jesus Christ" was greater than the "great power" of Simon (see v. 10). Sure Simon had amazed the people and boasted of his greatness, but the Samaritans had never seen anything like the signs performed by Philip. This demonstration of power gave credibility to Philip's message about Jesus,[71] and consequently many of the Samaritans, both men and women,[72] believed and were baptized (v. 12). Surprisingly, "Simon himself believed and was baptized" (v. 13).[73] So far so good in the interpretation of Acts, chapter 8. But the problem comes when Luke informs us that Peter and John came from Jerusalem to Samaria to pray for these believers that "they might receive the Holy Spirit, because the Holy Spirit had not yet come upon any of them; they had simply been baptized into the name of the Lord Jesus" (vv. 15-16). The perplexing question is, "If the Holy Spirit is given at baptism, why the delay in the case of the Samaritans?" One solution questions the sincerity of the faith of the Samaritans. Under this view some deficiency in their faith delayed the coming of the Spirit.[74] However,

It should be noticed first that the remedy for the absence of the Holy Spirit was not sought or found in any disposition or action of the Samaritans. . . . The Samaritans are asked no questions and

they are placed under no commands. The problem lies not with
the Samaritans. . . . The discovery in Acts 8:14-17 of insufficient
commitment on the part of any parties or finding of the imperfect
fulfilling of any conditions must be imported into the text.[75]

The faith of the Samaritans was not insufficient. They did believe
Philip's message, and they were baptized into the name of the
Lord Jesus. Their faith found fulfillment in commitment and obedience. Of faith they had no lack, but they did lack *the Holy
Spirit*. Another solution sees "the laying on of the apostles'
hands"[76] as the key to this delay of the Spirit. While the
Samaritans received the "ordinary" gift of the Spirit at their baptism, they waited to receive the "extraordinary" or "miraculous"
gifts of the Spirit at the laying on of the apostles' hands. Rogers
suggests that in this passage,

The Holy Spirit is expressly named four times when the 'gifts' are
meant. These people had heard the gospel; they had believed the
gospel; they had obeyed the gospel. They had, therefore, received the Holy Spirit. Yet Peter and John came down from
Jerusalem that the Samaritans might receive the Holy Spirit. The
key to the whole section is verse 18: 'Now when Simon *saw* that
through the laying on of the apostles' hands the Holy Spirit was
given, . . .' This is a metonymy. The Spirit is stated when the gifts
are meant.[77]

But this sort of interpretation is clearly misguided. It assumes the
Samaritans had received the Holy Spirit as a gift when the text
plainly states otherwise. Furthermore,

It is difficult to believe that St. Luke can mean to limit the expression *lambanein* ["to receive"] here to anything less than a
bestowal of that divine indwelling of the spirit which makes the
Christian the temple of God.[78]

That's the problem, and the fact that Simon "saw" that the gift of
the Spirit accompanied the apostles' ministrations does not lessen

the problem. Marshall correctly observes that,

> The story presupposes that it can be known whether or not a person has received the Spirit. This would be the case if charismatic gifts were involved; cf. how 10:46 gives the proof for 10:45. But there is no proof that charismatic gifts were manifest every time, and other less spectacular indications, such as a sense of joy, may have been regarded as adequate evidence of the presence of the Spirit (13:52; 16:34; 1 Thessalonians 1:6).[79]

So the Samaritans did not receive the Holy Spirit at their baptism, and the question remains, "Why was the Spirit withheld?" The best explanation is,

> God withheld the Spirit until the coming of Peter and John in order that the Samaritans might be seen to be fully incorporated into the community of Jerusalem Christians who had received the Spirit at Pentecost.[80]

This unusual working of the Spirit was God's way of telling the Jewish believers, "You accept the Samaritan believers, just as I have accepted you" (cf. 10:47; 11:17). Through this special outpouring of His Spirit, God was mending that ancient split between Jew and Samaritan (see John 4:9; cf. 8:48).

> If the Holy Spirit had been given immediately upon profession of faith and baptism by the Samaritans, this ancient schism would have continued, and there would have been two churches, out of fellowship with each other. . . . God did not give his Holy Spirit to the Samaritans at once: not until representatives from Jerusalem came down and expressed their solidarity with the converts by praying for them and laying their hands on them. Then they received the Holy Spirit; . . .it was not so much an authorization from Jerusalem or an extension of the Jerusalem church, as a divine veto on schism in the infant church, a schism which could have slipped almost unnoticed into the Christian fellowship, as converts from the two sides of the 'Samaritan curtain' found Christ without finding each other. That would have

been a denial of the one baptism and all it stood for. It was for this reason that God made delay on this occasion. Acts 8 is recorded precisely to show the abnormality of a baptism which does not lead to reception of the Holy Spirit.[81]

So the Samaritan's reception of the Spirit *after* baptism is a special case, and it would be foolish to make such a special case a general pattern for the working of the Spirit. However, the incident does represent another new beginning associated with baptism. "Samaria was the church's first decisive step out of and beyond Judaism."[82] As such it is the beginning of God's reaching out through the apostles "to the ends of the earth" (Acts 1:8).

A similar movement of the Spirit involved the Gentiles. But unlike the Samaritans, Cornelius, his relatives, and his close friends received the Holy Spirit *before* baptism (Acts 10:44-48)! By this wondrous proof of the "falling" (*epesen*, v. 44) of God's Spirit upon the Gentiles, "Peter and his Jewish brethren with him saw that, uncircumcised though they were, Cornelius and his household were no longer common or unclean."[83] Chase appropriately calls this episode "the Pentecost of the Gentile world."[84]

> Through a striking intervention by which the Gentiles were inaugurated into the church just as the Jews had been ("just as we have," 10:47; cf. 11:15), a certainty was provided that Gentiles stood on no less equal footing in the church than did the Jews.[85]

The Holy Spirit took the initiative on this occasion. He did so in order to break down that ancient "dividing wall of hostility" (Ephesians 2:14).[86] But this special working of God's Spirit did not render water baptism useless or unnecessary. In fact, it made water baptism all the more important. Peter replied, "Can anyone keep these people from being baptized in water? They have received the Holy Spirit just as we have" (v. 47). Convinced of God's acceptance of the Gentiles, the apostles "ordered that they be baptized in the name of Jesus Christ" (v. 48). Why did Peter immediately demand the Gentiles be baptized with water? It can only be because he connected water baptism "in the name of Jesus Christ" (*en to onomati Iesou Christou*) with the promised baptism "with the Holy Spirit" (*en pneumati hagio*; see 11:16). The Spirit and the water belonged together.

> Baptism was not considered a superfluous rite, dispensable now because the 'real thing' had already occurred. The gift of the Holy Spirit without baptism was as unthinkable to the church as baptism without the gift of the Holy Spirit (8:14-17; 19:2-7). . . . The Holy Spirit and baptism, they knew, belonged together in such a way as to form the 'one baptism' of the church (Ephesians 4:5; cf. 1 Corinthians 12:13).[87]

Peter later explained his actions to his critics in Jerusalem, "If God gave them the same gift, . . . who was I to think that I could oppose God!" (11:17).[88] In other words, to not baptize the Gentiles with water would have been to oppose God. God had taken the initiative, and He had given His approval of the Gentiles by bestowing upon them the gift of His Spirit. Now it remained for these Jewish Christians to complete the Gentile's turn unto God by baptizing them. This they did, because they understood the importance of baptism.

So the Gentiles, like the Samaritans, received the Spirit in an unusual way. But even though the immediacy of the working of the Spirit was removed from baptism in these instances (i.e., an indication of God's sovereignty in this "cross-racial evangelism"), the strong connection between Spirit and water in conversion was still strongly preserved.

Once again, however, God used baptism to lead His people to new beginnings; it was a fresh start for Cornelius and his friends, and in a real sense it was a fresh start for the faith of Peter and his Jewish brethren. The Gentiles experienced the newness of the power of God's Spirit. The Jews, however, experienced the newness of God's working in the church of Christ, namely that God in His sovereign grace would "bring Gentiles directly into relationship with Jesus Christ apart from any prior relationship with Judaism."[89] So God worked through baptism to fix a point of decisive change not only in the lives of individual believers, but also in the attitudes and development of the Christian community as a whole.

Finally, the case of a leading official[90] from Ethiopia provides yet another instance of the new life associated with baptism in the growing church (Acts 8:26-40). Under the guidance of the Spirit (vv. 29, 39), the hellenist Philip received an invitation to join this man in his chariot and teach him. Beginning with Isaiah's prophecy about "the suffering servant," Philip "told him the good news about Jesus" (euangelisato auto ton Iesoun; v. 35). Evidently this message about Jesus included a message about baptism (cf. 2:22ff.,38; 8:12). When they came upon some water, the official asked ,"Look, here is water. Why shouldn't I be baptized?" (v. 36). He understood that the proper response to the message about Jesus was baptism, so "both Philip and the eunuch went down into the water and Philip baptized him" (v. 38). Note the language used to describe the eunuch's baptism. They both "went down into the water," and they "came up out of the water." "The context indicates that baptism was by immersion, and there can be no doubt that this was the custom of the early church."[91] As a beautiful portrayal of death and resurrection, baptism by immersion appropriately corresponds to the message about Jesus (i.e., the kerygma). Furthermore, the "coming up out of the water" (i.e., the believer's resurrection to new life; see v. 39; cf. Matthew 3:16; Mark 1:10) prepares the candidate for the reception of the Spirit, God's gift of new life. The believer's ascending from the water also complements the picture of the Spirit as gift descending from heaven. In the case of the Ethiopian, a longer form of the text actually reads, "When they came up out of the water, the Holy Spirit fell upon the eunuch, but the angel of the Lord caught up Philip. . . ."[92] Whether this reading is original or not is debatable,[93] but the fact of the official's reception of the Holy Spirit is not in question, for he "went on his way rejoicing." Things are now different. The indwelling Spirit imparted joy to his heart (cf. 13:52; Galatians 5:22). He had experienced a new beginning for his life. This is because he had discovered Jesus, and he had received the Spirit of Jesus in baptism.

By connecting water baptism with the saving work of Jesus and the reception of the Holy Spirit, the early church did not act arbitrarily. The summons to baptize came from the lips of Jesus Himself. Thus the early church acted under His authority. After His resurrection and prior to His ascension, the Lord taught His disciples many lessons concerning the kingdom of God (see Acts 1:3). He taught His followers about baptism with the Holy Spirit (Acts 1:5; cf. John 20:21-23), about repentance and forgiveness of sins (Luke 24:45-49), and about faith, discipleship, baptism, and further teaching (Matthew 28:19-20; cf. Mark 16:15-16). The Lord made clear the need for proclamation of good news about Himself — His suffering, His death, His resurrection, and His exaltation.[94] This would be the foundation of the kingdom. But the Lord also made clear the need for proclamation of a way whereby men and women might accept the saving benefits of His life and enter the kingdom. He gave them a way that was specific, decisive, and meaningful. He gave them a way which strongly identified any follower with the very foundations of Christian faith.[95] He gave them baptism. He told His disciples,

> All authority in heaven and on earth has been given to me. Go therefore and make disciples of all nations, baptizing them in the name of the Father and of the Son and of the Holy Spirit, teaching them to observe all that I have commanded you; and lo, I am with you always, to the close of the age (RSV, Matthew 28:18-20; cf. Mark 16:15-16).

Herein lies the authority for Christian baptism; it came first from the authority of Jesus Himself. Baptism was His gift to His church; and by giving baptism, Jesus gave His followers an objective means by which to confer the forgiveness of sins,[96] entrance into the kingdom, the gift of the Holy Spirit, union with Christ, etc. The two participles in Jesus' commission, "baptizing" (*baptidzontes*) and "teaching" (*didaskontes*), describe how disciples are made. Carson, however, denies any strong connection between baptism and discipleship. Rather than the *means* of disciple-making, he sees baptism and teaching as actions "characterizing" discipleship.[97] But McNeile's comment on "baptizing them" (*baptidzontes autous*) is more to the point. "The present participle expresses a continuous activity [emphasizing the ongoing activity of the church in both baptizing and teaching, DF]; each forms part of a continuous *matheteuein* ['disciple making']."[98] Perhaps it is even better to see the commission as involving a threefold task. "The apostles are to make disciples of all men, to baptize them, and to instruct them."[99] Thus the apostolic pattern of teaching (i.e., evangelizing), baptizing, and post-baptismal teaching is preserved. But the necessary connection between the differing activities must not be obscured by the difficulty of the grammar. Just as baptism without further teaching would be inappropriate, so evangelism without baptism would be incomplete and lacking. Proclamation of good news without profession of that good news in baptism would be omitting the very necessary work of God to incorporate the sinner into the company or fellowship of the Father, Son, and Holy Spirit. Osborne indicates that,

> The baptized convert becomes the possession of and therefore enters into fellowship with the Trinity in the discipling process. Jesus' words here are thus more than just a liturgical formula; baptism is an experience which transcends any act of obedience or symbolic rite. It is the initiation of the disciple (cf. 1 Peter 3:19, 20) into the rights and obligations of his calling.[100]

Similarly, Plummer notes that,

> In the words before us our Lord was not ordering any particular form of administering baptism. . . . Our Lord may be explaining

what becoming a disciple really involves: it means no less than entering into communion with, into vital relationship with, the revealed persons of the Godhead. The divine name is often a reverent symbol for the divine nature, for God himself; and therefore baptizing into the name of the Trinity may mean immersing in the infinite ocean of the divine perfection. In Christian baptism the divine essence is the element *into* which the baptized are plunged, or *in* which they are bathed.[101]

So the early Christians vigorously entered into their profession of faith and into fellowship with the Trinity by gladly accepting and proclaiming salvation via baptism.[102] Unlike many modern believers, they did not balk at baptism. They gave baptism its due prominence. This was not done without cause. Baptism has historical associations with the death and resurrection of Jesus; it has existential associations with the risen Lord, the Godhead, and the gathered community of saints; and it has eschatological associations with the Holy Spirit and the promised return of Christ. Only because of these crucial associations was baptism given such prominence by those early disciples. Ridderbos rightly observes that,

Baptism is the means by which communion with the death and burial of Christ comes into being (*dia tou baptismatos*, "through baptism," Romans 6:4), the place where this union is effected (*en to baptismati*, "in baptism," Colossians 2:12), the means by which Christ cleanses his church (*katharisas to loutro*, "having been washed with water," Ephesians 5:26), and [the means whereby] God has saved it (*esosen hemas dia loutrou*, "he saved us through washing," Titus 3:5), . . . All these formulations speak clearly of the significance of baptism in mediating redemption; they speak of what happens in and by baptism and not merely of what happened before baptism and of which baptism would only be the confirmation. On the other hand, it is plain that baptism as means of salvation, does not have an exclusive significance. Thus what is here attributed to baptism can elsewhere be ascribed to faith, and thus what is here represented as appropriated to believers by baptism can elsewhere be ascribed to them already in

394

Christ's death. . . .[So] baptism accomplishes in its own way what already obtained in another way, and thus occupies its own place in the whole of the divine communication of redemption.[103]

It is precisely because of these connections "in the whole of the divine communication of redemption," connections with repentance, entry into the kingdom, forgiveness of sins, reception of the Spirit, union with Christ, etc., that it will not do to suppose that baptism is an optional extra or superfluous ordinance. Yes, baptism is God's ordinance of new life, and as such it surely depends upon God, Christ, and the Holy Spirit for its effectual working. They alone can make us new people; they alone can bring about the transformation of mind, body, spirit, and will so needed by sinful man. But baptism must not be decontextualized and then regarded as unnecessary to this process of transformation. Baptism should be viewed in its immensely rich and varied context, its biblical context; and when baptism is seen in this light, then baptism will be heralded and obeyed as one of God's greatest gifts to his church. If baptism is not this important, why did Jesus so will and so command His people to make disciples by baptizing and teaching until "the very end of the age"?

2. Baptism in the established church [Romans 6:3,4; I Corinthians 1:13,14,15,16,17; 10:2; 12:13; 15:29; Galatians 3:27; Ephesians 4:5; Colossians 2:12; I Peter 3:21).
When we move from the book of Acts to the epistles, the emphasis on baptism changes. Exhortation to be baptized now becomes exhortation *to the baptized*. Paul and the other writers do not address a hostile, unbelieving audience; they speak to an already Christian audience, to those of whom they can say, "That is what some of you were. But you were washed, you were sanctified, you were justified in the name of the Lord Jesus Christ and by the Spirit of our God" (I Corinthians 6:11). So the emphasis on baptism changes from invitation via proclamation (i.e., Peter's "Repent, and be baptized . . .") to exhortation via remembrance

(i.e., Paul's "Don't you know . . ."), a remembrance that recalls God's saving act and the Spirit's imparting of new life. Furthermore, baptism as hortatory instruction becomes a vital part of the early church's paraenetic tradition, a tradition indispensable for Christian maturation and growth.

> Paraenetic reminders are appeals to recall what happened when the addressees first became Christians, both the ritual of baptism and the instruction that accompanied it, and to behave in ways appropriate to that memory.[104]

This paraenetic use of baptism as "reminder" or as appealing to the "memory" should be emphasized. Baptism can function as *anamnesis* ("reminder")[105] only by an appeal to an already existing consciousness of baptism. This is an amazing fact about references to baptism in the epistles. The need for and necessity of baptism is never argued! Baptism is always assumed to be part of the believer's past experience. Thus the epistles address only those who have already been baptized, and this common experience of baptism becomes a powerful argument for holy and righteous living.

    a. *Baptism as death and resurrection with Christ*. In his letter to Christians at Rome (chapter 6), Paul introduces the matter of baptism because of a certain antinomian misconception of grace. However, Paul does not answer the "bogus logic"[106] echoed in verse 1 with an appeal to the law (cf. v. 14, "you are not under law, but under grace"). Rather, he emphasizes the importance of new life in Christ, a new life brought into existence by God's grace through baptism. In baptism the believer experiences death, burial, and resurrection with Christ. "We were baptized into his death" (*eis ton thanaton autou ebaptisthemen*, v. 3); "we were buried with him through baptism into death" (*sunetaphemen auto dia tou baptismatos eis ton thanaton*, v. 4).[107] In this rite of baptism "we died with Christ" (*apethanomen sun Christo*, v. 8); "our old self was crucified with him" (*ho palaios hemon anthropos sunestaurothe*, v. 6; cf. Galatians 2:20). But as Beasley-

Murray suggests, "The death we died is the death *he* died on Golgotha. . . . The action of baptism primarily means, not that the baptistry becomes our grave, but that we are laid in the grave of Christ."[108] The emphasis in baptism then, is that we died "with him," and likewise through baptism we were buried "with him."[109] However, this identification with Christ in His death, and the ratification and sealing of this death by burial, demands a corresponding resurrection unto new life. Thus Paul affirms, "So that as Christ was raised from the dead by the glory of the Father, we too might walk in newness of life" (RSV, v. 4). Just as the believer at baptism died with Christ, likewise at baptism the believer is raised to a new life. But the connection between death and resurrection at baptism goes much deeper.

> When the parenthetical material of [v. 4] is omitted we are left with the unambiguous statement: 'We were buried with him through baptism . . . *that we might walk in newness of life*'. Bornkamm maintains that the *hina* introduces the divine determination and demand under which we now stand. . . . The *hina* ('in order that') introduces the purpose of the convert as he submits to baptism. . . . He renounces the 'oldness' of his earlier life and commits himself to the 'newness of life' opened up for him through the resurrection life of Christ.[110]

So resurrection unto new life is the *purpose* for the believer's baptismal death. However, the transformation that God accomplished for Jesus historically (i.e., in Christ's own body), He accomplishes for the believer existentially and eschatologically (i.e., in the body of Christ's church).

> Descent into the water obviously did not mime Jesus' death, but it could be construed as "being buried with Christ" (Romans 6:4; Colossians 2:12), and rising from the water could very well signify "being raised with Christ" (Colossians 2:12; 3:1; Ephesians 2:6).[111]

In other words, the dying and rising in baptism is not to be construed in a crassly literal sense (*contra* ancient pagan initiation rites).[112] The bodily death and resurrection of Jesus is the pattern or prototype (i.e., the church's foundation), and those who are baptized "into Christ Jesus" do indeed experience death and resurrection, but with reference to sin, the world, the body of Christ's church, the coming resurrection, etc.[113] The dying and subsequent rising become a reality through faith, howbeit faith in an existential/eschatological context.

> The union of the individual with Christ is such that the experiences of Christ are re-enacted in the experience of the individual Christian. The life, death, resurrection and glorification of Jesus cease to be mere external facts of history but living realities in the Christian's own life. The latter appropriates to himself the past events of the historical and risen life of Jesus so that they become his own.[114]

Yet it must be further stressed that baptism is a *real* experience of this union with Christ; it is not simply a "mere sign." "That which baptism symbolizes also actually *happens*, and [it happens] precisely through baptism."[115] Christ Himself is both present and personally active in and through the "visible word of baptism."[116] Furthermore, the tangible element of water and the tangible movements of dipping and rising again in immersion enhance baptism's forceful realism. So much so that it is precisely this experience of death with Christ in baptism that brings death to sin (i.e., the Christian need sin no longer, because he has a new master or a new owner; see vv. 15ff.); and it is precisely this fellowship of resurrection with Christ in baptism that brings triumphant hope of the death of death itself (see vv. 8-10). Baptism thus unites the believer with Christ in His death, and likewise unites the believer with Christ in His resurrection.

Strikingly, however, Paul uses the aorist tense when referring to the believer's baptismal death, but he uses the future tense when referring to the Christian's resurrection (*esometha*, "we will be," v. 5; *sudzesomen*, "we will live," v. 8).[117] These references to resurrection in the future seem to be Paul's way of exhorting the Roman Christians to more diligence concerning sanctification.[118]

> His main emphasis is on dying with Christ, as, against any accusation of a deficient 'cheap' view of grace, he insists that the believer's present life cannot be one of living in sin because he or she has died to sin. But dying with Christ is only one side of the coin. It is a precondition which finds its intended completion in the sharing of the new resurrection life of Christ.[119]

In other words, if the rising with Christ prefigured in baptism is to become a future reality, then the dying with Christ also portrayed in baptism must find fulfillment in holy living. In this age of the "already, but not yet" (already raised with Christ, but not yet raised with Christ), the life of spiritual resurrection must be lived in hope of a future bodily resurrection. Until that time comes, however, "there is a present aspect of sharing in Christ's resurrection," a present reality that must be worked out by living a sanctified life. To the contrary, the libertine view of grace (vv. 1, 15) does not take God's gift of new life seriously. Furthermore, to adhere to such a notion of grace would be to quench the new life of the Spirit, and that would be a rejection of what was experienced with Christ at baptism. So the Roman Christians should "count" or "reckon" themselves "alive to God in Christ Jesus" (v. 11).

> Through his resurrection Christ now lives to God [v. 10], and since they are en Christou Iesou ["in Christ Jesus"] and identified with Christ in both his death and his life, believers are also to consider themselves alive to God.[120]

But equally they are "dead to sin" (v. 11). The new life of holiness and righteousness must be followed (see vv. 15ff.). To do otherwise would be to forfeit participation in God's greatest gift of new life, the life of the bodily resurrection. Such would also be a tragic reversion to living under law, under sin, and under the penalty of death.

    b. *Baptism as union with Christ and union with fellow Christians.* In his letter to churches of Galatia, Paul writes to believers struggling with the relationship of law and faith.[121] The attempt to impose circumcision, dietary restrictions, the observance of "appointed times," etc. upon all believers had caused certain of the Galatians to question their status as Christians and the ground of their reception into the church (see 1:7; 3:1-5; 4:8-11; 5:2-12).

> It appears that the Judaizers promoted circumcision [and other practices, DF] on the grounds that only those who submitted to [these rites] could enter fully into the elect community of the people of God and become the seed of Abraham.[122]

This separatistic leaven put a severe strain on associations in the churches (see 5:15). So much so that the problem threatened to tear apart the newly formed Christian communities. Such a crisis called for a decisive response. So Paul tells the Galatians "that they have already attained to the goals the agitators are holding before them, and that they have done so simply by faith in Christ."[123] He declares, "You are all sons of God through faith in Christ Jesus" (Galatians 3:26). Clearly, faith in Christ rather than works of law had been the basis of their justification before God. The law could add nothing; in fact, such would be contrary to the law's purpose and duration (3:15ff.).[124] But in verse 27, Paul delineates the means whereby God had worked to adopt these Galatian believers into His family (cf. 4:4-7). Paul's reminder focuses on the bodily confirmation of their faith via baptism. To allow the Galatians to forget *their exact starting point* in Christ would be too risky (cf. 3:2-5). So he states, " . . .for all of you who were baptized into Christ have been clothed with Christ" (*ho soi gar eis christon ebaptisthete, christon enedusasthe*). In other words, the faith that brought about their adoption into God's family was the faith that led to baptism, the faith by which they "put on" Christ. Rendtorff rightly maintains that "one sentence qualifies the other, [so that] the experience of baptism is the experience of faith."[125] Beasley-Murray adds,

> If Paul were pressed to define the relationship of the two statements in vv. 26-27, I cannot see how he could preserve the force of both sentences apart from affirming that baptism is the moment of faith in which the adoption is realized — in the dual sense of effected by God and grasped by man — which is the same as saying that in baptism faith receives the Christ in whom the adoption is effected.[126]

This connection that Paul makes between faith and baptism shows that baptism is not a work of law. Rather it is the acceptance of God's grace in Jesus based on faith. In baptism faith receives what the grace of God gives, and above everything else, God's grace freely gives Christ. Baptism brings about *union* with Christ; it is thus God's way of incorporating the sinner into the realm of Christ's saving life, the realm of justification, regeneration, and sanctification. The Galatians did not need the law to save them; God had already saved them by uniting them with Jesus at their baptism.

To describe this union with Christ, Paul uses the metaphor *enduein* ("to put on," "to be clothed with"). Possibly it signifies being clothed with the righteousness of Christ (i.e., His robe of righteousness; cf. Isaiah 61:10; Job 29:14; Psalm 132:9; Zechariah 3:3ff.), or perhaps it describes the putting on the new man that is recreated in the image of Christ (cf. Romans 13:14; Ephesians 4:20ff.; Colossians 3:9ff.).[127] The term could also refer to the symbolic practice of dressing the baptismal candidate or the newly baptized convert with a white robe. Richardson notes,

> Older commentators thought that this practice could hardly have begun in St. Paul's day. But there is no reason why the practice should be less likely to have arisen in A.D. 50 than in A.D. 150; Justin Martyr (*Dialogue with Trypho* 116) attests its prevalence in

the second century. After all, some such practice must have been necessary from the very beginning, since baptism was by total immersion in running water (cf. *Didache* 7:1-3; Hebrews 10:22), and the earliest Christians doubtless shared in full the aversion of the Jews [to] the state of *gumnotes* ["nakedness"]. What is more likely than that the putting on of the white robe should from the beginning have represented to the mind of the church the putting on of Christ, just as the actual immersion in the river represented the burial of the Christian with Christ in his death, and as the rising from the water symbolized his resurrection from the dead (cf. Romans 6:3f.)? . . . [Similarly], the seer's conception of the robes of the saints washed in the blood of the Lamb (Revelation 7:14; 22:14) is his way of expressing the great truth which the whole NT affirms, namely, baptismal justification.[128]

But whatever the precise reference might be, the "putting on" of Christ in baptism does indicate a close and strong association between the baptized and Christ. Such union with Christ is complete, real, and irreversible; it is a *once for all*[129] act of union with the risen Lord, and it is an act with extensive, spiritual consequences.

One obvious consequence of this union with Christ is *union with others who have likewise experienced union with Christ.* Baptism is much more than union with Christ on an individual basis. Because of their common baptism based upon like faith unto the same Lord (cf. Ephesians 4:5, "one Lord, one faith, one baptism"), Paul tells the Galatians,

There is neither Jew nor Greek, slave nor free, male nor female, for you are all one in Christ Jesus. If you belong to Christ, then you are Abraham's seed, and heirs according to the promise (3:28-29; cf. Colossians 3:11; 1 Corinthians 12:13).

The apostle here addresses these believers collectively, "For ye are all *one* in Christ Jesus, and if ye be Christ's, then are ye Abraham's seed" (KJV). Baptism in Christ effects union with others. Baptism into Christ creates community. Baptism gives

402

birth to family, to brothers and sisters in Christ, who share a common life, who are the people of God. To use the words of Paul, "So in Christ we who are many form *one body*, and each member belongs to all the others" (Romans 12:5; on "one body" cf. I Corinthians 6:15-17; 10:17; 12:12-13,20,27; Ephesians 2:16; 4:4,25; 5:30; Colossians 3:15). So great is this union with one another in Christ that,

> Every barrier is swept away. No special claims, no special disabilities exist in him, none can exist. The conventional distinctions of religious caste or of social rank, even the natural distinction of sex, are banished hence. One heart beats in all; one mind guides all; one life is lived by all. Ye are all *one man*, for ye are members of Christ.[130]

Thus union with Christ destroys faction, schism, and disunity; it is God's vigorous movement against the structures and forces of the prevailing godless culture.[131]

Similarly, when he writes to the Corinthian church, Paul connects baptism to this work of God in joining together individual believers as one body.[132] To a "church of God" wracked by squabbles, immorality, divisions, etc., he affirms the unity effected by God's Spirit at baptism.

> For indeed in *one* Spirit we *all* into *one* body were baptized — whether Jews or Greeks, whether bondmen or freemen — and we *all* of *one* Spirit were made to drink (12:13).[133]

Paul's stress on "oneness" is very clear. But what is equally clear is the means by which this oneness is effected. Note that both verbs in this verse are aorist passives ,"ye were baptized" (*ebaptisthemen*), "ye were given to drink" (*epotisthemen*). The emphasis definitely falls upon the action of God's Spirit. The Corinthians' baptism into one body was effected "in" or "by" one Spirit (*en heni pneumati*).[134] It was not brought about by their own merit nor by their own abilities. Rather it was the work of the Spirit

403

through water (en hudati)[135] that made them one. At baptism "one Spirit flooded their souls with the love and joy of a common faith in Christ."[136] At baptism they were drenched or saturated with God's Spirit which had at Pentecost been poured out for all to drink.[137] Paul's reminder exhorts the Corinthians to so live as people of the Spirit. "The argument of the passage as a whole is that the Christians at Corinth who have the most spectacular charismata ["gifts"] should not boast of them."[138] There are many gifts but one Spirit. There are many members but one body. The essential unity of God's people needed to be recognized and preserved. So Paul focuses on the Corinthians' common baptism by the same Spirit, something that "all" (pantes repeated twice in v. 13) received equally. As Althaus suggests,

> Since it is precisely the apostle's concern to show the inner con-solidation of Christians in one unified organism by means of a public-fact-of-experience, he could not use an inner, purely 'spiritual' event as his evidence; he could call upon only an historical event which had occurred in the same way to all members, by which their entrance into the spiritual 'body' came also outwardly into view.[139]

Appropriately, Paul calls forth something outward, public, and objective; he calls forth baptism, that "profound initiation event through which every Christian passes and by which every Christian is given the same spiritual gift" (i.e. the Holy Spirit).[140] But at baptism the Corinthians also received ordination to the ministry of Christ's spiritual body, the church; and every member received that personal charisma ("gift") of the Spirit to enable each one to fulfil his or her God-given diakonia ("service").[141] However, as Beasley-Murray indicates,

> The controlling idea of [the passage] is not a personal, in the sense of private, receiving of the Spirit, but the social concept of incorporation of the baptized through the Spirit into the body of Christ. . . . The unity of the body does not consist in uniformity

of character and function, but these differentiated functions are possible because the body is a unity, informed by one life and inspired by one Spirit. [So] baptism obliterates the disunities of man and harmonizes them in the unity of Christ's body in the one Spirit.[142]

Furthermore, this unity exists not because baptism is "into the name of Paul" (see 1:13-17), nor because of any certain individual that administered the baptism.[143] Rather, the unity of the body in baptism is made a reality solely "through the name of our Lord Jesus Christ" (*dia tou onomatos tou kuriou hemon Iesou Christou*, 1:10; cf. 1:2; 5:4; 6:11; 10:2).

> Christian baptism is 'in the name of the Lord Jesus', to the crucified and exalted redeemer, who has sent to his church the Spirit promised from the Father; and the Spirit he sends is his agent, communicating the benefits of his redemption.[144]

The Lord Jesus is thus for the church *the unifying personality*. All members of the church draw their common life from Him through the Spirit, a oneness of life received at baptism; and it is precisely because of such a valued sense of baptism that Paul "regarded with such abhorrence its debasement by Corinthian partisanship."[145]

c. *Baptism as spiritual* (acheiropoieton, *"made without hand"*) *circumcision*. In response to false teaching at Colossae about the heavenly world and about the employment of rigorous observances, esoteric knowledge, visionary experiences, etc. as means of attaining salvation,[146] Paul vigorously affirms the supremacy of Jesus as risen and exalted Lord and the believer's complete and secure incorporation in Him.[147] Against the heretics' syncretistic use of the Jewish circumcision as part of initiative procedures,[148] Paul strikingly makes a counterclaim that compares Christian baptism with circumcision; but Paul delicately phrases his analogy by describing baptism as a circumcision made without human hands.

> In him you were also circumcised, in the putting off of the sinful

nature, not with a circumcision done by the hands of men, but with the circumcision done by Christ (Colossians 2:11).

The qualification of "not done by the hands of men" (*acheiro-poieton*; cf. Mark 14:58; II Corinthians 5:1) shows that the believer's circumcision is not literal but of the heart (cf. Deuteronomy 10:16; 30:6; Jeremiah 4:4; 9:26; Ezekiel 44:7,9; Romans 2:28,29; Philippians 3:3). Christ Himself performs this cutting away of "the sinful nature" (*tou somatos tes sarkos*, "the body of the flesh"),[149] and He executes this spiritual surgery at baptism (*en to baptismo*, v. 12). Baptism is the time at which Christ circumcises the old nature and God resurrects the new creature. Paul nicely signals this connection by balancing the clause "having been buried with him in baptism" with a double use of the phrase "in whom also."

> *In whom also ye were circumcised,*
>> with a spiritual circumcision,
>>> by cutting off the carnal person,
>>>> by the circumcision [worked by] Christ;
>
> *Having been buried together with him in baptism;*
>
> *In whom also ye were raised,*
>> through faith,
>>> in the working of God,
>>>> who raised him from the dead.

This structure also indicates that the action of the aorist participle *suntaphentes* ("having been buried") should be taken as *coincident in time* with the actions of the two main verbs, *perietmethete*, "you were circumcised," and *sunegerthete*, "you were raised."[150] God so worked and man so received at baptism. The phrase "the working of God" (*tes energeias tou theou*) designates the activity of God, while the phrase "through faith" (*dia tes pisteos*) portrays the role of man in receiving. Baptism is thus "the grave of the old man, and the birth of the new."[151] But it

406

is only so through faith in the supreme manifestation of the power of God, the resurrection of Christ. The ordinance of baptism derives its efficacy "not from the water . . . but from the saving act of Christ and the regenerating work of the Holy Spirit."[152] Furthermore, it must not be forgotten that Paul lays emphasis on baptism as something that belongs to the Colossians' *past* experience (i.e., the verbs used are all aorists). In this way Paul urges the Colossians to recall their baptism. He wants them to know that God made obsolete any syncretistic attempt to achieve salvation through fleshly circumcision. God had given to them a far better circumcision at their baptism, a circumcision of the heart, performed without human hands, the spiritual operation of the risen Christ.

d. *Baptism as salvation from suffering through the resurrection of Jesus.* In writing to Christians of various provinces of Asia Minor (I Peter 1:1), the apostle addresses the problem of suffering, and especially suffering for doing what is right and good (see 3:13-17; cf. 1:6; 4:12-19; 5:9).[153] Peter himself is probably in Rome at the time of writing (see 5:13, "Babylon" as a cryptogram for Rome), and he had either seen with his own eyes or had heard eyewitness reports of what had happened there. "When Rome was burned (A.D. 64), Nero persecuted the Christians in order to divert suspicion from himself; it was a ludicrous charge, but the Christians in Rome suffered greatly."[154] The Roman annalist Tacitus describes some of the events in the following way,

First, Nero had self-acknowledged Christians arrested. Then, on their information, large numbers of others were condemned — not so much for incendiarism as for their anti-social tendencies.[155] Their deaths were made farcical. Dressed in wild animals' skins, they were torn to pieces by dogs, or crucified, or made into torches to be ignited after dark as substitutes for daylight. Nero provided his gardens for the spectacle, and exhibited displays in the circus, at which he mingled with the crowd — or stood in a chariot, dressed as a charioteer. Despite their guilt as Christians, and the ruthless punishment it deserved, the victims were pitied. For it was felt that they were being sacrificed to one man's brutality rather than to the national interest.[156]

True, the experience of Roman Christians should not be transferred uncritically to the situation of believers in Asia Minor of a
later time. But after the Neronian conflagration, Peter probably
knew what to expect![157] So he writes to encourage believers to
stand firm in their faith (see 5:12), because the persecution they
would face would only be temporary. "Who is there to harm
you?" he questions (RSV, 3:13). Who can corrupt you? Who will
cause you to lose your inheritance? Who can destroy your life in
Christ? The obvious answer is, "No one can!" (cf. Romans
8:31ff.). If you suffer because you have become a Christian,
God's blessing rests upon you (cf. Matthew 5:3ff.; Luke 6:22).
So "do not fear what they fear; do not be frightened" (3:14).[158]
Rather, "in your hearts reverence Christ as Lord" (RSV, 3:15).
Regard Christ (not Caesar) as holy, and do not fear those
persecuting you. Fear the Lord! (cf. Matthew 10:28). If
unbelievers bring you before the Roman tribunal, or if they accuse
you privately, be ready to make a reasoned defense (rather than
condemning or accusing in return; cf. 2:23; 3:9). Furthermore,
"keep your conscience clear," and put the accusations of the
pagans to rest by your good behaviour (3:16), because "it is better to suffer for doing right, if that should be God's will, than for
doing wrong" (RSV, 3:17; cf. 2:20).

At this point in his hortatory argument,[159] Peter introduces the
example and victory of Christ (3:18-22).[160] He shows to these
beleaguered saints the triumph of Jesus over all opposing
powers. "This triumph began in his redeeming death, was
established through his resurrection, and is now effective,
through his ascension and sitting at God's right hand."[161] Christ
died (v. 18); Christ was raised (vv. 19-21); Christ ascended and
now He reigns (v. 22)! Such a proclamation spoke powerfully to
the situation of these persecuted Christians.[162] Facing powers of
evil, the readers would know that in Christ hostile forces had
already been defeated, and that every baptized believer shares in

the triumph of his or her Master.

   i. *The death of Christ.* Christ died *for sins,*" affirms Peter (v.
18). His was a redemptive death. Furthermore, His sacrifice was
"once for all." It was a decisive and complete victory. No more
sacrifice for sins was necessary. He also died a substitutionary
death, for *guilty ones.* His death was "the righteous one *on behalf
of* the unrighteous ones" (*dikaios huper adikon*; cf. 1:19; 2:22).
Notice very carefully the cutting edge of Peter's focus on the
death of Jesus. His readers face possible torture, estrangement
from family, homelessness, even death! Definitely, they too (like
many others) struggle with these terrible experiences of suffering,
and especially suffering brought about by serving a crucified Lord!
So when Peter emphasizes the death of Jesus, the burning question seems to be, "Why? Why did He do this?" Furthermore, this
question cannot be far removed from their own negative experience; it is really two questions in one, "Why did *He* do this;
why must *I* go through with this?" Peter has a ready answer. He
focuses, however, upon the prior question. Christ died "in order
that He might lead you to God" (*hina humas prosagage to theo*).
But the answer is not completely unassociated with the latter
question. Peter is also saying,

> It is for this faith in Christ who died for you that you too are called
> to suffer. It's not an optional extra; it's the only way of salvation,
> the only way to God; but it's worth the cost![163]

   ii. *The resurrection of Christ.* The believer's suffering
possesses value, since in Christ the negative aspects of suffering
are radically revolutionized. What appear to be wounds of defeat
inflicted by the world become marks of glory borne by the disciple
(see Galatians 6:14,17). Such can be true only because "the apparent defeat of death was for Jesus the beginning of [his]
victory."[164] Death led to resurrection and and triumph. "God
raised him up again, putting an end to the agony of death, since it
was impossible for him to be held in its power" (NAS, Acts 2:24).

409

Even though "he was put to death in the flesh, (God) made him alive in the spirit" (cf. Romans 1:3f,; I Timothy 3:16). "Death could not keep its prey, he tore the bars away."[165] Furthermore, in His *resurrected state* ("in which also," *en ho kai*),[166] Jesus went and preached to the spirits in prison (v. 19; cf. Jude 6; II Peter 2:4).[167] While a myriad of interpretations of verse 19 have been suggested,[168] it seems best to see in this preaching of Jesus a post-resurrection *proclamation* or *announcement*[169] of His victory over sin, over death, over all evil, over all hostile spiritual powers (cf. Colossians 2:15). To these defeated powers in the "prison" where they awaited judgment, Christ declared His conquest. France paraphrases, "In the triumph of his resurrection he went to the fallen angels awaiting judgment in their place of confinement, and declared to them the victory won by his redeeming death."[170] Perhaps Jesus told them, "I am the Living One; I was dead, and behold I am alive for ever and ever! I hold the keys of death and Hades" (Revelation 1:18). No doubt, this message of Christ's proclamation of victory would assure Peter's suffering Christian readers that spiritual powers of evil influencing their pagan opponents had already been defeated. He says, in effect, "Even the most wicked powers had to recognize the authority of the risen Jesus. So whatever the forces against you, they are not his equal. Do not fear!"[171]

iii. *The antitype baptism.* Peter had mentioned these "spirits" of Noah's time in order to hearten his readers. Now he turns to the flood and God's salvation of Noah as the basis for further reassurance. It is true "God waited patiently in the days of Noah while the ark was being built" (v. 20). God is extremely patient with wicked humanity, but judgment will come! (cf. II Peter 3:8ff.). The proof that God's judgment did come in the days of Noah is that *few* were saved (only *okto psuchai*, "eight souls").

The persecuted Christians must have been painfully conscious of their small numbers and relative feebleness compared to the pagan majority among whom they lived. But Noah and his crew were an even smaller minority: only eight out of the whole wicked population of the world. Yet they were saved, and the world destroyed.[172]

Furthermore, these eight souls *were saved through water* (*diesothesan di' hudatos*).[173] The flood of waters separated those rescued from those destroyed; thus the waters became judgment for the unbelievers and salvation for the believers.[174] Peter's readers had likewise experienced salvation *by means of* water (instrumental sense).[175] So Peter adds, "Which [water] now saves even you, the antitype baptism" (*ho kai humas antitupon nun sodzei baptisma*, v. 21).[176] Note Peter's forceful use of "antitype," and the antitype he affirms is baptism.

> God works according to a regular pattern, so that what he has done in the past, as recorded in the Old Testament, can be expected to find its counterpart in his work in the decisive period of the New Testament.[177]

So just as Noah and his family were saved through water, Peter's readers are saved by the watery experience of Christian baptism. The confidence of Peter is that "baptism now saves you," and "any view of baptism which finds it a rather embarrassing ceremonial extra, irrelevent to Christian salvation, is not doing justice to [this] New Testament teaching."[178] But Peter is careful to qualify his statement, lest anyone accuse him of a "magical" view of baptism. In effect, he answers the question, "*How* does baptism save?" He says, "Not [by] the removal of dirt from the body, but [by] the pledge of a good conscience toward God." The outer act of washing in baptism does not bring salvation in and of itself. Baptism is not a matter of washing away ritual uncleanness (cf. the Jewish ritual washings). Rather, the outer washing saves only because it represents the proper inner response (i.e., the submission of the soul to God for cleansing). Baptism is a transaction with God concerning the conscience (*suneideseos agathes eperotema eis theon*, "an appeal to God for a clear conscience,"

RSV). Baptism is a pledge, a contract, an undertaking.[179] In baptism, the believer commits his or her life to God and to Jesus as Lord. Baptism thus functions as a pledge to maintain a good conscience by honoring Jesus and God in one's life (cf. Acts 8:37; Romans 10:9; I Timothy 6:12). Yet this pledge of the believer has saving relevance only because of the resurrection of Jesus. Baptism saves "by the resurrection of Jesus Christ" (*di' anastaseos Iesou Christou*). This is Peter's ultimate answer to the *why* of salvation in Christian baptism. This is also the reason why Peter can affirm, "baptism also *now* saves you" (the verb is in the present tense, *sodzei*). Because of the presence of the victory of the risen Christ, not only were Peter's readers saved at the occasion of their baptism, but even now they are being saved from persecution through hope in the resurrection, a hope that exists because of their union with Christ effected by baptism. Baptism is thus for them God's ark of safety from the floods of persecution through the power of Christ's resurrection; and it is a refuge of salvation both past, present, and future. Such is tremendous encouragement for these believers.

> Peter reminds [them] of what their baptism means. It marks them out as God's chosen few who, like Noah, will be saved though all around mock them and perish. Their baptismal pledge commits them to unswerving loyalty to God whatever the consequences. And their baptism is a symbol of their being united with the risen Christ, who in his resurrection has triumphed over all the powers of evil [v. 21]. It is a reminder, in fact, of all that they stand for, and of the strength in which they stand, the victory of the risen Christ.[180]

Endnotes

1. That this emphasis has been central in the movement's discussion of baptism is undeniable. For example, see J.B. Briney, "Baptism — Its Action, Subjects and Import," in *The Old Faith Restated*, ed. J.H. Garrison (St. Louis: Christian Publishing Company, 1891), pp. 222ff. Cf. references to baptism in

Leroy Garrett, *The Stone-Campbell Movement* (Joplin, MO: College Press, 1981), p. 731 (index). Even Campbell had to respond to an unhealthy overemphasis on baptism in his reply to a "conscientious sister" from Lunenberg, see his "Christians Among Protestant Parties" and "Christians Among the Sects," *Millennial Harbinger* (1837).

2. For the different interpretations of "water" in John 3:5, see C.K. Barrett, *The Gospel According to St. John* (2nd ed.; Philadelphia: Westminster, 1978), p. 209.

3. Herman Ridderbos, *Paul: An Outline of His Theology*, trans. J.R. De Witt (Grand Rapids: Eerdmans, 1975), p. 398.

4. G.R. Beasley-Murray, *Baptism in the New Testament* (Grand Rapids: Eerdmans, 1962), pp. 214-5.

5. Ridderbos, *Paul*, pp. 398,411.

6. Newport J.D. White, "The Epistle to Titus," *The Expositor's Greek Testament*, ed. W.. Nicoll (rpt.; Grand Rapids: Eerdmans, 1983), Vol IV, p. 199.

7. Ibid.

8. J. Beckman, cited by Beasley-Murray, *Baptism*, p. 302.

9. Jack Cottrell, "Doctrine of Baptism: Course Outline" (Cincinnati, OH: Cincinnati Christian Seminary, n.d.), pp. 3-4. See also Donald M. Baillie, *The Theology of the Sacraments* (New York: Charles Scribner's Sons, 1957), pp. 47ff.

10. See Joseph C. Aldrich, *Life-Style Evangelism* (Portland, OR: Multnomah, 1981), p. 234; also Rebecca Manley Pippert, *Out of the Saltshaker & Into the World* (Downers Grove, IL: InterVarsity, 1979), p. 147.

11. Elmer L. Towns, *The Complete Book of Church Growth* (Wheaton, IL:Tyndale, 1981), p. 264.

12. Will Metzger, *Tell the Truth* (Downers Grove, IL: InterVarsity, 1981), p. 63.

13. For example, see Beasley-Murray, *Baptism*, pp. 1-31.

14. See Acts 2:38; 8:16; 10:48; 19:5; compare Acts 8:12; 22:16; contrast I Corinthians 1:13,15.

15. See Ronald H. Nash, *Christianity & the Hellenistic World* (Grand Rapids: Zondervan, 1984), pp. 149-58. Cf. J. Gresham Machen, *The Origin of Paul's Religion* (1925; rpt. Grand Rapids: Eerdmans, 1978), pp. 255-90.

16. The particulars are set forth nicely by Wayne A. Meeks, *The First Urban Christians: The Social World of the Apostle Paul* (New Haven, CT: Yale, 1983), pp. 150-7. For a survey of the historical development of baptism as initiation, see Cheslyn Jones, Geoffrey Wainwright, Edward Yarnold, eds., *The Study of Liturgy* (New York: Oxford, 1978), pp. 79-146.

17. William L. Lane, *The Gospel According to Mark* (Grand Rapids: Eerdmans, 1974), p. 49. Cf. W.S. LaSor's unconvincing denial of the newness of John's work, "Discovering what Jewish Miqva'ot Can Tell Us About Christian Baptism," *Biblical Archaeology Review* (Jan/Feb, 1987), XIII, No. 1, pp. 58-9.

18. Clearly Apollos, or someone closely associated with him, administered the baptism of John to twelve men at Ephesus (Acts 18:25; 19:3), so perhaps an earlier precedent for this practice existed as was the case with the disciples of Jesus (see John 3:22; 4:1-2).

19. Cf. Matthew 26:28; Luke 24:47; and Acts 2:38. See also Herwart Vorlander, "Forgiveness," *The New International Dictionary of New Testament Theology*, gen. ed. Colin Brown (Grand Rapids: Zondervan, 1975), Vol. 1, pp. 697-703.

20. "What is meant [by *metanoeo*, "repent"] is . . . a fundamental turn-around involving mind and action and including overtones of grief, which results in 'fruit in keeping with repentance,' " D.A. Carson, "Matthew," *The Expositor's Bible Commentary*, gen. ed. Frank E. Gabelein (Grand Rapids: Zondervan, 1984), Vol. 8, p. 99.

21. Cf. Luke 20:1ff. and the parallels in Matthew 21:23ff.; Mark 11:27ff.

22. See Jack Finegan, *The Archaeology of the New Testament* (Princeton, NJ: Princeton University Press, 1969), pp. 8-10.

23. The infinitive of purpose is here used by Matthew, *tou baptisthenai hup' autou*. See Ernest De Witt Burton, *Syntax of the Moods and Tenses in New Testament Greek* (1900; rpt. Grand Rapids: Kregel, 1976), p. 146. Cf. F. Blass and A. Debrunner, *A Greek Grammar of the New Testament and Other Early Christian Literature*, trans. Robert W. Funk (Chicago: The University of Chicago Press, 1961), p. 197.

24. Compare a fragment from the Gospel of the Hebrews preserved by Jerome (*Against Pelagius* iii.2), "Behold the mother of the Lord and his brethren said to him, John the Baptist baptizes for the remission of sins; Let us go and be baptized by him. But he said to them, What sin have I committed that I should go and be baptized by him?" Alfred Plummer, *An Exegetical Commentary on the Gospel According to St. Matthew* (rpt. Minneapolis, MN: James Family Christian Publishers, n.d.), p. 31.

25. A mild imperative, *aphes arti*, by which Jesus extends an invitation to John to allow him to be baptized. See Blass and Debrunner, *Greek Grammar*, pp. 183-4.

26. See Jack P. Lewis, *The Gospel According to Matthew: Part I* (Austin, TX: Sweet, 1976), p. 65.

27. Compare Oscar Cullmann's interpretation, "At the moment of his baptism he receives the commission to undertake the role of the suffering servant of God, who takes on himself the sins of his people. Other Jews came to the Jordan to be baptized by John for their *own* sins. Jesus, on the contrary, . . . is baptised for [the sins] of the whole people. . . . This means that Jesus is baptised in view of his death, which effects forgiveness of sins for all men. For this reason Jesus must unite himself in solidarity with his whole people, and go down himself to Jordan, that 'all righteousness might be fulfilled.' . . . The baptism of Jesus is related to *dikaiosune*, not only his own but also that of the whole people." *Baptism in the New Testament*, trans. J.K.S. Reid (Philadelphia: Westminster, 1950), p. 18.

28. "Like John himself, his baptism has no independent significance; both exist in order to bear witness (v. 7) to Christ, who alone truly takes away sin and confers the Spirit as well." Barrett, *Gospel According to St. John*, p. 177. Notice the forceful *all' hina . . . dia toutou.*

29. *Emeinen ep' auton*, i.e., 'the Spirit abides permanently upon Jesus; the baptism was not a passing moment of inspiration." Ibid., p. 178.

30. Ibid.

31. See John 7:39; 14:16f.; 20:22.

32. The consistent use of the future tense, *autos batisei humas en pneumati hagio* (Mark 1:8; cf. Matthew 3:11; Luke 3:16; Acts 1:5) is very important to the "already but not yet" schema.

33. John 3:30. Compare the testimony of the synoptic gospels to the imprisonment of John by Herod Antipas shortly after the baptism of Jesus, Matthew 4:12; Mark 1:14; Luke 3:19-20.

34. "John *also* was baptizing," *en de kai ho Ioannes baptizon*, John 3:23. Given the context, verse 26 could be paraphrased, "he is baptizing *too*," *ide houtos baptidzei*.

35. John 4:1 makes clear the difference that captured the Pharisees' attention. It was not the baptizing itself; rather it was *hoti Iesous pleionas mathetas poiei kai baptidzei e Ionnes* ("that Jesus made and baptized more disciples than John," KJV).

36. Two other sayings, Matthew 28:19 and Mark 16:16, will be treated later.

37. Psalm 11:6; 75:8; Jeremiah 25:15,17,28.

38. Alfred Plummer, *The Gospel According to St. Mark* (1914; rpt. Grand Rapids: Baker, 1982), p. 247. For example, Psalm 69:1-2 vividly reads, "Save me, O God,, for the waters have come up to my neck. I sink in the miry depths, where there is no foothold. I have come into the deep waters; the floods engulf me." Cf. Psalm 124:3-4. Noteworthy is the reading *he anomia me baptidzei* ("lawlessness overwhelms me") in the Septuagint of Isaiah 21:4. Note Isaiah's extreme agitation because of the vision (vv. 3-4), even though the destruction of Babylon is something he has longed for. Compare the similar attitude of Jesus to His *cup*, especially in the garden of Gethsemane.

39. See F.F. Bruce, *The Hard Sayings of Jesus* (Downers Grove, IL: InterVarsity, 1983), p. 128.

40. Cullmann, *Baptism*, p. 10.

41. The connection between this outpouring of the Spirit and the Spirit-baptism promised by Jesus is unmistakable. See Frederick Dale Bruner, *A Theology of the Holy Spirit* (Grand Rapids: Eerdmans, 1970), pp. 155-65. It seems plausible that this would be the point at which the 120 disciples (see Acts 1:15) received the Spirit, and that in a special, extraordinary way (like the Samaritans and the Gentiles). For this reason, the 120 did not need Christian baptism; they already had the Spirit (from their Pentecostal experience), and they already had forgiveness of sins (from John's baptism). See also Addendum A at the end of the chapter.

42. Cullmann, *Baptism*, pp. 10,22.

43. Bruner, *Theology of HS*, p. 168.

44. The Greek phrase has two aorist imperatives, *metanoesate kai baptistheto*.

45. Bruner, *Theology of HS*, p. 168.

46. Luke's favorite word (see Acts 2:17,18,33) is *ekcheo* ("pour out") taken from the Septuagint, Joel 3:1,2.

47. "With *sothete* cf. *sothesetai* ['you will be saved'], quoted from Joel in verse 21. In both places the word applies to a 'remnant' (cf. Joel 11:32) which would be delivered from the judgment destined to overtake the mass of the people." F.F. Bruce, *The Acts of the Apostles* (Grand Rapids: Eerdmans, 1951), p. 99. Note too that the verb is passive, and this emphasizes God's initiative rather than man's.

48. Gareth L. Reese, *New Testament History: A Critical and Exegetical Commentary on the Book of Acts* (Joplin, MO: College Press, 1976), p. 80.

49. In verse 41 those who were baptized were added (*prosetethesan*). In verse 47 the Lord added (*prosetithei*) those who were being saved. The connection between baptism, salvation, and the Lord's work of adding to the body is plain.

50. Bruner, *Theology of HS*, p. 167.

51. "The imperatives [*baptisai kai apolousai*] are in the middle voice: get yourself baptized and get your sins washed away'." F.F. Bruce, *Acts*, p. 403.

52. "Paul is to get up, act straightway, and submit to baptism." I. Howard Marshall, *The Acts of the Apostles*, Tyndale New Testament Commentaries, gen. ed. R.V.G. Tasker (Grand Rapids: Eerdmans, 1980), p. 357.

53. Alan Richardson, *An Introduction to the Theology of the New Testament* (London: SCM, 1958), pp. 347-8. However, Beasley-Murray responds, "The view of Richardson, that faith without baptism is 'Christian Science' or 'docetism', is an unhappy exaggeration." *Baptism*, p. 303. But compare Addendum C on baptism and faith at the end of the chapter.

54. Ridderbos observes, "Baptism and faith are both means to the appropriation of the content of the gospel. However, while faith according to its nature is an act of man, baptism according to its nature is an activity of God and on the part of God. That which the believer appropriates to himself on the proclamation of the gospel God promises and bestows on him in baptism. One can therefore speak of a sequential order only in part. For although baptism presupposes faith, the place of faith is not only prior to baptism, but in and after baptism as well. Baptism, however, according to its essence is once for all, because it marks the transition from the mode of existence of the old man to that of the new. . . . For this reason faith is not without baptism, just as baptism is not without faith." *Paul*, p. 412.

55. Marshall, *Acts*, p. 274.

56. C.F.D. Moule, *An Idiom Book of New Testament Greek* (2nd ed.; Cambridge: University Press, 1959), p. 13.

57. See S.S. Smalley, "Seal," *The New Bible Dictionary*, ed. J.D.

Douglas (Grand Rapids: Eerdmans, 1962), pp. 1155-6, and the bibliography on baptism and the Spirit as a seal. Cf. also Ridderbos, *Paul*, pp. 399-400. See also II Corinthians 1:22; Ephesians 1:13; 4:30; cf. Revelation 7:2ff.; 9:4; I John 2:20,27.

58. Bruner, *Theology of HS*, p. 206.

59. Marshall, *Acts*, p. 306.

60. See Burton, *Moods and Tenses*, p. 64.

61. Notice the parallel role of John's baptism and Christian baptism in the confirmation of belief. However, the key difference lies in the *object* of that belief.

62. "These men can hardly have been Christians since they had not received the gift of the Spirit; it is safe to say that the NT does not recognize the possibility of being a Christian apart from possession of the Spirit (John 3:5; Acts 11:17; Romans 8:9; 1 Corinthians 12:3; Galatians 3:2; 1 Thessalonians 1:5f.; Titus 3:5; Hebrews 6:4; 1 Peter 1:2; 1 John 3:24; 4:13)." Marshall, *Acts*, p. 305. Cf. Michael Green, *I Believe in the Holy Spirit* (Grand Rapids: Eerdmans, 1975), pp. 134-6.

63. Green, *I Believe in HS*, pp. 128, 132.

64. Bruce, *Acts*, p. 354.

65. Beasley-Murray, *Baptism*, p. 112.

66. On the usages and meaning of *onoma* in relation to Jesus, see Hans Bietenhard, "*Onoma*, etc.," *Theological Dictionary of the New Testament*, eds. G. Kittel and G. Friedrich (Eng. trans.; Grand Rapids: Eerdmans, 1967), Vol. V, pp. 271ff. See also Grant Osborne, *The Resurrection Narratives: A Redactional Study* (Grand Rapids: Baker, 1984), pp. 93-4.

67. Paul's "laying on of hands" could simply be the administration of baptism itself, or a symbolic gesture subsequent to baptism indicating the impartation of the Holy Spirit. "This does not mean, however, that the moment of the laying on of hands was thought of as the moment of the imparting of the Holy Spirit. Still less does it mean that the apostolic church considered that baptism in water was not baptism in Holy Spirit at all, that it was the ceremony of the laying on of hands which was thought of as baptism in Holy Spirit. In the NT the whole baptismal action is a unity which cannot be analyzed into its component parts, and it is in the whole action that the Spirit is bestowed." Richardson, *Introduction to Theology*, p. 355; cf. p. 329. On the variety of blessings associated with the "laying on of hands" in the NT, see Addendum D at the end. Cf. also Noakes' comments, *The Study of Liturgy*, p. 87.

68. Marshall, *Acts*, p. 152. On the Samaritans, see George W.E. Nicklesburg and Michael E. Stone, *Faith and Piety in Early Judaism* (Philadelphia: Fortress, 1983), pp. 13-19; cf. T.H. Gaster, "Samaritans," *The Interpreter's Dictionary of the Bible*, ed. G.A. Buttrick (Nashville: Abingdon, 1962), Vol. 4, pp. 190-197; and James D. Purvis, "The Samaritans and Judaism," *Early Judaism and Its Modern Interpreters*, eds. R.A. Kraft and G.W.E. Nicklesburg (Philadelphia: Fortress, 1986), pp. 81-98.

69. Green, *I Believe in HS*, p. 136.

BAPTISM AND THE REMISSION OF SINS

70. "The RSV has 'a city of Samaria.' The oldest manuscripts have '*the city of Samaria*' which *Good News Bible* paraphrases as 'the principal city of Samaria'. The possible towns are Sebaste (Herod the Great's new name for OT Samaria), Shechem, or possibly Gitta, the birthplace of Simon." Marshall, *Acts*, p. 154.

71. On the evidential nature of miracles, see Bernard Ramm, *Protestant Christian Evidences* (Chicago: Moody, 1953), pp. 125-45. For a critical discussion of the philosophical problems involved, see Colin Brown, *Miracles and the Critical Mind* (Grand Rapids: Eerdmans, 1984).

72. For Luke's inclusion of the *gunaikes* ("women") among the believers, cf. 1:14; 2:17; 5:14; 8:3; 9:2; 16:1,13; 17:4,12,34; 18:2; 21:5; 22:4. In light of rabbinic statements like, "The daughters of the Samaritans are menstruants [i.e., ceremonially unclean] from their cradle" (*Niddah* 4.1, cited by Barrett, *Gospel According to St. John*, p. 232), Luke's mention of the women in Samaria is all the more significant.

73. There is no reason to doubt the sincerity of Simon's faith. See Reese's treatment, *NT History: Acts*, p. 322.

74. So J.D.G. Dunn, *Baptism in the Holy Spirit* (London: SCM, 1970), p. 65. Cf. Marshall's critique, *Acts*, p. 156.

75. Bruner, *Theology of HS*, p. 174.

76. See vv. 17,18,19; cf. 6:6; 9:12,17; 13:3; 19:6; contrast 4:3; 5:18; 21:27.

77. Richard Rogers, *The Holy Spirit of God* (Lubbock, TX: World Mission Publishing, 1968), p. 29.

78. R.J. Knowling, "The Acts of the Apostles," *The Expositor's Greek Testament*, Vol. II, p. 216.

79. Marshall, *Acts*, p. 158.

80. Ibid., p. 157; cf. G.W.H. Lampe, *The Seal of the Spirit* (London: Longmans, 1951), pp. 70-72. But see Green's critique of Lampe's view, *I Believe in HS*, p. 137. However, Green seems to wrongly argue an either/or case between Lampe's view and his own.

81. Green, *I Believe in HS*, pp. 138-9. Cf. Richard N. Longenecker, "The Acts of the Apostles," *Expositor's Bible Commentary*, gen. ed. F.E. Gaebelein (Grand Rapids:Zondervan, 1981), Vol. 9, pp. 159-60.

82. Bruner, *Theology of HS*, p. 174.

83. Knowling, "Acts," *Expositor's Greek Testament*, Vol. II, p. 262.

84. See Bruce, *Acts*, p. 227.

85. Bruner, *Theology of HS*, p. 191.

86. On Jewish/Gentile tensions in the early church, see John E. Stambaugh and David L. Balch, *The New Testament in Its Social Environment* (Philadelphia: Westminster, 1986), pp. 46ff.; Rudolph Bultmann, *Primitive Christianity*, trans. R.H. Fuller (Cleveland: World, 1956), especially pp. 175-9; and T.R. Glover, *The Conflict of Religions in the Early Roman Empire* (1909; rpt. Washington: Canon, 1974), pp. 167-95.

87. Bruner, *Theology of HS*, pp. 193-4.

88. See Cullmann, *Baptism*, pp. 71ff., for his argument that *koluein* ("prevent" or "forbid"; Matthew 3:14; Acts 8:36; 10:47; 11:17) indicates an early baptismal formula in the NT. Cf. Carson's critique, "Matthew," *Expositor's Bible Commentary*, Vol 8, pp. 420-1.

89. Longenecker, "Acts," *Expositor's Bible Commentary*, Vol. 9, p. 395.

90. On the question of the eunuch's relationship to Judaism, Ibid., p. 363.

91. Knowling, "Acts," *Expositor's Greek Testament*, Vol. II, p. 226. For an older treatment of the mode of baptism, see Alexander Campbell, *Christian Baptism* (rpt. Nashville: McQuiddy, 1913), pp. 85-159; cf. John Murray, *Christian Baptism* (rpt. Phillipsburg, NJ: Presbyterian & Reformed, 1980), pp. 6-30; also G.R. Beasley-Murray, "Baptism, Wash," *The New International Dictionary of New Testament Theology*, gen ed. Colin Brown (Grand Rapids: Zondervan, 1975), Vol. 1, pp. 143ff. Cf. Ezekiel 36:25; Zechariah 13:1; Isaiah 4:4 on the image of sprinkling.

92. Marshall's translation, *Acts*, p. 165.

93. See the discussion in Bruce M. Metzger, *A Textual Commentary on the Greek New Testament* (3rd. ed.; UBS, 1971), pp. 360-361.

94. See especially Luke 24:44ff., and Osborne's treatment, *Resurrection Narratives*, pp. 129-36. However, Osborne does not seem to place enough emphasis on the role of "suffering" in Luke's apostolic commission. Cf. Matthew 16:21; 17:12; Mark 8:31; 9:12; Luke 9:22; 17:25; 22:15; 24:26,46; Acts 1:3; 3:18; 17:3.

95. Note Cullmann's assessment, "Most theologians today agree that the distinctive element in the baptismal act of the primitive church at first consisted in the relation of that act to the individual who now dies and rises again with Christ (Romans 6:3). On the other hand, the explanations diverge widely as soon as the attempt is made to define more closely the nature of the relation and thus to establish what it is in the baptism of an individual that effects his participation in Christ's death and resurrection." *Baptism*, p. 23. Cf. Ridderbos' discussion of what happens in baptism and his critique of different views, *Paul*, pp. 406ff.

96. For example, see John 20:23; cf. Matthew 16:19; 18:18.

97. Carson, "Matthew," *Expositor's Bible Commentary*, Vol. 8, p. 597.

98. Alan Hugh McNeile, *The Gospel According to St. Matthew* (1915; rpt. Grand Rapids: Baker, 1980), pp. 435-6.

99. Plummer, *Gospel According to St. Matthew*, p. 435.

100. Osborne, *Resurrection Narratives*, p. 93.

101. Plummer, *Gospel According to St. Matthew*, p. 433. Noakes similarly remarks, "If we look at the writings of the NT we shall find much about the significance of baptism but little liturgical detail," *The Study of Liturgy*, p. 80.

102. Note the strong affirmation of Mark 16:16, *ho pisteusas kai baptistheis sothesetai* ("he who believes and is baptized will be saved," RSV), an early second century scribal gloss, so Metzger, *Textual Commentary*, p. 125. See also Osborne's fine treatment, *Resurrection Narratives*, pp. 58-65.

103. Ridderbos, *Paul*, pp. 409-10.

104. Meeks, *First Urban Christians*, p. 154. Cf. Abraham J. Malherbe, *Social Aspects of Early Christianity* (2nd ed.; Philadelphia: Fortress, 1983), pp. 23-24. See also Nils Alstrup Dahl, "Anamnesis: Memory and Commemoration in Early Christianity," *Jesus in the Memory of the Early Church* (Minneapolis: Augsburg, 1976), pp. 11-29.

105. While the various terms for "memory" and "remembrance" are not used directly in conjunction with baptism in the NT (see K.H. Bartels, "Remember, Remembrance," *The New International Dictionary of New Testament Theology*, Vol. 3, pp. 230-47), the conceptualization is surely present (i.e., see Paul's use of *agnoeite* "don't you know," in Romans 6:3).

106. C.E.B. Cranfield, *The Epistle to the Romans*, The International Critical Commentary, gen eds. J.A. Emerton and C.E.B. Cranfield (rpt. Edinburgh: T. & T. Clark, 1982), Vol. I, p. 297.

107. It seems pointless to wrangle over the exact meaning of "baptized into his death" (i.e., whether an ethical, sacramental, eschatological, judicial, etc. significance). Beasley-Murray nicely surveys three of a "veritable Babel of voices" on this question and concludes, "Each of these three views has essential truth and none is complete in isolation from the rest," *Baptism*, pp. 130-32.

108. Ibid., p. 133.

109. "The reason for Paul's stating that the baptized is *buried* as dead, . . . is the nature of baptism as immersion. The symbolism of immersion as representing burial is striking. . . . . It is the kerygma *in action.* . . . But the 'with him' of baptism is due to the gospel. . . . Christ and his dying, Christ and his rising give the rite all its meaning." Ibid. cf. Ridderbos' objection, *Paul*, p. 402.

110. Beasley-Murray, *Baptism*, pp. 143-4.

111. Meeks, *First Urban Christians*, p. 155.

112. For an example, see C.K. Barrett, ed., *The New Testament Background: Selected Documents* (New York: Harper & Row, 1961), pp. 96-100. Cf. Glover's survey of the mystery cults, *Conflict of Religions*, pp. 20ff.

113. Meeks nicely depicts the two nearly symmetrical movements associated with baptism. "The first, characterized by descending action, climaxes with the 'burial' in the water; it signifies the separation of the baptized from the outside world. The second, a rising action, marks the integration of the baptized into another world, the sect on one plane, the heavenly reality on another." *First Urban Christians*, pp. 156-7. In Romans 6 the contrast is not nearly so involved, but a definite life/death antithesis is to be noted. See Addendum E at end of paper.

114. W.D. Davies, *Paul and Rabbinic Judaism* (4th ed.; Philadelphia: Fortress, 1980), p.88.

115. Anders Nygren, *Commentary on Romans* (3rd ed.; Philadelphia: Fortress, 1975), p. 233. Contrast Cecil Hook's overreaction to a sacramental/magical view of baptism. "Baptism symbolizes and confirms the change that the convert has undergone rather than accomplishing the change. . . . Regeneration is a process finalized by baptism instead of being produced by it." "Our

THE DESIGN OF BAPTISM IN THE NEW TESTAMENT

Seven Sacraments," *Restoration Review* (Dec., 1986), Vol. 28, No. 10, pp. 297-8. Hook tends to argue an either/or position by putting too much weight on the parallel between human birth and the new birth and by neglecting the decisive, once for all work of the Spirit at baptism.

116. Cranfield, *Epistle to Romans* (ICC), Vol. I, p. 303.

117. Cf. Colossians 2:12, where Paul uses the aorist tense of both death and resurrection in baptism (*suntaphentes*, "having been buried"; *sunegerthete*, "you were raised").

118. Compare E.P. Sanders, *Paul and Palestinian Judaism* (Philadelphia: Fortress, 1977), pp. 449-50, who argues that Paul's soteriology involves *only* a future resurrection, but he has to dismiss Colossians 2:11-13 as not Pauline and a later theological development.

119. Andrew T. Lincoln, *Paradise Now and Not Yet*, Society for New Testament Studies, Monograph Series, gen. ed., R.M. Wilson (Cambridge: University Press, 1981), pp. 122-3.

120. Ibid., p. 123.

121. See Helmut Koester, *History and Literature of Early Christianity*, Volume Two of *Introduction to the New Testament* (Philadelphia: Fortress, 1982), pp. 116-20. Cf. Lincoln's treatment, *Paradise*, pp. 9-11.

122. Lincoln, *Paradise*, p. 11.

123. Ibid.

124. Ibid.

125. *Die Taufe in Urchristentum im Lichte der Neueren Forschungen* (Leipzig, 1905), p. 36, cited by Beasley-Murray, *Baptism*, p. 151.

126. Ibid.

127. See Richardson's fine treatment of these texts, *Introduction to Theology*, pp. 344-7.

128. Ibid., pp. 346-7. Cf. Meeks, *First Urban Christians*, pp. 155-7. Frederick Rendall observes that by this image of clothing, baptism is "likened to spiritual coming of age." Just as the Roman youth exchanges the *toga praetexta* for the *toga virilis* and passes into the rank of citizen, so the Christian at baptism receives the robe of spiritual maturity, a symbol of emancipation from earlier bondage to an outward law. "Hitherto bound to obey definite commandments and fulfil definite duties, the convert is now set free to learn God's will from the inward voice of the Spirit, and discharge the heavier obligations incumbent on a citizen of the heavenly commonwealth under the guidance of an enlightened conscience." "The Epistle to the Galatians," *The Expositor's Greek Testament*, Vol. III, p. 174.

129. "It is of the essence of the eucharist that it is *repeated*, whereas baptism *cannot be repeated* for the individual. . . . In baptism, the individual is, for the first time and once for all, set at the point in history where salvation operates — where even now, the death and resurrection of Christ, the forgiveness of sins and the Holy Ghost, are to be efficacious for him. . . . [Furthermore], what happens in the act of baptism is clearly defined, in the decisive Pauline texts 1 Corinthians 12:13 and Galatians 3:27-28, as a setting within the body of Christ.

God sets a man within the body of Christ; and *at this moment* therefore the reception of this act on the part of the person baptised consists in nothing else than that he is the passive object of God's dealing, that he *is really set within the body of Christ by God.*" Cullmann, *Baptism*, pp. 29,30,31. Cf. Richardson, *Introduction to Theology*, pp. 348-9.

130. J.B. Lightfoot, *The Epistle of St. Paul to the Galatians* (rpt. Grand Rapids: Zondervan, 1957), p. 150.

131. "The early Christians did not see themselves as isolated individuals. Their interdependence and love amazed pagans, helping to convert some of them to Christ. . . . In strong communities Christians also found protection from the corroding influences of the non-Christian culture. . . . But we would be mistaken to think Christians formed committed communities only for the sake of evangelism or resistance to pagan culture. The basic reason for their unity was an understanding of the gospel — that in Christ God [was] raising up a new race of men and women, the people of God, joined together as a body." Kevin Springer, "Brothers and Sisters in Christ," *Pastoral Renewal, (February, 1984), p. 84.*

132. On the church as the body of Christ, see Ridderbos, *Paul*, pp. 362ff.; cf. Sanders, *Paul and Palestinian Judaism*, pp. 453ff.; and Jerome Murphy-O'Connor's interesting comments, *St. Paul's Corinth: Texts and Archaeology*, Col. 6, Good News Studies, ed. R.J. Karris (Wilmington, DE: Michael Glazier, 1983), pp. 165, 167.

133. G.G. Findlay's translation and emphasis, 'St. Paul's First Epistle to the Corinthians," *The Expositor's Greek Testament*, Vol. II, p. 890.

134. The translation of 'by" is to be preferred "on the analogy of 1 Corinthians 6:11, . . . and the immediately preceding reference to the Spirit's agency in the church." Beasley-Murray, *Baptism*, p. 167.

135. "The baptism 'in or by one Spirit', 1 Corinthians 12:13, is Christian baptism in water." Ibid., p. 169.

136. Findlay, "Corinthians," *Expositor's Greek Testament*, Vol. II, p. 890.

137. On *potidzein* ("to give to drink"), cf. Isaiah 29:10; 43:20; Joel 3:18; Psalm 36:8.

138. Sanders, *Paul and Palestinian Judaism*, p. 457.

139. Paul Althaus, *Die Heilsbedeutung der Taufe* (Gutersloh: Bertelsmann, 1897), p. 48, cited by Bruner, *Theology of HS*, p. 292.

140. Ibid. Cf. I John 2:20; 2:27, where the Holy Spirit is referred to as an "anointing" (Greek *chrisma*).

141. Richardson, *Introduction to Theology*, pp. 350-351.

142. Beasley-Murray, *Baptism*, pp. 170-171.

143. This seems to be the thrust of Paul's disclaimer, "Christ did not send me to baptize, but to preach the gospel" (I Corinthians 1:17). To see in this statement a minimizing of the significance of baptism is to abuse and misunderstand Paul's sacramental teaching; see Beasley-Murray, *Baptism*, pp. 178ff.

144. Ibid., p. 169.

145. W.F. Flemington, *The New Testament Doctrine of Baptism* (London, 1948)

THE DESIGN OF BAPTISM IN THE NEW TESTAMENT

1948), p. 54, cited by Beasley-Murray, *Baptism*, p. 181.

146. See Lincoln, *Paradise*, pp. 110-118.

147. Ibid., pp. 118-22; cf. F.F. Bruce, *Paul: Apostle of the Heart Set Free* (Grand Rapids: Eerdmans, 1977), pp. 417-23.

148. See especially Stanislas Lyonnet, "Paul's Adversaries in Colossae," and compare Gunther Bornkamm, "The Heresy of Colossians," both in *Conflict at Colossae*, eds. F.O. Francis and W.A. Meeks (rev. ed.; Missoula, MT: Scholars Press, 1975), pp. 147-61, 123-45.

149. On Paul's use of *sarx* ("flesh") in general, see Davies, *Paul and Rabbinic Judaism*, pp. 18ff.

150. On usages and description of the aorist participle of identical action, see Burton, *Moods and Tenses*, pp. 64ff.

151. J.B. Lightfoot, *Saint Paul's Epistles to the Colossians and to Philemon* (1879: rpt. Grand Rapids: Zondervan, 1959), p. 184.

152. F.F. Bruce, *Commentary on the Epistle to the Colossians*, The New International Commentary on the New Testament (Grand Rapids: Eerdmans, 1957), p. 236.

153. See E.G. Selwyn, *The First Epistle of Peter* (London: Macmillan, 1946), pp. 78ff.

154. Ernest Best, *1 Peter*, The New Century Bible Commentary, gen. ed., Matthew Black (rpt. Grand Rapids: Eerdmans, 1977), p. 41.

155. The Latin phrase *odio humani generis* could also mean "detested [or] hated of the human race."

156. Tacitus (15:44), *The Annals of Imperial Rome*, trans. Michael Grant (rev. ed.; New York: Penguin, 1971), pp. 365-6. On the Neronian persecution of Christians, cf. Bo Reicke, *The New Testament Era*, trans. D.E. Green (Philadelphia: Fortress, 1968), pp. 245-51.

157. For the development of Roman persecution of Christians, see Philip Schaff, *History of the Christian Church*, Vol. II, Ante-Nicene Christianity, A.D. 100-325 (1910; rpt. Grand Rapids: Eerdmans, 1979), pp. 31-84. For source documents, see Naphtali Lewis and Meyer Reinhold, *Roman Civilization, Sourcebook II: The Empire* (New York: Harper & Row, 1966), pp. 552-610. For a good treatment of Pliny and the Christians, see Robert L. Wilken, *The Christians as the Romans Saw Them* (New Haven, CT: Yale University Press, 1984), pp. 1-30.

158. This is a quote from Isaiah 8 where the prophet is told not to fear the king of Assyria as the Israelites do. "Do not fear what they fear, and do not dread it. The Lord Almighty is the one you are to regard as holy, he is the one you are to fear, he is the one you are to dread" (vv. 12-13).

159. On whether or not the epistle of I Peter is a baptismal treatise, see Beasley-Murray, *Baptism*, pp. 251-8; cf. Best, *1 Peter*, pp. 21-7.

160. For an excellent treatment of this passage, see R.T. France, "Exegesis In Practice: Two Examples," *New Testament Interpretation*, ed. I.H. Marshall (Grand Rapids: Eerdmans, 1977), pp. 264-78.

161. Ibid., p. 266.

423

162. Even if some of these believers were not experiencing persecution at the time of Peter's writing, such would come eventually. Cf. Donald Guthrie, *New Testament Introduction* (Downer's Grove, IL: InterVarsity, 1970), pp. 781-4. Through these Christians, Peter speaks encouragement and hope to the church universal, for all ages.

163. France, "Exegesis," *NT Interpretation*, p. 277.

164. Ibid., . p266.

165. Robert Lowry, "Low in the Grave He Lay" (1874).

166. See France's treatment, "Exegesis," *NT Interpretation*, pp. 268-9.

167. "The evidence is more than sufficient to indicate that *ta en phulake pneumata* ('the spirits in prison') must be fallen angels who according to apocalyptic tradition, sinned at the time of Noah, and are in custody awaiting their final punishment." Ibid., p. 270.

168. See John S. Feinberg, "1 Peter 3:18-20, Ancient Mythology, and the Intermediate State," *Westminster Theological Journal*, XLVIII (Fall, 1986), pp. 303-36.

169. The Greek word *kerussein* can mean simply "to act as herald" or "to utter a proclamation" (so NAS).

170. France, "Exegesis," *NT Interpretation*, p. 277.

171. Ibid.

172. Ibid., p. 272.

173. Note again the passive voice of the verb. God as always does the saving!

174. "What is to unbelievers their judgment, is to believers their hope and trust." Best, *1 Peter*, p. 147.

175. Ibid. Cf. however, J.H.A. Hort, "both local and instrumental meanings of *di'* are contemplated." "The First Epistle General of Peter," *The Expositor's Greek testament*, Vol. V, p. 69; and note France's ambiguity, "Exegesis," *NT Interpretation*, p. 273.

176. For a brief exegetical discussion and translation, see France, "Exegesis," *NT Interpretation*, p. 273. Surely Beasley-Murray, *Baptism*, p. 259, is wrong to minimize the role of water as means of salvation.

177. France, "Exegesis," *NT Interpretation*, pp. 273-4.

178. Ibid.

179. Ibid., p. 275.

180. Ibid., p. 276.

ADDENDUM A

The Twelve or the One Hundred Twenty?

The limiting of the outpouring of the Spirit in Acts 2 to the apostles only, seems to labor under the conviction that "baptism in the Holy Spirit" is a special measure or bestowal of the Spirit intended only for the apostles and empowering them to work miracles, speak in tongues, teach and write with inspiration, etc. But the "baptizing with the Holy Spirit" promised by Jesus is better viewed as the general outpouring of God's Spirit which God's church received at Pentecost. Henceforth, the Spirit became available for everyone that God calls through the gospel (i.e., accepts the gift of the Spirit at baptism; apart from the special exceptions of the Samaritans and the Gentiles). This baptism is not limited to just a select few. It is strongly associated throughout the NT with the rite of water baptism; it is available to all who will receive. The bestowal of the Spirit is administered by Jesus on the occasion of the recipient's water baptism. It did not take place before Pentecost. It does not necessarily convey the power to perform miracles (i.e., the apostles had performed miracles before this promise came). It does not carry with it the promise of inspiration. It does not necessarily involve the speaking in tongues (although this did occur in certain situations). The idea of the miraculous as bound up with the gift of the Spirit (i.e., "baptism of the Spirit") is not justifiable by NT evidence. The baptism is not a mere clothing with the Spirit (i.e., power from on high). Yes, power is involved, but a distinction exists between the gift of the Spirit Himself and the power given by the Spirit (see I Corinthians 12:11). It is improper to confuse the power given by the Spirit with the gift of the Spirit Himself. See Richard Rogers, *The Holy Spirit of God*, pp. 18ff. Cf. Addendum B.

The use of "all" in Acts 2:1,4 seems to include the fuller number of disciples.

Luke is careful to preserve the special role of the twelve (see 1:2,13; 2:14), but he does so without excluding others (see 2:14-15). The special role of the twelve is not dependent upon the Spirit's baptism.

If the 120 did not receive the Spirit at this time, then when? Acts 2:41 seems to indicate only those who "received the word" of Peter were baptized (and hence, received the Spirit). The 120 had already received the word; they were part of those "numbered among us' '(Acts 1:17). The 120 (cf. the seventy Jesus sent out during His earthly ministry) comprise a group that included "men who have accompanied us during all the time that the Lord Jesus went in and out among us, beginning from the baptism of John until the day when he was taken up from us — one of these men must become with us a witness to his resurrection" (RSV, vv. 21-22; cf. I Corinthians 15:6, "five hundred brethren"). The fact that the disciples had a choice between Justus and Matthias (evidently selected from a larger group of possible candidates) would indicate a broader group than the twelve involved in this ministry. So the Spirit's falling upon all these who shared in Jesus' ministry from the beginning of John's baptism to the resurrection of Jesus is not at all surprising.

The identification of those speaking in tongues as Galileans (2:4,7) does not necessarily restrict the number to the twelve. Jesus spent the largest portion of His ministry in Galilee, and this is where He had the greatest following, especially true concerning those immediate, intimate disciples (and this seems to be the characteristics of the 120). See also Matthew 28:7,10,16,17, and the emphasis on the eleven, but not a neglect of a larger number. Cf. also Mark 16:7; Luke 24:6; and especially 24:33, "the eleven and those who were with them" and the promise to this larger group in vv. 44ff.! Also in John 20:19,20,24,26, 30, the number of the "disciples" is not to be restricted to the eleven.

ADDENDUM B

Baptism and the Gift of the Holy Spirit
Compiled by J. Cottrell

1. The fact that baptism is the point of time when regeneration occurs can be explained only in connection with the teaching that the gift of the Holy Spirit is received at baptism.

    a. The Holy Spirit is the life-giver. John 6:63; 7:37-39; Rom. 8:2, 6,11,13; I Cor. 15:45; II Cor. 3:6; Gal. 6:8.

    b. "The gift of life is prominently ascribed to the Spirit. . . . Whatever vitality man possesses is itself the gift of the Spirit of God" (G. Hendry, *The HS in Christian Theology*).

2. It is characteristic of many religious groups to separate baptism and the gift of the Holy Spirit.

    a. But NT passages connect baptism with the gift of the Spirit.
        Acts 2:38-39
        John 3:5
        Titus 3:5
        I Corinthians 6:11

    b. See also the following passages.
        Acts 3:9 and Acts 5:31-32
        I Corinthians 12:13
        Acts 9:12,17-18
        Col. 2:12 compared with Rom. 8:11
        Acts 18:8 compared with Eph. 1:13
        Acts 19:2-3

    c. See also the connection between joy/rejoicing and the HS.
        Acts 8:39; 13:52; 16:34
        Rom. 14:17; 15:13
        Gal. 5:22

3. The entrance of the Holy Spirit is a seal upon our hearts. See II Cor. 1:22; Eph. 1:13.

4. Is there any special terminology used for the different aspects of the Spirit's working? This does not seem to be the case. See the section on the following page.

New Testament Terminology Regarding the Giving of the Holy Spirit
Compiled by J. Cottrell

1. *Baptism in* the H.S.

Mark 1:8	Acts 1:4-5
Matt. 3:11	Acts 11:16
Luke 3:16	I Cor. 6:11
John 1:33	I Cor. 12:13

2. *Pouring out* of the H.S.

Acts 2:17,18	Acts 10:45
Acts 2:33	Titus 3:5-6

3. *Gift/Giving* of the H.S.

John 4:10,14; 7:39	Acts 8:18; 10:45
II Cor. 1:22	Acts 11:17
Acts 2:38; 5:32	Acts 15:8

4. *Receiving* the H.S.

John 7:39	Acts 2:38
Rom. 8:15	Acts 8:15,17,19; 10:47
Gal. 3:2,14	Acts 19:2

5. Other

   a. *Came upon,* Acts 1:8; 19:6
   b. *Fell upon,* Acts 8:16; 10:44; 11:15
   c. *Drink/Give to Drink/Partake,* John 4:14; 7:37; Heb. 6:4 (see Eph. 3:6); I Cor. 12:13
   d. *Sent forth,* Gal. 4:6
   e. *Sealed with,* Eph. 1:13; 4:30; II Cor. 1:22
   f. *Have from God,* I Cor. 6:19 (see Acts 3:19)

428

ADDENDUM C

Baptism and Faith

God's Gifts	Promised to Faith	Connected with Baptism
Forgiveness of sins	I John 1:9; Acts 15:9	Acts 2:38; 22:16
Union with Christ	Eph. 3:18; Gal. 2:20; Col. 2:12	Gal. 3:26; Col. 2:12; Rom. 6:1-11
Possession of Spirit	Gal. 3:2,14	Acts 2:38; Titus 3:5
Church membership	Acts 5:14; 4:32; Gal. 6:10	I Cor. 12:13; Gal. 3:27ff.
Inherit Kingdom	John 3:14; Mark 10:15	John 3:5
Justified/Sanctified	Rom., ch. 3-5	I Cor. 6:11
Sonship	Gal. 3:26	Gal. 3:26-27
Holy Living	Phil. 3:8-11	Col. 3:1ff.

—Compiled from G.A. Beasley-Murray, *Baptism Today and Tomorrow*, pp. 27-33, by J. Cottrell.

"In light of these statements I am compelled to conclude that the understanding of baptism as a 'beautiful and expressive symbol,' *and nothing more*, is irreconcilable with the NT" (Ibid., p. 32).

"It is evident that God's gift to baptism and to faith is one: it is salvation in Christ" (Ibid., p. 37).

"Baptism and faith are but the outside and the inside of the same thing" (James Denny, *The Death of Christ*, p. 185, cited by ibid., p. 33).

ADDENDUM D

Laying On of Hands in the NT

Reference	By Whom	Upon Whom	Purpose
Matt. 19:13 (cf. Mark 10:16)	Jesus	Little children	"to pray for them" (NIV; Gk. "pray"
Mark 5:23 (cf. 1:41)	Jesus	Jairus' daughter	Healing
Mark 6:5	Jesus	Few sick people	Healing
Mark 7:32	Jesus	Deaf man	Healing
Mark 8:23	Jesus	Blind man	Healing
Mark 16:18 (?)	Disciples	Sick people	Healing
Luke 4:40	Jesus	Sick; diseased	Healing
Luke 13:13	Jesus	Crippled woman	Healing
Acts 6:6	Apostles	Seven men . . . full of faith & Holy Spirit	App. to ministry; connected with prayer
Acts 8:17	Peter & John	Samaritans	After baptism, to impart Spirit
Acts 9:17	Ananias	Saul	Before baptism, to bless or heal (?)
Acts 13:3	Ch. leaders; whole ch. (?)	Barnabas & Saul	To set apart for work (v.2); connec. w/ prayer, fasting.
Acts 19:6	Paul	Disciples at Ephesus	To bestow Spirit; at baptism?
Acts 28:8	Paul	Publius' father	after? Healing, with prayer
I Tim. 4:14	Presbytery	Timothy	"Gift" given through prophecy, with laying on of hands; ref. to extraordinary gift (?)
I Tim. 5:22	Timothy	Others; someone	To bless, approve (?)
II Tim. 1:6 (cf. Heb. 6:2)	Paul	Timothy	"Gift" of God; ref. to Spirit which came upon Timothy at baptism (?)

ADDENDUM E

THE WORLD   THE BODY OF CHRIST

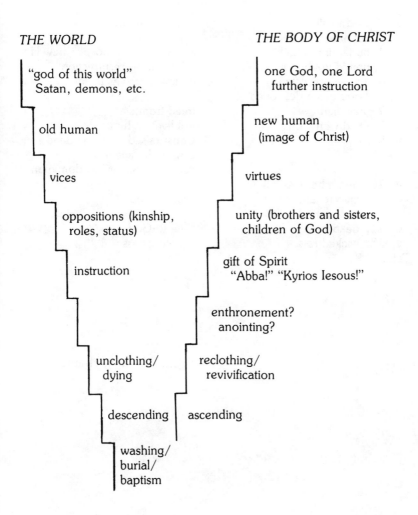

"god of this world"   one God, one Lord
Satan, demons, etc.   further instruction

old human   new human
                                          (image of Christ)

vices   virtues

oppositions (kinship,   unity (brothers and sisters,
roles, status)   children of God)

instruction   gift of Spirit
                                          "Abba!" "Kyrios Iesous!"

                                         enthronement?
                                         anointing?

unclothing/   reclothing/
dying   revivification

descending   ascending

washing/
burial/
baptism

—from Meeks, *First Urban Christians*, p. 156

DEATH	LIFE
v. 2, died to sin	how can we live in it
v. 3, baptized into death	
v. 4, buried into death	just as . . . we too . . . new life
v. 5, united w/ him in death	will be in his resurrection
v. 6, old self crucified; body of sin destroyed	no longer slaves to sin
v. 7, has died	freed from sin
v. 8, died with Christ	will live w/ him
v. 9,	Christ raised from the dead; cannot die again; death no longer has dominion
v. 10, death he died; died to sin; once for all	life he lives; lives to God
v. 11, dead to sin	alive to God
v. 13, wickedness	righteousness
etc.	

—From Romans, chapter 6